Re-Reading
LEVINAS

Studies in Continental Thought

JOHN SALLIS, GENERAL EDITOR

Consulting Editors

Re-Reading
LEVINAS

EDITED BY

**ROBERT BERNASCONI
and SIMON CRITCHLEY**

INDIANA UNIVERSITY PRESS
Bloomington and Indianapolis

The paper used in this publication meets the minimum
requirements of American National Standard for Information
Sciences—Permanence of Paper for Printed Library Materials,
ANSI Z39.48–1984.

⊗™

Manufactured in the United States of America

Library of Congress Cataloging-in-Publication Data
Re-reading Levinas / edited by Robert Bernasconi and Simon
Critchley.
p.   cm. — (Studies in Continental thought)
Includes bibliographical references and index.
ISBN 0-253-31179-9 (alk. paper). — ISBN 0-253-20624-3 (pbk. :
alk. paper)
1. Lévinas, Emmanuel.   I. Bernasconi, Robert.   II. Critchley, Simon,
date.   III. Title: Rereading Levinas.   IV. Series.
B2430.L484R47 1991
194—dc20   90-41833
                                                                    CIP

1   2   3   4   5   95   94   93   92   91

CONTENTS

Acknowledgments

"En ce moment même dans cet ouvrage me voici" first appeared in a collection of essays, *Textes pour Emmanuel Levinas* (Paris, Editions Jean-Michel Place, 1980). It was reprinted in *Psyche: Inventions de l'autre* (Paris, Galilée, 1987). "Tout Autrement" first appeared in the journal *L'Arc*, in a number devoted to Derrida's work (no. 54, 1973). It was reprinted in *Noms Propres* (Montpellier, Fata Morgana, 1976). The editors wish to express their gratitude to Jacques Derrida and Emmanuel Levinas for allowing these essays to be translated for this volume.

The papers collected in the rest of this volume, with the exception of those of Luce Irigaray and Simon Critchley, were presented at the international colloquium "Re-Reading Levinas" held at Wivenhoe House, University of Essex, May 29–31, 1987. The colloquium was organized by Robert Bernasconi and sponsored by the Philosophy Department, University of Essex with the generous support of the Service Culturel de l'Ambassade de France. An earlier version of Luce Irigaray's "Questions to Emmanuel Levinas: On the Divinity of Love" was presented on the occasion of her visit to Essex University in May 1987, and the editors wish to express their gratitude for allowing her essay to be translated and published here. Simon Critchley's essay was written especially for this volume.

Key to Abbreviations

LEVINAS'S WORKS

ADV   *L'au-delà du verset.* Paris, Minuit, 1982.

AE   *Autrement qu'être ou au-delà de l'essence.* The Hague, Martinus Nijhoff, 1974.

CP   *Collected Philosophical Papers.* Trans. Alphonso Lingis. The Hague, Martinus Nijhoff, 1987.

DE   *De l'existence à l'existant.* Paris, Vrin, 1947.

DL   *Difficile Liberté.* 2nd. ed. Paris, Albin Michel, 1976.

DVI   *De Dieu qui vient à l'idée.* Paris, Vrin, 1982.

EDE   *En découvrant l'existence avec Husserl et Heidegger.* 3rd ed. Paris, Vrin, 1974.

EE   *Existence and Existents.* Trans. Alphonso Lingis. The Hague, Martinus Nijhoff, 1978.

EeI   *Éthique et Infini.* Paris, Librairie Arthème Fayard, 1982.

EI   *Ethics and Infinity.* Trans. Richard Cohen. Pittsburgh, Duquesne University Press, 1985.

HH   *Humanisme de l'autre homme.* Montpellier, Fata Morgana, 1972.

ND   "Le nom de Dieu d'après quelques textes Talmudiques." *Archivio di Filosofia.* Rome, 1969, pp. 155-67.

NP   *Noms propres.* Montpellier, Fata Morgana, 1976.

OB   *Otherwise than Being or Beyond Essence.* Trans. Alphonso Lingis. The Hague, Martinus Nijhoff, 1981.

TA   *Le temps et l'autre,* Montpellier, Fata Morgana, 1979.

TeI   *Totalité et Infini.* The Hague, Martinus Nijhoff, 1961.

TI   *Totality and Infinity.* Trans. Alphonso Lingis. Pittsburgh, Duquesne University Press, 1969.

TO   *Time and the Other.* Trans. Richard Cohen. Pittsburgh, Duquesne University Press, 1987.

TTO   "The Trace of the Other." Trans. Alphonso Lingis. In *Deconstruction in Context,* ed. Mark Taylor. Chicago, University of Chicago Press, 1986, pp. 345-59.

WO   "Wholly Otherwise." Trans. Simon Critchley, below, chap. 1.

DERRIDA'S WORKS

AM   "At this very moment in this work here I am." Trans. Ruben Berezdivin, below, chap. 2.

ED   *L'écriture et la différence.* Paris, Seuil, 1967.

EM   "En ce moment même dans cet ouvrage me voici." In *Textes pour Emmanuel Levinas*, ed. F. Laruelle. Paris, Jean-Michel Place, 1980.
FC   *Feu la cendre*. Paris, Éditions des Femmes, 1987.
WD   *Writing and Difference*. Trans. Alan Bass. Chicago, University of Chicago Press, 1978.

Although for ease of reference the page numbers of the English translations have been given where one exists, the authors have sometimes provided their own translations.

Editors' Introduction

Re-Reading Levinas? Does the title of this volume imply that Levinas has already been read, understood, and appropriated? And is there a suggestion that understanding is a misunderstanding so that Levinas stands in need of a corrective re-reading, a certain re-appropriation of the proper meaning of his works? Why call for a re-reading of Levinas now, just when many people are taking up his writings for the first time?

Re-Reading Levinas: an invitation to respond to his work anew. The question of re-reading includes a reference to the issue of response and responsibility, what one might call the ethical structure of reading. Can such a structure be elucidated in terms drawn from Levinas's texts? One would notice, for example, that, for Levinas, the predominance accorded to ontology by the Western philosophical tradition from Parmenides to Heidegger has had the effect of suppressing alterity and transmuting it into what he calls the Same (*le Même*). Philosophy is the assimilation of otherness into Sameness, where the other is digested like food and drink. Levinas finds in the face of the Other (*autrui*) a point of irreducible alterity which resists the philosophical logos. The self finds itself put in question by and obliged to respond to the Other. The obligation to respond amounts to a responsibility that cannot be evaded, but that has been ignored or dissimulated within the philosophical tradition. Do such considerations apply beyond the face-to-face, understood empirically, to the relation a reader might have with a text? Does the activity of reading—often defined as a process of comprehension, even of digestion— itself betray the ethical space which is so carefully broached in Levinas's work? Or does Levinas's reinscription of the face-to-face in what he calls "Saying" (*le Dire*), which he himself in *Otherwise than Being* and elsewhere applies to written works as well as direct encounters, not suggest the possibility of a Levinasian hermeneutics? Such a hermeneutics would perhaps be defined by its readiness for re-reading because it would have no interest in distilling the content of a text into a "said," an encapsulation of its meaning, so that one could be satisfied that one had finished reading. That is an illustration of the kind of question which serves as an invitation to re-read Levinas, because it brings to his writings questions that a first reading of his works provokes without answering, precisely because they are not systematically pursued by him.

Re-Reading Levinas: reading at the limit of responsibility where the response itself tries to maintain an ethical space. What sort of re-reading of Levinas will be necessary in order not to betray this ethical responsibility? Perhaps it requires a re-reading that betrays Levinas in a radical way. A reading that works within a certain irreducible economy of betrayal, which, in the knowledge of the violence that any reading commits, tries to respond responsibly to the responsibility produced by Levinas's work. These considerations of responsibility and the ethics of reading are at the heart of a number of the contributions to this volume.

Re-Reading Levinas: buried in this title is the assumption of a prior reading of Levinas that has been determinate for the response to his work and provides the occasion for this re-reading. There are two contexts for such a prior reading which must briefly be mentioned: first, the initial reception of Levinas's work has been to a great extent determined by *Totality and Infinity*. Second, the questions addressed to *Totality and Infinity* by this initial reading have been largely and particularly in the English-speaking world determined by Derrida's "Violence and Metaphysics." Here the problems of reading multiply, for the reception of Levinas via Derrida has often been based upon the idea that one can read "Violence and Metaphysics" as a critique of Levinas. Simply stated, such a reading would claim to follow Derrida by arguing that because the ethical relation to the Other is based on discourse, it presupposes the very ontological language that Levinas claims it overcomes. Levinas therefore betrays his ethical intention in his philosophical discourse because as soon as the Other enters discourse, the Other is reduced to the Same. However, to understand "Violence and Metaphysics" as a critique of Levinas is to misunderstand Derridian deconstructive reading. Without rehearsing arguments set out at length elsewhere,[1] one can claim that what distinguishes deconstruction as a textual practice lies in double reading, that is, a reading that interlaces at least two motifs, most often first by following or repeating the intentions of a text, in the manner of a commentary, and second, within and through this repetition, leaving the order of commentary and opening up the blind spots or ellipses within the text's intentionality. It is not for a double reading to decide between these paths of reading, these two motifs, but rather to render such choice undecidable. Although "Violence and Metaphysics" is one of Derrida's earliest texts, it offers a double reading of Levinas, which, by following and eventually leaving the path of commentary, shows, on the one hand, the impossibility of escaping from logocentric conceptuality and, on the other, the necessity of such an escape arising from the impossibility of remaining wholly within the (Greek) logocentric tradition. Letting these two motifs interlace, Derrida's essay displays the necessity of these two impossibilities and suspends the critical moment of deciding between them.

Re-Reading Levinas: if the first generation of Levinas reading has hitherto been largely determined by the above two contexts, then this volume attempts to move the debate into its second generation, where reading Levinas will be determined by a further two texts: Levinas's *Otherwise than Being or Beyond Essence* and Derrida's "At this very moment in this work here I am." Most of the essays in this volume base their reading of Levinas on the arguments of *Otherwise than Being* rather than *Totality and Infinity*. Similarly, many of the essays take up the provocative issues raised by Derrida's major but hitherto largely ignored essay. Once again, questions of re-reading arise: is *Otherwise than Being* Levinas's response to and re-reading of the problems first described in *Totality and Infinity*? Certainly, the problematic that guides *Otherwise than Being* differs from that of the earlier work; whereas in *Totality and Infinity* Levinas had spoken of Being and employed a mainly ontological terminology in his discussion of ethics, the central preoccupation of *Otherwise than Being* concerns the possibility of an ethical Saying (*le Dire*) which ruptures the ontological language of the Said (*le Dit*). Although the relation between *Otherwise than Being* and *Totality and Infinity* is more complex and chiasmic than any simple, developmental thesis would suggest, it is clear that in the latter work Levinas is more aware of the logocentric recoils that occur when ethical Saying is thematized within the ontological Said. This provokes a further question of re-reading: to what extent is *Otherwise than Being* a response to Derrida's "Violence and Metaphysics?" Might not *Otherwise than Being* be seen as a re-reading of *Totality and Infinity* in the light of "Violence and Metaphysics"? Although the dialogue between Levinas and Derrida should not be reduced to a question of influence, a notion whose philosophical value is questionable, it seems clear that Levinas has carefully read and assimilated Derrida's essay. Because Levinas has not referred to "Violence and Metaphysics" by name in any of his books or essays, all such arguments, however plausible, are for the most part based upon allusion and conjecture. The questions surrounding Levinas's reading of Derrida are given a more concrete context with the translation of "Wholly Otherwise," which is the only piece by Levinas devoted exclusively to Derrida.

"Wholly Otherwise" provides a rare glimpse of what it might mean to respond responsibly to Derrida. Almost always Derrida's textual interlocutors construe themselves as victims and so try to resist or overturn the deconstructive reading. The responsibility of Levinas's response lies in the way in which he reads Derrida. He does not have the "ridiculous ambition of 'improving'" Derrida's reading; rather he wishes to draw Derrida into "a contact made in the heart of a chiasmus." The figure of the chiasmus, etymologically constituted by the two lines of the Greek letter χ, well describes the pattern of Levinas's reading in "Wholly Otherwise." The responsibility of Levinas's response to Derrida is due to what one can justifiably call the double reading that Levinas gives of deconstruction. On the one hand, Levinas sees Derrida's work as a continuation of the critique of metaphysics begun by Kant, a continuation which somehow "thinks through to the end" this epoch of critique. Deconstruction is distinguished by its critique of the determination of Being as presence, a critique which, paradoxically, "employs the present tense of the verb to be" and "seems to offer an ultimate refuge to presence." However, if one side of Levinas's reading stresses the dependence of deconstruction upon the tradition that it deconstructs and the difficulties and aporias involved in trying to escape that tradition—arguments which are hauntingly analogous to those that Derrida raised in "Violence and Metaphysics"—then this only tells half the story. For Levinas goes on to argue that the "rigorous reflection" that deconstructive reading practices also "lets us catch a glimpse of these interstices of Being where this very reflection unsays itself." Thus, the rigor that deconstruction brings to the tradition both remains bound to the ontological tradition of the determination of Being as presence while, at the same time, opening that tradition to the dimension of the otherwise than Being.

In short, concealed in the interstices of Derrida's texts is an attempt at ethical Saying, a claim that Levinas pursues elliptically through discussions of skepticism, creation, and the sign. Furthermore, the responsibility of Levinas's double reading of Derrida consists in the fact that Levinas does not choose between these two readings. He lets them interlace one with the other producing the figure of a chiasmus. Levinas locates the Saying within Derrida's texts but does not try and divorce it from its Said. The Saying is maintained within the Said as the permanent possibility of the latter's interruption. It is hoped that "Wholly Otherwise" will raise the vital issue of the ethics of deconstructive reading and prepare the way for the consideration of Derrida as an ethical thinker, understood in the particular sense Levinas gives to the word "ethics."

A similar pattern of double reading to that detected in "Wholly Otherwise" is at work in Derrida's "At this very moment," the essay which, for the moment at least, completes this chain of readings and responses between Derrida and Levinas. Two initial points need to be made here: first, Derrida's "At this very moment" is largely based upon *Otherwise than Being*, a text which, as has already been suggested, is far more attentive to the sort of problematic generated by deconstructive reading than *Totality and Infinity*. Second, one might also read "At this very moment" as a re-reading of "Violence and Metaphysics," an attempt to reformulate a response to Levinas's work in the light of Levinas's "response" to Derrida in *Otherwise than Being*. This second issue is explored in Robert Bernasconi's essay with specific reference to Levinas's discussion of skepticism, whereas Simon Critchley's essay offers a commentary on the complexities of "At this very moment." To prefigure briefly these analyses, it is claimed that there are two moments of reading operative in Derrida's essay, which together constitute a double reading. Simply stated, Derrida first tries to find out how Levinas's work works, and then shows how Levinas's work does not work. The first moment of reading describes how the Levinasian text works by resisting the ontological Said and achieving the ethical interruption of the Said by the Saying. The second moment of reading arises out of the problems involved in the ethics of reading outlined above. If the reader of Levinas responds to his work by gratefully repeating it and returning it to his proper name in an act of homage, then, Derrida asks, might this not deny the very structure of the ethical Saying that Levinas's work attempts to set to work, i.e., the movement from the Same to the Other? If this is the case, then the response to Levinas's work must become more nuanced and attempt to maintain the otherness which that work tries to establish. Derrida goes on to argue that perhaps the only responsible response to Levinas's work is that of ingratitude, and that it is precisely by being ungrateful and refusing to return the work to its author that the alterity that Levinasian ethics seeks to establish is maintained. Derrida demonstrates this necessary ingratitude in the second moment of reading by arguing that Levinas's work continually subordinates sexual difference to ethical difference and, in so doing, unwittingly subordinates woman to man, thereby repeating one of the most traditional and iniquitous of philosophical gestures. In Derrida's essay, the pattern of double reading is employed as the way of maintaining the ethical interruption sought by Levinas's work.

The essays which follow those by Levinas and Derrida in the present volume have been grouped under a number of thematic headings. In part 2, "The Later Levinas," the essays of Adriaan Peperzak, Jean Greisch, and Fabio Ciaramelli focus on the issues raised by Levinas's more recent work. Adriaan Peperzak begins from the problematic of the Saying and the Said in *Otherwise than Being* and explores the question of how a transcendence or evasion of the logos becomes possible in Levinas's work. After an extended exposition of skepticism and its relation to the Saying and the Said, Peperzak describes ethical Saying as the most common fact of everyday life, but one which accomplishes the transcendence sought but overlooked by philosophy. He continues by describing the structure of ethical subjectivity and its relation to alterity and concludes by further deepening and complicating the coupling of the Saying and the Said. In "The Face and Reading: Immediacy and Mediation," Jean Greisch offers what, borrowing a word from *Totality and Infinity*, he calls a "hypocritical" reading of Levinas. Such a reading plays the immediacy of the face-to-face relation against the mediation of the text and explores the question of the irreducible hypocrisy involved in reading Levinas insofar as reading loses sight of the ethical. This coupling of immediacy and mediation reveals the hypocritical reader as Hegelian, a reader whose name, it is eventually revealed, is Eric Weil. Although Greisch discusses many of the central issues in the later Levinas, the essay is of particular interest to an English-speaking audience because of its extended comparison of Levinas and Wittgenstein. Fabio Ciaramelli's "Levinas's Ethical Discourse between Individuation and Universality" offers a discussion of the serious problem of the relation between individual responsibility and ethical universality in Levinas's work. Ciaramelli examines the irreducibly individual character of ethical responsibility for Levinas, the fact that it is my own ipseity and nobody else's that is reponsible to the other person. He compares this with the Levinasian claim that ethics is not a private affair of solitary subjects, inasmuch as responsibility to the other is demanded of every person. Ciaramelli claims that it is in the notion of prophecy, understood as ethical Saying, that the link is forged between the individual and the universal.

The third part of the volume, "Levinas and the Feminine," comprises essays by Luce Irigaray, Catherine Chalier, and Tina Chanter. These essays take up the question of sexual difference, which, as already mentioned, dominates the final pages of Derrida's "At this very moment." Irigaray's "Questions to Emmanuel Levinas: On the Divinity of Love"—which itself develops and distills her reading of Levinas in "The Fecundity of the Caress"[2]—is significant for identifying a double gesture or tension in Levinas's work between two levels of discourse. On the one hand, one finds in *Totality and Infinity* Levinas's "Phenomenology of Eros," a radical phenomenology of carnality and of the alterity of the feminine that would indicate "that we are no longer in the order of metaphysics." On the other hand, Irigaray argues, the institution of ethics

xvi / *Editors' Introduction*

through the concepts of fecundity and paternity reinscribes Levinas's work within the metaphysics of patriarchy and male subjectivity. Thus, although Levinas's phenomenology of feminine alterity interrupts metaphysics, Irigaray claims that he always gives a privilege to the second component of the double gesture, where "Levinas clings on once more to this rock of patriarchy in the very place of carnal love." Whereas Irigaray's essay represents a powerful and compelling feminist critique of Levinas, Catherine Chalier is more conciliatory and pursues the first movement of the double gesture outlined above, emphasizing the unusual privilege given to the feminine in Levinas's work. Basing her exposition on analyses of both *Otherwise than Being* and Levinas's confessional texts devoted to the Judaic tradition, she first argues that the theme of the feminine plays a central role in Levinas's critique of the virility of Being, as that which puts ontology and masculinity into question. Second, she focuses on the Levinasian themes of substitution, as the fulfillment of responsibility, and maternity, as the very pattern of substitution and the ultimate meaning of the feminine in Levinas. Third, she shows the function of the feminine in the disruption of Being by goodness, a point illustrated by the story of Rebecca in Genesis, a passage that also appears as a leitmotif in Simon Critchley's essay. Tina Chanter, in "Antigone's Dilemma," begins by discussing Derrida's relation to feminism and goes on to show how this issue is broached in "At this very moment," before offering her own analysis of the theme of the feminine in Levinas's work. She pursues this theme through Hegel's interpretation of Sophocles's *Antigone* and goes on to offer a new reading in terms of Antigone's renunciation of motherhood. Finally, with reference to and in defense of Irigaray, she argues against the claim that the affirmation of feminine specificity exposes feminists to the charge of essentialism.

Two of the essays from the fourth section, "Levinas's Readers: Derrida and Blanchot," those by Robert Bernasconi and Simon Critchley, have already been mentioned for their discussion of "At this very moment." A third essay, Ruben Berezdivin's "3 2 1 CONTACT: Textuality, the Other, Death," is a meditation upon Derrida's essay which explores the complexities involved in the textual contact or dialogue between Derrida and Levinas. Berezdivin introduces the third party of Heidegger into this dialogue, focusing on the analysis of Being-towards-death in *Being and Time*, and eventually claiming that the relation to the other is founded upon the relation to the other's mortality: the death of the other is the source of obligation.

Paul Davies's essay shifts attention to another reader of Levinas, Maurice Blanchot. Blanchot and Levinas have been friends since the 1920s when they were students together in Strasbourg. Their work intersects at various points over a long period. In keeping with the focus of this volume, Davies considers Blanchot's reading of (and with) Levinas's *Otherwise than Being*. Blanchot seems to have far fewer reservations about this text than he expressed about *Totality and Infinity*. Davies finds an explanation for this change in the distinction between the Saying and the Said and he charts how Blanchot takes it up into his own texts.

The final part of the volume, "Levinas, Psychoanalysis, and Animality," provides further illustration of how a re-reading of Levinas allows questions that Levinas himself barely touches on to be explored for the first time. Noreen O'Connor explores the implications of Levinas's work for psychotherapy by focusing upon the themes of suffering and obsession. The latter concept is traced in Levinas's work from *Totality and Infinity* through *Otherwise than Being* to his 1982 essay "Useless Suffering." O'Connor argues that suffering has an ethical status insofar as the other's suffering opens the self to the interhuman order, where my suffering only becomes meaningful as a suffering for the other's suffering: compassion. O'Connor's point is that to become a psychotherapist is only possible through the interhuman emergence of one's own suffering. It is to enter into an ethics based upon the primacy of the relation between human beings. In this sense, the psychotherapeutic relation can become an exemplar of the ethical relation.

In "Am I Obsessed by Bobby? Humanism of the Other Animal," John Llewelyn pursues the question of whether Levinasian ethics can extend to relations with animals. Llewelyn asks "who is the neighbor?" and again "who is the Other (*autrui*)?" and seeks to establish whether animals—Llewelyn focuses on the example of a dog discussed by Levinas—can be neighbors or Others for human beings and therefore become a source of ethical obligation. Llewelyn criticizes Levinas on the grounds that in the latter's "metaphysical ethics" one has direct responsibilities only toward beings that are capable of speech and that have a rationality that is presupposed by the universalizing reason fundamental to Kant's metaphysics of ethics. In short, for Levinas, one is only ethically responsible for human beings. Indeed, Llewelyn finds considerable agreement between Levinas and Kant, where ethical obligations to animals are conceived on analogy with human ethical relations, and where, consequently, animals are considered secondary to humans. The essay also explores the specific religious background to Levinas's estimation of animality.

Re-Reading Levinas: a call to read Levinas anew, to respond responsibly to his work. In spite of their diverse intonations, these essays share a desire to be scrupulous and cautious, while being prepared to risk a provocative response. They are readings marked by the peculiar necessity of Levinas's work, of its radicality as well as its aporias and blind spots. Readings which suspend the hastiness of critique and the assumption of mastery which it entails. Readings which are re-readings, both in their acknowledgment of the task of reading and in their recognition that Levinas's thinking is a thinking on the move which continues to reformulate itself much beyond *Totality and Infinity*.

Notes

1. See, for example, Robert Bernasconi, "The Trace of Levinas in Derrida," in *Derrida and Différance*, ed. D. Wood and R. Bernasconi, Chicago, North-

western University Press, 1988, 13–29; *and Simon Critchley, "The Chiasmus: Levinas, Derrida and the Ethical Demand for Deconstruction," Textual Practice* 3, no. 1, 1989: 91–106.

2. *Ethique de la différence sexuelle,* Paris, Minuit, 1984, 173–99; trans. Carolyn Burke, "The Fecundity of the Caress," in *Face to Face with Levinas,* ed. Richard Cohen, Albany, State University of New York Press, 1986, 231–56.

PART ONE

Ethics and Deconstructive Reading

CHAPTER

1

WHOLLY OTHERWISE

Emmanuel Levinas

Translated by Simon Critchley[1]

IT'S TODAY TOMORROW

May not Derrida's work cut into the development of Western thinking with a line of demarcation similar to that of Kantianism, which separated dogmatic philosophy from critical philosophy? Are we again at the end of a naïveté, of an unsuspected dogmatism which slumbered at the base of that which we took for critical spirit? We may well ask ourselves. The Idea, as the completion of a series which begins in intuition without being able to end there; the Idea said to be "in the Kantian sense of the term"[2] would operate within intuition itself: a transcendental semblance itself generating metaphysics would create an illusion within presence itself, a presence that would ceaselessly be found to be wanting. A new break in the history of philosophy? One that would also mark its continuity. The history of philosophy is probably only a growing awareness of the difficulty of thinking.

[82] In the meantime we walk in a "no-man's land,"[3] in an in-between (*un entre-les-deux*) which is uncertain even of the uncertainties which flicker everywhere. Suspension of truths! Strange epoch! Perhaps in writing each of us feels this when we catch ourselves unawares using familiar notions with a surplus of precautions, while the new critique would challenge the sense of imprudence as the virtue of prudence. A new style of thinking is dawning on us in reading these exceptionally precise texts which are yet so strange. In *Voice and Phenomenon*, which overthrows logocentric discourse, not a scrap of a sentence is contingent. A marvelous rigor learnt, to be sure, at the phenomenological school, an extreme attention given to the discrete gestures of Husserl and the broad movements of Heidegger, but carried out with coherence and consummate art: the reversal of the "limit concept" into *precondition* (*préalable*), of default into source, of the abyss into condition, of discourse into site—the reversal of these very reversals into destiny. Concepts purged of their ontic resonance, liberated from the alternative of truth and falsehood.

At the start, everything is in its place, and then, at the end of a few pages or paragraphs, under the effects of a formidable questioning, nothing is left for thought to dwell in. This is, beyond the philosophical scope of propositions, a purely literary effect, a new *frisson*, the poetry of Derrida. When I read him, I always recall the exodus of 1940. A retreating military unit arrives in an as yet unsuspecting locality, where the cafés are open, where the ladies visit the "ladies' fashion store," where the hairdressers dress hair and bakers bake; where viscounts meet other viscounts and tell each other stories of viscounts, and where, an hour later, everything is deconstructed and devastated: houses closed up or left with their doors open, emptied of their occupants who are swept along in a current of cars and pedestrians, through [83] roads restored to their "former glory" as roads when, in an immemorial past, they were traced by great migrations. In these in-between days, a symbolic episode: somewhere in between Paris and Alençon, a half-drunk barber used to invite soldiers who were passing on the road to come and have a free shave in his shop; the "lads" ("*les petits gars*") he used to call them in a patriotic language which soared above the waters or floated up from the chaos. With his two companions he shaved them free of charge—and it was today. The essential procrastination—the future différance—was reabsorbed into the present. Time came to its end with the end or the interim period of France.[4] Unless the barber was as delirious as that fourth form of delirium described in the *Phaedrus*, in which, since Plato, the discourse of Western metaphysics has remained.

THE PASS-TIME

Philosophy as defeat, as a defection from an impossible presence. Western metaphysics—and probably the whole of our history in Europe—will have been, through a conceptual apparatus that Derrida dismantles or deconstructs, the edification and preservation of this presence: the foundation of the very idea of founding, the foundation of all the relations which turn into experience, that is to say, the manifestation of beings architectonically arranging themselves upon a base which supports them; the manifestation of a world capable of constructing itself or, as they say, constituting itself for a transcendental apperception. The presence of the present, gathering and synchrony. Leave nothing lying around! Let nothing be lost! Keep everything that you own (*en propre*)! The security of European peoples, behind their frontiers and the walls of their houses, assured of their property[5] (an *Eigenheit* which becomes *Eigentum*)[6] is [84] not the sociological condition of metaphysical thinking but the very project of such a thinking. A project whose accomplishment is impossible and which is always deferred—*messianic future* as this presence in default. *Voice and Phenomenon* denounces this metaphysical simulacrum of presence maintained by the voice which listens to itself: presence and possession united in self-consciousness. A simulacrum or illusion which is prior to ontical illusion or appearing and prior to the distinction of reality and fantasy. Every material-ism bears its mark, as does every idealism.

The defection from presence led up to the defection from the true, to significations which do not have to comply with the summation of Knowledge. Truth is no longer at the level of an eternal or omnitemporal truth—but this is a relativity that no historicism would ever have been able to suspect. A deportation or drifting of Knowledge beyond the skepticism which remained in love with the truth, even if it felt incapable of embracing it. Henceforth, significations do not converge on the truth—truth's no great matter! Being won't be able to go the whole way: its bankrupt way of life demands new respites, a recourse to signs in the midst of a presence which steals away from itself; but only other signs are produced in the signified of these signs. The Husserlian notion of infinite iteration, the comprehension of which was assured, for Husserl, by the "idea in the Kantian sense," ceaselessly postpones the contemporaneity of the signified with a presence. The latter, always indicated, escapes from prehension (*la préhension*). From which arises the wearing away of the signified. A system of signs is liberated, a language guided by no full meaning, signifiers without a signified. Différance is thus said by way of a dissemination in which presence is deconstructed, a postponement without limits to be respected, which time is, or, more precisely, which pass-time itself is. A play in the interstices of Being [85] where the centers of gravitation are not the same as those of the world. But are there centers? Is there gravitation? Is there? (*Y a-t-il?*) Everything is otherwise if one can still speak of Being.

What remains constructed after the deconstruction is, certainly, the stern architecture of the deconstructing discourse which employs the present tense of the verb "to be" in predicative propositions. Discourse in the course of which, amidst the shaking of the foundations of truth, against the self-evidence of present lived experience which seems to offer an ultimate refuge to presence, Derrida still has the strength to say "is it certain?"[7] as if anything could be secure at that moment and as if security and insecurity should still matter.

One might well be tempted to infer an argument from this use of logocentric language against that very language, in order to dispute the produced deconstruction: a path much followed by the refutation of skepticism, but where, although at first crushed and trampled underfoot, skepticism got back up on its feet to come back as the legitimate child of philosophy.[8] A path, perhaps, that Derrida himself has not always disdained from following in his polemic.

But, in following this path, one would risk missing one side of the signification which this very inconsequence bears. One would risk missing the incompressible nonsimultaneity of the Said and the Saying, the dislocation of their correlation. A dislocation which, although minimal, would be wide enough to swallow up skeptical discourse, but without stifling itself in the contradiction between what is signified by its Said and what is signified by the very fact of articulating a Said. As if simultaneity were lacking from the two significations, so that the contradiction broke the knot that tied them together. As if the correlation of the Saying and the Said was a diachrony of that which can't be brought together (*l'inassemblable*). As if the situation of the [86] Saying was already a "memory retention" for the Said, but without the *lapse* of the instants of the Saying letting themselves be recuperated in this memory.

The truth of truths would not therefore be capable of being gathered into an instant, nor into a synthesis where the supposed movement of the dialectic comes to a standstill. The truth of truths lies in the Said, in the Unsaid, and in the Otherwise Said—return, resumption, reduction: the history of philosophy or its preliminary. Is this what Blanchot suggests to us in *L'attente . . . L'oubli*, by successively making the subject of the proposition agree with the affirmative and negative forms of the predicate?[9] Perhaps the truth of truths does not have the style of verbal dissemination, but it is from the same nonworld (the end of "eternal truths") of which empiricism and historical relativism can imagine neither the agony nor the figures drawn by their convulsions. It is not therefore absurd that a rigorous reflection lets us catch a glimpse of these interstices of Being where this very reflection unsays itself. One can see nothing without thematization, or without the oblique rays which it reflects back, even when it is a question of the nonthematizable.

The path toward these pathless "places." ("*lieux*"), the subsoil of our empirical places, does not, in any case, open itself to the vertigo which we get from those who—dreadfully well-informed, prodigiously intelligent, and more Derridian than Derrida—interpret his extraordinary work with the assistance of all the key-words at once, without having or leaving time to return to the thinking of which these words are contemporary.

THE CHIASMUS

Derrida's critique, which liberates time from its subordination to the present, which no longer takes the past and the future as modes, modifications, or [87] modulations of presence, and which arrests a thinking which reasons upon signs as upon signifieds, thinks through to the end Bergson's critique of Being and Kant's critique of metaphysics. The evidence given by consciousness itself loses its Cartesian privilege in this deconstruction of presence. Must one apologize for quoting these ancient authors? That doesn't prevent this idea of "going the whole way" ("*jusqu'au boutisme*") from leading to the peculiar nonorder of the excluded middle, where one refuses to recognize the value of the disjunction between the yes and the no—imperious alternative, thanks to which computers decide the fate of the universe.

It will probably be less willingly acknowledged (and Derrida will probably deny it) that this critique of Being in its eternal presence of ideality allows, for the first time in the history of the West, the thought of the *Being of the creature*, without recourse to an ontic account of divine operation, without from the start treating "Being" ("*être*") as a being (*étant*), without using negative and empirical concepts like those of contingency and of "generation and corruption," which are as ontic as the idea of the incorruptibility of the Whole (*Tout*).

For the first time, the "lesser being" (*le "moins être"*) of the creature is shown in its verbality of verb. It is true that, to avoid a return of the metaphysics of presence in this thinking, he seeks, for the operative concept of the sign which supplements (*supplée*) a failed presence, another referent than the failure of this presence and another site than the Said of language (*langage*), oral or written; a site other than the language (*langue*) which, entirely at the disposal of the speaker, feigns synchrony itself, the presence par excellence of a system of signs which is already presupposed by any empirical simultaneity. But is not the attempt at a positive utterance of this failure of presence to itself still a way of returning to the presence with which this positivity merges? To say that this failure is still within Being is to revolve in the circle of Being and [88] nothingness—ultimate concepts but of the same degree—and to retain for Being only the taste of unhappiness. Doubtless, this unhappiness is more assured than the hoped for happiness which, beyond pleasures and intoxications, is the impossible plenitude of presence. But is there no way out of ontology?

That language be grafted upon the most invisible difference of time, that its Saying be dislocated from its Said, that the correlation be not rigorous (already breaking the unity of apperception and, consequently, already breaking the possibilities of experience), certainly sets language apart from everything empirical which exhausts itself in presence and in the lack of presence. Indeed, starting from the Saying and from its own signification, its correlation with the Said must, one day, be rediscovered—and this isn't impossible. But the Saying does not exhaust itself in this Said, and the sign has not grown on the soil of the ontology of the Said in order to receive its paradoxical relational structure from it (which so astonished Plato that it pushed him to parricide) and in order to supplement a presence slipping away from itself. Like the Saying, the sign is the extra-ordinary event—against the flow of presence—of exposure and subjection to the Other, the event of subjectivity. It's the one-for-the-other. It's the signification which does not exhaust itself in simple absence of intuition and presence. We ask: whence comes the sign that produces a presence deficient to itself or the diachrony of that which cannot be brought together which produces creaturality (*la créaturalité*)? It does not begin (if indeed it begins, if it is not an-archy from top to bottom) as a Said. As substitution, supplementing (*suppléance*), or the one-for-the-other, isn't the sign, in its decisive suspension of the *for-itself*, the for-the-other of my responsibility to the Other? The difference between the Same and the other is the nonindifference for the other of fraternity. What appears to deconstructive analysis as truly lacking in itself is not the *surplus*—which would still be a promise of happiness and a residue of ontology—but the *better* (*le mieux*) of [89] proximity; an excellence, an elevation, ethics before Being or the Good beyond Being, to quote once again an ancient author. The presence of the present that Descartes discovered in the *cogito*, without suspecting the unconscious which was eating away at it, immediately shattered between his fingers with the idea of God that presence could not contain.

We shall not prolong the trajectory of a thinking which is on the side opposite to the one on which its verb disseminates itself. Indeed, the ridiculous ambition* of "improving"[10] a true philosopher is not our intention. To meet him on his way is already very commendable and is probably the very modality of the philosophical encounter. In underlining the primordial importance of the questions posed by Derrida, we wished to express the pleasure of a contact made in the heart of a chiasmus.

Translator's Notes

1. An earlier draft of this translation was prepared by Olivier Serafinowicz, which I have consulted throughout. I am also very grateful to Geoff Bennington, who scrupulously corrected errors and suggested many invaluable improvements to the translation. Finally, my thanks go to John Llewelyn, who read the final draft and suggested at least a dozen crucial amendments, all of which have been silently incorporated into the present text.

The page numbers of the French text as published in NP have been included in square brackets.

2. This phrase appears in Husserl's *Ideas* (see paragraph 83 in *Ideas: General Introduction to Pure Phenomenology*, trans. W. R. Boyce-Gibson, London, Macmillan, 1931) and is discussed in Derrida's *Introduction à l'origine de la géométrie*, Paris, P.U.F., 1962 (see esp. 149 n. 1 with reference to Levinas). The phrase also appears in *La voix et le phénomène*, Paris, P.U.F., 1967, 8, 112, 114.

3. In English in the original. See also TeI 149; TI 174.

4. Levinas would here seem to be referring to the period of the Nazi occupation of France.

5. "Propriété"—Levinas would here seem to be playing with the manifold meanings of the French term "propre." The latter can mean proper, ownness, cleanliness, property, and possession. Thus, the idea of being self-possessed in one's own self-presence is connected with the idea of property ownership. This word assumes a fundamental importance in Derrida's writings and in particular in his reading of Heidegger: see "Les fins de l'homme" in *Marges*, Paris, Minuit, 1972 and *Eperons: Les styles de Nietzsche*, Paris, Flammarion, 1978, esp. 92–96.

6. This literally means, "a propriety which becomes a property." Levinas is here emphasizing the German term "Eigen" which is broadly equivalent to the French "propre."

---

*An ambition which Kant very mischievously ascribed to Salomon Maimon with respect to the critical philosophy, in his letter of 28 March 1789. It's true that the two situations are in no way alike, for several reasons![11]

7. See *La voix et le phénomène*, 106, "Est-ce sûr?"

8. "Pour revenir en enfant légitime de la philosophie." This phrase occurs at least three times in Levinas's *Autrement qu'être ou au-delà de l'essence*, AE 9, 108 n. 18, and 231. In *Otherwise than Being or Beyond Essence* (OB), it is systematically and, I believe, incorrectly translated as "philosophy's illegitimate child" (7) "a bastard child of the spirit" (192) and "a bastard child of philosophical research" (182).

9. For a discussion of the way in which the consecutive use of affirmatior and negation opens up a modality of transcendence, see Levinas's "La servante et son maître: A propos de 'L'attente . . . L'oubli,'" in *Sur Maurice Blanchot*, Montpellier, Fata Morgana, 1975.

10. Interestingly, Levinas employs exactly the same formulation of the futility of "improving" a true philosopher when outlining his questions and objections to Martin Buber:

> These objections or, better, questions, stem from a reflection on Heidegger and on certain passages of the *Phaedrus* where the problem of the absolutely other is encountered, and it is in this desire for the other that a definition of metaphysics has itself been sought. Buber's descriptions are essential to that metaphysics, and in formulating these objections or questions we deny ourselves the ridiculous position of him who wishes to "improve upon" the work of a creative spirit.

(From "Interrogation of Martin Buber, conducted by Maurice Friedman," *Philosophical Interrogations*, ed. S. and B. Rome, New York, Harper and Row, 1970, 25–26. One can find the same formulation in *Totality and Infinity*—TeI 40–41; TI 69—once again with reference to Buber.)

11. Levinas is exactly five years too early here. The letter to Reinhold which mentions Salomon Maimon's "improvement" to the critical philosophy is dated 28 March 1794. Levinas is probably confused about the date because there exists an earlier correspondence between Maimon and Kant which in fact dates from 1789. Upon the advice of Kant's friend Marcus Herz, Maimon sent a copy of his *Essay on Transcendental Philosophy* (1790) to Kant before its publication, in order to elicit Kant's "priceless judgment" (*Kant's Philosophical Correspondence 1755–99*, ed. and trans. Arnulf Zweig, Chicago, University of Chicago Press, 1967, 211. Subsequent citations refer to this volume). Some six weeks later, Kant replied to Maimon through the intermediary of Herz. Kant warmly praises the work, writing that, "not only had none of my critics understood me and the main questions as well as Mr. Maimon does but also very few men possess so much acumen for deep investigations as he" (151). Kant goes on to give a detailed examination and refutation of Maimon's revisions to the critical philosophy, which concludes with the following remark to Herz: "But, dearest friend, your request for a recommendation from me, to accompany the publication of this work, would not be feasible, since it is after all largely directed against me" (156). Maimon, unhappy with this response, would write to Kant on several further occasions, but the latter always

refused to reply. Finally, in the letter to which Levinas refers, Kant speaks of the "inexpressible difficulty" (211) he feels when he is forced to project himself into other people's ideas. As an example of this difficulty, Kant cites Maimon's "improvement" to the critical philosophy and confesses, "I have never really understood what he is after and must leave the reproof to others" (211). Strangely, in a parenthesis to the same letter, and with reference to Maimon, Kant makes the following antisemitic remark: "Jews always like to do that sort of thing, to gain an air of importance for themselves at someone else's expense" (212). Doubtless this is why Levinas concludes his article by claiming that the two situations (those obtaining between himself and Derrida and Maimon and Kant) are in no way alike!

CHAPTER
2

AT THIS VERY MOMENT IN THIS WORK HERE I AM

Jacques Derrida

Translated by Ruben Berezdivin[1]

— He will have obligated (*il aura obligé*).

At this very instant, you hear me, I have just said it. He will have obligated. If you hear me, already you are sensible to the strange event. Not that you have been visited, but as after the passing by of some singular visitor, you are no longer familiar with the places, those very places where nonetheless the little phrase—Where does it come from? Who pronounced it?—still leaves its resonance lingering (*égarée*).

As if from now on we didn't dwell there any longer, and to tell the truth, as if we had never been at home. But you aren't uneasy, what you feel—something unheard of yet so very ancient—is not a malaise; and even if something is affecting you without having touched you, [22] still you have been deprived of nothing. No negation ought to be able to measure itself up to what is happening so as to be able to describe it.

Notice, you can still hear yourself (*tu peux encore t'entendre*) all alone repeating the three words ["il aura obligé"], you have failed neither to hear its rumor nor understand its sense. You are no longer without them, without these words which are discrete, and thereby unlimited, overflowing with discretion. I myself no longer know where to stop them. What surrounds them? He will have obligated. The edges of the phrase remain drowned in a fog. Nevertheless it seems quite plain and clearly set off (*decoupée*) in its authoritarian brevity, complete without appeal, without requiring any adjective or complement, not even any noun: he will have obligated. But precisely, nothing surrounds it sufficiently to assure us of its limits. The sentence is not evasive but its border lies concealed. About the phrase, whose movement can't be resumed by any of the one, two, three words ["il aura obligé"] of one, two, three syllables, about it you can no longer say that nothing is happening at this very moment.

But what then? The shore is lacking, the edges of a phrase belong to the night.

He will have obligated—distanced (*éloigné*) from all context.

That's right, distanced, which does not forbid, on the contrary, proximity. What they call a context and which comes to shut in the sense of a discourse, always more or less, is never simply absent, only more or less strict. But no cut *is* there, no utterance is ever cut from all context, the context is never annulled without remainder. One must therefore negotiate, deal with, transact with marginal effects (*les effets de bord*). One must even negotiate what is nonnegotiable and which overflows all context.

Here at this very moment, when I am here trying to give you to understand, the border of a context is less narrow, less strictly determining than one is accustomed to believe. "Il aura obligé": there you have a phrase that may appear to some terribly indeterminate. But the distance that is granted to us here would not be due so much to a certain quite apparent absence of an edge ("il aura obligé," without a nameable subject, complement, attribute, or identifiable past or future on this page, in this work [*ouvrage*] at the moment when you hear yourself presently reading it), but rather because of a certain *inside* of what is said and of the saying of what is said *in* the phrase, and which, from within, if this may still be said, infinitely *overflows* at a stroke all possible context. And that at the very moment, in a work, for example —but you don't yet know what I mean by that word, work—when the wholly other who will have visited this phrase negotiates the nonnegotiable with a context, negotiates his economy *as* that of the other.

He will have obligated.

You must find me enigmatic, a bit glib or perverse in cultivating the enigma every time I repeat this little [23] phrase, always the same, and lacking context, becoming more and more obscure. No, and I say this without studying the effect, the possibility of this repetition is the very thing that interests me, interests you as well, even before we should happen to find it interesting, and I should like slowly to move closer (to you, maybe, but by a proximity that binds [*lie*], he would say, to the first comer, to the unmatched other, before all contract, without any present being able to gather together a contact), slowly to bring myself closer to this, namely that I can no longer formalize, since the event ["il aura obligé"] will have precisely defied within language (*la langue*) this power of formalization. He will have obligated to comprehend, let us say rather to receive, because affection, an affection more passive than passivity, is party to all this, he will have obligated to receive totally otherwise the little phrase. To my knowledge he has never pronounced it as such, it matters little. He will have obligated to "read" it totally otherwise. Now to make us (without making us) receive otherwise, and receive otherwise the otherwise, he has been unable to do otherwise than negotiate with the risk: in the same language, the language of the same, one may always ill receive what is thus otherwise said. Even before that fault, the risk contaminates its very proposition. What becomes of this fault then? And if it is inevitable, what sort of event is at issue? Where would it take place?

He will have obligated. However distanced it may remain, there is certainly some context in that phrase.

You hear it resonate, at this very moment, in this work.

What I thus call "this work" is not, especially not, dominated by the name of Emmanuel Levinas.

It is rather meant to be given to him. Given according to his name, in his name as much as to his name. Therefore there are multiple chances, probabilities, you cannot avoid surrendering to them, so that the subject of the phrase, "il aura obligé," might be Emmanuel Levinas.

Still it is not sure. And even if one could be sure of it, would one thereby have responded to the question: Who is the "He" ("*Il*") in that phrase?

Following a strange title that resembles a cryptic quotation in its invisible quotation marks, the site of this phrase "princeps" doesn't allow you yet to know by what right *He* carries a capital. Perhaps not only as an incipit, and, in this hypothesis of another capital letter or of the capital letter of the Other, be attentive to all the consequences. It is drawn into the play of the irreplaceable *He* submitting itself to substitution, like an object, into the irreplaceable itself. He, without italics.

I wonder why I have to address myself to you to say that. And why after so many attempts, so many failures, here I am obligated to renounce the anonymous neutrality of a discourse proposed, in its form at least, to no matter whom, pretending self-mastery and mastery of its object in a formalization without remainder? I won't pronounce your name nor inscribe it, but you [24] are not anonymous at the moment when here I am telling you this, *sending it* to you like a letter, giving it to you to hear or to read, *giving* being infinitely more important to me than what it might transmit at the moment I receive the desire from you, at the moment when I let you dictate to me what I would like to give you of myself. Why? Why at this very moment?

Suppose that in giving to you—it little matters what—I wanted to give to him, him Emmanuel Levinas. Not render him anything, homage for example, not even render myself to him, but to give him something which escapes from the circle of restitution or of the "rendez-vous." ("Proximity," he writes, "doesn't enter into that common time of clocks that makes the rendez-vous possible. It is derangement.") I would like to do it faultlessly (*sans faute*), with a "faultlessness" ("*sans-faute*") that no longer belongs to the time or logic of the rendez-vous. Beyond any possible restitution, there would be need for my gesture to operate without debt, in absolute ingratitude. The trap is that I then pay homage, the only possible homage, to his work (*oeuvre*), to what his work says of the Work (*Oeuvre*): "The Work thought to the end requires a radical generosity of the movement in which the Same goes toward the Other. Consequently, it requires an *ingratitude* from the other." He will have written this twice, in appearance literally identically, in *The Trace of the Other* and in *Signification and Sense*. But one cannot economize on this *seriality*. I will return to this.

Suppose then that I wished to *give* to him, to E.L., and beyond all restitution. I will have to do it in *conformance* with what he will have said of the

Work in his work, in the Work of his work. I will still be caught in the circle of debt and restitution with which the nonnegotiable will have to be negotiated. I would be debating with myself, interminably, forever, and even before having known it, up to the point, perhaps, when I would affirm the absolutely anachronic dissymetry of a debt without loan, acknowledgment, or possible restitution.

According to which he will have immemorially obligated even before calling himself by any name whatsoever or belonging to any genre whatsoever. The conformity of *conformance* is no longer thinkable within that logic of truth which dominates—without being able to command it—our language and the language of philosophy. If in order to give without restituting, I must still conform to what he says of the Work in his work, and to what he gives there as well as to a re-tracing of the giving; more precisely, if I must conform my gesture to what makes the Work in his Work, which is older than his work, and whose Saying according to his own terms is not reducible to the Said, there we are, engaged before all engagement, in an incredible logic, formal and nonformal. If I restitute, if I restitute without fault, I am at fault. And if I do not restitute, by *giving* beyond acknowledgment, I risk the fault. I leave for now in this word—fault—all the liberty of its registers, from crime to [25] a fault of spelling. As to the proper name of what finds itself at issue here, as to the proper name of the other, that would, perhaps, return/amount to the same (*cela reviendrait peut-être au même*).

There you are, forewarned: it is the risk or chance of that fault that fascinates or obsesses me at this very moment, and what can happen to a faulty writing, to a faulty letter (the one I write you), what can remain of it, what the ineluctable possibility of such a fault gives to think about a text or a remainder. Ineluctable since the structure of "faultiness" is, a priori, older even than any a priori. If anyone (He) tells you *from the start* (*d'abord*): "don't return to me what I give you," you are at fault even before he finishes talking. It suffices that you hear him, that you begin to understand and acknowledge. You have begun to receive his injunction, to give yourself to what he says, and the more you obey him in restituting nothing, the better you will disobey him and become deaf to what he addresses to you. All that might resemble a logical paradox or trap. But it is "anterior" to all logic. I spoke, *wrongly*, of a trap just now. It is only felt as a trap from the moment when one would pretend to escape from absolute dissymmetry through a will to mastery or coherence. It would be a way to acknowledge the gift in order to refuse it. Nothing is more difficult than to accept a gift. Now what I "want" to "do" here is to accept the gift, to affirm and reaffirm it as what I have received. Not from someone who would himself have had the initiative for it, but from someone who would have had the force to receive it and reaffirm it. And if it is thus that (in my turn) I give to you, it will no longer form a chain of restitutions, but another gift, the gift of the other. Is that possible? Will it have been possible? Shouldn't it have already taken place, before everything, so that the very question may emerge from it, which in advance renders the question obsolete?

The gift *is not*. One cannot ask "what is the gift?"; yet it is only on that *condition* that there will have been, by this name or another, a gift.

Hence, suppose that beyond all restitution, in radical ingratitude (but notice, not just any ingratitude, not in the ingratitude that still belongs to the circle of acknowledgment and reciprocity), I desire (it desires in me, but the it [*le ça*] is not a neutral non-me), I desire to try to give to E.L. This or that? Such and such a thing? A discourse, a thought, a writing? No, that would still give rise to exchange, commerce, economic reappropriation. No, to give him the very giving of giving, a giving which might no longer even be an object or a present said, because every present remains within the economic sphere of the same, nor an impersonal infinitive (the "giving" [*le "donner"*] therefore must perforate the grammatical phenomenon dominated by the current interpretation of language), nor any operation or action sufficiently self-identical to return to the same. That "giving" must be neither a thing nor an act, it must somehow be [26] someone (male or female) not *me*: nor him ("he"). Strange, isn't it, this excess that overflows language at every instant and yet requires it, sets it incessantly into motion at the very moment of traversing it? That traversal is not a transgression, the passage of a cutting limit; the very metaphor of overflowing (*débordement*) no longer fits insofar as it still implies some linearity.

Even before I attempt or desire to attempt it, suppose that the desire for that gift is evoked in me by the other, without however obligating me or at least before any obligation of constraint, of a contract, or gratitude, or acknowledgment of the debt: a duty without debt, a debt without contract. That should be able to do without him or happen with anyone: hence it demands, *at once*, this anonymity, this possibility of indefinitely equivalent substitution *and* the singularity, nay the absolute uniqueness of the proper name. Beyond any thing, beyond whatever might lead it astray or seduce it toward something else, beyond everything that could somehow or other return to me, such a gift should go right to the unique, to what his name will have *uniquely* named, to that uniqueness that his name will have given. This *right* does not derive from any right, from any jurisdiction transcendent to the gift itself; it is the right of what he calls, in a sense that perhaps you don't understand yet, because it disturbs language every time it visits it, *rectitude* or *sincerity*.

Which his name will have *uniquely* named or given. But (but it would require saying *but* for every word) uniquely in another sense than that of the singularity which jealously guards its propriety or property as irreplaceable subject within the proper name of an author or proprietor, in the sufficiency of a self assured of its signature. Finally, suppose that in the wake of the gift I commit a fault, that I let a fault, as they say, slip by, that I don't write straight (*que je n'écrive pas droit*), that I fail to write as one must (but *one must* [*il faut*], *one must* understand otherwise the *one must*), or that I fail to give him, *to him*, a gift that is not *his*. I am not at this very moment thinking of a fault on his name, on his forename or patronym, but with such a default in the writing that in the end would constitute a fault of spelling, a bad treatment inflicted on this proper name, whether done consciously or expressly by me or not.

Since in that fault your body is at issue (*il y va*), and since, as I previously said, the gift I would make him comes from you who dictate it to me, your unease grows. In what could such a fault consist? Shall one ever be able to avoid it? Were it inevitable, and hence in the final account irreparable, why should reparation require claiming? And especially, above all, on this hypothesis, What would have taken place? I mean: What would happen (and about what? Or whom?)? What would be the proper place of this text, of this faulty body? Will it have properly taken place? Where should you and I, we, let it be? [27]

— No, not let it be. Soon, we shall have to give it to him to eat, and drink, and you will listen to me.

— Does the body of a faulty text take place? He himself has an answer to this question, so it seems. There should be no protocols for gifts, nor preliminaries awaiting for conditions of possibility. Or the protocols should then already constitute a gift. It is under the heading of a protocol, and hence without knowing up to what point here a gift is probable, that I would like first (*d'abord*) to start interrogating his response to the question of the faulty text. His answer is first of all practical: he deals with the fault, deals with the fault by writing in a certain way and not in another. The interest I take in the manner he writes his works (*ouvrages*) may appear out of place: to write, in the current sense of the word, to concoct phrases and compose, exploit a rhetoric or a poetics, etc., is not in the last instance what matters to him, being a collection of subordinated gestures. And yet I believe that the obligation at issue in our little phrase quoted above *ties itself* (*se noue*) into a certain kind of binding (*lier*), not only of the Saying with the Said, but of Writing to the Said and of Saying to the written; and ties itself to a binding, a tightening, an enchaining together and an interlacing according to a serial structure of a singular type. Soon I will come back to what I am myself lacing together in the word *series*.

How, then, does he write? How does what he writes make a work (*ouvrage*), and make the Work (*Oeuvre*) in the work (*ouvrage*)? For instance, and most especially, what does he do when he writes in the present, in the grammatical form of the present, to say what cannot be nor ever will have been present, the *present said* only presenting itself in the name of a Saying that overflows it infinitely within and without, like a sort of absolute anachrony of the wholly other that, although incommensurably heterogeneous to the language of the present and the discourse of the same, nonetheless must leave a trace of it, always improbably but each time determinate, this one, and not another? How does he manage to inscribe or let the wholly other be inscribed within the language of being, of the present, of essence, of the same, of economy, etc., within its syntax and lexicon, under its law? How does he manage to give a place there to what remains absolutely foreign to that medium, absolutely unbound from that language, beyond being, the present, essence, the same, the economy, etc.? Mustn't one reverse the question, at least in appearance, and ask oneself if that language is not *of itself unbound* and hence open to the wholly other, to its own beyond, in such a way that it is less a matter of exceeding that language than of treating it otherwise with its own possibilities. Treating it otherwise, in other words to calculate the transaction, negotiate the compromise that would leave the nonnegotiable intact, and to do this in such a way as to make the fault, which consists in inscribing the wholly other within the empire of the same, alter the same enough to absolve itself from itself. According to me that is his answer, and that [28] de facto answer, if one may say so, that response in deed, at work rather in the series of strategic negotiations, that response does not respond to a problem or a question, it responds to the Other—for the Other—and approaches (*aborde*) writing in enjoining itself to that for-the-Other. It is by starting from the Other that writing thus gives a place and forms an event, for example this one: "Il aura obligé."

It is that response, the responsibility of that response, that I would like to interrogate in its turn. Interrogate, to be sure, is not the word, and I don't yet know how to qualify what is happening here between him, you, and me that doesn't belong to the order of questions and responses. It would be rather his responsibility—and what he says of responsibility—that interrogates us beyond all the coded discourses on the subject.

Hence: What is he doing, how does he work (*oeuvre*) when, under the false appearance of a present, in a more-than-present (*plus-que-présent*), he will have written this, for example, where I slowly read to you, at this very moment, listen:

> Responsibility for the other, going against intentionality and the will which intentionality does not succeed in dissimulating, signifies not the disclosure of a given and its reception, but the exposure of me to the other, prior to every decision. There is a claim laid on the Same by the Other in the core of myself, the extreme tension of the command exercised by the Other in me over me, a traumatic hold of the other on the Same, which does not allow the Same time to await the Other. . . . The subject in responsibility is alienated in the depths of its identity with an alienation that does not empty the Same of its identity, but constrains it to it, with an unimpeachable assignation, constrains it to it as no one else, where no one could replace it. The psyche, a uniqueness outside of concepts, is a seed of folly, already a psychosis. It is not an ego (*Moi*), but me (*moi*) under assignation. There is an assignation to an identity for the response of responsibility, where one cannot have oneself be replaced without fault. To this command continually put forth only a "here I am" (*me voici*) can answer, where the pronoun "I" is in the accusative, declined before any declension, possessed by the other, sick,[2] identical. Here I am—an inspired saying, which is not a gift for fine words or songs. There is constraint to give with full hands, and thus a constraint to corporeality. . . . It is the subjectivity of a man of flesh and blood, more passive in its extradition to the other than the passivity of effects in a causal chain, for it is beyond the unity of apperception of the *I think*, which is actuality itself. It is a being-torn-up-from-oneself-for-another in the giving-to-the-other-of-the-bread-out-of-one's-own-mouth. This is not an anodyne formal relation, but all the gravity

of the body extirpated from its *conatus essendi* [29] in the possibility of giving. The identity of the subject is here brought out, not by resting upon itself, but by a restlessness that drives me outside of the nucleus of my substantiality.

(I should have liked slowly to consider the title of the work (*ouvrage*) which I have just quoted: in a singular comparative locution that does not constitute a phrase, an adverb (*otherwise*) immeasurably wins out over a verb (and what a verb: to be) to say something "other" that cannot make nor even modify a noun or a verb, nor this noun-verb which always amounts/returns to *being*, in order to say something else, some "other" thing that is neither verb nor noun, and especially not the simple alter*ity* that would still submit the *otherwise* (that modality without substance) to the authority of a category, an essence or being again. The beyond of verbalization (constitution into a verb) or nominalization, the beyond of the *symplokè* binding the nouns and the verbs by playing the game of essence, that beyond leaves a chain of traces, an other *symplokè* already "within" the title, *beyond essence*, yet without allowing itself to be included, rather deforming the curvature of its natural edges [*bords*].)

You have just heard the "present" of the "Here I am" freed for the other and declined before any declension. That "present" was already very complicated in its structure, one could say almost contaminated by that very thing from which it should have been rent. It is not the presumed signatory of the work, E.L., who says: "Here I am," me, presently. He *quotes* a "Here I am," he thematizes what is nonthematizable (to use that vocabulary to which he will have assigned a regular—and somewhat strange—conceptual function in his writings). But beyond the Song of Songs or Poem of Poems, the citation of whoever would say "Here I am" should serve to mark out *this* extradition when responsibility for the other gives me over to the other. No grammatical marking as such, no language or context would suffice to determine it. That present-quotation, which, as a quotation, seems to efface the present event of any irreplaceable "here I am," also comes *to say* that in "here I am" the self is no longer presented as a self-present subject, making itself present to itself (I-myself), it is declined before all declension, "in the accusative," and he

— He or she, if the interruption of the discourse is required. Isn't it "she" in the Song of Songs? And who would "she" be? Does it matter?

Nearly always with him, this is how he sets his work in the fabric: by interrupting the weaving of our language and then by weaving together the interruptions themselves, another language comes to disturb the first one. It doesn't inhabit it, but haunts it. Another text, the text of the other, arrives in silence with a more or less regular cadence, without ever appearing in its original language, to dislodge the language of translation, converting the version, and refolding it while folding it upon the very thing [30] it pretended to import. It disassimilates it. But then, that phrase translated and quoted from the Song of Songs which, it should be recalled, is already a response, and a response that is more or less fictitious in its rhetoric, and what is more, a response meant in turn to be *quoted*, transmitted, and communicated in indirect discourse—this gives the accusative its greatest grammatical plausibility (various translations render it more or less exactly: "I opened to my beloved; / but my beloved had gone away, he had disappeared. / I was outside myself when he spoke to me. . . . I called him and he did not reply. . . . They have taken away my veil, the guards of the walls. / I implore you, daughters of Jerusalem / If you find my beloved, / What will you say to him? . . . / That I am sick of love." Or again "I open myself to my darling / but my darling has slipped away, he has passed. / My being goes out at his speaking: / I seek him and do not find him. / I call him: he does not reply. . . . On me they take away my shawl, / the guardians of the ramparts. / I appeal to you, daughters of Yeroushalaïm: if you find my darling, what will you declare to him? /— That sick of love, I . . ."), that phrase translated and quoted (in a footnote, so as to open up and deport the principal text); it is torn from the mouth of a woman, so as to be given to the other. Why doesn't he clarify that in this work?

— Doubtless because that remains in this context, and with regard to his most urgent purpose, secondary. Here, at least, he doesn't seem to answer that question. In the passage that quotes the "here I am," which I have in turn read to you, the structure of the utterances is complicated by the "astriction to giving." What is quoted here is what no quotation should be able to muffle; what is each time said only once, and henceforth exceeds not the saying but the said in language. The phrase describes or says what within the said interrupts it and at one stroke makes it anachronistic with respect to the saying, negotiated between the said and the saying and at the same time interrupting the negotiation while forthwith negotiating interruption itself. Such negotiation deals with a language, with the ordering of a grammar and a lexicon, with a system of normative constraints, which tend to interdict what here *must be said* (*il faut dire*), namely the astriction to giving and the extradition of subjectivity to the other. The negotiation thematizes what forbids thematization, while during the very trajectory of that transaction it forces language into a contract with the stranger, with what it can only incorporate without assimilating. With a nearly illegible stroke the other stands the contaminating negotiation up (*fait faux-bond*), furtively marking the effraction with a saying unreduced to silence although no longer *said in language*. The grammatical utterance is there, but dislodged so as to leave room for (though not to establish residence in) a sort of agrammaticality of the gift assigned from the other: *I* in the accusative, etc. The interdictory language [31] is interdicted but continues speaking; it can't help it, it can't avoid being continually and strangely interrupted and disconcerted by what traverses it with a single step, drawing it along while leaving it in place. Whence the essential function of a quotation, its unique setting to work, which consists in quoting the unquotable so as to lay stress on the language, citing it as a whole in order to summon *at once* as witness and as accused within its limits, (sur)rendered to a gift, as a gift to which language cannot open up on its own. It is not, then, simply a matter of transgression, a simple passage beyond language and its norms. It is not, then, a thought of the limit, at least not of that limit all too easily figured forth by the word "beyond" so necessary for the transaction. The passage beyond language requires language or rather a text as a place for the trace of a step that is not (present) elsewhere. That is why the movement of that trace, passing beyond language, is not classical nor does it render the *logos* either secondary or instrumental. *Logos* remains as indispensable as the fold folded onto the gift, just like the tongue (*langue*) of my mouth when I tear bread from it to give it to the other. It is also my body.

The description of this discursive structure could be further refined, but it doesn't matter much. Whatever the complications, the example we have just encountered remains held within quite strict limits. Which? Due to the (in some manner) first order quotationality of the "here I am," which is not the glib exhibition of the self but the unreserved exposition of its secret staying secret, the presumed signatory, E.L., does not directly say *I* in the text. He does speak of the "I think," to be sure otherwise, and sometimes the indecision as to whether he says "I" or the "I," myself or the self, remains undecidable (for example: "The identity of the subject is here accused, not by a self-repose but by an unease that chases me out of the nucleus of my substantiality." Earlier in the same text he writes: "I have always been at issue: persecuted. Ipseity, in its passivity without the *arche* of identity, is hostage. The word *I* means *here I am*, answering for everything and everybody" [AE 145; OB 114]), according to a rhetoric that may appear traditional within philosophical discourse. But nothing in the discourse you have listened to *remarks* upon a certain present of the scription, at this very moment, the phenomenal maintenance of writing, the "I say now (*maintenant*) that I say (the Saying)" or "I write now that I write (the Saying)," which you are at this very moment reading. At least it is not thematized. When that comes about, and it does, the protocols will have to be further complicated, the protocols of the negotiation with the contagious or contaminant powers of a reappropriative language, of the language of the Same, strange or allergic to the Other. And one will then have to produce or recognize therein the symptoms of that allergy, particularly when something like a "this is what is going on at this moment," "that's what I mean [32] and how I say it in this work," "that's how I write certain of my books," comes to describe the law of that negotiation and by the same stroke to interrupt, *not without* recounting, the interruption. For that negotiation is not merely a negotiation like any other. It negotiates the nonnegotiable and not with just any partner or adversary, but with The negotiation itself, with the negotiating power that believes itself able to negotiate everything. *This* negotiation (which passively and one would almost say idly interrupts the negotiating activity, which denies it by a double negation) should negotiate the treatment of the nonnegotiable so as to keep (*garder*) its chance for it, that is to say so that it gives and does not keep itself intact like the same.

Here is an example (I will limit myself to a few examples, taking into account the economy regulated at this very moment by the time of writing, the mode of composition, and the editorial facture of this work [*ouvrage*] here). Listen:

But the reason of justice, the State, thematization, synchronization, of the re-presentation of logos and of being, doesn't it manage *to absorb within its coherence the intelligibility of that proximity in which it blossoms*? Must one not subordinate proximity to coherence, since the very discourse we are holding *at this moment* [my italics, J. D.] counts by what is *Said*, since, in thematizing, we synchronize the terms, form a system among them, use the verb to be, place within *being* whatever signification pretends to signify beyond being? Or must we recall alternation and diachrony as the time of philosophy. . . .

And a little further on, the following, where you will notice around the "at this very moment" the metaphor of the *retied thread* (*fil renoué*). This metaphor belongs to a very singular fabric, a relation (this time in the sense of a *récit*, a narrative, a relation of the same which resumes [*reprend*] the interruption of the Relation to the Other within its knots) by which the philosophical *logos* reappropriates itself, resumes into its web the history of all its ruptures:

Every contesting and interruption of this power of discourse is at once related by the discourse. Thus it recommences as soon as one interrupts it. . . . This discourse will be affirmed to be coherent and one. In relating the interruption of discourse or my being ravished by it, I retie its thread. . . . And are we not *at this very moment* [my italics, J. D.] in the process of barring up the exit which our whole essay is attempting, thus encircling our position from all sides? The exceptional words by which the trace of the past and the extravagance of the approach are said—One, God— become terms, rejoin the vocabulary, and are put at the disposal of philosophers instead of unseating philosophical language. Their very explosions are recounted. . . . Thus signifies the inextricable equivocity woven by language. (AE 215; OB 169)

Within the question just posed ("And are we not at this very moment . . ."), the "at this very moment" would constitute the enveloping form or web of a text resuming without end all its tears within itself. But two pages later, the same "at this very [33] moment," otherwise said within the text, caught within another enchaining-unchaining, says something wholly other, namely, that "at this very moment" the interruptive breakthrough has taken place, ineluctable *at the very moment* when the discursive relation, the philosophical *récit*, pretends to reappropriate for itself the tear within the continuum of its texture:

. . . the intervals are not recuperated. The discourse which suppresses the interruptions of discourse in relating them together, does it not maintain the discontinuity behind the knots where the thread is retied?

The interruptions of discourse, recovered and related within the immanence of the said, are conserved as the knots in a retied thread, the tracing of a diachrony which does not enter into the present, refusing itself to simultaneity.

But the ultimate discourse, where all the discourses are uttered, I still interrupt it, in telling it to he who listens and is situated outside the Said which discourse says, outside all that discourse embraces. Which is true of the discourse I am in the process of holding *at this very moment* [my italics, J. D.]. This reference to the interlocutor permanently pierces the text that discourse pretends to weave in thematising and enveloping all things. In totalising being, discourse as *Discourse* belies the very pretension to totalise.

At a two-page interval, an interval which neither can nor should be reduced, that here constitutes an absolutely singular seriality, the same "at this very moment" seems to repeat itself only to be dis-lodged without return. The "same" "very" (*le "même" du "même"*) of the "at this very moment" has remarked upon its own alteration, one which will have ever since opened it up to the other. The "first" one, which formed the element of reappropriation in the continuum, will have been *obligated* by the "second," the other one, the one of interruption, even before being produced, and in order to be produced. It will have constituted a text and context with the other, but only within a series where the text coheres with its own (if this may still be said) tear. The "at this very moment" only coheres with itself by means of an immeasurable anachrony incommensurable with itself. The singular textuality of this "series" does not enclose the Other but on the contrary opens itself up to it from out of irreducible difference, the past before any present, before any present moment, before anything we think we understand when we say "at this very moment."

This time, the "at this very moment" quoted in the meanwhile (recited or quoted again from one page to the next in order to mark the interruption of the *récit*) will not, as in the earlier "here I am," have been a quotation. Its iteration—for it is iterable and iterated in the series—is not of the same type. If language is there *at once used* and *mentioned* (as the theoreticians of *speech acts* would say), the mention is not of the same type as that of the "here I am" that earlier found itself quoted as well, in the traditional sense of the term. It is thus a strange event. The words there describe (constate) [34] and produce (perform) undecidably a written and a writing immediately implying the "I-now-here" of the scriptor. That strange event holds within itself a serial repetition, but it is repeated later once again, as a series, regularly. For example, it is repeated at the end of "Le nom de Dieu d'après quelques textes Talmudiques." The expression "at this very moment" or "at this moment" appears there twice within a three-line interval, the second one appearing as the deliberate if not strictly citational resumption of the first. The calculated allusion remarks there, in any case, the *same moment* (each time it is now) and the same expression, although from one moment to the next the same moment is no longer the same. But if it is no longer the same, it is not, as in the chapter on "Sense-Certainty" in Hegel's *Phenomenology*, due to time having passed (after writing down *das Jetzt ist die Nacht*), so that the now is now no longer the same. It is due, rather, to something else, to the thing as Other. Listen:

Responsibility which, before the discourse bearing on the *said*, is probably the essence of language.

(I cut across my reading to admire this "probably": it contains nothing empirical or approximative, it removes no rigor from the utterance it determines. As ethical responsibility [ethics before ontology], the essence of language doesn't belong to discourse about the *said*, which can only determine certainties. Here essence does not define the being of what is but of what should be or will have been, which cannot be proved within the language of being-present in the language of essence insofar as it suffers no improbability. Even though language can also be that which, bringing back to presence, to the same, to the economy of being, etc., has not *surely* got its essence in that responsibility responsive [to and for] the other as a past which will never have been present, nevertheless it "is" such responsibility that sets language in motion. Without that [ethical] responsibility there would be no language, but it *is never sure* that language surrenders itself to the responsibility that makes it possible [surrenders to its simply probable essence]: it may always [and to a certain extent it is probably even ineluctible that it will] betray it, tending to enclose it within the same. This liberty of betrayal must be allowed in order for language to be rendered back to its essence, which is the ethical. For once, for a unique time, essence is freed for probability, risk, and uncertainty. From this point on the essence of essence remains to be rethought in accordance with responsibility for the other, etc.)

> It will of course be objected that if any other relation than thematisation may exist between the Soul and the Absolute, then would not the act of talking and thinking about it *at this very moment* [my italics, J.D.], the fact of enveloping it in our dialectic, mean that language and dialectic are superior with respect to that Relation?
> But the language of thematisation, which *at this* [35] *moment* [my italics, J.D.] we are using, has perhaps only been made possible itself by means of that Relation, and is only ancillary.

A "perhaps" ("has perhaps only been made possible") still affects this assertion: yet it nonetheless concerns a condition of possibility, the very thing philosophy subtracts from every "perhaps." This is consonant with the earlier "probably," and the "only" making possible is to be read also, perhaps, in two ways: (1) It has *not* been made *possible* except by that Relation (classical form of a statement on a condition of possibility); (2) It has only been rendered *possible* (probable), a reading that better corresponds with the ordinary syntactic order, and with the insecurity of a *perhaps*.

You will have noticed that the two occurrences of "at this moment" are inscribed and interpreted, drawn along according to two different gestures. In the first case, the present moment is determined from the movement of a present thematization, a presentation that pretends to encompass within itself the Relation which yet exceeds it, pretends to exceed it, precede it, and overflow it. That first "moment" makes the other return to the same. But the other, the second "moment," if it is rendered possible by the excessive relation, is no longer nor shall it ever have been, a present "same." Its "same" is (will have been) dislocated by the very same thing which will have (probably, perhaps) been its "essence," namely, the Relation. It is in itself anachronic, in itself disparate, it no longer closes in upon itself. It is not what it is, in that strange and only probable essence, except by allowing itself beforehand to be opened up and deported by the Relation which makes it possible. The Relation *will have* made it possible—and, by the same stroke, impossible as presence, sameness, and assured essence.

To be more precise: between the two occurrences of "at this moment," the link is not one of distinction. It is the "same" moment which is each time repeated and divided each time in its link to its own essence, in its link to the responsibility that makes it possible. In the first case, E.L. thematizes the thematization that envelops, covers up, and dissimulates the Relation. In the second case, E.L. thematizes the nonthematizable of a Relation that does not allow further envelopment within the tissue of the same. But although, between the two "moments," there is a chronological, logical, rhetorical, and even an ontological interval—to the extent that the first belongs to ontology while the second escapes it in making it possible—it is nevertheless the *same moment*, written and read in its difference, in its double difference, one belonging to dialectic and the other different from and deferring from (*différant*) the first, infinitely and in advance overflowing it. The second moment has an infinite advance on the first. And yet it is the same.

But there must be a *series*, a beginning of a series of that "same" (at least two occurrences) in order for the writing that dislocates the Same toward the Relation to have a hold and a chance. E.L. would have been unable to make understandable the *probable* essence of language without that [36] singular repetition, without that citation or recitation which makes the Same come (*venir*) to rather than returning (*revenir*) to the Other. I said a "chance" because one is never constrained, even when obligated, to read what is thus rendered legible. Certainly, it appears clear, and clearly said, that, in the second occurrence, the "at this moment" which determines the language of thematization finds itself, one cannot say determined any longer, but disturbed from its normal signification of presence, by that Relation which makes it possible by opening (having opened) it up to the Other, outside of the theme, outside presence, beyond the circle of the Same, beyond Being. Such an opening doesn't open something (that would have an identity) to something else. Perhaps it isn't even an opening, but what bids (*ordonne*) to the Other, from out of the order of the other, a "this very moment" which can no longer return to itself. But nothing forces us to read it like that. It can always be interpreted without passing beyond, the beyond here not opening out to anyone or anything at all. The second "at this very moment" can always be made to return to the first, enveloping it anew, ignoring the series effect or reducing it to a homogeneous concept of seriality, ignoring what this seriality bears of the singularly other and of the out-of-series (*hors-série*). Everything would then return to the same.

But what does that mean? That the dialectic of the first moment would triumph? Not even that. The Relation will have taken place anyway, will have already made possible the relation (as a *récit* of the interruptions) which pretends to sew everything up again within the discursive text. Everything would return to the same but the same could as well already be the other, the one of the second "at this very moment," the one—probably—of responsibility. It follows that the responsibility in question is not merely said, named, thematized, in one or other occurrence of "this moment," it is first of all yours, the one of reading to which "this moment" is given, confided, or delivered over. Your reading is thus no longer merely a simple reading that deciphers the sense of what is already found in the text; it has a limitless (ethical) initiative. It is freely self-obligated from the text of the Other, whose text one could abusively say today, wrongly, today that it *produces* it. But that it is freely self-obligated in no way signifies any auto-nomy. To be sure, you are the author of the text you read here, that can be said, but you remain within an absolute heteronomy. You are responsible for the other, who makes you responsible. *Who will have obligated you.* And even if you don't read *as one must*, as E.L. says one must read, still, beyond the dominant interpretation (that of domination) integral to the philosophy of grammar and to the grammar of philosophy, the Relation of dislocation *will have taken place*, there is nothing you can do about it, and unwittingly you will have read what will have made only possible, from out of the Other, what is happening "at this very moment."

That is the strange force of a text which frees itself to you without apparent defense, a force not that of the written, to be sure, in the current sense of the term, which obligates the written in simply making it possible. The [37] disturbance which it *refers* (the Relation it relates to the other in linking to it the *récit*) is never assured, perceptible, or *demonstrable*: neither a demonstrative conclusion nor a phenomenal showing. By definition it is not a controllable disturbance, it is not readable within the *inside* of logic, semiotics, language, grammaticality, lexicon, or rhetoric with their supposedly internal criteria, because nothing is less certain than the rigorous limits of such an inside.

That internal element must have been holed or broken through (to the light of day), torn, even *more than once*, in more or less regular fashion, so that the regularity of the tear (I would say the *strategy* of the tear if this word, strategy, did not betoken too much—for him, not for me—toward economic calculation, the ruse of a stratagem and warring violence at the very point when on the contrary everything must be so calculated that calculation should not have the last word [*avoir raison de*] over everything) may have obligated you to receive the order which is gently given to you, confided to you, in order to read thus and not otherwise, to read *otherwise* and not thus. What I would like to give you here (to read, think, love, eat, drink, whatever you wish) is what he himself will have given, and how he gives "at this very moment." The gesture is very subtle, almost unapparent. Because of what's at stake it must remain almost unapparent, merely probable, not so as to be decisive (which it must rather avoid being) but in order to respond to chance before the Other. Hence the second "at this moment," the one that gives its time to this language that "has perhaps only been made possible by that Relation" to the other of all presence, is nothing other than the first, it is the same in the language, he repeats it a few lines further on and its reference remains the same. Yet everything will have changed, sovereignty will have become ancillary. The first "moment" gave its form or its temporal place, its "presence," to a thought, a language, a dialectic "sovereign in regard to that Relation." So what will have happened—probably, perhaps—is this: the second "moment" will have forced the first toward its own condition of possibility, toward its "essence," beyond the Said and the Theme. It will have in advance —but after the fact within the serial rhetoric—torn the envelope. But that very tear would not have been possible without a certain hooking back (*échancrure*) of the second moment and a sort of analogical contamination between the two, a relation between two incommensurables, a relation between the relation as ontological *récit* and the Relation as responsibility for the Other.

Apparently he likes the tear (*déchirure*) but detests contamination. Yet what holds his writing in suspense is that one must welcome contamination, the *risk* of contamination, in enchaining the tears and regularly *resuming them* within the philosophical text or tissue of a *récit*. This *resumption* is even the condition upon which what is beyond essence may keep (*garder*) its chance against the enveloping seam of the thematical or dialectical. The tear must be saved, for [38] which one must play off seam against seam. The risk of contamination must be regularly accepted (in series) in order to leave its chance to the noncontamination of the other by the rule of the same. His "text" (and I would even say *the* text without wishing to efface an irreplaceable idiom) is always that heterogeneous tissue that interlaces both texture and atexture, without uniting them. And whoever (as was written elsewhere of an other, very close and very distant) "ventures to plot the absolute tear, absolutely tears his own tissue, once more become solid and servile in once more giving itself to be read." I propose this rapprochement without complacency, in order to try to think a necessity: one which, although unformalizable, regularly reproduces the relation of the formalizable to the nonformalizable.

The "metaphors" of seam and tear obsess his text. Is it merely a matter of "metaphors," once they envelop or tear the very element (the text) of the metaphorical? It matters little for the moment. In any case they seem to be organized as follows. Let us call by one word, *interruption* (which he uses often), that which regularly puts an end to the authority of the Said, the thematical, the dialectical, the same, the economical, etc., whatever is demarcated from this series so as to go beyond essence: to the Other, toward the Other, from the Other. The interruption will have come to tear the continuum of a tissue which naturally tends to envelop, shut in upon itself, sew itself back up again, mend, resume its own tears, and to make it appear as if they were still its own and could return to it. For example, in "Le Nom de Dieu," the first "moment" gathers together the continuum of a tissue that "envelops" the beyond in the same and forbids the interruption. Now, in the following phrase, yet still within the language of thematization, the other moment, the moment of the Other, marks the instance of the tear by a Relation which *will have made* "only possible" the continuum itself, that will therefore not have been (or have come to be) the continuum it seemed to be. The absolutely future anterior of that tear—as an absolutely past anterior—will have made possible the effect of the seam. And not vice versa. But only on the condition of letting itself be contaminated, resumed, and sewn up within what it has made possible. It follows that the resumption is not any more logical than the interruption. *Otherwise than Being*:

> Are the tears in the logical text, sewn up again by logic alone? It is in the association of philosophy and the State, philosophy and medicine, that the rupture of discourse is surmounted. The interlocutor who does not yield himself to logic is threatened either with imprisonment or internment, or is submitted to the prestige of the master and the medication of the doctor. . . . It is by means of the State that Reason and knowledge are forceful and efficient. But the State discounts neither irrevocable madness nor even intervals of madness. It doesn't untie the knots, it cuts them. The Said thematises the interrupted dialogue or the dialogue delayed by silences, by failures or by delirium; but the intervals are not recuperated. The discourse which suppresses the interruptions by relating [39] them, does it not maintain the discontinuity under the knots which retie the thread? The interruptions of discourse, found and related within the immanence of the said, are conserved as though in the knots of a retied thread, trace of a diachrony which does not enter into the present, refusing itself to simultaneity.

Whether it severs or reties, the discourse of philosophy, medicine, or the State retains the trace of interruption despite itself. Despite itself. Yet in order to re-mark the interruption, which is what E.L.'s writing does, one must *also* retie the thread, despite oneself, within the book not left intact by philosophy, medicine, or the logic of the State. The analogy between the book, philosophy, medicine, logic, and the State is very strong. "Interrupted discourse recapturing its own ruptures—this is the book. But books have their destinies, they belong to a world they do not englobe but acknowledge by writing and imprinting themselves within it, allowing themselves to be pre-faced and preceded by some introduction. They interrupt themselves, calling forth other books in the final count interpreting each other in a saying distinct from the said."

So he writes books that should not be books of State (of philosophy, medicine, or logic). How does he do it? In his books, as in those of others, the interruption leaves its marks, but otherwise. Knotted threads are formed in it, recapturing the tears, but otherwise. They allow the discontinuous to appear in its trace, but since the trace is not to be reassembled into its appearance, it can always resemble the trace which discontinuity leaves within the logical discourse of the State, of philosophy, or of medicine. The trace should therefore "present" itself there, without presenting itself, *otherwise*. But how? *This* book (*livre*) here, the one composed of *his* books beyond all totality, how is it freed (*comment se livre-t-il*) otherwise to the other? From one moment to the next, the difference must have been infinitely subtle, the one recapturing the other in its meshes (*mailles*) must leave another trace of the interruption in its meshes, and by thematizing the trace make another knot (left to the discretion of the other in the reading). But another knot remains insufficient; what is needed is another chain of multiple knots having the peculiarity that they do not tie together continuous threads (as a State book pretends to do) but retie cut threads while keeping the hardly apparent trace (perhaps, probably) of absolute interruptions, of the ab-solute as interruption. The trace of this interruption within the knot is never simply visible, sensible, or assured. That trace does not belong to discourse and only comes to it from the Other. That is also true of State discourse, to be sure, but here, nonphenomenality must obligate us, without constraint, to read the trace as trace, the interruption as interruption according to an *as such* no longer appropriable as a phenomenon of essence. The structure of the knot must be other, although it resembles it quite a lot. You are never required to read or recognize the trace of interruption, it only comes about through you for whom it is freed, and yet he will have, wholly otherwise, obligated you to read what one is not obligated to read. Unlike [40] everyone, the State, philosophy, medicine, he doesn't simply make knots and interruptions in his text. I say like everyone, since if there is interruption everywhere, there are knots everywhere. But there is in his text, perhaps, a supplementary nodal complication, another way of retying without retying.

How is this supplement of the knot to be figured? It must enchain together the knots in such a way that the text holds together, but also that the interruptions "remain" ("*restent*") *numerous* (one alone is never enough): not merely as a present, apparent, or substantial remainder (*restance*), which would merely be another way for the supplementary knot to disappear, but tracing out in passing by to leave more opportunity for the trace of the other. Now to achieve that, one sole knot, keeping the trace of one sole interruption, would not suffice, nor one chain exhibiting the trace of a sole hiatus. One sole interruption in a discourse does not do its work and thus allows itself to be immediately reappropriated. The hiatus must insist, whence the necessity of the *series*, of the series of knots. The absolute paradox (of the ab-solute) is that *this series*, incommensurable with any other, series out-of-series, does not tie up threads but the interruptions between threads, traces of intervals which the knot should only remark, give to be remarked. I have chosen to name this structure by the word *series* so as to tie together, in my turn, *series* (file, sequence, range, consequence, ordered enchainment of a regular multiplicity, interlacing, line descendance) and *seira* (cord, chain, lasso, lace, etc.). We will accept the chance of finding in the net of the same lineage at least one of four Latin *seros* (to interlace, plait, enchain, reattach) and the Greek *eiro* which says (or ties) together the interlacing of lace and saying, the *symplokè* of discourse and binding. This ab-solute series is *without a single knot*, but ties a multiplicity of retied knots, and does not re-tie threads but the interruptions without thread, leaving open the interruptions between interruptions. This interruption is not a cut (*coupure*) nor does it fall under a logic of the cut, but rather that of ab-solute de-stricturation. That is why the opening of interruption is never pure. And in order to distinguish itself, for instance, from the discontinuous as a symptom within the discourse of the State or of the book, it can break its resemblance only by being *not just any* interruption, and thus also by determining itself within the element of the same. *Not just any*: here is situated the enormous responsibility of a work—within the State, philosophy, medicine, economy, etc. And the risk is ineluctable, it is inscribed in the *necessity* (another word for speaking about the bond one cannot cut) of stricture, the necessity of enchaining the moments, be they of rupture, and of negotiating the chain, albeit in nondialectical fashion. This risk is itself regularly thematized in his text. For example, concerning precisely the opening: "How is one to think the opening onto the *other than being* without that opening as such signifying at once a gathering in conjunction, in the unity of essence in which the subject would at once get bogged down, the very subject to which this gathering would unveil itself, the bond [41] *with* essence immediately tightening itself up *within* the intimacy of essence?" etc. (OB).

There are thus many ways of enchaining together the interruptions and the passages beyond essence, enchaining them not simply *within* the logic of the same, but in the contact (in the contact without contact, in proximity) of the same with the Other; there are many ways of confecting such an inextricable mesh rather than another, since the risk has to do with their not all being equivalent. There a philosophy, or an aesthetics, a rhetoric, a poetics, a psychagogy, an economy, a politics still remains to be negotiated: between, if this could still be said, the before and the beyond. With a vigilance one could probably say was operating at every instant, in order to save the interruption without, by safe-keeping it, losing it all the more, without the fatality of retying coming to interrupt structurally the interruption, E.L. takes calculated risks in this regard, risks as calculated as possible. But how does he calculate? How does the Other calculate in him so as to leave room for the incalculable? What will have been the style of this calculation, if one may call style this idiom which marks the negotiation with a singular and irreplaceable seal? And what if the pledges he will give to the other of the Other, which will make of himself, according to his work, a hostage, are no longer absolutely replaceable?

What I here call the risk of obligated negotiation (since if the interruption is not negotiated, it is even more surely interrupted, abandoning the nonnegotiable to the marketplace), that toward which his attention is perhaps incessantly drawn, in the extreme, is what he himself also calls the inevitable "concession" (" 'Go beyond'—that is to already make a concession to theoretical and ontological language, as if the *beyond* were still a term or an entity or a mode of being, or the negative counterweight of all that" [OB]), the always threatening risk of "betrayal" (AE 214; OB 168) or of "contamination" ("there you have the propositions of this book, which names the *beyond essence*. A notion which certainly could not pretend originality, but whose access has lost none of its ancient steepness. The difficulties of the ascent—and of its failures and resumptions—are inscribed within a writing which doubtless also attests to the breathlessness of the searcher. But, to *hear to a God uncontaminated by Being* is a human possibility no less important or precarious than to *draw Being from the forgetfulness*, into which it would have fallen in metaphysics and onto-theology" [AE x; OB xlii; see also ND 160]). Yielding on the one hand to the arbitrary, that of an example in a series, and on the other to the economy of the discourse I am enchaining here, let us thematize "contamination." Usually it implies the stain or poisoning by the contagion of some improper body. Here simple contact would suffice, since it will have interrupted the interruption. Contact would be a priori contaminating. Graver yet, the risk of contamination would surface even *before* contact, in the simple *necessity of tying* together interruptions as such, in the [42] very seriality of traces and the insistence on rupture. And even if that unheard of chain does not retie threads but hiatuses. Contamination then is no longer a risk but a fatality that must be assumed. The knots in the series contaminate without contact, as if the two edges established continuity at a distance by the simple vis-à-vis of their lines. Still, it is no longer a matter of edges since there is no longer any line, only filed points absolutely disjoint from one shore to the other of the interruption.

Once tied, the point of each thread remains without contact with the other, but the contamination will have taken place between the (internal and external) borders, between the two points of the same and the other that have been linked together, the one maintaining (*maintenant*) the other within the diachrony of the "moment."

The lace of obligation is in place. It is not a trap; I have previously said why. Its incomparable stricture contaminates one obligation by another, the one that unbinds by the one that binds, yet without reciprocity. Playing—but scarcely, perhaps—one could say that the obligation binds and unbinds. He will have obligated: bound and unbound, bound in unbinding "together," in the "same" seriasure (*sériature*) in the same dia-synchrony, in a serial *at once*, the "many times" that will have taken place only once. He will have bound/unbound an obligation that obligates, a *religion*, and an ob-ligation that un-binds without merely raising an ob-stacle or ob-jection to the ligature, that opens up religion within the very unbinding.

This lace of obligation holds language. It maintains it, preventing it from falling apart in passing through the eyelets of a texture: alternatively inside and outside, below and above, before and beyond. It does it in measure, regularly tightening the body into its form. It is in allowing this lace to be made that he will have obligated.

But who, "he"? Who says the *"one must"* of this obligation that is made into a fault so as to be freed up to your discretion?

Here now is another example. He speaks of "this book," even here, of the fabrication of "this work," of the "present work," these expressions repeat themselves as with the above "at this moment," but this time interlaced with a series of "one musts." A "me" and "here I am" slide incessantly from the quotation to an interminable oscillation between "use" and "mention." This happens in the last two pages of *Otherwise than Being* (chapter 6: "Outside"). I select the following, not without some artificial abstraction: "Signification—one-for-the-other—relation with alterity—has already been analysed *in the present work* [my italics, J.D.] as proximity, proximity as responsibility for the Other (*autrui*), and responsibility for the Other—as substitution: in its subjectivity, in its very bearing as separated substance, the subject has shown itself as expiation-for-the-other, condition or uncondition of hostage." I interrupt for an instant; *"in the present work"* the impresentable has therefore presented itself, a relation with the Other (*Autre*) that defeats any gathering into presence, to the point where no "work" can be rebound or shut in upon its presence, nor plotted or enchained [43] in order to form a book. The present work makes a present of what can only be given outside the book. And even outside the framework. "The problem overflows the framework of this book." These are the last words of the last chapter of *Totality and Infinity* (immediately before the conclusion). But what overflows has just been announced—it is the very announcement, messianic consciousness—on the internal border of that utterance, *on the frame* of the book if not *in* it. And yet what is wrought and set to work in the present work only makes a work outside the book. The expression "in the present work" mimics the thesis and the code of the university community; it is ironic. It has to be so as discretely as possible, for there would still be too great an assurance and too much glibness to break the code with a fracas. Effraction does not ridicule, it indeed makes a present of the "present work."

Let's continue: "This book interprets the *subject* as *hostage*, and the subjectivity of the subject as substitution breaking with the *essence* of being. The thesis exposes itself imprudently to the reproach of utopianism, in the opinion that modern man takes himself for a being among beings, while his modernity explodes as an impossibility of staying at home. This book escapes the reproach of utopianism—if utopianism be a reproach, if thought can escape being utopian—by recalling that *what humanely took place has never been able to remain shut in its place.*" *"The thesis"* is therefore not posed, it is imprudently and defenselessly exposed, and yet that very vulnerability is ("this weakness is necessary," we will read a little later on) the provocation to responsibility for the other, it leaves place for the other in a taking-place of *this* book where the *this here* no longer shuts in upon itself, upon its own subject. The same dehiscence that opened up the series of "at this moment," is there at work in "the present work," "this book," "the thesis," etc. But the series is always complicated by the fact that the inextricable equivocation, contamination, soon it will be called "hypocrisy," is at once described and denounced in its necessity *by* "this book," by "the present work," by "the thesis," and *in* them, out of them, in them, but destined in them to an outside that no dialectic will be able to reappropriate into its book. Thus (I underline *it is necessary* [*il faut*], *it was necessary* [il fallait]):

Each individual is virtually an elect, called forth to leave, in his turn—or without awaiting his turn—from the concept of the self, from his extension into the people, to respond to responsibility: *me* that is to say, *here I am for the others*, called forth radically to lose his place—or his refuge within being, to enter within a ubiquity that is also a utopia. Here I am for the others—e-normous responsibility whose lack of measure is attenuated by hypocrisy from the moment it enters into my own ears, warned, as they are, of the *essence* of being, that is to say, of the way in which it carries on. Hyprocrisy immediately denounced. But the norms to which the denunciation refers have been understood within the enormity of their sense, and in the full resonance of their utterance, true like an unbridled witness. *No less*, at any rate, *is necessary* for the little humanity that adorns the earth. . . . There must be [44] a de-regulation of essence by means of which essence may not solely find violence repugnant. This repugnance attests only to the phase of an inaugural or savage humanity, ready to forget its disgusts, to be invested as "essence of de-regulation," surrounding itself like all essence with honors and military virtues, inevitably jealous of its perseverance. For the little humanity that adorns the earth there must be a relaxing of essence to the second power: *in the just war made on war, to tremble—even shiver —every instant, because of that very justice.* There *must* be this weakness. This relaxing of virility, without cowardice, *was necessary* for the little cruelty that our hands repudiate. This is the sense, notably, which should have been suggested by the formulas repeated in *this book* [my italics, J.D.] about the passivity more passive than any passivity, the fission of the Self as far as myself, or about the consummation for the other without the act being able to be reborn from out of the ashes of that consummation.

I again interrupt: no Hegelian Phoenix after this consummation. *This book* is not only singular in not being put together like the others, its singularity has to do with *this* seriality here, ab-solute enchainment, rigorous yet with a rigor that knows how to relax itself as is necessary so as not to become totalitarian again, even *virile*, hence to free itself to the discretion of the other in the hiatus. It is in this seriality here and not another (the array in its homogeneous arrangement), in this seriality of derangement that one must hear each philosopheme deranged, dislocated, disarticulated, made inadequate and anterior to itself, absolutely anachronic to whatever is said about it, for example, "the passivity more passive than any passivity" and the whole "series" of analogous syntaxes, all the "formulas repeated in this book." Now you understand the necessity of this repetition. You thus approach the "he" ("*il*") which occurs in this work and from which the "one must" ("*il faut*") is said. Here are the last lines:

In this work [my italics, J.D.] which does not seek to restore any ruined concept, the destitution and de-situation of the subject do not remain without meaning: following the death of a certain god inhabiting the hinter-worlds, the substitution of the hostage discovers the trace—unpronounceable writing —of what, always already past, always "he" ("*il*") never enters any present and to whom no names designating beings, nor verbs where their *essence* resounds, are any longer appropriate, but who, Pro-noun (*Pro-nom*), marks with his seal anything that can carry a name.

— Will it be said of "this work" (*ouvrage*) that it makes a work? From which moment? Of what? Of whom? Whatever the stages may be, the responsibility comes back to him, "he," to him, who "*undersigns*" every signature. Pro-noun without pronounceable name that "marks with its seal whatever can carry a name." This last phrase comes at the end of the book as if in place of a signature. Emmanuel Levinas recalls [45] the preceding Pro-noun that replaces and makes possible every nominal signature, by the same double stroke, he gives to it and withdraws from it, his signature. Is it him, "he," that then is set to work? *Of him* that the work responds? Of him that one will have said, "Il aura obligé" (he will have obligated)? I do not think that between such a pro-noun and a name or the bearer of a name there is what one could call a difference or a distinction. This link between "he" and the bearer of a name is other. Each time different, never anonymous, "*he*" is (without sustaining it with any substantial presence) the bearer of the name. If I now transform the utterance, which came from I know not where and from which we took our point of departure ("Il aura obligé"), by this one, "the work of Emmanuel Levinas will have obligated," would he subscribe to that? Would he accept my replacing "he" by Emmanuel Levinas in order to say (who) will have made the work in his work? Would it be a fault, as to "he" or as to him, E.L.?

— Now, I write at your dictation, "the work of E.L. will have obligated." You have dictated it to me and yet what I write at this very moment, "the work of E.L. will have obligated," articulating together those common nouns and proper names, you don't yet know what that means. You don't know yet how *one must* read. You don't even know how, at this moment, *one must* hear this "one must" (*il faut*).

The work of E.L. *comprehends* an *other* manner to think obligation in the "one must," an *other* manner of thinking the work, and even of thinking thought. One must therefore read it otherwise, read there otherwise the "one must," and otherwise the otherwise.

The dislocation to which this work will have obligated is a dislocation without name; toward another thought of the name, a thought that is wholly other because it is open *to the name of the other*. Inaugural *and* immemorial dislocation, it will have taken place—another place, in the place of the other—only on the condition of another topic. An extravagant topic (u-topic, they will say, believing they know what takes place and what takes the place of) and absolutely other. But to hear the absolute of this "absolutely," one must have read the serial work that displaces, replaces, and substitutes this word "absolute." And to start with, the word "work." We endlessly get caught up in the network of quotation marks. We no longer know how to efface them, nor how to pile them up, one on top of the other. We no longer even know how to quote his "work" any longer, since it already quotes, under quotation marks, the whole language—French, Western, and even beyond—even if it is only from the moment and because of the fact that "he" must put in quotation marks, the pronominal signatory, the nameless signatory without authorial signature, "he" who undersigns every work, sets every work (*ouvrage*) to work (*met en oeuvre*), and "marks by his seal whatever can carry a name." If "he" is between quotation marks, nothing more can be said, [46] about him, for him, from him, in his place or before him, that wouldn't require a tightly knit, tied up, and wrought (*ouvragée*) series, a whole fabric of quotation marks knitting a text without edge. A text exceeding language and yet in all rigor untranslatable from one tongue to another. Seriality irreducibly knots it to *a* language.

If you wish to talk of E.L.'s operation when he sets himself into "this work" (*ouvrage*), when he writes "at this moment," and if you ask "What is he doing?" and "How does he do it?" then not only must you dis-locate the "he" who is no longer the subject of an operation, agent, producer or worker, but you must right away clarify that the Work, as his work gives and gives again to be thought is no longer of the technical or productive order of the operation (*poiein, facere, agere, tun, wirken, erzeugen,* or however it may be translated). You cannot therefore speak—pertinently—of the Work before what "his" work says of the Work, in its Saying and beyond its Said, because that gap (*écart*) remains irreducible. Nor is there any circle here, especially not a hermeneutic one, because the Work—according to his work—"is" precisely what breaks all circularity. There, near but infinitely distanced, the dislocation is to be found in the interior without inside of language which is yet opened out to the outside of the wholly other. The infinite law of quotation marks seems to suspend any reference, enclosing the work upon the borderless context which it gives to itself: yet behold here this law making absolute reference to the commandment of the wholly other, obligating beyond any delimitable context.

If, therefore, I now write "the work of E.L. will have obligated to an absolute dislocation," the obligation, as the work that teaches it, teaching also how one must teach, will have been without constraint, without contract, anterior to any engagement, to any nominal signature, which through the other responds for the other before any question or requisition, ab-solute thereby and ab-solving. "He" will have subtracted dissymmetrical responsibility from the circle, the circulation of the pact, the debt, acknowledgment, from synchronic reciprocity, I would even dare say from the annular alliance, from the *rounds* (*tour*), from whatever makes a round from a finger and I dare say from a sex.

Can it be said? How difficult, probably impossible, to write or describe here what I seem on the verge of describing. Perhaps it is impossible to hold a discourse which holds itself at this moment, saying, explaining, constating (a constative discourse) E.L.'s work. There would have to be (*faudrait*) a writing that performs, but with a performative without present (who has ever defined such a performative?), one that would respond to his, a performative without a present event, a performative whose essence cannot be resumed as to presence ("at this very moment," at this *present* moment I write this, I say *I*, presently; and it has been said that the simple utterance of an *I* was already performative), a performative heretofore never described, whose performance must not, however, be experienced as a glib success, as an act of prowess. For at the same time it is [47] the most quotidian exercise of a discourse with the other, the condition of the least virtuoso writing. Such a performance does not correspond to (*répond à*) the canonical description of a performative, perhaps. Well then, let the description be changed, or renounce here the word "performative"! What is pretty certain is that *that* performance derives nothing from the "constative" proposition, nor from any proposition at all; but inversely and dissymmetrically, every so-called constative proposition, every proposition in general *presupposes* this structure before anything else, this responsibility of the trace (*per*forming or *per*formed).

For example, I wrote earlier: " 'he' will have withdrawn it from the circle. . . ." Now it would already be necessary—infinitely—that I take back and displace each written word in series. Displacing being insufficient, I must rip away each word from itself, *absolutely* rip it away from it-self (as, for example, in his manner of writing "passivity more passive then passivity," an expression which undetermines itself, can just as well pass into its opposite, unless the ripping off stops somewhere, as if by a piece of skin symbolically ripped off from the body and remaining, behind the cut, adhered to it), I must absolutely detach it and absolve it from itself while nevertheless leaving upon it a mark of attachment (the expression "passivity more passive than passivity," does not just become any other expression, it does not mean "activity more active than activity"); in order that two annulments or two excesses not be equivalent, within indetermination, the ab-solving erasure must not be absolutely absolute. I must therefore make each atom of an utterance appear faulty and absolved; faulty in regard to what or whom? And why? When I write, for example, " 'he' will have withdrawn it, etc." the very syntax of my phrase, according to the dominant norms that interpret the French language, the "he" appears to be constituted into an active subject, author and initiator of an operation. If "he" were the simple pronoun of the signatory (and not the Pro-noun marking with its seal whatever may carry a name . . .), it could be thought that the signatory has the authority of an author, and that "he" is the agent of the action that "will have withdrawn," etc. Now *it would have been necessary* (*aurait fallu*) to say, it must therefore be said, that "he" has withdrawn nothing whatever, "he" has *made appear* the possibility of that withdrawal, he has not *made* it appear, he has *let* it appear, he has not let it *appear*, since what he has let (not to be but to make a sign, and not a sign but an enigma), what he has let produce itself as enigma, and to produce itself is still too much, is not of the phenomenal order, he has "let" "appear" the non-appearing as such (but the non-appearing never dis-appears into its "as such," etc.) on the limit of the beyond, a limit that is not a determinable, visible, or thinkable line, and that has no definable edges, on the "limit," therefore, of the "beyond" of phenomena and of essence: that is to say (!) the "he" himself. That's it, the "he" himself, that is to say (!), the Other. "He" has said "He," even before "I" may say "I" and in order that, if that is possible, "I" may say "I." [48]

That other "he," the "he" as wholly other, was only able to arrive at the end of my phrase (unless my phrase never arrived, indefinitely arrested on its own linguistic shore [*rive*]) by means of a series of words that are all faulty, and that I have, as it were, erased in passing, in measure, regularly, the one after the other, while leaving to them the force of their tracing, the wake of their tracement (*tracement*), the force (without force) of a trace that will have allowed passage for the other. I have written in marking them, in letting them be marked, by the other. That is why it is inexact to say that I have erased those words. In any case, I should not have erased them, I should have let them be drawn into a *series* (a stringed sequence of enlaced *erasures*), an interrupted series, a *series* of interlaced interruptions, series of *hiatuses* (gaping mouth, mouth opened out to the cut-off word, or to the gift of the other and to the-bread-in-his-mouth) that I shall henceforth call, in order to formalize in economical fashion and so as not to dissociate what is not dissociable within this fabric, the *seriasure* (*sériature*). That other "he" could have only arrived at the end of my phrase within the interminable mobility of this seriasure. He is not the subject-author-signer-proprietor of the work (*ouvrage*); it is a "he" without authority. It could just as well be said that he is the Pro-noun leaving its presignature sealed under the name of the author, for example, E.L., or conversely that E.L. is but a pronoun replacing the singular pronoun, the seal that comes before whatever can carry a name. From this point of view, E.L. would be the *personal* pronoun of "he." Without authority, he does not make a work, he is not the agent or creator of his work, yet if I say that he *lets* the work work (a word that remains to be drawn along), it must immediately be specified that this letting is not a simple passivity, not a letting of thought within the horizon of letting-be. This letting beyond essence, "more passive than passivity," hear it as the most provocative thought today. It is not provocative in the sense of the transgressive, and glibly shocking, exhibition. It is a thought also provoked, *first of all* provoked. Outside the law as law of the other. It is only provoked from its absolute exposure to the provocation of the other, exposure stretched out with all possible force in order not to reduce the *past anterior* of the other, so as not to turn inside out the surface of the self who, *in advance*, finds itself delivered to it body and soul.

"Past anterior" (in the past, in the present past), "first of all," "in advance": amongst the words or syntax whose setting in seriasure I have not yet sketched, there is the future anterior, which I shall have nonetheless used frequently, having no alternative recourse. For example, in the little phrase "Il aura obligé," or "the work of E.L. will have obligated" (Obligated to what? and who, in the first place? I have not yet said thou [*tu*], me, you [*vous*], us, them, they [*ils, elles*], it). The future anterior could turn out to be—and this resemblance is irreducible—the time of Hegelian teleology. Indeed, that is how the properly philosophical intelligence is usually administered, in accord with what [49] I called above the dominant interpretation of language—in which the philosophical interpretation precisely consists. Yet *here indeed* (*ici même*), within *this* seriasure drawn along the "Il aura obligé," (he will have obligated), in this and not in another quite similar seriasure, but determining otherwise the same utterance, the future anterior, "here indeed," will have designated "within" language that which remains most irreducible to the economy of Hegelian teleology and to the dominant interpretation of language. From the moment when it is in accord with the "he" as Pro-noun of the wholly-other "always already past," it will have drawn us toward an eschatology without philosophical teleology, beyond it in any case, otherwise than it. It will have engulfed the future anterior in the bottomless bottom of a past anterior to any past, to all present past, toward that past of the trace that has never been present. Its future anteriority will have been *irreducible* to ontology. An ontology, moreover, made in order to attempt this impossible reduction. This reduction is the finality of ontological movement, its power but also its fatality of defeat: what it attempts to reduce is its own condition.

That future anteriority *there* would no longer decline a verb saying the action of a subject in an operation that would have been *present*. To say "il aura obligé"—in *this* work, taking into account what sets things to work within *this* seriasure—is not to designate, describe, define, show, etc., but, let us say, to *entrace* (*entracer*), otherwise said to perform within the intr(el)acement (*entr(el)acement*) of a seriasure that obligation whose "he" will not have been the present subject but for which "I" hereby respond: Here I am, (I) come. *He* will not have been (a) present but he will have made a gift by not disappearing without leaving a trace. But leaving the trace is also to *leave* it, to abandon it, not to insist upon it in a sign. It is to efface it. In the concept of trace is inscribed in advance the re-treat (*re-trait*) of effacement. The trace is inscribed in being effaced and leaving the traced wake of its effacement (etc.) in the *re*treat, or in what E.L. calls the "superimposition." ("The authentic trace, on the other hand, disturbs the order of the world. It comes 'superimposed.' . . . Whoever has left traces in effacing his traces did not mean to say or do anything by the traces he left" [HH 60; CP 104.]) The structure of superimposition thus described menaces by its very rigor, which is that of contamination, any *authenticity* assured of its trace ("the authentic trace") and any rigorous dissociation between sign and trace. ("The trace is not a sign like any other. But it also plays the role of a sign. . . . Yet every sign, in this sense, is a trace," ibid.) The word "leave" (*laisser*) in the locution "leave a trace" now seems to be charged with the whole enigma. It would no longer announce itself starting from anything other than the trace, and especially not from a letting-be, unless letting-be be understood *otherwise*, following the sign the trace makes to it where it is allowed to be effaced.

What am I saying to you when I pronounce "leave me"? Or when you say "he has left me," or as in the Song of Songs, "he has slipped away, he has passed by"? [50]

Otherwise said (the serial enchainment should no longer slip through a "that is to say" but instead it should be interrupted and retied at the border of the interruptions by an "otherwise said"), for this not-without-trace (*pas-sans-*

trace), the contamination between the "he" beyond language and the "he" within the economic immanence of language and its dominant interpretation, is not merely an evil or a "negative" contamination, rather it describes the very process of the trace insofar as it makes a work, in a work-making (*faire-oeuvre*) that must neither be grasped by means of work nor of making, but instead by means of what is said of the work in his work, by the saying of the said, by its intr(el)aced performance. There is no more a "negative" contamination than there is a simple beyond or a simple inside of language, on the one side and the other of some border.

Once again you find the logical paradox of *this* seriasure (but this one in its irreplaceable singularity counts for every other): one must, even though nobody constrains anybody, read his work, otherwise said, respond to it and even respond for it, not by means of what one understands by *work* according to the dominant interpretation of language, but according to what *his* work says, *in its manner*, of Work, about what it is, otherwise said, about what it *should* (*be*), otherwise said about it should have (to be), as work at work in the work.

That is its dislocation: the work does not deport some utterance, or series of utterances, it re-marks in each atom of the said a marking effraction of the saying, a saying no longer a present infinitive, but already a past of the trace, a performance (of the) wholly other. And if you wish to have access to "his" work, you will have to have passed by what it will have said of the Work, namely, that it does not return to him. That is why you have to respond for it, you. It is in your hands, that can give it to him, I will even say more —dedicate it to him. At this moment, indeed:

> The Other can dispossess me of my work, take it or buy it, thus controlling my very conduct. I am exposed to instigation. The work is vowed to this foreign *Sinngebung* from its very origin in me. . . . Willing escapes the will. The work is always, in a certain sense, an unsuccessful act (*acte manqué*). I do not fully know what I want to do. Whence an unlimited field of investigation for psychoanalysis or sociology seizing the will in its apparition within the work, in its conduct and within its products." (TeI 202–4; TI 227–28)

The Work, such as it is at work, *wrought*, in the work of E.L., as one should read it if one must read "his" work, does not return—from the origin—to the Same; which does not imply that it *signifies* waste or pure loss within a *game*. Such a game would still, in its waste, be determined by economy. The gratuity of this work, what he still calls *liturgy*, "a losing investment" (*"mise de fonds à perte"*), or "working without remuneration" (HH; CP), resembles playing a game but is not a game, "it is ethics itself," beyond even thinking and the thinkable. For the liturgy of work should not [51] even be *subordinated* to thinking. A work that would be "subordinated to thinking" (TTO and HH; CP) still understood as economic calculation, would not make a Work.

What E.L.'s work will therefore have succeeded in doing—in the unsuccessful act it claims to be, like any work—is to have obligated us, before all contract of acknowledgment, to this dissymmetry which it has itself so violently and gently provoked: impossible to approach his work without first of all passing, already, by the re-treat of its inside, namely, the remarkable saying of the work. Not only what can be found said on this subject, but the intr(el)aced saying which comes to it from out of the other and never returns it to itself, and which comes (for example, exemplarily) from you (come), obligated female reader (*lectrice obligée*). You can still refuse to grant him that sense, or only lend yourself to that *Sinngebung* while still not approaching that singular ellipsis where nevertheless you are already caught, perhaps.

— I knew. In listening I was nonetheless wondering whether I was comprehended, myself, and how to stop that word: comprehended. And how the work knew me, whatever it knew of me. So be it: to begin by reading his work, giving it to him, in order to approach the Work, which itself does not begin with "his" work nor with whoever would pretend to say "my" work. Going toward the Other, coming from the Same so as not to return to it, the work does not come from there, but from the Other. And his work makes a work in the re-treat which re-marks this heteronomous movement. The retreat is not unique, although it remarks the unique, but its seriasure is unique. Not his signature—the "he" undersigning and under seal—but his seriasure. So be it. Now if, in reading what he shall have had to give, I take account of the unique seriasure, I should, for example, ascertain that the word "work" no more than any other has a fixed sense outside of the mobile syntax of marks, outside of the contextual transformation. The variation is not arbitrary, the transformation is regulated in its irregularity and in its very disturbance. But how? By what? By whom? I shall give or take an example of it. More or perhaps another thing than an example, that of the "son" in *Totality and Infinity*, of the "unique" son or sons: "The son is not merely my work like a poem or an object." That is on page 254 of *Totalité et Infini* (TI 277), and I assume that the context is re-read. Although defined as beyond "my work," "the son" *here* seems rather to have the traits of what in other contexts, doubtless later on, is called, with a capital letter, the Work. Otherwise said, the word *work* has neither the same *sense* nor the same *reference* in the two contexts, without however there being any incoherence or contradiction among them. *They even have a wholly other link to sense and reference.*

"The son"—movement without return toward the other beyond the work —thus resembles what is called elsewhere and later on, the Work. Elsewhere and later on, I also read: "The link with the Other by means of the son" (*Du sacré au saint*). [52]

Now, in the same paragraph of *Totality and Infinity* (and elsewhere) where it is nearly always "son" (and "paternity") that is said, a sentence talks of the "child." ("I don't have my child, I am my child. Paternity is a relation with the stranger who while being Other [*autrui*] . . . *is* me; a relationship of the ego with a self which is nevertheless not me.") Is it that "son" is another word for "child," a child who could be of one or the other sex? If so, whence comes that equivalence, and what does it mean? And why couldn't the "daughter" play an analogous role? Why should the son be more or better than the daughter, than me, the Work beyond "my work"? If there were no differences from this point of view, why should "son" better represent, in advance, this indifference? This unmarked indifference?

Around this question which I here abandon to its elliptical course, I interrogate the link, in E.L.'s Work, between sexual difference—the Other as the other sex, otherwise said as otherwise sexed—and the Other as wholly other, beyond or before sexual difference. To himself, his text marks its signature by a masculine "I-he," a strange matter as was elsewhere noted "in passing," a while back, by an other. ("Let us observe in passing that *Totality and Infinity* pushes the respect for dissymmetry to the point where it seems to us impossible, essentially impossible, that it could have been written by a woman. The philosophical subject of it is man [*vir*].") And on the same page that says "the son" lying beyond "my work," I can also read: "Neither knowledge nor power. In voluptuousity, the Other—the feminine—retires into its mystery. The relation with it (the Other) is a relation with its absence." His signature thus assumes the sexual mark, a remarkable phenomenon in the history of philosophical writing, if the latter has always been interested in occupying that position without re-marking upon it or assuming it on, without signing its mark. But, as well as this, E.L.'s work seems to me to have always rendered secondary, derivative, and subordinate, alterity as sexual difference, the trait of sexual difference, to the alterity of a sexually non-marked wholly other. It is not woman or the feminine that he has rendered secondary, derivative, or subordinate, but sexual difference. Once sexual difference is subordinated, it is always the case that the wholly other, who is *not yet marked* is *already* found to be marked by masculinity (he before he/she, son before son/daughter, father before father/mother, etc.). An operation whose logic has seemed to me as constant as it is illogical (last example to date, Freudian psychoanalysis and everything that returns to it), yet with an illogicality that will have made possible and thus marked all logic—from the moment it exists as such—with this prolegomenal "he." How can one mark as masculine the very thing said to be anterior, or even foreign, to sexual difference? My question will be clearer if I content myself with quoting. Quoting not all of those passages where he affirms femininity as an "ontological category," ("The feminine figures among the categories of Being"), a gesture [53] which always leaves me wondering as to whether it understands (*comprend*) me to be *against* a tradition that would have refused me that ontological dignity, or whether better than ever it understands me to be *within* that very tradition, profoundly repeating it. But rather quoting these passages:

> Within Judaism woman will only have the destiny of a human being, whose femininity will solely count as an attribute . . . the feminity of the woman would know neither how to deform or absorb its human essence. In Hebrew "woman" is called *Ichah*, because, the bible says, she comes from man, *Iche*. The doctors seize hold of this etymology in order to affirm the unique dignity of the Hebrew that expresses the very mystery of creation, woman derived

quasi-grammatically from man. . . . "Flesh of my flesh and bone of my bones" signifies therefore an identity of nature between man and woman, an identity of destiny and dignity and also a subordination of sexual life to the personal link that is equality in itself. An idea more ancient than the principles on behalf of which modern woman fights for emancipation, yet the *truth* of all those principles in a sphere where the thesis which opposes itself to the image of an initial androgyny is supported as well, attached to the popular idea of the rib-side. That truth maintains a certain priority of the masculine; he remains the prototype of the human and determines eschatology. The differences of the masculine and the feminine are blotted out in those messianic times. (*"Judaism and the Feminine,"* in DL)

Very recently:

The sense of the feminine will be found clarified by taking as a point of departure the human essence, the *Ischa* following the *Isch*: not the feminine following the masculine, but the partition—the dichotomy—between masculine and feminine following the human. . . . beyond the personal relationship which establishes itself between these two beings issued from two creative acts, the particularity of the feminine is a secondary matter. It isn't woman who is secondary, it is the relation to woman *qua* woman that doesn't belong to the primordial human plan. What is primary are the tasks accomplished by man as a human being, and by woman as a human being. . . . The problem, in each of these lines we are commenting upon at this moment, consists in reconciling the humanity of men and women with the hypothesis of a spirituality of the masculine, the feminine being not his correlative but his corollary; feminine specificity or the difference of the sexes that it announces are not straight away situated at the height of the oppositions constitutive of Spirit. Audacious question: How can the equality of the sexes proceed from a masculine property? . . . There had to be a difference that would not compromise equity, a sexual difference; and consequently, a certain pre-eminence of man, a woman arrived later and *qua* woman as an appendix to the human. Now we understand the lesson: Humanity cannot be thought beginning from two entirely different principles. There must be some *sameness* common to these *others*: woman has been chosen above man, but has come after him: *the very femininity of woman consists in this initial afterwards (après coup).* ("Et Dieu Créa la Femme," in *Du sacré au saint*, 132–42) [54]

Strange logic, that of the "audacious" question. It would be necessary to comment upon each step and verify that each time the secondary status of sexual difference signifies the secondary status of the feminine (But why is this so?) and that the initial status of the predifferential is each time marked by this masculinity that should, however, have come only afterwards, like every other sexual mark. It would be necessary to comment, but I prefer, under the heading of a protocol, to underline the following: he is commenting himself, and says that he is commenting; it must be taken into account that this discourse is not literally that of E. L. While holding discourse, he says that he is commenting upon the doctors *at this very moment* ("the lines we are commenting upon at this moment," and further on: "I am not taking sides; today, I comment").

But the distance of the commentary is not neutral. What he comments upon is consonant with a whole network of affirmations which are his, or those of him, "he." Furthermore, the position of commentator corresponds to a choice: to at least accompany and not displace, transform, or even reverse what is written in the text that is commented upon. I do not wish to dominate the discourse on this subject. Concerning an unpublished (*inédit*) writing, here is the discourse of an other:

> If woman, therefore, quasi-grammatically derives from man, this indeed implies, as Levinas affirms, the same identity of destiny and dignity, an identity which it is suitable to think of as "the recurrence of self in responsibility-for-other," yet that also forms part of a double regime for the separated existence of man and woman. And if Levinas refuses to see in this separation a fall from some primary unity, if he repugns indifferentiation because separation is worth more than primary unity, he nevertheless establishes an order of precedence. If the derivation is thought with relation to a grammar, it is doubtless not due to chance. For grammar here testifies to the privilege of a name which always associates eschatological disinterestedness to the Work of paternity. That name can still be taken as what effectively determines eschatology within the derivation of a genealogy.
>
> To write grammar otherwise or invent some surprising (*inédites*) faults is not to wish a reversal of that determination. It is not a defiance equating itself with pride. It is to become aware that language is not a simple modality of thinking. That the logos is not neutral, as Levinas had also recognized. That the difficulty confronting him in his election—which seems to him that it cannot be exceeded—of using the Greek site in order to make a thought which comes from elsewhere be understood is not perhaps foreign to a certain mutism of the feminine. As if the surprise (*l'inédit*) of another syntax loses its way in the necessity of borrowing the path of a unique logos. (Catherine Chalier, *Figures du féminin: Lecture d'Emmanuel Levinas*, unpublished [*inédit*])[3]

I come then to my question. Since it (*elle*) is under-signed by the Pro-noun He (*Il*) (before he/she, certainly, but it is not She), could it be that in making sexual alterity secondary, far from allowing itself to be approached from the Work, his, or the one said to be, becomes [55] a mastery, the mastery of sexual difference posed as the origin of femininity? Hence mastery *of* femininity? The very thing that *must not have been* mastered, and that one—therefore—has been unable to avoid mastering, or at least attempting to master? The very thing that must not have been derived from an *arche* (neutral, and therefore, he says, masculine) in order to be subjected to it? The aneconomical, that must not have been *economized*, situated in the house, *within* or *as* the law of the *oikos*? The secondary status of the sexual, and therefore, He says, of feminine difference, does it not thus come to stand for the wholly-other of this Saying of the wholly other within the seriasure here determined and within the idiom of this negotiation? Does it not show, on the inside of the work, a surfeit of un-said alterity? Or said, precisely as a secret or as a symptomatic mutism? Then things would become more complicated. The other as feminine (me), far from being derived or secondary, would become the other of the Saying of the wholly other, of this one in any case; and this last one *insofar* as it would have tried to dominate alterity, would risk, (at least to this extent) enclosing *itself* within the economy of the same.

Wholly otherwise said: made secondary by responsibility for the wholly other, sexual difference (and hence, He says, femininity) is retained, as other, within the economic zone of the same. Included in the same, it is by the same stroke excluded: enclosed within, foreclosed within the immanence of a crypt, incorporated in the Saying which says itself to the wholly other. To desexualise the link to the wholly-other (or equally well, the unconscious as a certain philosophical interpretation of psychoanalysis tends to do today), to make sexuality secondary with respect to a wholly-other that in itself would not be sexually marked ("beneath erotic alterity, the alterity of the one for the other; responsibility before eros" [AE 113n; OB 192 n. 27]), is always to make sexual difference secondary *as* femininity. Here I would situate his profound complicity with such an interpretation of psychoanalysis. This complicity, more profound than the abyss he wishes to put between his thinking and psychoanalysis, always gathers around one fundamental design: their common link to me, to the other as woman. That is what I would like to give them (first of all, to read).

Shall I abuse this hypothesis? The effect of secondarization, allegedly demanded by the wholly-other (as He), would become the cause, otherwise said the other of the wholly other, the other of a wholly other who is no longer sexually neutral but *posed* (*posé*) (outside the series within the seriasure) and suddenly determined as He. Then the Work, apparently signed by the Pronoun He, would be dictated, aspired, and inspired by the desire to make She secondary, therefore *by* She (*Elle*). She would then under-sign the undersigned work from her place of derivable dependence or condition as last or first "Hostage." Not in the sense that undersigning would amount to confirming the signature, but countersigning the work, again not in the sense that countersigning would amount to redoubling the signature, according to the same or the contrary—but *otherwise than signing*.

The whole system of *this* seriasure would silently comment upon the [56] absolute heteronomy in respect to She who would be the wholly other. *This* heteronomy was writing the text from its other side like a weaver its fabric (*ouvrage*); yet it would be necessary here to undo a metaphor of weaving which has not imposed itself by chance: we know to what kind of interpretative investments it has given rise as regards to a feminine specificity which Freudian psychoanalysis *also regularly* derives.

I knew it. What I here suggest is not without violence, not even free of the redoubled violence of what he calls "traumatism," the nonsymbolizable wound that comes, before any other effraction, from the past anterior of the other. A terrifying wound, a wound *of life*, the only one that life opens up (*fraye*) today. Violence faulty in regard to his name, his work, insofar as it inscribes his proper name in a way that is no longer that of property. For, in the end, the derivation of femininity is not a simple movement in the seriasure of his text. The feminine is also described there as a figure of the wholly other. And then, we have recognized that this work is one of the first and rare ones, in this history of philosophy to which it does not simply belong, not to feign effacing the sexual mark of his signature: hence, he would be the last one surprised by the fact that the other (of the whole system of his saying of the other) happens to be a woman, and commands him from that place. Also, it is not a matter of reversing places and putting woman against him in the place of the wholly other as *arche*. If what I say remains false, falsifying, faulty, it is also to the extent that dissymmetry (I speak from my place as woman, and supposing that she be definable) can also reverse the perspectives, while leaving the schema intact.

It has been shown above that ingratitude and contamination did not occur as an accidental evil. It's a sort of fatality of the Saying. It is to be negotiated. It would be worse without negotiation. Let's accept it: what I am writing at this very moment is faulty. Faulty up to a certain point, in touching, or so as not to touch, his name, or what he sets to work in his rigorously proper name in this unsuccessful act (as he says) within a work. If his proper name, E.L., is in the place of the Pronoun (He) which preseals everything that can carry a name, it isn't him, but Him, that my fault comes to wound in his body. Where, then, will my fault have taken bodily form? Where in his body will it have left a mark, in his body to Him, I mean? What is the body of a fault in this writing where the traces of the wholly other are exchanged, without circulating or ever becoming present? If I wished to destroy or annul my fault, I would have to know what is happening to the text being written at this very moment, where it can take place or what can remain of its remains.

In order to make my question better understood, I shall take a detour around what he tells us of the name of God, in the nonneutral commentary which he proposes (ND). According to the treatise *Chevouoth* (35a), it is forbidden [57] to efface the names of God, even in the case when a copyist would have altered the form. The whole manuscript then has to be buried. Such a manuscript, E.L. says, "has to be placed into the earth like a dead body." But what does placing in earth mean? And what does a "dead body" mean, since it is not effaced or destroyed but "placed in the earth"? If one simply wanted to annihilate it—to no longer keep (*garder*) it—the whole thing would be burned, everything would be effaced without remains. The dys-graphy (*dis-graphie*) would be replaced, without remnant, by orthography. In inhuming it, on the contrary, the fault on the proper name is not destroyed, at bottom one keeps guard of it, as a fault, one keeps it at the bottom. It will slowly decompose, taking its time, in the course of a work of mourning in which, achieved successfully in spiritual interiorization, an idealization that certain psychoanalysts call introjection, or paralyzed in a melancholic pathology (incorporation), the other as other will be kept in guard, wounded, wounding, impossible utterance. The topic of such a faulty text remains highly improbable, like the taking-place of its remains in this theonymic cemetery.

If I now ask at this very moment where I should return my fault, it is because of a certain *analogy*: what he recalls about the names of God is something one would be tempted to say analogically for every proper name. He would be the Pro-noun (*Pro-nom*) or the First name (*Pré-nom*) of every name. Just as there is a resemblance between the face of God and the face of man (even if this resemblance is neither an "ontological mark" of the worker on his work nor "sign" or "effect" of God), in the same way there would be an analogy between all proper names and the names of God, which are, in their turn, analogous among themselves. Consequently, I transport by analogy to the proper name of man or woman what is said of the names of God. And of the "fault" on the body of these names.

But things are more complicated. If, in *Totality and Infinity*, the analogy is kept, though not quite in a classical sense, between the face of God and the face of man, here, on the contrary, in the commentary on the Talmudic texts, a whole movement is sketched in order to mark the necessity of interrupting that analogy, of "refusing to God any analogy with beings that are certainly unique, but who compose with other beings a world or a structure. To approach through a proper name is to affirm a relation irreducible to the knowledge which thematises or defines or synthesises, and which, by that very fact, understands the correlate of that knowledge as being, as finite, and as immanent." Yet the analogy once interrupted is again resumed as an analogy between absolute heterogeneities by means of the enigma, the ambiguity of uncertain and precarious epiphany. Monotheistic humanity has a *link* to this trace of a past which is absolutely anterior to any memory, to the ab-solute re-treat (*re-trait*) of the revealed name, to its very inaccessibility. "Square letters are a precarious dwelling whence the revealed Name already withdraws itself; effaceable letters at the mercy of the man who traces them or recopies them." Man, therefore, can be linked with this retreat, despite the infinite distance of the non-thematizable, with the [58] precariousness and uncertainty of this revelation.

> But this uncertain epiphany, on the verge of evanescence, is precisely that which *man alone can retain.* This is why he is the essential moment both of this transcendence and of its manifestation. That is why, through this ineffaceable revelation, he is called forth with an unparalleled straightforwardness.
> But is that revelation precarious enough? Is the Name free enough in regard to the context where it lodges? Is it preserved in writing from all contamination by being or culture? Is it preserved from man, who has indeed a vocation to retain it, but who is capable of every abuse?

Paradox: the precariousness of the revelation is never precarious enough. But should it be? And if it was, wouldn't that be worse?

Once the analogy is resumed, as one resumes the interruptions and not the threads, it should be recalled, I should be able to transpose the discourse on the names of God to the discourse on human names; for example, where there is no longer an example, that of E.L.

And thus to the fault to which the one and the other expose themselves in body. The fault will always, already, have taken place: as soon as I thematize what, in his work, is borne beyond the thematizable and is put in a regular seriasure within which he cannot not sign himself. Certainly, there is already contamination in his work, in that which he thematizes "at this very moment" of the nonthematizable. I am contaminating this irrepressible thematization in my turn; and not merely according to a common structural law, but just as much with a fault of my own that I will not seek to resolve or absolve within the general necessity. As a woman, for example, and in reversing the dissymmetry, I have added rape (*viol*) to it. I should have been even more unfaithful to him, more ungrateful, but was it not then in order to give myself up to what his work says of the Work: that it provokes ingratitude? Here to absolute ingratitude, the least forseeable in his work itself?

I give and play ingratitude against jealousy. Everything I say concerns jealousy. The thought of the trace as put in seriasure by E.L., thinks a singular link of God (not contaminated by being) to jealousy. He, the one who has passed beyond all Being, must be exempt from all jealousy, from all desire for possession, guarding, property, exclusivity, nonsubstitution, etc. And the link to Him must be pure of all jealous economy. But this without-jealousy (*sans-jalousie*) cannot not jealously guard itself, and insofar as it is an absolutely reserved past, it is the very possibility of all jealousy. Ellipsis of jealousy: seriasure is always a jealousy through which, seeing without seeing everything, and especially without being seen, before and beyond the phenomenon, the without-jealousy jealously guards itself, otherwise said, loses itself, keeps-itself-loses-itself. By means of a series of regular traits and re-treats (*re-traits*): the figure of jealousy, beyond the face. Never more jealousy, ever, never more zeal, is it possible? [59]

If feminine difference presealed, perhaps and nearly illegibly, his work, if she became, in the depths of the same, the other of his other, will I then have deformed his name, to him, in writing, at this moment, in this work, here indeed, "she will have obligated" (*elle aura obligé*)?

— I no longer know if you are saying what his work says. Perhaps that comes back to the same. I no longer know if you are saying the contrary, or if you have already written something wholly other. I no longer hear your voice, I have difficulty distinguishing it from mine, from any other, your fault suddenly becomes illegible to me. Interrupt me.

— HERE AT THIS VERY MOMENT I ROLL UP THE BODY OF OUR INTERLACED VOICES CONSONANTS VOWELS ACCENTS FAULTY IN THIS MANUSCRIPT ∼ I MUST PLACE IT IN THE EARTH FOR YOU ∼ COME LEAN DOWN OUR GESTURES WILL HAVE HAD THE INCONSOLABLE SLOWNESS THE GIFT REQUIRES AS IF IT WERE NECESSARY TO DELAY THE ENDLESS FALLING DUE OF A REPETITION ∼ IT'S OUR MUTE INFANT A GIRL PERHAPS STILLBORN OF AN INCEST WILL ONE EVER KNOW PROMISE TO THE INCEST ∼ FAULTY OR LACKING IN HER BODY SHE WILL HAVE LET HERSELF BE DE-

STROYED ONE DAY WITHOUT REMAINDER ONE MUST HOPE ONE MUST GUARD ONESELF FROM HOPE EVEN THAT THUS ALWAYS MORE AND NO MORE JEALOUSY THE BETTER SHE WILL BE KEPT GUARDED ~ MORE AND NO MORE THAN ENOUGH DIFFERENCE THERE AMONG THEM (*ELLES*) BETWEEN THE INHUMED OR THE ASHES OF A BURN-ALL (*BRÛLE-TOUT*) ~ NOW HERE EVEN THE THING OF THIS LITURGY KEEPS OR GUARDS ITSELF LIKE A TRACE OTHERWISE SAID LOSES ITSELF BEYOND PLAY AND EXPENSE ALL IN ALL AND ALL ACCOUNTING FOR OTHERS DONE ALREADY SHE LETS HERSELF BE EATEN ~ BY THE OTHER BY YOU WHO WILL HAVE GIVEN HER TO ME ~ YOU [60] ALWAYS KNEW HER TO BE THE PROPER BODY OF THE FAULT SHE WILL ONLY HAVE BEEN CALLED BY HER LEGIBLE NAME BY YOU AND THEREBY DISAPPEARED IN ADVANCE ~ BUT IN THE BOTTOMLESS CRYPT THE INDECIPHERABLE STILL GIVES READING FOR A LAPSE ABOVE HER BODY WHICH SLOWLY DECOMPOSES IN ANALYSIS ~ WE MUST HAVE A NEW BODY ANOTHER WITHOUT ANY MORE JEALOUSY THE MOST ANCIENT STILL TO COME ~ SHE DOESN'T SPEAK THE UNNAMEABLE YET YOU HEAR HER BETTER THAN ME AHEAD OF ME AT THIS VERY MOMENT WHERE NONETHELESS ON THE OTHER SIDE OF THE MONUMENTAL WORK I WEAVE MY VOICE SO AS TO BE EFFACED THIS TAKE IT HERE I AM EAT ~ GET NEARER ~ IN ORDER TO GIVE HIM /HER ~ DRINK[4]

Editors' Notes

1. The translator would like to thank Geoff Bennington for his generous advice on an earlier version of this translation and Simon Critchley for his work on later versions. The page numbers of the French original have been included in square brackets.

2. "I am sick of love," Song of Songs, v. 8, (AE 180 –81; OB 141–42).

3. Since published in a modified version in the series *La nuit surveillée*, Paris, 1982. See p. 97.

4. The final lines of the essay, almost as strange in French as they are in English, contain a number of undecidable ambiguities which the English cannot capture. Most notably, the phrase "plus de jalousie," which also appears on the preceding page, can signify both "more jealousy" and "no more jealousy," while "plus assez de différence" can be rendered as both "more than enough difference" and "no more than enough difference." In addition, "en faute de" can be translated as both "faulty" and "lacking," while "se garder" means both "to keep oneself" and "to guard oneself." Hence the phrase translated as "one

must guard oneself from hope" might also have been translated "one must keep some hope for oneself." The words "toute compte" suggest at once the translations "all in all," "everything counts," and "all accounting." Finally, an English translation cannot hope to evoke the resonances between "il faut," "il me faut," "il nous faut," "fautifs," "en faute de," and "la faute" that recur in these lines and throughout the essay. With Derrida's encouragement we are including the original French of the final lines of his essay.

~ VOICI EN CE MOMENT MÊME J'ENROULE LE CORPS DE NOS VOIX ENTRELACÉES CONSONNES VOYELLES ACCENTS FAUTIFS DANS CE MANUSCRIT ~ IL ME FAUT POUR TOI LE METTRE EN TERRE ~ VIENS PENCHE-TOI NOS GESTES AURONT EU LA LENTEUR IN-CONSOLABLE QUI CONVIENT AU DON COMME S'IL FALLAIT RE-TARDER L'ÉCHÉANCE SANS FIN D'UNE RÉPÉTITION ~ C'EST NOTRE ENFANT MUET UNE FILLE PEUT-ÊTRE D'UN INCESTE MORT-NÉE A L'INCESTE SAURA-T-ON JAMAIS PROMISE ~ EN FAUTE DE SON CORPS ELLE SE SERA LAISSÉ DÉTRUIRE UN JOUR ET SANS RESTE IL FAUT L'ESPÉRER IL FAUT SE GARDER DE L'ESPOIR MÊME QU'AINSI TOUJOURS PLUS DE JALOUSIE ELLE SE GARDERA MIEUX ~ PLUS ASSEZ DE DIFFÉRENCE LA ENTRE ELLES ENTRE L'INHU-MÉE OU LES CENDRES D'UN BRULE-TOUT ~ MAINTENANT ICI MÊME LA CHOSE DE CETTE LITURGIE SE GARDE COMME UNE TRACE AUTREMENT DIT SE PERD AU-DELA DU JEU ET DE LA DÉ-PENSE TOUT COMPTE POUR D'AUTRES FAIT ELLE SE LAISSE DÉJA MANGER ~ PAR L'AUTRE PAR TOI QUI ME L'AURAS DONNÉE ~ TU SAVAIS DEPUIS TOUJOURS QU'ELLE EST LE CORPS PROPRE DE LA FAUTE ELLE N'AURA ÉTÉ APPELÉE DE SON NOM LISIBLE QUE PAR TOI EN CELA D'AVANCE DISPARUE ~ MAIS DANS LA CRYPTE SANS FOND L'INDÉCHIFFRABLE DONNE ENCORE A LIRE POUR UN LAPS AU-DESSUS DE SON CORPS QUI LENTEMENT SE DÉCOMPOSE A L'A-NALYSE ~ IL NOUS FAUT UN NOUVEAU CORPS UN AUTRE SANS PLUS DE JALOUSIE LE PLUS ANCIEN ENCORE A VENIR ~ ELLE NE PARLE PAS L'INNOMMÉE OR TU L'ENTENDS MIEUX QUE MOI AVANT MOI EN CE MOMENT MÊME OU POURTANT SUR L'AUTRE COTÉ DE CET OUVRAGE MONUMENTAL JE TISSE DE MA VOIX POUR M'Y EF-FACER CECI TIENS ME VOICI MANGE ~ APPROCHE-TOI ~ POUR LUI DONNER ~ BOIS

PART TWO

The Later Levinas

CHAPTER
3

PRESENTATION
Adriaan Peperzak

What does it mean that here and now, yesterday and tomorrow, we are "re-reading Levinas"? Has "Levinas" become the title of an *oeuvre*? Is it the name of a production process resulting in materials for a reading-club? Or do we still hear "Levinas," even in "re-reading Levinas," as the name of someone who is present in being absent, speaking to us from a distance, although never coinciding with his written words? Isn't Levinas in a way more present at this conference than any one of us? But how? What is the presence of an absent author who sits in Paris, perhaps remembers that we told him about this conference, perhaps also thinks of the strengths and weaknesses of the books he wrote . . . ?

How much distance separates us from Levinas's voice and remarkable personality! How many approximations are necessary to get in touch with the man, whose name has become part of the title of this book? Or shall we simply forget about that person in order to concentrate on certain texts that can be classified "Levinas," just as other textual ensembles are called "Homer," "Moses," "Pseudo-Dionysius," or "Anonymous"?

LOGOS AND TEXTS

To begin with, the author's absence from a philosophical text signed by its writer might be clarified somewhat by the analysis of the sort of discourse that plays the main role in philosophy.[1]

As *logos*, language thematizes and arranges the world of beings from the perspective of systematic coherence, in which principles, structures, horizons, etc. play the leading part. Philosophical discourse is the most explicit example of such a systematic and foundational language. It gathers beings by asking how they fit into the order of a whole. As the search for foundations, philosophy has a fondness for *archai*, be they source or germ, end or completion, cause or matter. Philosophical discourse is totalitarian and "archaic." As the gathering of reason, it is "logical" and systematic.

As a concatenation of judgments, a *text* has what we could call a "syllogical" or "syllogistic" structure. By its composition it tries to outline different wholes as integral parts of a complete totality called "the truth." The idea of such a totality is, however, destroyed by the fact that every text relies on a host of texts and conditions whose legitimacy it cannot prove, but necessarily takes for granted. And yet, that idea(l) of the total truth cannot be suppressed altogether, even after we have discovered that truth does not have a direct and immediate rapport with the totality of beings, events, principles, and thoughts. From the perspective of philosophical research, the history of textual *oeuvres* and successions appears as an endless series of attempts to bring a complete and universal truth into the perspective of the reader.

The *synoptic* and *synchronical* character of a text manifests itself in the fact that we can start our reading from many different points: not only from its beginning to its end, but equally from the end to the beginning or from the center to both ends and so on. All the elements of a text are contemporaneous within one space: the space of their being present at once in the form of a book or paper. All reading demands time, but the order of priorities depends, to a great extent, on our choice. Such a choice is not completely arbitrary because a text has its own tricks of imposing a specific order and specific demands on the reader, but the very discovery of such demands presupposes a survey of the text as a limited whole that can and must be deciphered from all sides successively.

The independence of a text with regard to its author seems to be its main distinction, if we compare it to the spoken word. After writing his paper the author leaves it to the reader, who may do with it whatever he wants. Everybody can appropriate it in his own way. Whether this appearance is completely true will be one of the questions to which I would like to come back when we reflect upon the peculiarities of speaking and speech. For the moment we may leave the question at the stage where Plato answered it in the *Phaedrus* and his Seventh Letter by stating that the text cannot be assisted—helped, defended, developed further—by its author, whereas the spoken word can.[2]

Between its writing and reading, a text is as dead as a fossil that can still come back to life. As written but not yet read, it is a score before performance. Its kerygmatic character is not noticed, the meaning of its themes and structures has vanished, but it can be brought back to life by a new understanding. A thinking that is other than that of the author's is needed to take care of the inscriptions and transform them into a way of seeing and arranging the order of reality. Another voice is needed to change the never spoken words into an audible message. Left to itself, a text does not mean anything. *Someone* is needed—a loud or silent reader, a commentator or believer (and the author himself may fulfill this second function)—in order to be presented with a meaningful paper. An initiative presenting or representing the text is an indispensable condition for the possibility of understanding, explaining, or discussing —and in this sense for "reading"—(e.g., Levinas's) "texts."

LOGOS AND EVASION

Is it the overwhelming multiplicity of texts and textual procedures in which we find ourselves involved—and almost buried—that has created (or at least has intensified) our feeling that the space of systematic *logos* is too narrow to be true? From the beginning of European civilization, the "archaic" order of synchronizing and syllogistic reason has been seen as a most eminent, but problematic, enterprise. Platonism itself, for instance, developed a double movement of thought: beyond the phenomenal order which was contemplated in the light of its own ideal truth, another orientation, born of desire, pointed toward something nonphenomenal and nonideal, to which the ideal and phenomenal order of beings owed its possibility of becoming true—a source of light for the work of *logos*. The universe of logical and syllogistic thematization is felt to be too narrow. The whole idea of an *embracing* truth has indeed been problematic from the beginning. Neoplatonism and its Christian transformations might be understood as systematic attempts to evade the prison into which philosophy—not only as hedonism or materialism, but even more so as idealism and faith in *logos*—threatened to force the human search for . . . for what? A desire for transcendence has manifested itself[3] in the endless discussions of Greek, medieval, modern, and contemporary philosophy about the limits of philosophical thought and the possibility of a more radical dimension which would not be irrational. Why and how can the logic of a noncaricatured kerygmatic thinking be felt as a narrowing of "what there really is" (to be lived, enjoyed, celebrated, etc.)? Which experiences, adventures of the mind, or events of history do not permit the gathering of *logos* to enclose them within its horizons?

The main direction in which Western philosophy has sought a possibility of evasion and transcendence, was the "up there" (*ekeise*), the "height" or the "*epekeina*" of some One that would not fit into the possibilities of *logos*—not even as its summit or first and last being, principle, idea, or ground. A careful reading of Plotinus, St. Augustine, Pseudo-Dionysius, Bonaventure, and Kant —to name only a few pillars of our spirituality—shows that the Transcendent has never been seen by them as the highest of all beings. If the name "ontotheology" is applicable at all to their thoughts, it should not be forgotten nor left unsaid that they dedicated the utmost of their thinking energy to the attempt to show that the "*theon*" could not be seized by the patterns of ontology and that there was infinitely more difference between God and phenomenal being than between a highest being and the rest, just as there was an infinite abyss between God and reason, whereas the highest form of *logos* differed from other forms only in degree. It is, however, true that the Western attempt to transcend the system of logical discourse by taking the way of an ascension toward the divine is a Greek heritage and that Christian theology had a lot of trouble trying to prevent its combination of biblical revelation and Greek logic from degenerating into an absolutization of philosophy. In the best examples of Christian thought, however, like that of Anselm, philosophy takes a turn or a bow by which it changes its kerygmatic language into adoration or gratitude.

Levinas's novelty consists in the fact that—without denying the necessity of attributing "transcendence" to God—he shows: (1) that the circle of philosophical logic is interrupted and opened up by the fact that all discourses are necessarily addressed to another human, and (2) that the transcendence of God destroys itself, if it is separated from the transcendence of the other human. Moreover, the latter transcendence implies a sort of radical descendence into the depth of the subject indicated by the words "me" or "I." Neither God, the other, nor I can be thought of in terms of kerygmatic discourse alone.

In order to prepare an interpretation of Levinas's analysis of transcendence, we might reflect on that other attempt of evading philosophy, in which Levinas sees a certain affinity with his own way of thought: the skeptical attempt.

SKEPTICISM

Skepticism may be understood as an expression of an extreme form of dissatisfaction with the *logos* in its philosophical form. Skepticism tries to evade philosophy; but is there any *logos*-free space where it could settle in order to enjoy a human life?

Since skepticism is a historical fact as persistent as philosophy itself, it must have a meaning. Its recurrence after every refutation suggests that its logical impossibility does not prevent something else in it being true or valuable or at least worth meditating upon. Skepticism is a child of philosophy; but is it also a "legitimate child of philosophy"?[4]

As an attempt to state something totally and absolutely negative, skepticism tries to give short shrift to philosophy as the logic of truth. But is there a realm outside of philosophy? Where can one find another dimension from which one could deliver a total condemnation without falling into the traps of universal logic? Is this realm outside of philosophy a sort of postphilosophical naïveté? Or is it still philosophical? But how, in the latter case, could skepticism save itself from its own condemnation?

The inspiration that prompts the negativities of skepticism looks like an expiration: not only were all the answers given to the important questions of humanity not true, but there is not even the possibility of true answers. Boredom, fatigue, and the exhaustion of an epoch are fertile soils for such a spirit of negation. Another mask of it is, however, the haughtiness of an acute intelligence which has tested every theory without meeting any view that imposed respect. Could skepticism itself be a mask? For instance, the reverse of a positive orientation or position? Or would this destroy it as efficiently as the universality of its negation?

What skepticism says, its thesis or "said," can be formulated in a sentence like the following one: "All (philosophical) theses are false" or "None of the possible theses (in philosophy) is true." We must perhaps distinguish (1) a skepticism that limits itself to a critical judgment about philosophy, from (2) a less careful and more absolute kind of skepticism. The latter condemns all statements, including the extraphilosophical ones; the former limits itself to the universal negation of the possibility of *philosophical* truths.

The classical refutation of skepticism consists in a simple analysis of the thesis or "said" in which skepticism takes a stand with regard to the universe of all possible theses (or "saids"). If the skeptical said is true, every thesis —the skeptical one as much as any other thesis—is false. This falsehood follows from the *implication* of the skeptical said in the universal said of skepticism. The difference between both saids is the difference between an *explicit* (and universal) thesis and an *implicit* (equally universal) thesis. It is not a difference of time, at least if we consider a thought that is logically entailed in another thought to be *simultaneous* with the latter.

If this analysis is right, skepticism can neither defend itself by pointing out that (1) the contradiction found by the refutation is a misinterpretation of the divergence between its saying and its said, nor by claiming that (2) its main thesis (which according to skepticism is true) *precedes* the thesis that skepticism on that very premise must be false. For (a) the refutation does not uncover an opposition between a saying and a said, but between an *explicit said* and an *implicit said*, and (b) although there may be a temporal difference between the moment in which the skeptical thesis is understood in a global sense and the moment in which it becomes evident that it is a self-contradictory statement, the insight contained in its contradiction destroys it as a philosophical statement. At least *within the realm of philosophy*, it must be considered to be nonsensical.

Could the skeptic defend himself by claiming that his thesis belongs to a metaphilosophical level? The question that he must answer in this case, is the following: Where do you find a metaphilosophical level from which you can state some thesis about all philosophical theses, without either becoming yourself hopelessly naïve or being refuted by the inner contradiction of your very thesis? Is there place for a *logos* or thought above or outside of philosophy?

If skepticism is defenseless against its classical refutation, how can we then save the passages in which Levinas claims that the refutation puts the saying and the said of skepticism on the same level and neglects the diachrony by which they are separated?

> The periodic return of skepticism and of its refutation signify a temporality in which the instants refuse memory which recuperates and re-presents. Skepticism, which traverses the rationality or logic of knowledge, is a refusal to synchronize the implicit affirmation contained in saying and the *negation* which this affirmation states in the said. The contradiction is visible to reflection, which refutes it, but skepticism is insensitive to the refutation, as though the affirmation and negation did not resound in the same time. Skepticism then contests the thesis which claims that *between the saying and the said* the *relationship that connects* in synchrony a *condition* with the *conditioned*

is repeated. It is as though skepticism were sensitive to the *difference* between *my exposure* without reserve to the other, which is saying, and the exposition or statement of the said in its equilibrium and justice.[5]

With regard to the diagnosis of skepticism given here, I would like to make the following remarks.

It does not seem to be true that skepticism distinguishes itself from all other forms of classical philosophy by a contestation of the thesis—be it only implicit —that the saying and the said must be seen as simultaneous and connected synchronically. Its way of stating and arguing does not differ from the traditional way of philosophy, except in its impossible attempt to be absolutely negative about everything. Its very thesis appeals to everybody's memory in order to gather all possible sentences and systems and to grasp them as a collection of positions which claim to be true. It does not present another alternative than the traditional one of true or false theses and theories. It claims to embrace all possibilities of truth but destroys the representation of this universe immediately. If skepticism is "a refusal to synchronize the implicit affirmation contained in saying and the *negation* which this affirmation states in the said," then the implicit affirmation itself is not a form of saying, but a said: a said it cannot refuse to affirm because of the absolutist thesis in which this said is contained. The structure of both saids is not different; both are parts of the same logic. If the (implicit) affirmation and the (explicit) negation do not *resound* at the same time, this is due to the fact that a discourse cannot tell all the aspects and moments of a thesis at once, but this is nothing special in skepticism. A trained logician, however, hears immediately the simultaneity of the affirmation and the contradictory negation in the statement that "all theses (including this one) are false."

If the skeptical thesis is meant to be a philosophical one, it cannot be saved. If it cannot find a way out, in order to condemn philosophy from a nonphilosophical, nonthetic, and nonsystematic standpoint, it should either give up and die, or show the possibility of another form of thought—a metaphilosophy or transformed philosophy—in which the *logos* of traditional philosophy is overcome. This would perhaps convince us that it "traversed the rationality of logic of knowledge" before it launched its presumptuous claim upon all attempts of stating truths.

However, the uneasy feeling that remains after the classical refutation of skepticism and the latter's insensitivity to the force of that refutation can be interpreted otherwise. There must be some hidden affirmation in the skeptical position. The strength of its logical refutation is exactly the—as a matter of fact very formal—truth that an absolutely negative statement is impossible. The weakness of skepticism is its incapacity or unwillingness to make the affirmative moments of its position—its positivity—explicit. In order to save some sort of skepticism, the positive side of its negation must be recognized. But can it be stated, posited, taken, defined, and located within the archaic and totalizing order of philosophy?

Both Kant and Hegel are exemplary in exploiting hidden possibilities of (a mitigated form of) skepticism. Kant even calls the "skeptical method" indispensable for acquiring access to the most radical questions of philosophy.[6] In order to show the incapacity of experiential and scientific knowledge with regard to the truths of metaphysics and the dimension of transcendence, Kant shows the necessary destruction of a certain form of philosophy by proving the inevitable simultaneity of contradictory theses about the world as the universe of phenomenal being. This insight gives access to another dimension and procedure of thought than the traditional one. Skepticism is a good weapon against the dogmatism of traditional metaphysics. A new, positive but very strange dimension of truth, full of negations, limitations, and impossibilities, is opened up for those who dare traverse the contradictions of skepticism. But how shall we call the sort of *Fürwahrhalten* (holding-as-true) which becomes possible after the suffered loss?

Less cautious than Kant, Hegel follows his example by acknowledging the most radical form of skepticism, while submitting it at the same time to an equally universalistic but positive position. Faithful to the syllogistic framework of Western philosophy, Hegel converts and integrates skepticism by showing that all its explicit and implicit negations are true, except its negation of the unique truth of the Absolute itself, which is also the whole. By neutralizing all those finite negations through corresponding affirmations, Hegel imprisons the spirit of negativity by extending the horizons of truth just a little beyond that spirit's range.

The radicalism of skepticism and its affinity with true metaphysics lies, however, in its pointing beyond totality. This is the reason why Levinas writes phrases like the following: "Philosophy is not separable from skepticism,"[7] "Language is already skepticism,"[8] and "the history of Western philosophy has been the refutation of transcendence."[9] From the standpoint of logic, Hegel argued that such a "beyond" is possible only if the "beyond" (the Absolute itself) somehow coincides with the totality of truth in which it unfolds itself by means of a universal and double negation. Like Plato and Plotinus, but in a different vein, Levinas maintains that the One beyond the whole of being is separated from it.

From Hegel we can learn that truth is infinitely more dramatic than most antiskeptical *and skeptical* philosophers think: the force and width of negation are as universal and almost as absolute as the Absolute itself. Absolute skepticism, however, is absurd, because in denying whatever is said, it does not say anything and therefore exists as if it did not exist. The skeptical position must be "traversed" because the *logos* of kerygmatic philosophy is not wide enough. But what comes after both?

Kant's traversal of the skepticism that results from the inevitable antinomies of metaphysical cosmology was an attempt to break out of a well-assured and solid knowledge toward an ambiguous sort of "holding-as-true" which must awaken many suspicions because it looks like an illogical faith. Did this sort of relation to the true belong inside or outside of philosophy?

Levinas's appraisal of skepticism, too, seems to be inspired by the search for a dimension beyond the order of well-founded and self-assured *logos*—

a dimension in which the eminence and strangeness of the transcendent expresses itself in the loss of syllogistic certainty and in the preference for words like "perhaps" and "it is as if" or "everything seems to suggest" over the bold statements of conceptual comprehension and kerygmatic language. Levinas's great discovery is that he found a way beyond the solidarity of logic and its skeptical denial in the difference between the said and its saying.

The order of the said—the dimension of the *logos* and its synoptic structures —refers to and depends on the saying, which can never become an element of it. Skepticism is seen by Levinas as a position in which that difference is recognized more clearly—be it in the form of a feeling only—than it is within the logic of traditional philosophy. The mild and perhaps too positive diagnosis of skepticism given by Levinas becomes illuminating if we read it as a description of his own attempt to think the relation between the logical way of doing philosophy and the beyond which does not contradict the dimension of *logos* and phenomenology, but is incommensurate to it.

Before we reflect on the importance of this discovery, I would, however, like to come back to the problem of textuality and ask the question that we postponed: Is it altogether true that the author is *absent* from his texts once they are written or after his death?

PRESENTATION

A writer cannot address himself to us from the shelves of the library where his books are located. He at least needs the assistance of some other instance —person, group, or tradition—to present his text to us. In this case he is represented and in a way existent behind or even *in* the text, coming from our and his past but provoking us, here and now, to read his words. At least the echo of his voice is perceptible, even when his name is unknown. Can the voice of an author be silenced totally? Is it true that "in a written text the saying certainly becomes a pure said, a simultaneity of the saying and its conditions?"[10] Perhaps synchrony is not the whole truth of a text, because it only "functions" if it provokes us to an understanding, interpretation, or discussion. No text could affect us if it were not brought to our notice by a *presentation*. Is it essential to the meaning of a text that it be addressed to possible readers or listeners? The presentation of a text to me by a third person or by myself not only reminds me of its known or unknown author, but represents and revives the author's position as someone who calls to me.

When we re-read Levinas, who saves his texts from fossilization? Who addresses them to us? Is it the contributors to this volume? To what extent is it Levinas himself? Or isn't there any instance in particular responsible for our being provoked by these texts? Are they "interesting" because we decided (or something in us decided) to read them or to make them readable? But how could we take this initiative? Must our initiative not be preceded by an initiative that belongs to the past and is a constituent of it? Does this lead us to an infinite regression?[11]

Even if we were capable of deciding with sovereignty to treat texts as ownerless property or free "food for our souls," our treatment meets with voices and provocations whose absence would kill all their meaning. The meaning of a kerygma depends on its being proclaimed *and addressed* by a Voice. Reading a text is always responding to a call that summons us, although it is true also that the presenting voice comes from the past when the text was born from its author. Representation is essential to reading. Our discussing "Levinas" presupposes and implies our addressing his writings to one another and when we are doing this, the master's voice is echoing in ours.

If this analysis is acceptable, we should not overemphasize the distance by which a text is separated from its writer. A text is not a tool made by someone before it was given to us, who, in turn, took it into our possession, neither can it be compared to the bread which I will not eat because I want to give it to someone else. A tool can be understood and handled perfectly without any reference to its maker (except when it is a very original work, but then it is not only an artifact, but also some sort of "poem"). The giving of bread is not analogous to the offering of a text because I cannot eat or assimilate a text of my own (except, perhaps, later, when I have become different from the writer that I once was), but only give it away. An author is not a maker, because in presenting his text, he presents *himself*. To utter words is to address and to expose myself to the benevolence or the violence of readers over whom I have no power, but whom I cannot help invoking.

Levinas's analyses of saying and responsibility can be applied to the necessary presentation of a text. In order to get an idea of this analogy, let's turn to the analysis of speaking and spoken words.[12]

SPEAKING

A kerygma is always addressed to one or more addressees. Saying is a condition of the possibility of all discourse. What is communication insofar as it is not the production of a message but an address to possible listeners?

When I direct myself to someone by saying "Hello!" I enter into a relation with the person who is there, in front of me or at the end of the line, while I am here, speaking to her. In telling what I have to tell, I count on the other's memory: she must synchronize the succession of words in which I unfold my narration or my argument. My saying itself, however, "precedes" that which, by my communication, is told or argued for. What sort of "precedence" separates the saying from the said?

When I say "Good morning!" I am not delivering a message, but through a sort of benediction, I am wishing you a happy or successful morning. Here, too, the saying—which now has a content of its own—differs from the story or the discourse that can be unfolded thereafter. If we reserve the said for the message, then, too, the saying precedes the said. Within this saying we can, however, distinguish between the fact of addressing oneself to another and the wish ("Please . . .") or accusation ("Bastard!") or command ("Come!"

or "Away!") worded by it. In his analyses of the saying Levinas concentrates on the moment of addressing. The said indicates primarily the order of kerygmatic language and especially theoretical discourse. There is, thus, still space for other distinctions and elaborations.

The precedence of saying differs from the precedence by which an author has a distance from his text. Between a speaker and his speech the unity is closer: he himself actually exists in the proffering of his said. Yet, there is a sort of interval, a nonsimultaneity, between his saying and the said. Not only is a saying possible without kerygma, whereas the reverse needs at least a representant of the original voice, but "Hello" or "Here I am" are not meant to communicate a story or a thesis; they are an appeal to the addressee to pay attention to the presence, here and now, of the speaker, who may deliver a message hereafter. By saying "Good morning" I might be initiating a communication, but it is also possible that nothing else will follow. Saying is a sort of foreword or "preface" to the message that follows. Saying and said do not coincide perfectly; they are not completely simultaneous: the said comes from a saying which takes the initiative, resounds before and stays behind it. The interval between the saying and the said is, however, much smaller than the distance between author and text. The speaking voice is a much more intense presence than the style, the souvenirs, and the echoes by which a writer is recognizable in his writings.

To speak to someone is not identical with the reading of a paper or the delivery of an address. Indeed, it is essential to speaking that the speaker not only directs himself to one or more listeners, but also invites and provokes them to a response. To deliver a speech without intending it to be the beginning of a discussion in which my speech will be subjected to other perspectives, is a hybridic form of language holding the middle between speaking and reading. If we not only want to "read Levinas," but also intend to give his and our saying(s) a chance, we must hear his texts as calls and provocations to which we respond with words of our own.

To sum up the difference between texts and spoken words the following features might be stressed. The synoptic character of a text is less obvious in speech. Not only does a series of spoken words miss the completion of a text, whose elements are all present here and now in one piece of paper, but the intention of speaking is also less totalitarian. Spoken words are meant to be fragments of intersubjective chains of exchange and conversation. Normally they do not claim to constitute a well-rounded whole; by scanning the flow of time they trust that there will be more time for speaking in order to respond, correct, augment, and relativize what has been said before.

Since the speaker is present in his words, he thereby addresses *himself* to the listener. The temporal distance and the "diachrony" between an author and his text are more obvious, but even here he is not altogether absent from his writings. This difference in distance is the reason why Levinas, in some passages of *Totality and Infinity*, quotes Plato's defense of oral teaching against the pretensions of written texts. Authors cannot defend their message when it is distorted by misunderstandings or attacked by objections, because their presence in the text is a diminished one. A speaker can elucidate, interpret, and correct her words by prolongating or adjusting her discourse.[13]

A spoken word is not a score, like a text before it is read. Speech cannot exist in separation from the speaker. Even a tape-recorded speech differs from a text by (re-)presenting the speaker's voice and intonation, which is another form of existence than the style. Speech is, however, not to be compared to writing, but rather to the *reading* of a text: both are the presentation of a message by voices in which the author is present or represented.

Whatever the differences between speaking, writing, and reading may be, all these ways of language present us with a radical difference between the *said*, whose structure was clarified by the analysis of kerygmatic language, and the *saying* of it. This difference cannot be reduced to the traditional opposition of an autonomous interiority and its exteriorization, nor can saying be understood as a complication of a said, and certainly not as an anonymous *saga* or *Sage* coming from the past of our traditions. *Language does not speak*, although everybody recognizes that all our commonplaces and dicta, and even the most original sayings of our history, are shaped and marked by that forceful past.

Against the domination of anonymous powers and mores it is not sufficient —although it may be useful—to stress the originality of a personal style. Through a style of her own, an author shows that her assimilation of the current usages and patterns, stories and discourses is not the simple repetition of everybody's *Gerede* (idle talk). The more she transforms the commonplaces into a said of her own, the more she emerges from anonymity. A personal style is, however, not the most important characteristic of language. Above, before, and behind all features of a personality as expressed in style, the *addressing* of the said to someone is at once the most common and the most radical distinction by which language transcends the whole range of things that can be said.

SAYINGS AND ADHESION

In addressing words to someone, I present and expose myself to that person. This most common event of everybody's daily life realizes the transcendence that philosophy is looking for without finding it in the realm of *logos*. *Saying* (1) is the condition that precedes all said, all systematic discourse, thematization, and phenomenology; (2) it cannot be understood as a modulation or modification of a human or superhuman said; (3) it cannot be reduced to the act of an autonomous subject or the free initiative of human self-consciousness.

In directing myself to another person saying exposes me. What I present cannot be named by summing up my material or spiritual qualities, my words or the phenomenal characteristics by which I could be recognized as this specific person. Through and behind or beyond all my masks and appearances, I am present to the other as a naked subject whose "essence" is to be given, delivered up, and extradited to the other. Being present to another in saying is spoliation and extradition. I am hostage to the other and nobody can replace me in this service, which constitutes me as this unique individual. Subjectivity as the relation of the-one-for-the-other interrupts and forbids the absolutization of a narcissistic way of life prompted by the spontaneous drives of an isolated ego. By the other's very existence—not by her decisions—she poses an infinite claim on me: I will never be able to fulfill the obligations contained in this claim, but this does not dispense me from fulfilling them. The opposition between the other's claim and my spontaneous narcissism expresses itself in the humiliation and injuring of my egocentrism. This is the reason why being-offered-to-the-other implies pain and suffering. Everybody has been chosen to suffer for the other. Suffering and vulnerability are essential to human subjectivity.

A crucial point in the analysis of the relation of the-one-for-the-other is the impossibility of understanding this relation as the result of a decision, a contract, or a convention based on acts of some human will. Human freedom is not capable of creating its own meaning and orientation. The foundation of ethics cannot be found in the self-determination (*Selbstbestimmung*) of one or more wills by themselves. If I try to fulfill my obligations, I obey a law that was there before I awoke to consciousness: the law regards and orders me from the eyes of someone who—by this existence alone—deserves esteem. My devotion to others does not begin with dedicating myself to them. It was already there before I discovered it.

The same must be said of my directing myself to another by *saying*. My act and my intention, not only my work of exteriorization but the whole dynamism of my inner life, is preceded, caught, and carried on by an already-being-addressed, -given, and -dedicated to the other, which comes from an immemorial and irretrievable past. I discover what I am when I discover that I have been given to the other before I could agree to it. My first agreement occurs when I obey the order that constitutes me more radically than autonomy. It is in obedience that I get an inkling of what subjectivity or being-human is. Although I never wanted or even accepted to be responsible for another, I cannot escape from this infinite responsibility. My devotion to the other is a past where neither my consciousness nor my will have been present, but this past determines all the presents of my life. The core of human subjectivity is the extreme passivity of someone who always comes too late to accept his task and autonomy.

One may, however, ask whether it is not possible at all that a human subject, in the course of a life, approaches the point where free will coincides completely with responsibility and obligations never contracted willingly. Isn't it possible and isn't it the basic task of a moral life that we learn to agree with our subjectivity *afterwards* and that we assent progressively to our having become infinitely responsible before all memorable time? Levinas stresses the interval between the election and the emergence of consciousness and autonomy; upon awakening, our spontaneous egoism is not ready to agree with the infinite demands of responsibility which took possession of us without our consent and against the desires of our spontaneity. But this excludes neither the possibility of a future agreement with the orders of the good nor the perspective of a final peace by full adhesion to the law of infinite obligation. Isn't death, after all, the possibility of a full payment of all debts? Even if we are justly aware that the extent and intensity of responsibility are so enormous that they will always exceed our capacity for accomplishing what should be done, a certain peace is ideally possible, on the condition that one also accepts the exact measure of one's destiny or election. Mustn't we conclude that the two strains of our existence suggest and demand that we consider a certain union of goodness and peace to be the destination and final meaning of an individual's life?

Being exposed to others and being responsible for them is to be animated by a spirit of devotion. It is to have a soul. Every reminiscence of the vulgar opposition between matter and spirit should be banished from our understanding of subjectivity. Human spirituality is a particular position and movement of earthly bodies with regard to other bodies. Inspiration is not a mysterious insufflation taking place within some inner cave, but the extradition of a subject in flesh and blood. It does not leave any private property to a subjective interiority that could extract solitary pleasures from it. By agreeing to the reversal that has taken place before I became conscious of it, I lose all possibilities of isolation and spiritualization.

The transcendence practiced in the most simple acts and gestures of everyday life, like speaking, suffering, or helping, is not at all heroic in the sense of an ensemble of impressive plans and actions; it realizes itself as endurance and patience. Instead of an ascension by means of elitist projects and originality, it demands a descent to service and devotion.

Saying, responsibility, goodness, proximity, subjectivity, inspiration, and spirituality do not fit into the horizons of kerygmatic discourse and logical appropriation. My own saying captures me in a movement that started before I could move my will. It takes me away from my attempt at identifying myself as the central or transcendental point of reference. The presentation of myself in my addressing words to someone cannot be welcomed within the system of *logos* and phenomenology. It cannot be gathered or synchronized within the said. At the same time, however, the saying and the said are united in the very act of speaking in spite of their being "diachronically" related to one another. Their combination in one and the same time is possible because their difference does not produce a contradiction. The saying and the said are not contradictory, but incommensurable. If they were related as contradictory terms, skepticism would be inevitable and the only possible defense—a narrow escape!—would be in stressing the temporal precedence of saying, which would be separated by an interval from the said. Against the synchrony of the kerygmatic synopsis the duplicity of saying and said would have to realize an authentic diachrony without any overlapping.

By taking up once again Levinas's analyses I have insisted on the presence by which the author, the speaker, and the saying subject present themselves or are (re-)presented in their message. I have thereby diminished the importance of the diachrony by which Levinas distinguishes saying, responsibility, and subjectivity from all possible objects and subjects of logical thematization. That the saying "precedes" every said, that the obligation in which I discover myself belongs to an immemorial past that precedes my awakening to consciousness, that "He" from whom that obligation comes (and thereby the ultimate meaning of world and history) will have always already passed away—all these references to an irretrievable "Before" must be affirmed and meditated upon. Transcendence must be practiced and described as an exodus out of the logical and archaic temporality of Western philosophy, but what sort of time is introduced by pointing to the *before* of God, Law, and subjectivity? It is not merely the precedence of civilization, history, and the traditions that support us and our language as *Sage* and *sprechende Sprache*. Which sense is applicable to the "somewhere else" that affects us? In which sense is the "beyond" a *temporal* before?

In a degenerated form of metaphysics, which for giants like Nietzsche became a bugbear, transcendence was understood as a transition from this empirical world to a higher world "behind" this one. The hinter-world of the hinterland has lost its spell. As a matter of fact, it never had any attraction for philosophers; they have always known that the image of a *Hinterwelt* is only an awkward spatial metaphor and that its value depends exclusively on its capacity to adjust the orientation of our being in a unique world of natural phenomena and human history.

In Levinas's later works the spatial metaphors like "a higher order," "the highest being," "the deepest ground," "the fundamental or basic principle," "that which is behind the phenomena," and so on, which were used in the context of old metaphysical reflection, are replaced by adverbs of time, and principally by expressions that indicate the *past*. "An immemorial and irretrievable past," "He, who passed away," "a past that has never been present," "a passivity more passive than all passivity," and similar expressions suppress the metaphorical "behind" and "above."[14] Must we also understand Levinas's *diachrony* in a metaphorical way? What then is the meaning of *temporal metaphors*? They are not absent from the philosophical and theological traditions of Western civilization, in which, e.g., God also was imagined as He who already existed before creation and as He who will exist when it is completed, but even more so as He, whose presence is the "first principle" (*principium*) of all principles. If Levinas's characterization of transcendence by its diachronical structure must be understood as a metaphorical language, the question arises whether temporal metaphors are better suited to a consideration of transcendence and to what extent their power of evocation and suggestion differs from that of spatial metaphors. Could it be that the preference for the quasi-spatial eminence of the transcendent is connected to a cosmological vision in which the main attention is given to the space of nature, whereas temporality occupies the center of our symbolic language when human history—or its elementary and everlasting emergence in intersubjective relationships—has become the principal concern?

THE UNITY OF SAYING AND SAID

My conclusion must remain very sketchy. I will only suggest a few possibilities that should be tested, rejected, or amended in further meditations.

(1) The noncontradictory incommensurability of the saying and the said makes their combination, unity, and simultaneity possible, in spite of the "diachronic" primacy of the saying.

(2) At the same time, their difference makes it very difficult to clarify the peculiarity of the saying, *but also to determine the characteristics of the said,* which is always a said presented by a saying (or reading).[15]

If the saying and the said cannot be isolated from one another, we come to two main difficulties: (a) The first is the classical difficulty of how it is possible to thematize and objectify constitutive *moments* of an object or theme, like, for instance, matter and form or noumenality and phenomenality. If a thing is essentially composed of matter and form, it is obvious that we cannot treat the form as if it were a thing, but how can we treat it, then, as the subject of our predications? (b) The second difficulty results from the very special essence of the saying, and the impact it has on the peculiarities of the said. If every said is necessarily presented by a saying and if there is no saying without any said, their interwovenness must be constitutive for the modes of being characteristic of both of them.

(3) The simultaneity of the said and the saying, which is not abolished by their difference, must be thought as such. The transition between the two and their belonging together is formulated many times, but how can it be thought? This question is even more urgent than the question about the relation between myself and the other in the separation that does not abolish this belonging together. But finally both questions coincide.

The alternation of the *dire-dédire-redire* and so on proposed by Levinas does not seem to be the final word on this question. Indeed, to know that we must jump from one dimension (the dimension of *logos*) to the other dimension (the dimension of saying, exposure, and responsibility) and again to *logos*, and repeat this jumping back and forth an infinite number of times, implies that we somehow "know" about the secret passage that binds them together. The alternation of "yes" and "no" in our saying-denying-saying-again in a time of repetition (in which—in a sense—"the same" is said and denied again and again) implies at least the repetition of a moment in which the transition of "yes" in "no" and of "no" in the selfsame "yes" testifies to their simultaneity —albeit briefly. That this simultaneity can be *accomplished* is evident; that there is also some secret awareness of it seems to be plausible; but can it be transformed into a part of philosophy? Responsibility is better than reflection, but philosophy cannot give up reflecting upon its extradition to the better. As long as responsibility remains reflexive, it cannot evade philosophy. Repetitive reflexion may, however, be a final attempt to avoid the pain of radical passivity.

Notes

1. Cf. "Langage et proximité," EDE 217–22; CP 109–13; and AE 43–47; OB 34–37. About the difference between writings and oral utterances, some hints can be found in AE 217; OB 170–71. See also TeI 69, 150–53; TI 95, 175–78.

2. *Phaedrus* 275b–277a; Seventh Letter 341b–344d; cf. TeI 45, 69–71; TI 73, 95–98.

3. Cf. the analysis of Desire at the beginning of TeI 18–23; TI 33–36. If the later work does not often come back to the radical human desire for the Absolute, this does not mean that Levinas rejects the analyses of TI or deems them unimportant. His silence about desire may be explained by his emphasis on the denucleation of the subject and its extradition. Not only is there a danger of mistaking desire for a sort of *eros* that is our eminent *need*, but the subject (the I) does not have an interiority of its own that would be protected from its being delivered to the other. In EDE 230; CP 120, proximity is described as "a hunger, glorious in its insatiable desire." This desire is "hungry" from an absence that is the presence of the infinite.

4. Cf. AE 231: "A legitimate child of philosophical research" ("enfant légitime de la recherche philosophique"); cf. OB 231, which reads "illégitime" ("bastard") instead of "légitime."

5. AE 213; OB 167–68.

6. Cf. *Kritik der reinen Vernunft*, B 514, 785–86, 797.

7. AE 213; OB 168.

8. AE 216; OB 170.

9. AE 214; OB 169: "l'histoire de la philosophie occidentale n'a été que la réfutation du scepticisme autant que la réfutation de la transcendence." I translate this phrase as if the end of the sentence runs: "n'a été la réfutation du scepticisme que pour autant qu'elle a été la réfutation de la transcendence." It seems to me that the French is a mixture of this phrase and the phrase: "l'histoire de la philosophie occidentale a été la réfutation du scepticisme autant que la réfutation de la transcendence" (. . . has been as much . . . as . . .).

10. AE 217; OB 170–71. Cf. AE 211; OB 166: "the *simultaneity of writing*, the *eternal present* of a writing that records or presents results."

11. Compare what Levinas writes on the infinite regression as expression of our finitude in EDE 224; CP 115: "infinite regression—to the bad infinity—jeopardizes, all the more, the certitude of truth and is precisely for this reason also finite."

12. Cf. EDE 223–34; CP 114–15; AE 6–9; OB 5–9; and AE 43–65; OB 34–51.

13. Cf. TeI 45 and 69–71; TI 73 and 95–98; and Plato's *Phaedrus* 274b–277a.

14. The dimension of height (*hauteur*) is still very much present in *Totality and Infinity*. Cf., for example, TeI 59; TI 86.

15. A similar conclusion imposes itself with regard to the relationship between the other as *Thou* and the other as the *third*. A further complication is that I experience myself, too, as an individual for whom I must care and as someone who is spoken to as well as one who is speaking to the other who speaks to me.

CHAPTER

4

THE FACE AND READING
Immediacy and Mediation
Jean Greisch
Translated by Simon Critchley

A recent work devoted to Emmanuel Levinas carries the suggestive title: *Face to Face with Levinas*.[1] The present book is entitled simply *Re-Reading Levinas*. The confrontation of these two titles is an invitation to relate together, through the labor of reading which is also a labor of thinking, two experiences which play an essential role in Levinas's thinking: the experience of the epiphany of the face, of which we realize the capital importance for his conception of ethics, and the experience of reading which also plays an important role in his thinking, since Levinas is one of the rare authors who suggest making a fundamental existential category of the relationship to the Book.[2] Of course, it will not be a question of setting these two experiences one against the other, under the guise of a philosophy of Hegelian inspiration which opposes the rule of immediacy to that of mediation. The authors who are grouped together under the title *Face to Face with Levinas* are, of course, readers of Levinas, just as we, the contributors to this book, cannot withdraw ourselves from the *obligation* which speaks in those texts of Levinas which offer themselves to our reading. *Re-Reading Levinas*: that does not only mean engaging oneself in an extremely demanding labor of reading, seeing that we venture into a jungle of texts as difficult as the pages of *Otherwise than Being*. It signifies, as Jacques Derrida suggests in a text entitled "At this very moment in this work here I am,"[3] the attempt to intersect two instances, the instance of the letter and of the reading that has always already begun, necessarily making a plurality of contexts intervene, and the ethical instance of the "Here I am" which implies the assignation and obligation by the other who takes me hostage, without me having chosen him.

The intersection of these two instances, which everything would seem to oppose, is no easy thing. If, as Paul Ricoeur thinks, reading is an operation of refiguration, situating itself at the intersection of two "worlds," those of the text and the reader,[4] it would be, in the case of the work that we read here, a simple defiguration if it lost sight of the face-to-face of responsibility. Now, at first sight, everything indeed takes place as if the labor of reading, labor of contextualization, would be in this sense also a "hypocritical" enterprise. It is clearly necessary to understand this expression in terms of the signification that Levinas gives to it at the beginning of *Totality and Infinity*.[5] The act of reading is "hypocritical" insofar as the encounter with the voice of a determinate text awakens other voices, the fruit of previous readings. Is this to say that, from this fact, reading bears within it the inevitable risk of losing sight of the very tenor of the ethical face-to-face? The "height" of the face against the immanence of the text, the immediacy of the relation with the near or distant Other (*autrui*) against textual mediation, the infinity that comes to the idea against the bad infinity of the text, itself accompanied by its cortege of paratexts (Gérard Genette)[6] of every order: we would not be able to count all the oppositions which crop up here. And yet, Levinas's thinking forbids us to transform these oppositions into antinomies. On the contrary, his thinking invites us to overcome them. Which is where the stakes of the work of reading attempted here arise from: in focusing the reading on *Otherwise than Being*, it will be our concern to identify this point of possible intersection and consequently to see in what sense it allows us to take up "otherwise" the Heideggerian question "What is philosophy?" This will oblige me to construct a fictive reader of *Otherwise than Being*, a reader who, at all costs, wishes to discover the Hegelian movement of immediacy and mediation, at risk of becoming a sort of "evil genius" to the thinking of our author.

THE INTRIGUE OF ETHICS AND LANGUAGE

We know what the meeting with the face of the Other in its very straightforwardness signifies for Levinas: it is a rupture of context, the discovery of a "signification without context,"[7] which, when it is considered in its final consequences, compels a complete rethinking of the relation between transcendence and intelligibility. This experience of the epiphany of the face—which in Levinas's eyes is "the experience par excellence"[8]—is also the condition for the possibility of language, to such a point that it is from the perspective of this experience that the meaning of speech and expression must be thought. In a different terminology, elaborated in *Otherwise than Being*, but speaking of the same thing, it is a matter of thinking the signifyingness (*signifiance*) anterior to all signification (*signification*). In *Totality and Infinity* we have already met the affirmation that, "The face opens the primordial discourse whose first word is obligation, which no 'interiority' permits avoiding."[9] *Otherwise than Being* will be an intense effort to unpack all the implications of "the intrigue which forms in the face of the Other."[10]

The term "intrigue" takes on a particular importance here. To read Levinas, to understand the bearing of his philosophical enterprise, consists in deciphering this "intrigue" which admits of no narrative connotations, contrary to what takes place in the recent work of Paul Ricoeur. But, in the same way, Levinasian intrigue overflows that other "intrigue" that we would call "speculative," which Hegel puts forward in his doctrine of the speculative proposition and which decides, let us not forget, the form of presentation (*Darstellung*) in the entirety of Hegel's thinking. From whence the question arises: what connection is there between "the intrigue which forms in the face of the Other" and the Levinasian formulations of the problem "What is philosophy?"

The order of language signifies the establishment of an "absolute difference, inconceivable in terms of formal logic."[11] On this point, Levinas finds himself deeply in agreement with Franz Rosenzweig, who also clearly affirmed that the entry into the order of linguistic signification compels us to turn our back on the atomistic language of logic and mathematical thinking. Confronted with a similar "intrigue" a Hegelian reader will undergo some perplexity to the extent that "intrigue" seems to disrupt profoundly the economy of immediacy and mediation such as it is defined by the Hegelian doctrine of the Concept. At first sight, everything takes place as if ethical intrigue necessarily marked a triumph of immediacy over the performances of the Concept. But it is essential to analyze more closely these Levinasian figures of immediacy in order to understand what makes them so unwilling to accept the Concept. The inflation of the values of immediacy seems particularly pregnant in the section of *Otherwise than Being* entitled "The Exposition." In the first place, my reading will limit itself to this section. It will be the question of an attempt to enter into the procession of signifiers "maternity, vulnerability, responsibility, proximity, contact,"[12] which must be traversed if we want to have access to Levinas's "philosophy of language." We will only have access to the latter once the phenomenological signification of all these figures of immediacy has been elucidated. It seems to me that the nucleus of this philosophy of language is formed by the idea that language begins in the pure saying of sincerity, which unites immediacy and obligation: "The saying could not be interpreted as sincerity, if one takes a language as a system of signs. One only enters into language as a system of signs out of an already spoken language, which in turn cannot consist in a system of signs. The system in which the significations are thematised has already come out of signification, the-one-for-the-other, approach and sincerity."[13]

It is as "simple as hello" as our author often reminds us, especially in those circumstances when the reader finds his thinking extremely difficult! Indeed, what could be more evident than the insistence on the fact that the first and fundamental value of immediacy is sincerity. The implications of this thesis must be examined more closely. It seems to me that two affirmations must hold our attention here.

(1) On the one hand, everything takes place as if "the pre-original saying which is prior to all civilisation and every beginning in the spoken speech that signifies,"[14] crystalized itself into a very specific "language game": namely, the prophetic "here I am." In Levinas's eyes, the prophetic "here I am" also defines "the very psychism of the soul,"[15] in that it contains the answer to the question of the essence of language. Read from a Wittgensteinian perspec-

tive, this is a very surprising declaration. Whereas, in the later Wittgenstein, "the great question" which underlies all linguistic investigation, namely that of knowing "what the essence of a language game, and hence of language is,"[16] finds its solution by referring to the diversity of language games; the whole of Levinas's philosophy is an attempt to identify *the* language game—which could be called "transcendental"—which contains in itself the condition for the possibility of all other language games, regardless of their real diversity or their family resemblance which brings them together while differentiating them. But, paradoxically, this "transcendental language game," the "signifyingness anterior to signification" (a formula which contains the Levinasian version of the famous question: "what is the meaning of meaning?"), is as well placed inside of language as prior to it. This is why Levinas can place two theories of signification in the same basket, when they would seem to oppose each other: on the one hand, the Heideggerian conception of speech as the "resonance" or the "reverberation" of Being across the saying, like to that of certain mystics who thought to discern the resonance of the creative Verb across the multiplicity of human *verba*; and on the other hand, the structuralist conception of language which regards it as a closed system of signs. Everything occurs as if those two rationalities which, in other respects, are so opposed, discover themselves to be accomplices when it is a question of making the subject a simple epiphenomenon of the system or a simple moment of Being.[17]

(2) This entire problematic of language which seeks to identify a signifyingness anterior to signification is dominated by a further opposition which runs through all of the analyses in *Otherwise than Being* like a red thread: the opposition of the *Saying* and the *Said*. In showing how these two interrogations are related, we are led to the point of intersection that we sought, which allows us access into Levinas's approach to the Heideggerian question: "What is philosophy?" To begin with, let us remind ourselves that the opposition of the Saying and the Said doesn't possess a purely regional signification, as if the opposition were only a theme within a much larger philosophy of language. Its signification is much more fundamental. It is this opposition which ultimately decides Levinas's "gesture" or "style of thinking."

How do these two themes tally with one another? Several of the notes in *Otherwise than Being* (in Genette's terminology we must consider them as a particular style of *paratext*) affirm that the donation of the originary sign, the signifyingness of the saying, is not an immediate certitude conquered once and for all. On the contrary, the "scandal of sincerity" is that it always yet remains to be said! How can it be said? Precisely in the register of the *unsaying* (*dédire*)! "There is therefore a need to unsay (*dédire*) all that comes after the nakedness of signs, to set aside all that is said in the pure saying proper to proximity."[18] It is a question of "breaking through the wall of meaning said, so as to revert to the hither side of civilisation." A comparable enterprise has been attempted by other speculative projects, the difference being that their preoccupation was more that of reuniting with the *beyond* (*l'au-delà*) of all simply established signification. It was a question of reuniting with the ineffable

One, at the risk of seeing oneself accused by certain people of wanting thinking to sink into "the night of the Absolute where all cows are black." The analogy with negative theologies and meontologies is evidently not only fortuitous in this context. It is not only a "hypocritical" reader who establishes such a rapprochement in Levinas's discourse. It is a rapprochement which we can read in the text. A rapprochement which, moreover, duplicates itself upon the refusal to engage oneself in such a line of research; insofar as it is not a question of overcoming the intrinsic limits of an affirmative language through a recourse to a liberating negativity. If the "unsaying" implies negation, then it is solely a question of a "negation of the present and of representation which finds in the 'positivity' of proximity, in responsibility and in substitution a difference with the propositions of negative theology."[19]

If we recall that, in *Totality and Infinity*, the neo-Platonic reading of the *epekeina tes ousias* is mobilized alongside the Cartesian infinite in order to bring about a rupture with the thinking of totality, we can better understand why this allusion does not simply concern a relation to a trend in the history of philosophy. As a matter of fact, this allusion is essential as a qualification to the style of thinking that is being sought here.

OTHERWISE READ: WITTGENSTEIN AND LEVINAS FACING ETHICS

But the "unsaying" may still present itself in a different form, probably more familiar to certain of our contemporaries. Thus, before even pursuing my reading in the direction of the Levinasian deployment of the question "What is philosophy?" I would like to extend the results already acquired in the direction of a philosophical context at first sight absolutely foreign to Levinasian questioning. By that I mean Wittgensteinian philosophy and, more specifically, the Wittgensteinian manner of approaching (some will say of clearly avoiding) the problem of ethics. What authorizes such an untimely rapprochement? Thus far, we have seen that the "primordiality of the intrigue of ethics and language" forbids us from only seeing the latter as an act amongst acts: "Before placing oneself at the service of life as the exchange of information across a linguistic system, the Saying is testimony, Saying without a said, a sign given to the Other."[20] On this subject, Levinas speaks of a "complicity for nothing." A subsequent reading would clearly have to confront this ethical "for nothing" with the "without why" of Silesius's rose, which allows Heidegger to deconstruct the Principle of Reason. An important philosophical consequence of this ethical "for nothing" is that such an ethics gives up the pretense of wanting to found a morality. In the course of his conversations with Philippe Nemo, Levinas says, "My task does not consist in constructing ethics, I am simply trying to find its meaning."[21] It is precisely this refusal to give oneself over to a foundational enterprise that Levinas has in common with Wittgenstein.

The refusal becomes yet more eloquent if one puts it alongside the numerous recent philosophical attempts which seek to constitute a philosophical morality independent of religious and metaphysical presuppositions. Jürgen Habermas in particular, supporting himself on the researches of Singer, Rawls, Lorenzen, Tugendhat, and especially K. O. Apel, has recently become the eloquent advocate of a "discursive ethics"[22] which claims to found ethics upon a logic of moral argumentation. One can clearly see where the interest lies in this concern to recover a cognitivist approach to the problem of ethics, based on the concept of communicative action and a supposedly "communicative" reason. It is a question of escaping from the mournful consequences of value-skepticism and affirming the possibility of rationally argued discussion in a public space that is fundamentally marked by a pluralism of values.[23] Is it still necessary to remind ourselves that each philosopher has for an interlocutor and adversary the skeptic that he deserves? Consequently, it seems that the attempt to make sure of a transcendental-pragmatic foundation for the ethical demand only triumphs over the skeptical objection upon a very limited terrain. Habermas himself is conscious of the fact that, from a certain moment, the cognitivist "will only be able to discourse *upon* the sceptic and not *with* him."[24] Let us retain this confession, which implies a definition of skepticism that we will return to later on. As a matter of fact, the program of a discursive ethics comprises still another and yet more severe limit than that which skepticism allowed to appear. Indeed, on the one hand, discursive ethics professes a formalism which has no reason to be envious of Kantian formalism, since the price that must be paid for the attainment of a principle of universalization of the ethical demand is the severing of the link between the "Good" and the "Just."[25] On the other hand, everything takes place as if the principle of such an ethics was simply a procedure for argumentation that was obliged to renounce the generation of content. For Habermas, practical discourse "is a procedure not for the generation of justified norms, but for the examination of the validity of proposed or possible norms by way of hypothesis."[26]

In correctly understanding the very confined limits which circumscribe the field for the application of a discursive ethics, it would therefore seem that the latter necessarily presupposes the one thing which interests Levinas as well as Wittgenstein: the very constitution of the field of ethical significations; or, to put it in the language of Levinas himself, "the intrigue of ethics and language" which, by right, precedes all controversy and all rational argumentation upon ethical choices. On this subject, Wittgenstein would thus represent the possibility of an original and insurmountable "skepticism." The signification of such a skepticism would clearly not be the artful ruination of ethical certitudes or of the subject's ethical choice. On the contrary, through his insistence on the transcendental character of ethics, he would call philosophy to the point where the ethical significations themselves emerge, conscious of the fact that it is a question of an absolutely specific intrigue which a cognitivist approach is, almost of necessity, bound to disregard in its specificity. To my mind, it is at this point that the necessity of a labor of reading is opened, whose task would be the systematic confrontation of the Wittgensteinian and Levinasian ethical problematics.

To suppose that Wittgenstein might indeed be one of the representatives of the skeptical attitude that Habermas seeks to nullify in the name of a cognitivist approach to ethics demands the qualification of the exact nature of this attitude. Now, to do that, a recourse to the distinction of the Said and the Saying is inevitable. In order to determine the Wittgensteinian attitude, we must take into account those few, and very laconic, aphorisms in the *Tractatus* which show the transcendental status of ethics:

> 6.41. The sense of the world must lie outside the world. In the world everything is as it is, and everything happens as it does happen: *in* it no value exists—and if it did exist, it would have no value.
>
> If there is any value that does have value, it must lie outside the whole sphere of what happens and is the case. For all that happens and is the case is accidental. What makes it non-accidental cannot lie *within* the world, since if it did it would itself be accidental.
>
> It must lie outside the world.
> 6.42. So too it is impossible for there to be propositions of ethics.
> Propositions can express nothing that is higher.
> 6.421. It is clear that ethics cannot be put into words.
> Ethics is transcendental.
> (Ethics and aesthetics are one and the same.)[27]

In order to understand the bearing of these aphorisms which hit you like a sock on the jaw, it is important to refer them to different "paratexts" of Wittgenstein himself. Indeed, the central affirmation that the ethical order in its entirety belongs to the "mystical" and the unsayable in the Wittgensteinian sense, that is to say, the universe of meaning which only lets itself be *shown* since it exceeds the possibilities of saying, refers us to two series of paratexts.

In the first place, it is significant that Wittgenstein felt the need, in those writings which correspond rigorously with the definition of the paratext elaborated by Genette, to assign an ethical finality to the *Tractatus* in its entirety. In a letter to Ludwig von Ficker, he sets out an unwritten preface, which should have included the following declaration, which it would be suitable to analyze at length in the perspective of the general theory of destination for which Jacques Derrida outlined the program in *La Carte Postale*.

> The book's point is an ethical one. I once meant to include in the preface a sentence which is not in fact there now but which I will write out for you here because it will perhaps be a key to the work for you. What I meant to write, then, was this: my work consists in two parts: the one presented here plus all that I have *not* written. And it is precisely this second part that is the important one. My book draws limits to the sphere of the ethical from the inside as it were, and I am convinced that this is the *only rigourous* way of drawing these limits. In short, I believe that where *many* others today are just *gassing*, I have managed in my book to put everything firmly into place by being silent about it.[28]

Provided that one is attentive to the extremely subtle equilibrium of the said, the saying, and the unsaying which structures this apocryphal "please insert," the Wittgensteinian silence becomes extraordinarily eloquent, in the same way as the veritable signification of his skepticism on the subject of ethics begins to manifest itself. Another paratext, a letter to Paul Engelmann, states in a much more brutal way the Wittgensteinian refusal to found a morality: "Only let's cut out the transcendental twaddle when the whole thing is as plain as a sock on the jaw!"[29] This brutal statement should not let us overlook the fact that the term "transcendental" is here given a depreciative signification, whereas in the *Tractatus* it was precisely a question of affirming the transcendental character of ethics. It clearly remains for us to ask ourselves why, in this domain, things are as clear as a sock on the jaw!

A second series of Wittgensteinian "paratexts" allow us to deepen still further the rapprochement that we have carried out. This time it is a question of certain passages from the *Notebooks*. Here again, it is important to note that we are dealing with an unsophisticated working sketch rather than a full-blown theory. Wittgenstein himself points out to his reader (who, in the *Notebooks*, is above all himself) the straightforwardly interrogative character of these reflections.[30] And yet, in this heteroclite working sketch, it is possible to isolate several motivating ideas, which, overlooking "the characteristic absence of reference to the problem of the other,"[31] it is possible to place in relation with Levinas's thinking. The important thing is that from all sides we must start from the principle that "ethics presupposes the *uniqueness* of life."[32] But whereas in Wittgenstein this presupposed unity is not grounded, Levinas, on the contrary, obliges us to examine its origin. What is it that gives the subject the guarantee that he is not just "one amongst others"? Is it a solipsistic certitude that he discovers in the most intimate nucleus of his ipseity? Or is it the primordial fact of being himself put into the accusative by the presence of the Other? Even if he does not speak the language of alterity, but the more traditional language of the voice of conscience, all of Wittgenstein's reflections, which sometimes tend to reduce the ethical problem to a straightforward business of "decency," seem to presuppose such an eventuality. For decency, in the Wittgensteinian sense, is perhaps only one aspect of the "respect" analyzed by Kant, to which Levinas's thinking gives an unrivaled pre-eminence.

If, despite everything, a fundamental difference separates the two approaches to ethics, this is not, contrary to appearances, connected with the fact that the Wittgensteinian formulation of the ethical problem finds itself in unstable equilibrium between a Kantian approach, with which it shares the marked distinction of fact and right and a Spinozist approach, seeking in the *acquiescientia in se ipsum* the secret of the whole ethical attitude. More properly, what is at question here is the difference in the ancestry of the two philosophical projects: the one which stands shoulder to shoulder with a phenomenological order of monstration ("the other who looks at me": the epiphany of the face), the other which has no other reference points than linguistic indications, for example the deep grammar which governs language games of an ethical type. My own conviction is that this difference in the style and tone of thinking should not transform itself into an insurmountable abyss.

FROM RESPONSIBILITY TO THE PROBLEM: PHILOSOPHICAL MEDIATION

> From responsibility to the problem—such is the way. The problem is posed through proximity itself, which, in other respects, as the immediate itself, is without problems.[33]

For want of being able to prolong the outline of a confrontation between two authors, who both gave a crucial place to the problem of the style of thinking, the third part of my "hypocritical" reading will be an attempt to specify what the Levinasian response to the question "What is philosophy?" consists in. We can recall the Heideggerian attempt to lay out this question in his paper "Was ist das—die Philosophie?" at Cerisy-la-Salle. It is clear that we are only faced with the question from the moment when the answer is no longer evident; that is to say, from the moment when thought's mutants arise, who are in search of "another thinking" which inevitably calls for "other words." Thus, the question requires a "philosophizing response," that is to say, a response which, in its very tenor, gives proof of philosophy. For Heidegger, this means that the response is in search of a more originary cor-respondence; the very response that is laid out at greater length in *Was heißt Denken?* The response enters into the complicity of essence which is itself in correspondence with Being. The latter is, in its turn, inseparable from a disposition or mood (*Stimmung*) which is the principle of all philosophy, not only the earliest kind: namely, *thaumazein*. This correspondence implies a specific conception of language which forbids us from only seeing language as an instrument at the service of thinking, when, as a matter of fact, the thinking which thinks itself as cor-respondence is at the service of speech.

It suffices to recall to mind this general structure of Heideggerian questioning in order to take account of the fact that, for a line of research entitled *Otherwise than Being or Beyond Essence* such a determination of the task of thinking is absolutely forbidden. And yet, the question cannot be avoided in all its acuteness, because for Levinas as for Heidegger, although for other reasons, philosophy has become profoundly *fragwürdig*. The difficulty could be formulated in the following terms: If it be admitted that the primary fact is the intrigue of ethics and language, how do we place philosophy in the latter, given that it is only the discourse and work of discursive reason? Or again, in other words, how do we pass from the glory of the infinite, which manifests itself in the pure saying of language, to the order of philosophical demonstration, which is that of the said and thematization? How can we surmount the apparent dichotomy between the prophetic essence of language and the philosophical usage of language which has nothing inspired about it?

Paradoxically enough, this transition is made possible by the regime of transcendence which characterizes the infinite: the ambiguity, or what Levinas sometimes calls the "flickering of meaning" (*clignotement du sens*—an expres-

sion that takes on a capital importance for his conception of Revelation). "Transcendence, the beyond of essence which is also Being-in-the-world, requires
ambiguity: a flickering of meaning which is not only a chance certainty, but
a frontier both ineffacable and finer than the tracing of an ideal line."[34] The
domain of the religious offers a particularly exemplary verification of this situation, to such an extent that Levinas feels able to make of the apparent dilemma
of a thinking that is divided between the affirmation of the infinite and its
negation in myself "the very point of Revelation, of its flickering light."[35] Once
again, the shadow of negative theology arises. But once again the affirmation
of a difference prevails over the admission of a proximity. Indeed, negative
theologies are dominated by an ineradicable henological postulate. By explor-
ing as far as possible the flaw that pertains between the cause which reproduces
itself in its effects and the principle which has nothing in common with that
which derives from it, negative theologies seek to identify a first principle,
even if the latter sometimes has a disconcerting appearance, which certain
of the particularly vertiginous texts of the *Enneads* allow us to catch a glimpse
of. But ethical intrigue demands that "the revelation of the beyond Being is
perhaps indeed but a word, but this 'perhaps' belongs to an ambiguity in which
the anarchy of the Infinite resists the univocity of an originary or principle."[36]

The "flickering of meaning" entails that there is not a complete dichotomy
between the saying and the said. The way from the saying to the said is negotia-
ble without the primary signification of ethical intrigue being betrayed. It is
precisely here that philosophical mediation intervenes, which raises the question: "Why knowledge? Why is there a problem? Why philosophy?"[37] Why
indeed? For after all that has been said, the response can no longer follow
the way of an analysis of the formal structure of the *Seinsfrage*, and no longer
perhaps even the formal structure of the question as questioning, for questioning is no longer "the piety of thought." The problem here becomes that of
describing "the latent birth of the *question* in responsibility."[38] It is clearly
not by chance that I speak here of "mediation." For the problem is clearly
one of passing from the order of ethical immediacy to the one where ethical
intrigue discovers the presence of the third party (*tiers*). "The responsibility
for the other is an immediacy antecedent to the question: It is proximity. It
is troubled and becomes a problem when a third party enters."[39] By way of
an attempt at a Wittgensteinian gloss on Levinasian analysis, I would claim
that responsibility for the other "is as clear as a sock on the jaw." In no way
does it become a problem, and all transcendental twaddle on this subject is
inadmissable. On the contrary, what "becomes a problem" is the inscription
of the third party into ethical intrigue. For Levinas, this uneasiness of proximity
when connected with the appearance of the third party coincides with philosophy. Philosophy is this very unease and not some astonishment before the
fact that there may be something rather than nothing. It is this supplement
of contradiction that demands the effort of comparison, of coappearance (*com-
parution*), of gathering, that is to say, the ensemble of operations and values which define the order of philosophical discourse. Philosophy is the "comparison of the incomparable."[40]

A constitutive paradox of philosophy is that in the infinite excessiveness (*démesure*) of responsibility—the an-archy of the infinite—philosophy traces out a principle of measure (*mesure*): "Philosophy is this measure brought to the infinity of the being-for-the-other of proximity, and is like the wisdom of love."[41] It is essential to size up (*prendre la mesure*) the reversal that takes place in this formula. Philosophy is no longer *philo-sophia*, the love of wisdom, it is only the "wisdom of love." To read Levinas is also to attempt the thought of this reversal, which allows access into the specifically philosophical order of problematization or thematization and which yet does not dissolve ethical intrigue, for at least as long as philosophy remains faithful to its vocation of being "the wisdom of love at the service of love."[42]

Contrary to what we might have feared, the tension of the saying and the said does therefore transform itself into an antinomy, which would irremediably oppose the voice of prophetic language to the voice of the philosophical *logos*. The transition from the saying to the said coincides with the passage from the trace to the order of monstration. While Wittgenstein opposes saying and showing (*montrer*), Levinas, heir to Husserlian phenomenology, derives monstration from saying itself. But it is a question of monstration that is entirely dominated by the idea of justice, because "*everything shows itself for justice.*"[43] Once the thesis that "Being as Being is a function of justice"[44] is admitted, the way is clear for a "systematic re-reading" of the figures of immediacy that would make philosophical categories of them. Substitution can thus be interpreted as coexistence. Proximity becomes "a historical world, that is to say, simultaneously in a book."[45] This shows at what point the book and reading are crucial figures of mediation in Levinas's thinking. The diachrony that is constitutive of ethical intrigue can, in its turn, take on the shape of the continuous and indefinite time of historical memory. Subjectivity finally loses the privilege of uniqueness that it maintained in its exposition to the other. It becomes that of an ego capable of the present, commencement, and liberty.

In the background of this transcendental deduction of philosophical categories starting from the idea of justice, which allows the unmatched terms of the one-for-the-other to appear as terms of a comparison, we can thus ask ourselves how the demand for critique, which is also constitutive of philosophical discourse, can be founded. We may then ask ourselves how, from this starting point, the critical requirements which constitute discourse can be founded. Now, everything takes place in Levinas as if his critique proceeded directly from the fact that in so far as it is the wisdom of love, philosophy is at the service of justice. "Philosophy serves justice by thematising the difference and reducing the thematised to difference." In its very project, philosophy is "the consciousness of the rupture of consciousness."[46] If philosophy is the consciousness of rupture, *Krisis*, we will perhaps understand in what sense it is necessarily critique.

An important aspect of this determination of critique is that, henceforth, philosophical rationality will no longer be able to dispense with skepticism. Skepticism is not the more or less perverse practice of the subversion of all position-taking and all affirmation. As in Wittgenstein, it is the constant reminder of the distance between the saying and the said, which philosophical discourse always risks ignoring or reducing. "Scepticism in fact makes a difference, and puts an interval between the saying and the said."⁴⁷ Although it is always already "undone" by the force of philosophical affirmation, skepticism in its turn undoes the said by recalling the originary force of the saying. And it is only thus that it is possible to affirm that "the philosophical speaking that betrays in its said the proximity it conveys before us still remains, as a saying, a proximity and a responsibility."⁴⁸ We should recall here what place Hegel reserves for the moment of skepticism on the threshold of his logic. It occupies, for Hegel, a very specific moment in the economy of logico-real comprehension: it is the negative-rational moment of dia-lectic which, in the first place, comes to disturb all the certainties of the understanding in order to be able to raise itself to the level of the speculative, that is to say, the positive-rational.⁴⁹ In Levinas, as in Hegel, skepticism is not a philosophical trend relevant to the history of ideas; it is an internal moment of philosophical comprehension itself. But the Levinasian rehabilitation of skepticism follows very different paths from those of the Hegelian dialectic. Skepticism cannot be eliminated, because "language is already scepticism."⁵⁰ Wanting to get rid of it once and for all—which indeed a certain type of philosophy has always sought to do—would mean wanting to get rid of transcendence itself.

Clearly, the confrontation between the discourse of comprehension made possible by the Hegelian doctrine of the Concept and the Levinasian response to the question "What is philosophy?" does not only concern the interpretation of skepticism. Levinas's question "Are the rendings of the logical text mended by logic alone?"⁵¹ echoes the Hegelian declaration that what is characteristic of the wounds of Spirit is that they heal without leaving any scars; but this is thrown into sharp relief when it is referred to all the images of the wound and of incurable traumatisms which define the one-for-the-other and found the psychism of the soul. Moreover, this line of investigation raises a crucial question concerning the very status of philosophical discourse: What has happened to the demand for coherence expressed by the philosophical *logos*? A careful reading of *Otherwise than Being* must, it seems to me, take over this more subterranean and intriguing question, rather than focusing on the constant polemic against Heideggerian ontology which still dominates the entire afterword of *Otherwise than Being*, which is entitled "Outside," and in which we read the following: "one has to find for man another kinship than that which ties him to Being."⁵²

In order to specify the stakes of this question it is not necessary that we immediately return to Hegel. A much more recent interlocutor of Levinas is Eric Weil, who, in his *Logique de la philosophie*⁵³ sought to establish a new philosophical discourse, described as "post-Hegelian Kantianism." If Eric Weil commands our attention in this context, it is because his own response to the question "What is philosophy?" is entirely dominated by the problem of violence, as is Levinas's thinking in *Totality and Infinity*. In referring to the work of Eric Weil, the fictive reader whose existence I have thus far only postulated, by simply outlining his ideal portrait, takes on a more determinate face. For Eric Weil, philosophy has no other secret than the fear of violence, and there is no other philosophical desire than that of seeking the disappearance of the world's violence. In short, there is no other philosophical challenge than that which consists in admitting that such an elimination demands the rigor of reasonable discourse.[54]

Now, for Eric Weil, a simple philosophy of dialogue, seeking to abolish the differences between interlocutors by resorting to the strategy of logical coherence, will not suffice for this task. For the "political" substructure of dialogue is a community of equals who recognize each other as such. All dialogue is inhabited by a "harmless violence" which is incapable of questioning itself on its own presuppositions. In this sense, excluding inequality, the dialogue, which represents one of the native forms of philosophical discourse, is inhabited by an anonymous and unavowable violence. For Weil, the "crisis" that explodes this initial consensus coincides with the birth of ontology. It is at this moment that dialogue becomes *discourse*, a discourse of *comprehension*.[55] This is what we risk losing sight of if we interpret the Levinasian accusation against ontological discourse too unilaterally. The advent of ontological discourse signifies a progress in the analysis of the violence which has always already invested human discourse. With regard to this ineradicable violence, the wager of ontological discourse could itself be stated thus: "Before violence, everyone is equal, and the discourse of each person is valid for everyone if it is valid in itself, which is to say, in the face of what may happen to every man, in the face of violence."[56]

If, in spite of everything, we must speak of a failure of ontological discourse, the latter is simply connected to the discovery that there exists an irreducible plurality of incommensurable primary discourses. This means that "the recourse to Being does not allow the establishment of a *unique* discourse upon which *all* men may agree, a discourse which is not perhaps that of such and such a community or some other, but *the* discourse of man."[57] In the *Logique de la philosophie*, skepticism is connected with the discovery of the irreducibility of the primary sciences. In the same way as the advent of ontology coincides with the failure of a certain form of dialogue, skepticism, as an internal moment of philosophical comprehension, is nothing other than this discovery of the plurality of incommensurable primary sciences.

But he who discovered that "violence between men constitutes a danger for man"[58] can no longer fall back on this side of the demand for rational coherence formulated by ontological discourses. But how, therefore, is this new challenge of reason to be defined? This question goes straight to the heart of Eric Weil's post-Hegelian Kantianism. The *Logique de la philosophie* is the attempt to invent a first philosophy which will no longer be an ontology, but a logic: "*First philosophy* is . . . not a theory of Being but the development of the *logos* and of discourse for itself and by itself, which understands itself by its accomplishments, to the extent that first philosophy *wants* to understand itself. First philosophy is not ontology, it is logic; not of Being but of concrete human discourse, of the discourse which establishes the unity of discourse."[59] With Kant, the latter wagers "reasonable force opposing itself to the violence of the given."[60] With Hegel, it wagers that the coherence of the discourse that bears on that which is and shows itself, is itself historically incarnated in a coherent ensemble of attitudes and categories which it pertains to the "logic of philosophy" to locate and identify as such.

On this point, I will stop this "hypocritical" reading, which has let itself be guided, rightly or wrongly, by the Hegelian coupling of immediacy and mediation. My conclusion will itself be "skeptical" in Levinas's sense. Recall to mind that the concern for coherence which animates a "logic of philosophy" like that of Eric Weil, clearly does not take the direction of a refutation of the Levinasian attempt to make ethics a first philosophy. It would perhaps be more of an invitation to question ourselves on the enigmatic equilibrium of the saying and the said. This equilibrium desires that even the demand for the absolute coherence of the discourse of comprehension finds itself perturbed by the "an-archical" call of ethical intrigue; for "I still interrupt the ultimate discourse in which all the discourses are slated, in saying it to the one that listens to it and who is situated outside the said that the discourse says outside all it includes."[61]

Notes

1. *Face to Face with Levinas*, ed. R. A. Cohen, Albany, State University of New York Press, 1986.

2. "Aristotle's animal gifted with language has never been thought, in its ontology, as far as the book; nor has it been questioned as to the status of its religious relation to the book. This relation has never merited, in the philosophically 'preferred' categories, the rank of a modality as determinant for the human condition (or incondition) as language itself, thinking, or technical activity; as if reading was only one of the vicissitudes in the circulation of information and the book only a thing among things, showing, like a hammer in the hands of manual workers, its affinity with the hand" (ADV 8). This affirmation contains the key to Levinas's hermeneutics, as I have shown in my work *L'age herméneutique de la raison*, Paris, Editions du Cerf, 1985, 177–90.

3. Jacques Derrida, EM 21–60; AM.

4. Paul Ricoeur, "Temps et recit III," *Le temps raconté*, Paris, Editions du Seuil, 1985, 228–63.

5. "It is perhaps time to see in hypocrisy not only a base contingent defect of man, but the underlying rending of world attached to both the philosophers and the prophets" (TeI xii; TI 24).

6. For Gérard Genette, the paratext is "that by which a text becomes a book and offers itself as such to its readers and, more generally, to the public" (*Seuils*, Paris, Editions du Seuil, 1987, 7). The necessity of such paratexts "imposes itself on every type of book" (9).

7. EeI 90; EI 86.

8. TeI 170; TI 196.

9. TeI 175; TI 201.

10. AE 123; OB 97.

11. TeI 168; TI 195.

12. AE 96; OB 76.

13. AE 183n; OB 199.

14. AE 182n; OB 198.

15. AE 190; OB 148.

16. Ludwig Wittgenstein, *Philosophical Investigations*, Oxford, Basil Blackwell, 1958, §65: "Here we come up against the great question that lies behind all these considerations. —For someone might object against me: "You take the easy way out! You talk about all sorts of language-games, but have nowhere said what the essence of a language-game, and hence of language is: what is common to all these activities, and what makes them into language or parts of language."

17. AE 171; OB 134.

18. AE 182n; OB 198.

19. AE 193; OB 151.

20. AE 192; OB 150.

21. EeI 95; EI 90.

22. Jürgen Habermas, *Moralbewußtsein und kommunikatives Handeln*, Frankfurt, Suhrkamp, 1983, chap. 3, "Diskursethik—Notizen zu einem Begründungsprogramm," 53–126.

23. Ibid., 87.

24. Ibid., 109.

25. Ibid., 113.

26. Ibid., 113.

27. Cf. Ludwig Wittgenstein, *Tractatus Logico-Philosophicus*, trans. D. F. Pears and B. F. McGuiness, London, Routledge & Kegan Paul, 1961, 6.4–6.421.

28. "Briefe an Ludwig Ficker," in *Brenner Studien*, Salzburg, Otto Müller, 1929, 35. The letter is translated in Georg Henrik von Wright, "Historical Introduction" in Ludwig Wittgenstein, *Prototractatus*, trans. D. F. Pears and B. F. McGuiness, London, Routledge & Kegan Paul, 1971, 16.

29. "Nur kein transzendentales Geschwätz, wenn alles kar ist wie eine Watschen!" cited by Paul Engelmann, *Letters from Ludwig Wittgenstein: With a Memoir*, Oxford, Basil Blackwell, 1967, 10.

30. "Die völlige Unklarheit dieser Sätze ist mir bewußt" (Ludwig Wittgenstein, *Notebooks 1914–1916*, Oxford, Basil Blackwell, 1961, 79).

31. Jacques Bouveresse, *Wittgenstein, la rime et la raison: Science, ethique et esthétique*. Paris, Editions de Minuit, 1973, 100. The second chapter of this work (73–118) puts forward an excellent presentation of the Wittgensteinian ethical problematic, to which my own analysis is indebted.

32. Cf. Wittgenstein, *Notebooks 1914–1916*, 79.

33. AE 205; OB 161.

34. AE 194; OB 152.

35. AE 196; OB 154.

36. AE 199; OB 156.

37. AE 199; OB 157.

38. AE 200; OB 157.

39. AE 200; OB 157.

40. AE 202; OB 158.

41. AE 205; OB 161.

42. AE 207; OB 162.

43. AE 207; OB 163.

44. AE 207; OB 162.

45. AE 207; OB 162.

46. AE 210; OB 165.

47. AE 213; OB 168.

48. AE 214; OB 168.

49. G.W.F. Hegel, *Encyclopaedia of the Philosophical Sciences*, Oxford, Oxford University Press, 1975, §81, *Zusatz*.

50. AE 216; OB 170.

51. AE 216; OB 170.

52. AE 223; OB 177.

53. Eric Weil, *Logique de la philosophie*, Paris, Vrin, 1967.

54. In an important note to "Violence and Metaphysics," Jacques Derrida had already pointed to the interesting confrontation between two different ways of determining the distinction between discourse and violence. ED 171–72n; WD 315 n. 42.

55. *Logique de la philosophie*, 29.

56. Ibid.

57. Ibid., 36.

58. Ibid., 40.

59. Ibid., 69.

60. Ibid., 48.

61. AE 216; OB 170.

CHAPTER
5

LEVINAS'S ETHICAL DISCOURSE BETWEEN INDIVIDUATION AND UNIVERSALITY

Fabio Ciaramelli

> Indem die *Sprache* das Werk des Gedankens
> ist, so kann auch in ihr nichts gesagt werden,
> was nicht allgemein ist. Was ich nur *meine*, ist
> *mein*, gehört mir als diesen besonderen
> Individuum an; wenn aber die Sprache nur
> Allgemeines ausdrückt, so kann ich nicht
> sagen, was ich nur *meine*.[1]

The thought of Emmanuel Levinas presents us with a most unusual conception of ethics as based on the radical asymmetry of a responsibility which is mine even before my freedom. With this we are also brought to a new understanding of subjectivity and a reformulation of the traditional problem of individuation. For Levinas, my own ineradicable ethical responsibility becomes the only valid *principium individuationis*.

The problem upon which I would like to focus in this text is the modality adopted by Levinas in his philosophical work as a result of the need to safeguard the radically individual foundation of asymmetric responsibility at the very moment in which it declares itself to be universal and of absolute value. A declaration of this kind is indispensable to ethical discourse if it is, subsequently, to serve as the basis for the justification of politics and ontology, which, in their turn, bring an attenuation of the asymmetry of proximity. Reserving an explicit examination of the passage from the ethical to the political for another occasion, I would like to restrict myself here to suggesting a possible reading of the relation between my ethical individuation as a responsible and irreplaceable subject and the universality of ethics as a discourse that is not addressed to me alone. My hypothesis concerns the connection between the problem of this relation and Levinas's reflection on the prophetic. In saying this, prophetism should be considered not only as a moment of the human condition as such, but also in the light of the unique and exceptional character of biblical prophetism. The prophetic declaration of the messianic vocation of each individual is made by each the responsible and irreplacable subject that is exclusively "I." Yet ultimately it introduces into the Said, and manifests there, the universality of the ethical, constituting a Saying which exceeds and transcends each Said.

This appeal to prophetism does not, I believe, resolve without paradox the problem of the relation between individuation and universality. It may, however, offer a concrete example—and a particularly delicate one—for the analysis of the equally problematic relation between the Saying and the Said which subtends Levinas's entire thought. Adriaan Peperzak has recently written: "Insofar as we remain within philosophical reflection . . . we would not know how to escape from the *universalization of the asymmetrical relation*, separating and inseparably binding together every ego and every Other. Thus *asymmetry* shows itself to be a universal and universally *reciprocal* relation."[2] The necessity of this universalization is sharply questioned by Peperzak within the framework of the passage from the anarchy of responsibility to the universal order of justice. Concentrating on Levinas's specifically ethical discourse, my own reading will also be led, at least initially, by the question of this necessity. In the final part of the text I shall go on to suggest that one can recognize in the prophetic dimension of language a possible satisfaction of such a necessity.

ETHICS AND INDIVIDUAL RESPONSIBILITY

The Western philosophical tradition has always reserved a special place for ontology as the discourse uniquely able to discover and to describe the ultimate structure of reality. From the perspective of the absolute, philosophers have speculated upon the very meaning of Being, seeking to comprehend that which mediates between particularity and the universal and intelligible.

To pass from ontology to ethics—by which we designate the sphere of human deeds—requires a step, or, more precisely, an inversion. In taking such a step we must first postulate freedom of will, since human freedom is absent from the ontological realm, governed as it is by theoretical necessity. The ethical project, then, is to submit freedom of will to the rule of rationality in the attempt to find criteria for human action that are universally intelligible and valid for everyone. In this way, particular human situations are subsumed under a general and universal order from which they receive their meaning. Philosophers speak in the name of the *logos*, which, by virtue of its universality, places them under obligation in two ways. First, it is intelligible and manifests to us the structure of reality; second, everyone is able to recognize himself in this rationality. To obey the *logos*, therefore, is to be autonomous. The demand made upon us by the ethical also has its source in the universality of reason, since moral obligation is initially determined and justified by referring to the inherent rationality of the *ethos*. This submission to the authority of the *logos* goes hand in hand with the primacy of ontology. When the philosopher speaks about ethics, he or she does so not as an individual, but always with regard for the universality of reason. Philosophers may believe that they have left their own particular perspectives and interests behind them. Viewed less sympathetically, however, this smacks of vanity and the appeal to universality could easily be construed as a kind of *escamotage* or conjuring away of responsibility.

The understanding of ethical discourse that we find in the work of Levinas is quite divorced from this view. Levinas does not treat "ethics" as one branch of philosophy amongst others. And neither does he attempt to construct a normative moral philosophy. Rather, his work is a search for the significance of ethics and the ethical.[3] For Levinas, as we shall see, "ethics" means an anarchical assignation of the particular subject to morality by the appeal of the other. And insofar as he maintains that the very origination of meaning —desired by all philosophy—is the occurrence of ethics, ethics becomes the radical basis of philosophy. "First philosophy" is no longer ontology or ontological metaphysics, but ethics.[4] Ethical obligation arises not from the logical and ontological universality of reason which discloses to knowledge criteria for freely determined action, but rather immediately from the uniqueness of the moral situation itself. In a reversal of the classical order of privilege which promoted speculative reason, obligation is no longer first disclosed in its universality and intelligibility, known and then evaluated. On the contrary, moral obligation binds us because it takes hold immediately, before understanding or decision on the part of the subject. Such an absolute obligation properly defines the status of prophetic discourse which grounds itself solely on the authority of its source and bypasses the mediatory role of reason.

In the light of the question of universality, there are two points that can be made concerning the intelligibility and value of obligation. The first of these was developed by Jean-François Lyotard in his paper on Levinas's logic, where he stresses that moral obligation for Levinas is quite different from the experience of law for Kant. Obligation is "an order having its authority in itself." It does not need a universal place—"*neutre*," *arche* or Being—to acquire its meaning and its power to bind a subject. "In pragmatic terms," Levinas's "repudiation of *arche* and Being," that is, his inversion of the traditional privilege accorded to ontology and knowing, corresponds to a decision "not to conduct a discourse having as its reference and model a prior discourse, even an enigmatic one, given by no matter whom." A neutral discourse of this kind implies that the philosopher, far from remaining "addressee" (*destinataire*) of it, "places himself in the position of addresser."[5] He speaks in the name of the absolute *arche*, impersonal and silent. Levinas, by contrast, looks for the original significance of an unmediated obligation (placed upon a subject). However—and here we come to the second of our two points—in the very particularity of such an unmediated obligation of the subject there also lies a dimension of universality. This springs not from the abstract character of the concept, but from the prescriptive power of the appeal and its pretention to concern each and every one of us, always and everywhere. Even if it arises in the *hic et nunc* of a subject affected by an infinite otherness, it transcends the *hic et nunc* because it grasps and displays the very meaning of subjectivity.

Philosophical discourse as such harbors an undeniable pretension to universality, and moreover, according to Levinas, it must always be in some sense "verifiable."[6] Yet in Levinas's work we are faced with a discourse about ethics conceived as the immediacy of an individual obligation prior to any universality whatsoever. How is it possible to express in philosophical language a situation so strange that it takes place in the most extreme particularity, yet concerns the universal meaning of subjectivity? How is it possible to "translate into Greek," that is, into philosophical language, this inspiration and this situation that belong to "prophetic eschatology"?[7]

Totality and Infinity and *Otherwise than Being* each take a different line of approach to these questions. Both seek to prevent the reduction of this exceptional moment of subjectivity to a purely psychological or theological account. However, whereas the former attempts to do this within the constraints of ontological language, *Otherwise than Being*, in a more radical effort, attempts, as far as possible, to disengage itself from the language of ontology altogether.[8]

As I hope to suggest in this paper, the renunciation of ontological language proves to be inseparable from so deep a revision of our understanding of the responsibility that one bears for another that, from this point on, Levinas conceives individuality not in general terms, but as uniquely *my own* ipseity, and *my own* substitution for another. Insofar as it dispenses with the resources of ontological language in order to further articulate its ethical intention, this development in Levinas's thinking renders our problem still more acute. It is, therefore, to *Otherwise than Being*, where Levinas's thought is given perhaps its most extreme formulation, that I shall address the question of the possibility of Levinas's remarkable discourse.

ETHICAL FREEDOM BEYOND BEING

In *Otherwise than Being*, then, Levinas avoids using the language of ontology. Since it is primarily a meditation on the exceptional "position" of subjectivity with respect to Being, Levinas is compelled, therefore, to attempt a description of subjectivity before its ontological constitution, before its identity as an entity among others, before its free activity in the world, indeed, before consciousness as such at all.

His response is to describe subjectivity as a radical passivity, that is, as being "subject to" the other in an ethical relation that precedes the ontological constitution of subjectivity in any more familiar sense. Yet can one define such an analysis of passive subjectivity as ethical? And indeed we could ask also whether Levinas's renunciation of ontological terminology entails an immediate access to a genuine ethical language adequate to the somewhat paradoxical task at hand. Subjectivity—as Levinas presents it—"in patience *above* nonfreedom"—precedes freedom, and for this reason appears to precede ethics as well. If "the individuation of the ego in me" prior to identity is achieved through my being summoned to answer for my neighbor,[9] then this radical passivity begins to look like a *metaphysical structure*, irreducible to the ethical context of my relation with the other. According to Levinas, however, such an interpretation of subjectivity in its passive destitution not only makes sense, but represents the very genesis and development of meaning. Philosophy, therefore, has to adopt an ethical language as the only language able to show "the metaphysical *hither side* itself, contradictorily enough."[10] The use of ethical language allows philosophy to give voice to this "metaphysical extraction from Being," that has previously been given only fleeting recognition in the history of philosophy.

The break with Being takes place in subjectivity. Yet it is consistently betrayed by language and its meaning is reduced to the ontological order of the Said, which restores the exception to the essence. In order to preserve this paradoxical moment from such a reduction, therefore, Levinas proposes that we attend not to the Said, but to the ethical Saying—in its exposure to the other—as the very meaning of subjectivity beyond Being. But in this ethical language, linked to the extreme passivity of the subject, an ambiguity remains. We can see this clearly in the following observations of an interpreter as careful as Adriaan Peperzak. "As an adequate description of the subject," he writes, "insofar as he escapes the order of Being, ethical language is pre- or meta-ontological. As a characteristic of a situation which precedes freedom, it is also pre- or meta-ethical."[11] We have, therefore, in Levinas's writing, an ethical language which is paradoxically, if only in a limited sense, pre- or meta-ethical. Nevertheless, when Levinas speaks about a subject beyond Being and describes subjectivity as a passive subjection to the other, he claims precisely to think the subject in terms of its *ethical* destitution and the displacement of its freedom when faced by the other.[12] We are forced at this point to reconsider what may be for Levinas the relation between ethics and freedom.

The very origin—the *pré-originaire*—of the subject is the subjection to the other that precedes freedom, consciousness, and identity. It is neither an empirical submission nor an event which befalls an existing subject. At this point ethics is not yet constituted. Indeed, it is this nascent subjectivity, prior to every *arche*, that is the origin and meaning of ethics. Ethics, therefore, has no connection with ontological freedom (in contrast to its conception within the philosophical tradition, where freedom of will is its necessary presupposition), but involves another modality of freedom—that which Levinas has called the extraction from Being.

Ethical language is uniquely suited to the task of expressing a subjectivity released from the *conatus essendi* toward that which occurs otherwise than Being. It is not merely an instrument to describe the situation prior to ontology, and neither is the appeal to categories like responsibility, substitution, and sacrifice simply a reflection of the absence of freedom that precedes a normative ethics. Levinas gives a new meaning to the categories of ethical thought and submits them to a profound torsion, so that they might signify that which is above and beyond ontological freedom, namely, a metaphysical structure of human passivity as subjection to infinite otherness in which only a situation named "ethics" can make sense. In this way, ethical freedom is to be understood as the liberation from ontological necessities and cares, a refusal of the *conatus essendi* and a "deliverance" from Being. In addition a positive, if unfamiliar, determination of ethical freedom can be recognized in the claim made upon me by the other. This calls, however, for an entirely new way of understanding and displaying what is irreducibly my own in subjectivity. At this stage it is possible only to sketch the horizon opened up by such a revision of ethical thought, without developing all the implications that follow from it. "Freedom would therefore signify the acceptance of a vocation to which I alone can respond, or again, the power to respond to it when called. To be free is only to do what nobody else can do in my place."[13]

FROM THE EGO TO ME: THE ETHICAL ELECTION OF IPSEITY

> It is by virtue of this supplementary responsibility that subjectivity is not the Ego, but me.[14]

Even though the claim made upon me by another precedes freedom, it takes place within an order—or disorder—having an ethical meaning. I am free only insofar as I am delivered from my ontological self-concern and become radically opened to hear the appeal from the face of the other.

I am obliged to respond to the other, without being ontologically *compelled* to do so (since I can still refuse myself to the other). Levinas stresses that I am the only one who can respond to an appeal so personal and so direct that it arises immediately from my orientation toward the other, from my position in the relation. The relation, characterized by a radical nonreciprocity, is prior to the relata—before the "I am"—and I cannot escape its orientation. Hence, in the same event which displays my own ipseity prior to any intelligible ontological identity whose form I might share with others, an absolute obligation arises concerning that which is irreducibly mine, not only now, in the contingency of this event, but always. The authority of this obligation, upon which the meaning of my subjectivity depends, is grounded not in the universality of the *logos*, but in the immediacy of the transcendence of the other who places me under obligation. In my position as a subject, responsible for another, I am affected by an infinite transcendence that I am unable to comprehend through the (*arche* of the) *logos*.[15] In order to express this an-archy of subjective responsibility without resorting to the abstractions and generalizations of ontological language, *Otherwise than Being* states repeatedly that this situation concerns my own ipseity, my own privacy above and beyond any conceptualization in which the concept of the I arises *après coup*. The other addresses *me* and not the universal concept of the ego. Levinas conveys this by the expression, the "fission of the Ego unto me" (*fission du Moi jusqu'à moi*) to which he returns on many occasions throughout the book. For the time being, however, our attention shall be confined to the first appearance of this unusual and provocative idea: "Here the unicity of the ego first acquires a meaning—where it is no longer a question of the ego, but of me. The subject which is not an ego, but which I am (*le sujet qui n'est plus un moi—mais que je suis moi*), cannot be generalized, is not a subject in general; we have moved from the Ego to me who am me and no one else (*ce qui revient à passer du Moi à moi qui suis moi et pas un autre*)."[16]

But, even given this movement, are we not left still facing the same problem as before? If ethics arises in and concerns only me, how is it possible to speak of it as an absolute obligation having its authority in itself, which has a value whose universality is derived not from the *logos*, but from the transcendent orientation of the *ethos*? If the subject of ethical language is no longer impersonal and general, but is rather my own ipseity affected by the infinite otherness of the face in the responsibility that is solely mine, is it still conceivable that there may be an ethics which is not only "verifiable," not only beyond all the relativity and contingency of the empirical world, but which is above all universally intelligible and valid?

These questions are woven deeply into Levinas's work. Our interrogation, therefore, does not stand outside his text, but follows one of the more radical movements of this thought itself. I would like simply to draw our attention to this complex issue of individuation and universality, since it represents one of the most extreme and controversial points in Levinas's thought.

Levinas writes that "indiscretion with regard to the unsayable . . . is probably the very task of philosophy."[17] Now, it seems to me that what is wholly and utterly unsayable in the language of ontology—and which is thus to be submitted to an indiscretion—is precisely this passage from the "I" to "me." My "position" as a particular subject is an inconceivable and incommunicable ipseity beyond the ontological identity of the individual. This is my radical secret, my sensibility, my *psychism*, and the solitude of my *Selbstheit*.[18] In *Totality and Infinity*, it was expressed as the concealment of enjoyment, that is, as a resistance to totalization in which I withdraw myself from participation in Being and become ontologically autonomous.[19] But this alone is not enough. The ontological separation of a subject, even if it breaks with the totality, is not in itself sufficient to establish transcendence. *Totality and Infinity* showed that this inwardness of the I identifying itself in the Same is not the Absolute.[20] The real experience of the other does indeed lie outside totality, yet it cannot be reduced to subjective inwardness. It requires not only "a being which tears itself away from totality," but also "one which does not encompass it."[21] Only the transcendence of the face of the other—thought in the light of Descartes's idea of the infinite[22]—escapes the conceptual reduction to the Same. "It is not the I who resists the system, as Kierkegaard thought, it is the other."[23]

In order to avoid the selfish contestation of totality by the "pure subjectivism of the I" with which Levinas reproaches Kierkegaard, *Totality and Infinity* was compelled, as Jacques Derrida wrote in "Violence and Metaphysics," to recognize the "passage from Ego to other as *an Ego*." As a result, *Totality and Infinity* was obliged to acknowledge also the passage to the "essential and not empirical, *egoity* of subjective existence *in general.*"[24] As Derrida continues, "no philosophy responsible for its language can renounce ipseity in general, and the philosophy or eschatology of separation may do so less than any other."[25]

Although the above may be true of *Totality and Infinity*, I believe that *Otherwise than Being* succeeds in renouncing ipseity in general, because it gives up ontological language and shifts its focus from the ego to *me*. Moreover, it can do so without forfeiting its status as philosophical discourse. In *Totality and Infinity*, we were to be introduced to a relation in which the Other did not limit, but rather established and justified the freedom of the I.[26] But the ontological language used to describe the constitution of subjectivity betrayed this intention by reintroducing, albeit implicitly, ipseity in general. To aggravate the problem, according to Derrida, the recourse to ipseity in general was not merely an accidental consequence of the analyses, but a necessary condition of possibility for the work as such. At the very least, therefore, Levinas has to accompany the rejection of ipseity in general with an alternative understanding of the constitution of subjectivity. The relation with the other concerns individuation from the very beginning in such a way that it is no longer a question of individuation in general, but of *my own* personal individuation. Since *Otherwise than Being*, Levinas has written, "The ultimate knot of the psychism is not that which assures the unity of the subject, but rather, if we can put it this way, the '*supple separation*' (*séparation liante*) of society."[27]

It is *my psyche* and not some abstract process that is the "undoing of the substantial nucleus (*dénucléation du noyau substantiel*) of the Ego that is formed in the Same, a fission of the 'mysterious' nucleus of the 'inwardness' of the subject by this assignation to respond, which does not leave any place of refuge, any chance to slip away, and is thus despite the ego, or, more exactly, *despite me.*"[28] Here the subject does not go forward to meet the other in the world outside and, similarly, the other is no longer the stranger coming from beyond to the ontologically separated psyche/subject. As Robert Bernasconi writes, "The emphasis on separation in the former [*Totality and Infinity*] is appropriate to an initial attempt to establish exteriority, the surplus which exceeds totality. The crucial point is that when we look to the relation itself we find that in responsibility for the stranger he is the neighbour."[29] Thus after *Totality and Infinity*, Levinas prefers to think of subjectivity in terms of proximity. Indeed, in one of his more recent writings Levinas adopts the formula of a "supple separation" in order to introduce into the heart of subjectivity a radical and an-archical reference to the other which in fact constitutes the very inwardness of the subject. This heterological affection is as old as subjectivity itself. Proximity, therefore, has nothing to do with self-presence, self-appropriation, or reflexivity of any kind. It is, rather, the subject's "position." Instead of treating the individuation of the Ego in me as an original closure (*clôture*) constituting the identity of an entity, we can take it as an openness that undoes my ontological identity and which, in the same movement, individuates me. My individuation in this case is ethical: I am linked to the other by the responsibility that I bear toward him or her. Proximity is only possible as responsibility, which, in turn, is only possible as substitution. "*My* substitution—it is only as *my own* that substitution for the neighbour is produced."[30]

Totality and Infinity spoke of a "relation without relation"[31] in order to convey the impossibility of reducing the ethical relation to an abstract conceptual coordination. Its nonreciprocity indicated the primacy of its orientation, whose point of departure is always my subjective "position." Pursuing the same point, *Otherwise than Being* suggests that "it is not simply a passage to a subjective point of view. One can no longer say what the Ego or I is (*ce qu'est le Moi ou le Je*). From now on one has to speak in the first person."[32] I am compelled to speak in the first person by the exigencies of the subject. This is not the uniqueness of a "once only" (*hapax*) and it is due neither to some distinctive quality, nor to the inertia of a quiddity individuated by an ultimate specific difference. "It is in the uniqueness of someone summoned (*l'unicité de l'assigné*)."[33] And the only one summoned to respond for the other, submitted to a groundless accusation, is me: "for in me alone innocence can be accused without absurdity. To accuse the innocence of the other, to ask of the other more than he owes, is criminal."[34] I can demand the sacrifice and moral effort called for by proximity and substitution of no one but myself. Levinas makes this perfectly clear when he writes, "To say that the other has to sacrifice himself to others would be to preach human sacrifice!"[35] This radical asymmetry grounds itself in a "concrete moral experience" which cannot be overcome and which implies the impossibility of speaking about myself and others in the same sense.[36]

Only the ego that is quite distinct from any generalization can hear the assignation of the other and respond to him or her. Accordingly, the subject, in its preoriginal link with the other, is beyond Being and has already received the enigmatic message of transcendence: "In order to tear itself from the ontological weight must not the subjectivity have to have received some most private convocation to appear from beyond Being and the rational enchainment of its significations?" This subjectivity is the "extreme privacy of the singular ego," "the subjectivity, alone, unique, secret, which Kierkegaard caught sight of."[37] Called by the transcendence beyond essence which shows itself only in human disinterestedness, this subjectivity is no longer a merely selfish contestation of totality. It is the only possible modality of the otherwise than Being. In this extraction from ontological cares, subjectivity is a descent or elevation of the abstract Ego to "me."

THE ETHICAL VOCATION OF EACH INDIVIDUAL

We can now see still more clearly the paradox in which ethical discourse is caught: it will have a universal and absolute meaning only if it is rooted in the extreme particularity of my own personal response to transcendence. For its part, philosophy is faced with the difficult task of giving universal meaning to this particularity, and to this end, it would seem compelled to generalize the disinterestedness, the infinite responsibility, and the sacrifice that are specifically required of *me*. Yet any move toward generalization would mark the reversal of the passage from the Ego to me and the return to the abstractions of ontology. The an-archy of the proximity between the Other and myself renders my responsibility infinite. Indeed, it reaches a limit only with the arrival of the third party, on whose account there has to be justice.[38] In the radical asymmetry of the ethical, on the other hand, I am responsible even for the responsibility of the other. I am not a mere psychological ego, equal to others; I am me, released from the concept of the "I" and summoned to respond for the other. As Lingis explains, "the approach of the other holding me responsible for everything, even for what I did not do—this unlimited accusation —is what singularises me utterly."[39] It would be immoral to extend to others an ethical demand so strong and so specific that it individualizes *me* and calls me to the point of *substitution*, that is, to the fact that I have to take the place of the other. "Immorality begins when we start saying that someone must substitute him or herself for me." The responsibility of the other for me is his or her affair. "My business is my responsibility and my substitution inscribed in my *ego*, inscribed as *ego*."[40]

If Levinas's discourse were to stop here, we would be troubled perhaps less by any question of its coherence, than by its apparent reduction of ethics to the tale of an entirely private adventure. We must ask, therefore, if Levinas's discourse negotiates this danger, and if so how. For Levinas, the ethical shows itself as the prophetical: this means that ethics expresses a vocation for humanity. The Bible itself is revelation precisely insofar as it is "ethical Kerygma." Each and every person is called upon to become a "me" in a relation of responsibility for the other.[41] In this we can recognize the universal dimension necessary for an ethical discourse. Indeed, Levinas emphasizes the prophetic ground of such a universality. The claim made upon me by another, insofar as it is addressed not only to me but to everyone, is the basis of the universality of ethics. Nevertheless, we cannot escape the fact that this assignation can be said only as my own individuation, brought about by the approach of the other. Levinas's aim of demonstrating a universal and absolute meaning to the ethical is expressed clearly and concisely in the closing paragraphs of *Otherwise than Being*, and we can see here the ultimate intention of the book and the real significance of Levinas's "humanism of the other man": "But each individual . . . is virtually a chosen one, called to leave in his turn, or without waiting for his turn, the concept of the ego, its extension in the people, to respond with responsibility: *me*, that is, *here I am for the others*."[42] Yet again, however, we must remember that even if there is a universality of the ethical by virtue of the fact that each subject is called to a responsibility as infinite as mine, it is only from the perspective of my own assignation and election that I can put it into words. My own particular situation remains nonreciprocal and my position cannot be generalized. The subject of philosophical discourse is in all cases a particular individual, that is, one who speaks or writes.

The three parts to the title of Derrida's second paper on Levinas, *En ce moment même, dans cet ouvrage, me voici*, exhibit very clearly the *hic et nunc* that are uniquely *me*, beyond any conceptual determination. Derrida writes that, in Levinas's work, "words indecidably describe (constate) and produce (perform) a written and a writing, immediately implicating the 'I-now-here' (*je-maintenant-ici*) of the scriptor."[43] Yet, insofar as Levinas speaks and writes about the meaning of subjectivity—even if this meaning arises beyond the abstract generality of the ontological difference[44]—he is not referring only to himself and his own interiority. He claims a universal value for the ethical import of his work.

The exceptional place of the particular subject, that is, the one who speaks and writes, remains the only possible point of departure for ethical discourse. But this position—as exceptional—is unstable and must be repeatedly reachieved by the subject speaking and also, on occasion, responding for the Other. Derrida, in his second essay on Levinas, refers to this insuperable necessity, writing of seriality (*sérialité*) as the repetition and multiplication of a singular point. This effect, which in my opinion is grounded in the diachrony of time, language, and subjectivity, might offer us the possibility of an exit from the impasse reached by a thought which refuses every logical and conceptual access to universality, yet which will not settle for anything less.

In other words, it has to be recognized that the unique site from whence the Saying comes is unsayable as such. While on the other hand, insofar as it is Said, it is always universal, tangible, and public. And in this objective dimension each subject becomes equal, or equivalent, to every other. Yet even here, in this climate of uniformity, it is possible to express the exceptional ethical significance of a particular Saying producing itself as *me* and capable of repetition, that is, of re-producing itself as me time after time, again and again. In the dimension of the Said the meaning of such a situation becomes universal, while its unsayable origin precedes the Said and lies in the ipseity of the subject in the Saying. Faced with the Saying and the Said, we should not make the mistake of looking for too rigid a hierarchical relation between the two orders. In fact, their interdependency and the fluctuation between them open an endless field of ambiguity with reference to subjectivity. In *Otherwise than Being* Levinas deliberately courts this ambiguity in order to preserve the particularity of the subject *alongside* its universal ethical significance. The ambiguity allows Levinas to speak and to write of *both* of these possibilities in the dislocation of a diachronic thought. He thinks "a thought that is *one* but not thought at the same time (*pensée une, mais non pensée en même temps*)."[45] As I have already suggested, I believe that the site of this diachrony is the preoriginary Saying which springs from a particular subject speaking and thereby exposing himself to the other as being vulnerable. Derrida is not mistaken, therefore, when he writes "the indecision remains irreducible as to whether he [Levinas] speaks of 'I' or the 'I' myself or the self."[46] Despite the renunciation of ipseity in general, when the philosopher says "I," he is, in a sense, still using a pseudonym.

THE SUBJECT OF THE SAYING AND THE UNIVERSAL SIGNIFICANCE OF ITS UNSAYABLE PARTICULARITY

If we wish to grasp the genuine universality of ethics without losing sight of its origin in the assignation of a particular subject, we must renounce the ontological dimension of consciousness altogether. However, this does not necessarily entail the renunciation of universality as such, for, as Levinas attempts to make clear, it is still possible to think through the ethical situation in ethical terms, without recourse to the language of ontology. Ethical universality differs pointedly from the universality of the *logos* in which language is valued for its semantic content alone. Indeed, the ontological order of the Said has only a derivative function inasmuch as it confines itself to the task of *showing* the preoriginal meaning of the Saying.

The nonreciprocity of the Saying, offered by one subject to another, disrupts the reduction of subjectivity to the ontological and affords us a glimpse of subjectivity prior to consciousness. "Consciousness is perhaps the very locus of the *reverting of the facticity of individuation into a concept of an individual*, and thus into consciousness of its death, in which its singularity is lost in its universality."[47] That which is taken to be the very uniqueness of the ego, when apprehended as consciousness, is, in fact, a multiplicity of egos subsumed under a universal. Each subject or ego asserts his own irreducible particularity through a denial of the universality of the concept. Yet, the differences between them are indiscernable. Levinas makes a reference here to Hegel's dialectical inversion of sense certainty, whereby one succeeds in *saying* only the strict contrary of what one *means*.[48] Extreme particularity, once articulated, becomes general universality, and the individual, or more precisely, the facticity of individuation, is lost. As Hegel says in the *Encyclopaedia*, "I cannot say what I merely *mean*."[49] And this "unsayable" has neither the status nor the fascination of a mystery. It is simply "the least significant" (*das Unbedeutendeste*).

But for Levinas, on the contrary, it is precisely because of its unsayable character and because of its irreducibility to the Said that the particularity of the subject saying "I" makes any sense at all. The difference here lies in the understanding of the "unsayable." For Hegel the "unsayable"—which is meaninglessness *par excellence*–concerns the impossibility of saying *this* particularity which I can only mean. "When I say 'I,' I *mean* my single self to the exclusion of all others: but what I *say*, viz. 'I,' is just every 'I,' which in like manner excludes all others from itself."[50]

In Levinas's view, however, the particularity of the subject is unsayable because it *exceeds* the Said, in which Hegel's dialectic takes place. Levinas, therefore, does not merely invert the Hegelian argument, he completely displaces it. Levinas shifts our attention toward the self that is presupposed by consciousness and demonstrates that conceptual universality is always derivative insofar as it is only the manifestation of subjectivity in the Said. The Saying of this subjectivity continues to be a hostage to the neighbor and testifies in this way to an unmistakable relation between two absolutely singular individuals beyond the universality of the concept.

Hegel argues that Saying, insofar as language is the work of thought, exceeds the merely subjective *Meinen*, which remains unsayable and hence also meaningless. If language is understood as the medium of sensibility, that is, of the approach of the other beyond conceptuality, it is possible to find in Saying a dimension that transcends *Meinung*. In fact, Levinas sees in *Meinung* an essential reference to the will, even to the point of supporting its translation as *vouloir-dire*. But the preliminary Saying precedes the will (and thus also consciousness and ontological freedom). It involves the an-archical passivity of responsibility: "responsibility as response is the prior (*préalable*) Saying."[51] Such a Saying exceeds its content, just as the surplus of meaning transcends the will of the subject. It is a *pouvoir-dire* beyond any *vouloir-dire*. This structure of Saying, which also belongs to the Book, is founded in the notion of *Mehrmeinung* by virtue of which Levinas is able to think the transcendence of *pouvoir-dire* with respect to *vouloir-dire*.[52] Subjectivity says more than it ever means as such, and in this surplus lies its vulnerability and its subjection to the other, that is, its individuation. Without this irreducible preontological occurence and recurrence of the self it would be impossible to grasp the subject as an individual at all. It is the subject's "position" of responsibility, presupposed by the transcendence of language, and thus by the preoriginary saying, that is the ultimate principle of individuation.

The element of universality that we find in the particular subject should not be taken as anything other than ethical. It is the universality of the "*otherwise*," of what Derrida calls the "modality without substance."[53] "Not to turn into relations that reverse," writes Levinas, "is the *universal* 'subjectiveness' of the subject (*c'est la 'subjectité' du sujet*, universel), of which the subject's ignorance bears witness . . . to the pre-originary *hither side* of abnegation."[54] I am individualized by my nonreciprocal relation with another. And in the very impossibility of my absenting myself from this relation, the subjectiveness of the subject becomes universal. That which is universal in this case is the ethical significance of my being the hostage of my neighbor, and I can remain blind to it since, by virtue of its very immediacy, it precedes consciousness and knowledge. It is neither a moral disposition nor a spontaneous benevolence destined to become aware of itself. In this context, universality is beyond the *logos* and does not concern "knowledge" of any kind. The abnegation of substitution is thus "a passive effect, which one does not succeed in converting into an active initiative or into one's own virtue."[55] Nevertheless, it is still possible for discourse to express this passivity "without healing the affection that rends consciousness."[56] Without reducing myself to the level of a thematic object, I show myself in a Saying, thereby declaring my exceptional position. And in this Saying an "overdetermination of the ontological categories" manifests itself "which transforms them into ethical terms."[57] Quite apart from any question of knowledge, ethical language is unique in its capacity to express the enigma of the transcendence which is irreducible to the Said. Only ethical language can express "the self without a concept, unequal in identity," the self that "signifies itself in the first person, sketching the plan of Saying, producing itself in Saying as an *ego* or as *me* (*se pro-duisant dans le Dire moi ou je*), that is utterly different from any other ego, that is, or equivalently, having a meaning despite death."[58]

The absolute and disinterested generosity of responsibility implies, by virtue of the sacrifice it performs, a radical individuation transcending the generality or the generalizing power of death. However, by no means does this signify a search for personal immortality. On the contrary, it calls upon the subject to refrain from assisting in the accomplishment of his or her own actions. In such a radical passivity or patience, subjectivity is being-for-beyond-my-death.[59] Responsibility does not triumph over mortality, but the very moment of my betrayal by language is set in a crucial ambiguity to which we have already referred. The Said succeeds by an abuse of language in expressing my extraction from Being, only to see its illicit gains reduced immediately to a new Said. As Levinas writes, "Language is ancillary and thus indispensable. At this moment language is serving a research conducted in view of disengaging the *otherwise than Being* [which] is stated in a Saying that must also be unsaid in order thus to extract the *otherwise than Being* from the said in which it already comes to signify but a *being otherwise*."[60]

The transcendence in play here cannot be described as in any way definitive. It is a transcendence whose movement is always frustrated by the medium in which it is set and on which it depends, namely, language. Perpetually in the moment of betrayal, the movement is always "to be made." And the same ambiguity or indecision can be seen between the individuation and universality of subjectivity. "The subject posited as deposed is me; I universalise myself. And it is also my truth, my truth of being mortal. . . . But the concept of the Ego can correspond to me only inasmuch as it can signify responsibility, which summons me as irreplaceable. . . . Thus there is a true movement (*D'où course à l'envi*) between the conceptuality of the Ego and the patience of a refusal of concepts, between universality and individuation, between mortality and responsibility. The very diachrony of truth is in this alternation."[61] At this point we can begin to see a fracture open up in time: that which, however ambiguously, resists conceptualization is not itself contemporary with this resistance. In other words, the transcendence of conceptualization is marked by diachrony.

The Ego can correspond to me only if it signifies nothing more than a nonreciprocal responsibility. The ontological concept is thus ethically overdetermined by the preoriginal ethical situation of the subject. The Saying overdetermines, or transcends, the Said. Even when overdetermined by the ethical, ontological concepts can—and must—still be reduced. But the very possibility of such a reduction depends upon the concept in question already having an ethical significance and upon it retaining a trace of this significance in its own meaning. The Saying breaks with the structure of the Said. It signifies in its separation, in its own time and in its reference to the unique responsibility of the first person, I. The significance of this Saying exceeds its thematic statement in the Said which, in turn, always bears within it traces of the Saying.

It is possible, therefore, to speak in general terms about the Ego without making any ontological generalizations. It is enough to show, in language, the universal ethical significance of individuation. "To say that the Ego is a substitution is then not to state the universality of a principle, the quiddity of an Ego, but, quite the contrary, it is to restore to the soul its egoity which supports no generalisation."[62]

The basis of this ethical overdetermination of ontological categories is the situation—we could almost say the "limit situation"—of speaking or writing. Derrida has emphasized the central position held by writing in *Otherwise than Being*. However, we can already find the same importance of speaking or writing in *Totality and Infinity*, where the priority of metaphysics over ontology (in Levinas's usage of these terms) was argued in the following way: "Already the comprehension of Being is said to the existent, who again arises behind the theme in which he is presented. This 'saying to the Other'—this relationship with the Other as interlocutor, this relation with an *existent*—precedes all ontology; it is the ultimate relation in Being."[63] One can also see the same move being made in the following passage on the social relation as the ultimate event in Being. "The very utterance by which I state it and whose claim to truth, postulating a total reflection, refutes the unsurpassable character of the face to face relation, nonetheless confirms it by the very fact of stating this truth—of saying it to the Other."[64] It is only by attending to the actual conjuncture in which a statement is made, the concrete situation of speaking and its inescapable orientation toward the Other, that the interruption of totality and the extraction from Being become possible, since only in this way does the Saying come into play.

Otherwise than Being's reflection on the relationship between the Saying and the Said shows that, despite the unfailing significance of the speaking subject's "position," insofar as it is said, the uniqueness of the first person becomes universal and thus requires a further reduction. We must remember that ethical language does not reach any definitive formulation. It calls, rather, for an endless thinking back from the Said to the Saying.

If it were possible, Levinas would speak of himself only "in the passivity of an undeclinable assignation"; not "as a particular case of the universal, an ego belonging to the concept of Ego, but as I (*moi*) said in the first person —I, unique in my genus." He is, however, the first to admit that language is never so generous as to grant him this opportunity. "It is indeed true that this I has already become a universal in the present exposition itself." However, the case is not without its possibilities, elusive yet persistent, for, as Levinas goes on to say, "I am capable of conceiving of a break with this universal, and the apparition of the unique *I* which *always* precedes the reflection which comes again . . . to include me in the concept—which I again evade or am torn up from."[65] This perpetual recurrence of the I in the alternation between the Saying and the Said is the same movement as one finds in the endless refutation and rebirth of skepticism. We could even add that skepticism cannot ever be successfully laid to rest since language itself, between the Saying and the Said, individuation and universality, "is already scepticism."[66]

ETHICS AS PROPHETIC WITNESS

Although it is inevitably performed in the Said, the task of philosophy is to reduce the Said to the signification of the Saying that precedes it. The subject of this Saying says himself not by offering information, but simply by exposing himself, by announcing himself, that is, by *expressing* himself in his Saying. Far from being the tale of a private adventure such as may befall a reflective consciousness, expression is a disinterested bearing witness. It is the response of the one for the Other, and since the Saying responds even before hearing the appeal of the Other, Levinas calls it anachronistic and diachronic. There is a paradoxical immediacy to the Saying, a sort of unthinkable immediacy which escapes the present. In the words of Blanchot, "one must manage somehow to understand the immediate in the past tense. This renders the paradox unbearable."[67] If the time of the Said is always the present (and its recollection is re-presentation), that of the preoriginary Saying arises from an immemorial past which precedes the activity of the understanding. Saying offers and obeys before any order has been given. It is, therefore, inspired. It is prophetic. Indeed, prophecy belongs to the essence of human language.

The Saying cannot be rationally grounded or guaranteed. (Again, we may be reminded of its affinity with skepticism, which cannot be either justified or extinguished by reason.) Upholding the possibility of nonsense, it testifies to its own disinterestedness. Its testimony is therefore ethical, but also enigmatic, cast in the modality of hint and allusion. As such, it is ever vulnerable to refutation, if interpreted only with respect to the Said. Only the preliminary Saying survives the universality of ontology insofar as it says nothing but the self-exposure of its subject and is addressed immediately to an interlocutor who transcends the *logos*. The preliminary Saying has always to be said in the first person singular, beyond any generality, and it testifies to my own exceptional uniqueness. While it is true that only in the Said can each individual posit him or herself and say "I," Hegel's argument against the particularity to which each individual aspires in saying "I" does not tell the whole story. It applies only to the Said and fails to recognize the possibilities promised by the Saying. Beyond its *Meinen*, the preoriginary Saying bears witness to the ultimate individuation of *me* as the one responsible and summoned to bear that responsibility. In the Saying, I am the only speaking subject, the one who responds for another, the one who is enigmatically elect. Considered as a "Saying without a Said," therefore, language is in itself always ethical, prophetic, skeptical, religious, and inspired.

As Catherine Chalier has made very clear in her paper on Jewish singularity, there is a crucial link between Levinas's thinking of ipseity and messianism.[68] The election of the subject is thought in the light of the election of Israel, which is itself a privilege only in the sense of a "charge écrasante" that one has to bear. Such an election is, in Levinas's words, "no doubt a *malheur*."[69] The parallel holds provided we recognize that despite its insurmountable particularity, Israel's election has, just as in the case of the individual, a meaning that is universal and which concerns the whole of humanity. Each and every person is called upon to accomplish this "destinée" which shows itself in the history and spirituality of Hebraism.

For the ethical subject, prophetic testimony of one's own election is the inspired Saying of the ethical as the vocation of humanity. As such, it cannot be objective and thematic in character, for this would be to gather transcendence into the universality of the *logos*. And neither can it be a confession of an inner condition or conviction, for then transcendence would be a matter for empirical psychology.[70] No, it is the simple statement of a truth, neither anonymous nor neutral, but entirely personal and even ideologically pure. Its universal ethical significance can be seen in Jewish singularity and in biblical history, continued in Israel's passion, "a history which calls more to the resources of the 'I' in each person."[71]

Ultimately, the same issue is at stake in Levinas's meditation on Jewish messianism and its difference from the Christian identification of the Messiah in the person of Jesus. Hebraism "would announce a form of existence beyond the individual Messiah, whose individuation is not realised in a single being." All people are the Messiah to the extent that they become a *me*, responsible for others. "The Messiah is Me. To be Me is to be the Messiah."[72] The themes of ipseity beyond Being and the responsibility that individuates a subject as *me* are developed most fully in *Otherwise than Being*. Yet they do not appear in Levinas's later writings alone, and we can find passages in *Totality and Infinity* that make the same point.[73] This is not surprising if we accept that these themes, and all of the meditations on them, are deeply inspired by messianism. In this sense, as Adriaan Peperzak, among others, has shown, the Jewish tradition is the principal prephilosophical experience on which Levinas draws in his philosophical writings.[74] It seems to me, therefore—and this has been the central theme of this paper—that the prophetic message is, for Levinas, the essential modality of the ethical. Yet if this message is addressed to everyone and demands of each of us that we heed the call as if it were our true vocation, does this not transform *my* nonreciprocal and infinite responsibility into "a theatrical role"[75] in precisely the way that Levinas is at pains to avoid? And is this danger not inevitable if we wish to preserve the universal value of ethics?

Blanchot interprets responsibility in Levinas as "disindividuation" (*désindividuation*), involving the loss of the ethical in its own right.[76] In a paper on Blanchot, Jacques Rolland criticizes this interpretation while conceding that the "position" of the *me* can be taken up by any one of many effectively equivalent subjects.[77] However, the radicality of Levinas's point of view demands that we conceive proximity to exclude the possibility of theater: "le rôle du moi" is mine alone and no one can play this part except me. In this respect, Levinas cannot possibly accept Blanchot's interpretation of "subjectivity without a subject" and responsibility that desingularizes me. On the contrary, only in this situation do I become myself, the one who cannot turn in flight and for whom no one can stand in. This is, once again, the nonreciprocity of language, of the Saying, delivered in the first person singular, I. "Here I am," "Me voici," in responding to the other before he speaks, this preoriginary Saying is really nothing less than a "delirium."[78] The reduction of each Said to the signification of Saying was the first step for philosophy. But now it must perform a second reduction different from the first, moving from this delirium "to signification, to the one-for-another."[79] In effect, philosophy has to turn about and retrace its steps from the Saying back to the Said in order to become, in Levinas's words, "the wisdom of desire."

Within this paradoxical conjuncture of individuation and universality, the ethical can be said as the memory of the preoriginary Saying, and, moreover, with the utmost simplicity, "Language is the fact that only one word is ever uttered: God."[80] We should not be too hasty and dismiss this as an unwelcome reversion to traditional metaphysical practices and formulae. In fact, the word "God" is still absent from God's first epiphany in language.[81] In this respect, we must recognize the significance of the ethical moment of the Saying, the declaration of my own vulnerability and responsibility, *me voici*: here I am in the name of God. We could say, therefore, that in language, even before "God," only one word is ever uttered: "me." It is no doubt paradoxical to ground the universal signification of the ethical on this extreme particularity, that is, on the facticity of my individuation. But Levinas's whole effort is precisely to show in a philosophical Said the universal signification of such a radical preoriginary Saying.

Now, finally, we must still ask if this preoriginary Saying has an absolute and universal significance which is both intelligible and immediately compelling in itself, that is to say, without the intervention and mediation of a specific historical and cultural context. Or could it be that it is conceivable as ethically absolute and universal in its extreme particularity only because our tradition —at once both Greek and Jewish—has seen fit to institute and then to privilege the ipseity of the individual in its ethical significance? Could it also be that this preoriginary Saying which says only "me" or "God" would be inconceivable ethically were it not for the prior recognition of an inner voice that calls *me*? How else could my Saying be already a response?

In conclusion, to what extent is it the prophetic—whether beyond history or within it—that allows the universality of the ethical to manifest itself? This must remain an open question. In spite of everything, the prophetic message is voiced in a *said* and cannot help, therefore, but obey the rules of the *logos*, while remaining unable to turn the conceptual resources at its disposal to its own advantage. If the prophetic word were language subjected to an extreme tension and had indeed to interpret itself as an "irreducible moment of a discourse which by essence is aroused by the epiphany of the face inasmuch as it attests the presence of the third, the whole of humanity, in the eyes that look at me,"[82] then perhaps it could open the way—*prior* to the passage to justice and *within* the originary ethical situation itself—to a more positive evaluation of reciprocity and symmetry. In this way, the universalization of the ethical demands that throw my freedom into question would be derived directly from the appeal of the other: an appeal which "commands me to command": thus the other does not address me alone but "is posited in front of a *we*."[83] If this were the case, the recognition of the Other's responsibility for me would have an eminently *ethical* sense. Yet when Levinas says that I am responsible also for the responsibility of the Other for me, one has the impression that he is using "extreme phrases" solely in order to emphasize the infinity of my own responsibility. Within the framework of radical asymmetry, however, to say that the other is *responsible* does not mean the same as "I am responsible," for the simple reason that the only subject is I, and I alone am responsible. Is the Other not also responsible? Perhaps, but that is entirely his or her own affair. In the end this means that one cannot attribute the status of "subject" to the Other. Derrida has discussed the paradoxes and aporia of this asymmetry at some length, showing that we may find harbored within them "the very gesture of all violence."[84]

But when we pass on to the manifestation of the ethical in the sphere of the prophetic—whether one looks to the exemplarity of biblical prophetism, or whether one says, as in the conclusion of *Otherwise than Being*, that each individual is virtually elect—are we not in spite of everything obliged to concede some form of universality and reciprocity to asymmetric responsibility? I cannot help returning to the observation of Adriaan Peperzak with which I began this text. Not without noting, however, that it would undoubtedly appear deeply problematic to Levinas who, in *Ethics and Infinity*, recently confirmed that the prophetic dimension—"beside the unlimited ethical demand"—constitutes "the fundamental fact of man's humanity." And—in order to explain that in spite of the universalization effected by the prophetic "which interprets itself in concrete forms" and "becomes religions"—he immediately added that "this by no means puts back into doubt the rigorous structure that I have tried to define where it is always I who am responsible and I who supports the universe, regardless of whatever happens next."[85]

Notes

Author's Note: I would like to express my thanks to David Webb for his generous assistance in preparing the English version of this paper.

1. G.W.F. Hegel, *Enzyklopädie der Philosophischen Wissenschaften*, Hamburg, Meiner, 1969, § 20, p. 56; trans. W. Wallace, *The Logic of Hegel*, Oxford University Press, 1968, p. 38: "Now language is the work of thought: and hence all that is expressed in language must be universal. What I only mean or suppose is mine: it belongs to me—this particular individual. But language expresses nothing but universality; and so I cannot say what I merely *mean*."

2. A. Peperzak, "Autrui, société, peuple de Dieu," *Intersoggettività Socialità Religione, Archivio di Filosofia* 54, 1986; 314.

3. Cf. E. Levinas, EeI 95; EI 90.

4. Levinas says that his thinking "does not push the original modalities of the *signifi-cant* into the knowledge where Being is given and grasped, but into the relation-of-*myself*-to-the-*Other*. The signification of meaning (*sens*), the *for-the-other* by which the significant given overflows the limits of its proper definition, does not reduce itself to the intended meaning (*la visée*) of the sign which lives within it and which is worth less than the presence of the signified 'in person'; nor does it reduce itself to finality, poorer than the contentment of the obtained and realised end. The *for-the-other* would adhere to the Other's placing me in question, to the truth 'which accuses'—Saint Augustine's *veritas redarguens*—to my responsibility for the *other man* which says itself silently in his face: meaning would adhere to human fraternity. Ethics which thus tends to affirm itself as first philosophy is therefore not at all privileged here because of whatever concern with edification or values (which it is not a question of denigrating), but because of the *meaning* that philosophy seeks" (preface to *La traccia dell' altro*, trans. F. Ciaramelli, Naples, Pironti, 1979, xv).

5. J.-F. Lyotard, "Logique de Levinas" in *Textes pour Emmanuel Levinas*, ed. F. Laruelle, Paris, Jean-Michel Place, 1980, 128; trans. I. McLeod, "Levinas's Logic," in *Face to Face with Levinas*, ed. R. Cohen, Albany, State University of New York Press, 1986, 129–30. Moral obligation disrupts the power of knowing and implies the radical obedience required of Israel by God: cf. Levinas's reflection on the Talmudic privilege of doing over hearing in *Quatre lectures talmudiques*, Paris, Minuit, 1969, 67–109. See also E. Wyschogrod, "Doing before hearing," in *Textes pour Emmanuel Levinas*, 179–203, and my analysis of this Talmudic reading in "Le rôle du judaïsme dans l'oeuvre de Levinas," *Revue philosophique de Louvain* 81, 1983: 580–600 (esp. 583–92).

6. Levinas has expressed unhappiness with Heidegger's later philosophy because of its way of thinking which "seems to me much less verifiable than that of *Being and Time*" (EeI 39; EI 42).

7. "Everywhere my concern is rightly to translate this non-Hellenism of the Bible into Hellenic terms. . . . There is nothing to be done: philosophy speaks Greek" (E. Levinas, DVI 137). Levinas also refers to "prophetic eschatology" in the preface to *Totality and Infinity*, TeI x; TI 22.

8. "The ontological language which *Totality and Infinity* maintains in order to ex-clude the purely psychological significance of the proposed analyses is hereafter avoided." E. Levinas, "Signature," ed. A. Peperzak, *Research in Phenomenology* 8, 1978: 189. See also DVI 133, where Levinas says that the ontological language in *Totality and Infinity* is not at all "definitive" and is already an investigation of the "beyond being." S. Strasser in his major work on Levinas, *Jenseits von Sein und Zeit: Eine Einführung in Emmanuel Levinas' Philosophie* (The Hague, Martinus Nijhoff, 1978) speaks about a *Kehre* in Levinas's thought with respect to this renunciation of ontological language after *Totality and Infinity* (219–51).

9. AE 162; OB 126.

10. AE 8 n. 4; OB 187 n. 5.

11. A. Peperzak, "Beyond Being," in *Research in Phenomenology* 8, 1978: 252.

12. For example the following passage: "To be responsible over and beyond one's freedom is certainly not to remain a pure result of the world." In other words we are, in spite of everything, within an ethical dimension. "*To support the universe is a crushing charge, but a divine discomfort.* . . . If ethical terms arise in our discourse, before the terms 'freedom' and 'non-freedom,' it is because, before the bipolarity of good and evil presented to choice, the subject finds himself committed to the Good in the very passivity of the *supporter*" (AE 157; OB 122). The meaning of such a passivity is ethical.

13. ADV 178 n. 6, 172.

14. "C'est par cette responsabilité supplémentaire que la subjectivité n'est pas le Moi, mais moi" (HH 99; CP 150).

15. Levinas, "Signature," 188–89.

16. AE 16–17; OB 13–14.

17. AE 8; OB 7.

18. The opposition between the *individual*, always equal to others and interchangeable with them, and the solitude of *Selbstheit* is taken up from Rosenzweig, as Levinas notes in *De Dieu qui vient à l'idée*, 221–22.

19. Cf. TeI 81–160; TI 109–80. Cf. C. M. Vasey, "Le corps et l'autre," *Exercises de la patience* 1980, no. 1: 33–42.

20. Cf. TeI 153; TI 178.

21. Levinas, "Signature," 182.

22. Cf. TeI 18–23; TI 48–52.

23. TeI 10; TI 40.

24. ED 162–63; WD 110–11. See especially the following passage: "The philosopher Kierkegaard does not *only* plead for Sören Kierkegaard . . . but for subjective existence in general (a non-contradictory expression). . . . In order to reject the Kierkegaardian notion of subjective existence Levinas should eliminate even the notions of an *essence* and a *truth* of subjective existence (of the Ego, and primarily of the Ego of the Other). . . . The least one might say is that Levinas does not do so, and cannot do so, without renouncing philosophical discourse" (ED 163; WD 110). But this is only true for *Totality and Infinity*.

25. ED 192; WD 131.

26. Cf. TeI 171; TI 197.

27. E. Levinas, preface to S. Mosès, *Système et révélation: La philosophie de Franz Rosenzweig*, Paris, Seuil, 1982, 16.

28. AE 180; OB 141.

29. R. Bernasconi, "Levinas Face to Face with Hegel," *Journal of the British Society for Phenomenology* 13, no. 3, 1982: 274–75.

30. AE 161; OB 126.

31. E.g., TeI 52; TI 80.

32. AE 104; OB 82.

33. AE 133 n. 9; OB 194 n. 9.

34. AE 144 n. 18; OB 195 n. 18.

35. AE 162; OB 126.

36. TeI 24; TI 53. The same movement—although not couched in terms of experience —is made at AE 12; OB 10.

37. "Énigme et phénomène," EDE 213, 215; "Enigma and Phenomena," CP 70, 72.

38. Cf. AE 199–207; OB 156–62. See also "Paix et proximité," in *Emmanuel Levinas*, ed. J. Rolland, *Les Cahiers de La nuit surveillée* 3, Lagrasse, Verdier, 1984, 339–48.

39. A. Lingis, "Translator's Introduction," OB xxx.

40. DVI 135, 148.

41. Levinas continually underlines the ethical dimension of Revelation in Hebraism (ethical because prophetic and at the same time prophetic because ethical), especially in the second section of *L'au-delà du verset*, 125–206. For example, "que dans cette relation [de responsabilité] l'homme se fasse 'moi' . . . , voilà la voie que je serais porté à prendre pour résoudre le paradoxe de la Révélation: l'éthique est le modèle à la mesure de la transcendance et c'est en tant que kérygme éthique que la Bible est Révélation" (178). Here man, every man, is the elect, the unique, the "non-interchangeable," summoned to an infinite responsibility. I would emphasize that this inevitable generalization is not founded in logic, but in prophetical assignation. Prophecy is the real modality of the manifestation—and universal significance—of the ethical: "L'éthique—*apparaissant comme le prophétique*—n'est pas une 'région,' une couche ou un ornement de l'être. Il est, de soi, le dés-inter-essement même" (138, my emphasis).

42. AE 232–33; OB 184–85.

43. J. Derrida, EM 33–34; AM.

44. In the preface to the second edition of *De l'existence à l'existant* Levinas writes of an "ethics older than ontology" which "will let the significations beyond the ontological differences signify, which, all things considered, doubtless is the signification of Infinity itself" (12).

45. AE 108 n. 18; OB 192 n. 18.

46. EM 31; AM.

47. AE 105; OB 83 (my emphasis).

48. AE 105; OB 84. Levinas is thinking of G.W.F. Hegel, *Phänomenologie des Geistes*, Hamburg, Meiner, 1952, 82; trans. A. V. Miller, *Phenomenology of Spirit*, Oxford University Press, 1977, 60.

49. *Enzyklopädie der Philosophischen Wissenschaften*, § 20, p. 56; trans. *The Logic of Hegel*, p. 38.

50. Ibid.

51. DVI 33.

52. Cf. J. Greisch, "Du vouloir-dire au pouvoir-dire," in *Emmanuel Levinas*, ed. J. Rolland, 211–21, esp. 219–20. On the notion of *Mehrmeinung*, which is very important in Levinas's interpretation of phenomenology, see J. Colette, "Levinas et la phénoménologie Husserlienne" ibid., 19–36.

53. EM 29; AM.

54. AE 106; OB 84.

55. Lingis, "Translator's Introduction," OB xxxi.

56. AE 105; OB 84.

57. AE 146; OB 115.

58. AE 147; OB 115.

59. "La trace de l'autre," EDE 191; trans. A Lingis, "The Trace of the Other," *Deconstruction in Context*, ed. M. Taylor, University of Chicago Press, 1986, 349.

60. AE 7, 8; OB 6, 7.

61. AE 162; OB 126.

62. AE 163–64; OB 127.

63. TeI 18; TI 47–48.

64. TI 196; TI 221.

65. AE 177; OB 139. The same movement is described at AE 217; OB 171, and at DVI 254–55.

66. AE 216; OB 170.

67. M. Blanchot, *L'écriture du désastre*, Paris, Gallimard, 1980, 44; trans. A. Smock, *Writing of the Disaster*, Lincoln, University of Nebraska Press, 1986, 24.

68. C. Chalier, "Singularité juive et philosophie," in *Emmanuel Levinas*, ed. J. Rolland, 78–98, esp. 96–97.

69. "Sans nom," NP 182. See also this passage from the conclusion of *Otherwise than Being*: "that the beyond or the liberation would be the support of a crushing charge, is to be sure surprising. It is this wonder that has been the object of the book proposed here" (AE 228; OB 181).

70. AE 212; OB 167. Here Levinas rejects the alternative of ontology (as thematic objectification which gathers transcendence) and psychology (as reduction of transcendence to an empirical state of mind) which induced *Totality and Infinity* to use an ontological language.

71. "La souffrance inutile," in *Emmanuel Levinas*, ed. J. Rolland, 337.

72. "Textes messianiques," in DL 118, 120.

73. Cf., for example, TeI 223; TI 245.

74. A. Peperzak, "Emmanuel Levinas: Jewish Experience and Philosophy," *Philosophy Today*, Winter 1983: 297–306. When Levinas admits in the first chapter of *Otherwise than Being* that his thought "is not completely disengaged from pre-philosophical experiences" (AE 24; OB 20) and when he refers to the independence of what "Alphonse de Waelhens called non-philosophical experiences" (AE 154; OB 120) I think that we

have to recognize the central place of Hebraism. This is confirmed by his recent observation that "every philosophical thought rests on pre-philosophical experiences, and . . . for me reading of the Bible has belonged to these founding experiences. It has thus played an essential role—and in large measure without my knowing it —in addressing all mankind" (EeI 19; EI 24).

75. AE 173; OB 136: "the uniqueness of the ego, my uniqueness as a respondent, a hostage, for whom no one else could be substituted without transforming responsibility into a theatrical role (*en rôle joué sur le théâtre*)."

76. When Blanchot writes: "In the patience of passivity, I am he whom anyone at all can replace . . . but one for whom nonetheless there is no dispensation: he must answer to and for what he is not. His is a borrowed, happenstance singularity —that, in fact, of the *hostage* (as Levinas says)" (*L'écriture du désastre*, 35; trans. *Writing of the Disaster*, 18), he distorts radically Levinas's understanding of the hostage's condition (or uncondition). Even if Levinas refers to a situation which precedes ontological identity of the subject (see "Sans Identité," HH 83–101; trans. "Without Identity," CP 141–52), this does not mean that the *self* in ethical responsibility loses his individuality. On the contrary, it is precisely this infinite responsibility that singularizes the subject who is radically irreplaceable and elect. This is contrary to Blanchot's reading where "the responsibility with which I am charged is not mine and causes me not to be I" (*L'écriture du désastre*, 35; trans. *Writing of the Disaster*, 18). For Blanchot, therefore, it is not only a question of a loss of identity but also of a loss of individuality (*L'écriture du désastre*, 36, 39; trans. *Writing of the Disaster*, 19, 21). The basis of ethical discourse in Levinas's sense is thereby completely destroyed.

77. J. Rolland, "Pour une approche de la question du neutre," *Exercices de la patience* 1981, no. 2: 32: "Each time, the unexpected arrival of this Other (*autrui*) translates itself *in the one who plays the role of the ego* by a loosening of the for-itself which is swallowed up within the measureless call of the Most-Weak (*Très-Faible*)" (my emphasis).

78. "Langage et proximité," EDE 236; trans. "Language and Proximity," CP 126.

79. AE 194; OB 152.

80. NP 137. See also EDE 236; CP 126.

81. AE 190; OB 149.

82. TeI 188; TI 213.

83. Id.

84. ED 184; WD 125.

85. EeI 122; EI 114.

PART THREE

Levinas and the Feminine

CHAPTER
6

QUESTIONS TO EMMANUEL LEVINAS
On the Divinity of Love
Luce Irigaray
Translated by Margaret Whitford

1.

Is there otherness outside of sexual difference? The feminine, as it is characterized by Levinas, is not other than himself. Defined by "modesty," "a mode of being which consists in shunning the light" (see *Time and the Other*),[1] the feminine appears as the underside or reverse side of man's aspiration toward the light, as its negative. The feminine is apprehended not in relation to itself, but from the point of view of man, and through a purely erotic strategy, a strategy moreover which is dictated by masculine pleasure (*jouissance*), even if man does not recognize to what limited degree his own erotic intentions and gestures are ethical. It is the culture of men-amongst-themselves, and in particular the monopoly of divine power by male gods, which is responsible for female sexuality, in so far as it is visible at all, being kept from the light and left without representation in terms of the divine. During the period when there were goddesses, female sexual organs always appear in the representation of the bodies of women, particularly goddesses, and not merely in the form of the triangle indicating the womb, but also in the form of the labia, an inscription which will later be erased. The cult of goddesses who are exclusively mothers, and mothers of sons, is a late episode in the history of women. In the symbolism of social exchanges, it is accompanied by the representation of the woman's sexual organs as the figure of the triangle representing the womb and standing as a symbol of the maternal function. This epoch also emphasizes the transition to a writing useful to trade and for this reason becoming phonogrammatic. One of the places where this transition can be pinpointed is at the junction of Mesopotamian and Sumerian culture, a place where the songs celebrating sacred unions or marriages (in this connection, see S. N. Kramer's work) give birth to the Song of Solomon, which tells of the complexity of the nuptials between the two lovers (*l'amante et l'amant*), the two beloveds (*l'aimée et l'aimé*), who are born of different mothers and so do not belong to the same traditions, to the same genealogies, or to the same gods.

Of this love and this grief in the Song of Solomon, of the sensual delight (*volupté*) of the lovers who wed each other with all their senses, with their whole body, inviting to their encounters the most succulent fruits of the earth, but who are already compelled to shun each other, to flee each other, to separate, nothing remains in the pleasure (*volupté*)² of which Levinas speaks. For Levinas, the feminine merely represents that which sustains desire, that which rekindles pleasure. The caress, that "fundamental disorder" (TA 82; TO 89) does not touch the other. What Levinas is seeking is neither the qualities of the other's flesh nor of his own, he seeks "a play with something elusive, a play absolutely without aim or plan [there is no union intended, therefore —Irigaray] not with that which may become ours and ourself, but with something other, always inaccessible, always in the future. The caress is the anticipation of this pure becoming, without content. It is made up of this intensified hunger, of promises ever richer, opening new perspectives onto the ungraspable. It is nourished by innumerable hungers. This intentionality of pleasure, directed purely and simply towards the future itself, and not an anticipation of any future event, has always been misrecognised by philosophical analysis" (TA 82–83; TO 89). To caress, for Levinas, consists, therefore, not in approaching the other in its most vital dimension, the touch, but in the reduction of that vital dimension of the other's body to the elaboration of a future for himself. To caress could thus constitute the hidden intention of philosophical temporality. But in this "play," the only function of the feminine other is to satisfy the hungers of the philosopher, to renourish the intentionality of his pleasure in the direction of a future without a "future event," a future where no day is named for the encounter with the other in an embodied love. This description of the caress (of which I have already spoken at length in "Fécondité de la caresse")³ is a good example of the way in which the temporality of the male subject, of Emmanuel Levinas at any rate, makes use of the support of the feminine in the intentionality of pleasure for its own becoming. In this tranformation of the flesh of the other into his own temporality, it is clear that the masculine subject loses the feminine as other.

To become other to himself, to return to self via the other, Levinas needs the son. The son is his being as same/other, in a simultaneous engenderment that he seems to forget somewhat.

The function of the other sex as an alterity irreducible to myself eludes Levinas for at least two reasons:

He knows nothing of communion in pleasure. Levinas does not ever seem to have experienced the transcendence of the other which becomes im-mediate ecstasy (*extase instante*) in me and with him— or her. For Levinas, the distance is always maintained with the other in the experience of love. The other is "close" to him in "duality." This autistic, egological, solitary love does not correspond to the shared outpouring, to the loss of boundaries which takes place for both lovers when they cross the boundary of the skin into the mucous membranes of the body, leaving the circle which encloses my solitude to meet in a shared space, a shared breath, abandoning the relatively dry and precise outlines of each body's solid exterior to enter a fluid universe where the perception of being two persons (*de la dualité*) becomes indistinct, and above all, acceding to another energy, neither that of the one nor that of the other, but an energy produced together and as a result of the irreducible difference of sex. Pleasure between the same sex does not result in that im-mediate ecstasy between the other and myself. It may be more or less intense, quantitatively and qualitatively different; it does not produce in us that ecstasy which is our child, prior to any child (*enfant avant tout enfant*). In this relation, we are at least three, each of which is irreducible to any of the others: you, me, and our work (*oeuvre*), that ecstasy of ourself in us (*de nous en nous*), that transcendence of the flesh of one to that of the other become ourself in us (*devenue nous en nous*), at any rate "in me" as a woman, prior to any child.[4]

Is it the fact that Levinas is a man that makes him unaware of this creation of pleasure prior to any son? Of pleasures neither mine nor thine, pleasure transcendent and immanent to one and to the other, and which gives birth to a third, a mediator between us thanks to which we return to ourselves other than we were?

Is what I am describing here only my pleasure as a woman? My pleasure with the lover of my flesh? My pleasure in an act in which neither can be substituted for the other. We cannot be interchangeable, in so far as he is a man and I am a woman, and in so far as he is he and I am I. And because we are not interchangeable, pleasure is no longer proximity nor duality, neither loss nor regression, nor more or less infantile perversity, nor failure of communion or of communication, etc. Pleasure is engendering in us and between us, an engendering associated with the world and the universe, with which the work (*oeuvre*) of the flesh is never unconnected. Either pleasure is a mere expenditure of fire, of water, of seed, of body, and of spirit . . . or else it is a unique and definitive creation. In this sense, it is time. It is ineffaceable, unrepeatable, even by the child.

The second reason Levinas does not perceive the feminine as other is that he substitutes the son for the feminine. However, the child belongs to another time. The child should be for himself, not for the parent. When one intends to create a child, giving the child to himself appears as an ethical necessity. The son should not be the place where the father confers being or existence on himself, the place where he finds the resources to return to himself in relation to this same as and other than himself constituted by the son. From my point of view, this gesture fails to achieve the relation to the other, and doubly so: it does not recognize the feminine other and the self as other in relation to her; it does not leave the child to his own generation. It seems to me pertinent to add that it does not recognize God in love.

2.

Who is the other, the Other (*l'autre, autrui*), etc.? How can the other be defined? Levinas speaks of "the Other" (*autrui*), of "respect for the Other" (*respect d'autrui*), of the "face of the Other" (*visage d'autrui*), etc. But how to define this Other which seems so self-evident to him, and which I see as a postulate, the projection or the remnant of a system, a hermeneutic locus of crystallization of meaning, etc.? Who is the other, if the other of sexual difference is not recognized or known? Does it not mean in that case a sort of mask or lure? Or an effect of the consumption of an other (*Autre*)? But how is transcendence defined?

Furthermore, this nondefinition of the other, when the other is not considered to have anything to do with sexual difference, gives rise to an infinite series of substitutions, an operation which seems to me nonethical. No one can be radically substituted for the other, without depriving the other of identity. Even a substitution which is authorized by proxy is questionable, given the irreducibility of each.

What Levinas does not see is that the locus of paternity, to which he accords the privilege of ethical alterity, has already assumed the place of the genealogy of the feminine, has already covered over the relationships between mothers and daughters, in which formerly transmission of the divine word was located.

Everything can slide in this historical and genealogical deracination. There is no longer any irreducible difference of the other. From this it results that ethics becomes indistinguishable from a kind of formalism or a disordered drift, whatever the nature of its passion (*pathos*).

Although temporarily useful and worthy of respect up to a certain point, this ethics no longer knows its faults. For such an ethics, the only faults are those which it openly produces. It turns on itself, in itself, failing to recognize its hidden faults; the fault remains invisible, nor is it recognized within the couple and the family, the nucleus of the socioreligious organization in which ethics is articulated.

The other sex, then, would represent the possible locus of the definition of the fault, of imperfection, of the unheard, of the unfulfilled, etc. But this fault cannot be named except by my other or its substitute. More precisely, there are at least two interpretations of the fault: that which corresponds to the failed fulfillment (*défault de l'accomplissement*) of my sex, to the failure to become the ideal of my genus (*genre*),[5] and that which is defined in relation to the ideal of the other genus. These faults are not the same. For centuries, one has been cruelly masked by the other. This puts society permanently in the position of being ethically at fault, a position which often has the backing of religion.

3.

How to articulate the question of the cosmic economy with, on the one hand, that of sexual difference, and on the other, that of the gods, or more generally, the divine, the other? The question of the face of the natural universe does not seem to me to figure much in the work of Levinas. Without interrogating him here on the issue of what the creation or the culture of the world might mean for him, I would like to pause at this question: who is the other if it is not rooted and situated in the natural universe? Is otherness defined uniquely in terms of the social body? Are its identity and its status sociological or ethnological? From such a conception of the other, I would distinguish that of an other with its roots also in the natural universe, in the body, and which, starting from this irreducible incarnation, continually elaborates a human universe, a human identity. We are not only culturally determined, we remain natural, and nature is the basis from which we can continue to create culture.

4.

Levinas uses a certain number of words without always defining or redefining them. Other (*autre*) is one of these. That gives a very insistent hermeneutical, metaphysical, or theological tone to his writings, even though the same writings sometimes have recourse to phenomenological methods from which metaphysical entities have been detached. This means that Levinas's discourse has two levels. The phenomenological approach—in particular through the caress, to the carnal relation, to the alterity of the feminine, to the unseen of the flesh—would belong to the descriptive methods, indicating that we are no longer in the order of metaphysics. The assertion that the other is always situated within the realm of the father, of the father-son, man-God relation, and that it is there and only there that ethics may be established, seems to me to belong to the imperatives of the metaphysical tradition. So the phenomenology of the caress in Levinas falls back within the boundaries staked out by the philosophical constitution of the masculine subject. It does not lead either to the other, or to God, or to a new spiritual or rational level. It is submerged in animality, perversity, childhood (which/whose?), of which the feminine other is the condition of representation. After having been so far—or so close—in the approach to the other sex, in my view to the other, to the mystery of the other, Levinas clings on once more to this rock of patriarchy in the very place of carnal love.

Although he takes pleasure in caressing, he abandons the feminine other, leaves her to sink, in particular into the darkness of a pseudoanimality, in order to return to his responsibilities in the world of men-amongst-themselves. For him, the feminine does not stand for an other to be respected in her human freedom and human identity. The feminine other is left without her own specific face. On this point, his philosophy falls radically short of ethics.

To go beyond the face of metaphysics would mean precisely to leave the woman her face, and even to assist her to discover it and to keep it. Levinas scarcely unveils the disfigurements brought about by ontotheology. His phenomenology of the caress is still implicated in it.

5.

The philosophy of Levinas does not resolve the question (shelved by Heidegger) of the relations between philosophy and theology: being as thought and being as other. Levinas, usually intentionally, fails to distinguish between the foundations of philosophy and the foundations of theology. Thus, unlike Heidegger, he writes that Being is the other or he points to the other as Being. According to Heidegger, Being corresponds to an operation of thought, to a logical and grammatical economy. No other is ever Being. We consider the other within the dimension of Being, or outside this dimension. But Being (*être*) does not correspond to any being (*étant*), neither the Other nor God. Being (*être*) is used to refer to a disposition which leads me to approach any being (*étant*) in a certain way. In this sense, the philosophy of Heidegger cannot be seen simply as an "ethics of the 'fruits of the earth'" (*nourritures terrestres*)[6] nor of the enjoyment (*jouissance*) of objects, such as the other in sexual love (cf. TA 45–46; TO 62–64). The philosophy of Heidegger is more ethical than that expression conveys, than his philosophy itself says explicitly. To consider the other within the horizon of Being should mean to respect the other. It is true that the definition of Being in terms of mortal destiny rather than in terms of living existence raises a question about the nature of respect. And in addition, this philosophy is more or less silent on man's sexual dimension (*la dimension de l'homme comme sexué*), an irreducible dimension of human existence. Perhaps Heidegger's thought was preparing the way for thinking the sexually identified subject (*sujet comme sexué*), in particular as a possible future for thought. The dissociation between philosophy and (patriarchal) theology can also be understood as an opening for a new epoch of Being.

To assimilate philosophy and theology as Levinas often does, is it not equivalent to assimilating philosophy and the thought of a people at a particular moment in their history, to assimilating philosophy and ethnology or sociology? Is this still philosophy? And further, is it possible to assimilate philosophy and theology until one has interpreted what is at stake in monotheism? In my opinion, it is not. Is monotheism wisdom or a patriarchal and masculine passion? The obligation to believe or to give one's allegiance, the injunction not to touch, form an integral part of a monotheism which conceals its passional nature. But monotheistic religions cannot claim to be ethical unless they submit themselves to a radical interrogation relative to the sexual attribution (*caractère sexué*) of their paradigms, whether these be of God, the ways in which God is referred to (in particular the masculine gender used by language, when he is not represented pictorially), God's commandments, etc.

6.

In this connection, I would like to return to the question of substitution, and point out once again that a place of irreducible nonsubstitutability exists within sexual difference. If an example is needed, let me suggest this question: Are the peoples of monotheism ready to assert that their God is a woman? How will they realign their entire socioreligious economy if this substitution is made? What upheaval in the symbolic order will be a necessary prerequisite for such a substitution?

7.

In "Fecundity of the Caress," I used the term "woman lover" (*l'amante*) and not only, as Levinas does, the word "beloved" (*aimée*). In this way, I wanted to signify that the woman can be a subject in love (*un sujet amoureux*) and is not reducible to a more or less immediate object of desire. Man and woman, woman and man can love each other in reciprocity as subjects, and not only in that transitive fashion whereby the man loves the woman, one accomplishing the act of love to which the other submits, already in the past tense,[7] in the passive. This description of pleasure given by Levinas is unacceptable to the extent that it presents man as the sole subject exercising his desire and his appetite upon the woman who is deprived of subjectivity except to seduce him. So the woman's pleasure is alienated to that of the man, according to the most traditional of scenarios of temptation and fall. In my opinion, if there is a fall, it is located in the reduction of the feminine to the passive, to the past tense, and to the object of man's pleasure, in the identification of the woman with the beloved (*aimée*).

This economy of love does indeed lead to despair. . . . But this is because of the obliteration of the woman as subject desiring *along with* man as subject. Such a situation exists in certain traditions. So it is not merely a woman's utopia or imagination. It is possible to live and simultaneously create sexual love. Here would lie the way out from the fall, for in this case, love can become spiritual and divine.

But what chance has it to exist in the genealogical economy of patriarchy? Without relationships between both natural and spiritual mothers and daughters, that are relationships between subjects, without cultural recognition of the divinity of this genealogy, how can a woman remain the lover (*l'amante*) of a man who belongs to the line of a Father God? And does not the latter need a Mother God? The two genealogies must be divinized in each of the two sexes and for the two sexes: mother and father, woman and man, for it to be possible for female and male lovers (*amante et amant*) to love each other.

The most precious thing that I wanted to say in "Fecundity of the Caress" has unfortunately not been possible to translate into English. For in fact English—in which, so I have been told many times, there is no hierarchy of sex or gender[8]—has no specific word for woman as lover (*amante*). How is sexual nonhierarchy in the act of love expressed in this language?

8.

When it is not traditional metaphysics, what governs the ethical order in Levinas is fundamentally a law deriving from God. His work displays a hesitation or oscillation between these two principles or measures, linked perhaps to an evolution in the process of his thought. But how are God's commandments brought to bear in the relationship between lovers? If this relationship is not divinized, does that not pervert any divinity, any ethics, any society which does not recognize God in carnality? And who is the other if the divine is excluded from the carnal act? If these gestures of ultimate relations between living humans are not a privileged approach to God, who is he? Who are those who testify to such a God? Who are, where are, the others? And why, and how long ago did God withdraw from the act of carnal love?

9.

In so far as I am acquainted with him, Levinas has little taste for mysticism. What is the link between this lack of interest and his conception of sexual difference? In other words, is mysticism not linked to the flesh in its sexual dimension (*comme sexuée*)? But outside of mysticism, who is God? What is God? What is the point of flesh without mysticism? Is it to commit sacrileges, since the subjectivity of the other is not respected if the woman is reduced to animality, perversity, or a kind of pseudochildhood? To exploit the woman as reproducer, depriving her of her desire as a virgin-daughter or as a woman? To expend like an animal—or worse?—an excess of energy that men have? No longer even art. It is forbidden or impossible. So the caress sinks into despair, the fall, for Levinas too.

He certainly aspires to something else and to the Other (*Autrui*). But the other, woman, he does not notice her existence. And what other or Other (*Autre*) is possible outside of this realization? Except for that or those which are substituted by authority.

10.

That brings me to my last question. What radical difference distinguishes the God who makes his presence known in the law from the one who gives himself, through his presence, as nourishment, including nourishment of the senses? How does it come about that the God of the writing of the law cannot be looked upon? What relation in particular is established between nonfigurative writing and this God? For God, in this period of theophany, does not share, he dictates (*il impose*). He separates himself, when he gives Moses the inscription of the law, an inscription which is not immediately legible. He no longer provides anything to be eaten or grasped by the senses. He imposes forms on a nation of men as he might have given forms to a man's body. But the man's body remains a visible creation, while the law, in a sense, does not. The law creates invisibility, so that God (in his glory?) cannot be looked upon. What happens to seeing, to flesh, in this disappearance of God? Where can one's eye alight if the divine is no longer to be seen? And if it does not continue to dwell in the flesh of the other in order to illuminate it, to offer up to the look the other's flesh as divine, as the locus of a divine to be shared? For this exchange, do not figurative writing and art represent necessary articulations? In particular to harmonize listening and seeing.

Why, at this period of the covenant, does God suspend the link between the two most spiritual of the senses, thereby depriving men of the carnal representation of the covenant? Is this not a gesture that breaks with the more feminine cultures? The Song of Solomon harks back to the break and evokes the painful separation between she who wants to be initiated in her mother's chamber, he who awakes her beneath the tree, the apple tree where her mother is said to have conceived her, and that which takes them into a banqueting house, the chamber or the armies of the king. The two lovers are separated. The nations of women and of men are also divided; they no longer occupy the same places, they are no longer faithful to the same genealogy, or to the same tradition. But the Song of Solomon bears the trace of the woman as lover (*l'amante*), for it says, and repeats: "do not awaken (my) love until *she* please."[9] She, the lover, remains a subject in the act of love.

Translator's Notes

1. TA 79; TO 87. Richard Cohen translates this phrase as "a mode of being that consists in slipping away from the light." *Se dérober* can be translated both as "shun" and as "slip away"; it does not exclude either meaning.

2. "Pleasure" translates *volupté* except where otherwise stated. Other translators prefer to use "voluptuousness" or "voluptuosity."

3. In *Éthique de la différence sexuelle*, Paris, Minuit, 1984, 173–99; "The Fecundity of the Caress," trans. Carolyn Burke, in *Face to Face with Levinas*, ed. Richard A. Cohen, Albany, State University of New York Press, 1985, 231–56.

4. Syntax imitates content here. Although the meaning seems to be fairly clear from the rest of the paragraph—a union/communion of two sexes, in a crossing of boundaries or exchange, in itself produces a third, a work, an ecstasy, a "child" which is not yet necessarily a physical child—the grammar of this sentence makes it difficult to disentangle. *Devenue* (become) agrees

with *transcendance* (transcendence), *chair* (flesh), *celle de l'autre* (that of the other), and possibly also *l'autre* (the other), so that it is difficult to know exactly what has become *nous en nous* (ourself in us). The fusion of syntax perhaps poetically echoes the fusion of bodies.

5. *Genre* can mean grammatical gender. It also means kind, sort, race (human race), species (animal), genre (literary or artistic). Irigaray uses it in "Femmes divines" (*Sexes et parentés*, Paris, Minuit, 1987, 67–85) in a discussion of Feuerbach's *Essence of Christianity* to mean "kind" as in "mankind," and to suggest that there should be "womankind" too.

6. *Les nourritures terrestres* is the title of a well-known book by André Gide, first published in 1897. Its English title is *The Fruits of the Earth*. (Cohen translates this phrase as "morality of 'earthly nourishments.'")

7. *Aimée*, "beloved," is a past participle in French as well.

8. In French, because of grammatical gender, the masculine subsumes the feminine, so that, for example, to refer to a group of men and women, the masculine plural, *ils*, is used, even if there is only one man and a hundred women. The feminine plural, *elles*, is only used where the reference is exclusively female. There is no neutral plural corresponding to *they*. I think this is what Irigaray means by her reference to absence of hierarchy in English. (In the singular, of course, there is the now much-contested generic "he.")

9. The Song of Solomon, 2:7, 3:5, and 8:4. In French: "ne réveillez pas l'amour avant qu'elle le veuille." In the King James Bible, the translation is quite different; it reads: "nor awake my love, till he please." The New English Bible gives: "Do not rouse her, do not disturb my love until she is ready [or: while she is resting]." This paragraph needs to be related back to the first question; the two lovers are "born of different mothers"—on the one side, the feminine cultures represented by the mother's chamber and the apple tree, on the other side, the patriarchal culture linked to the king.

CHAPTER
7

ETHICS AND THE FEMININE
Catherine Chalier

One major characteristic of Levinas's philosophy is his criticism of the priority of ontology. He wants to think "otherwise than being," that is to say he wants to free a space of transcendence which will enable us to understand the meaning of the word "ethics."

I shall explain three things. First, how Levinas puts into question the virility of being and how he analyzes its conversion into the gentleness of a being that is for the Other, whereby natural life turns into ethical life. We shall see how the feminine plays a leading part in this process. Second, how maternity can be understood as the excellence of responsibility and, above all, of substitution. I shall have to explain the meaning of these concepts for Levinas before dealing with maternity proper. Third, how it is possible to think of the feminine, beyond maternity, as a disruption of being by goodness. In this part I shall deal with an excerpt from the Bible.

HOW LEVINAS CALLS INTO QUESTION THE VIRILITY OF BEING

this still natural tension of being on itself that we above called egoism, which is not a bad failing of the subject but its ontology, and that we find in the sixth proposition in the third part of Spinoza's *Ethics*: "each being strives as much as he can to persevere in his own being"[1]

To overcome an alienation which, fundamentally, arises from the very virility of the universal and conquering *logos*, and which stalks even the shadows that could have sheltered it—such would be the ontological function of the feminine, the vocation of her "who does not conquer."[2]

Levinas's criticism of the *conatus*

If we agree with Levinas's analysis of the *conatus*, that is to say, of the endeavor that each being makes to persevere in his own being, we must also accept that it issues in a dramatic and violent view of reality, a view in which ethics is subordinated to the traditional priority of ontology. What does this mean?

If we accept the preeminence of the task of being, if we think it is the meaning of the dynamism animating essences, we are prone to think that egoism is the unavoidable fate of the one who must at any rate persevere in his being, that it is this which determines an essence "inevitably jealous for its perseverance,"[3] and thus in conflict with others. Such is life in the forest, according to Vassili Grossman:

> Once when I lived in the Northern Forests, I thought that good was to be found neither in man, nor in the predatory world of animals and insects, but in the silent kingdom of the trees. Far from it! I saw the forest's slow movement, the treacherous way it battled against the grass and bushes for each inch of soil. . . . First, billions of seeds fly through the air and begin to sprout, destroying the grass and bushes. Then millions of victorious shoots wage war against one another. And it is only the survivors who enter into an alliance of equals to form the seamless canopy of the young deciduous forest. Beneath the canopy the spruces and beeches freeze to death in the twilight of penal servitude. In time the deciduous trees become decrepit; then the heavyweight spruces burst through to the light beneath their canopy, executing the alders and the beeches. This is the life of the forest—a constant struggle of everything against everything. Only the blind conceive of the kingdom of trees and grass as the world of good. . . . Is it that life itself is evil?"[4]

In the same way, if the perseverance in my being and the desire to enforce it and to increase it charms me and is my only worry, everything must accept an inferior position to this perseverance; nothing seems able to call it into question.

Thus we are prone to think that we have to go beyond death that befalls us in spite of everything and that we must not bother about the lot of those it strikes. Does not popular wisdom say that life must go on, that it "has" to go on and persevere on the way of its life? Does this wisdom not try to persuade the one who is affected by misfortune that time, after all, mends everything, that is to say, sets everything right in the order of being and of its positivity? This order does not admit tears, it does not mix with yearning and scruples, it clings to a blameless and reproachless doggedness. As if, from the point of view of being, every one had to go on his own way, indifferent, happy, and bumptious. And it is true that one has to be deaf to the suffering of others (and perhaps also to one's own suffering) if persistence in one's being is the highest value, if it is "at any price" and if the phrase "such is life" is the only wisdom that we can think to offer the oppressed.

However, the persistence in one's being is not restful. There is no question of settling peacefully and serenely in some haven, remote from the uproar of the crowds, since one must constantly fight against what threatens one's being: one's own death. "The dialectic of being and nothingness within essence is an anxiety over nothingness and struggle for existence."[5]

It is a struggle to persevere in one's being and thus scrupulously to keep away the obstacles of nature and society and also to brush aside all that connotes death in itself. It is a struggle to increase and fulfill one's being at the price of the negation of its present representations and the ceaseless overstepping of its present limits.

There is another necessity in this way of thinking: the present is subordinate to future years, years that will be richer and more total than the present ones. This is the way of thinking of those who subordinate the burden of evil and suffering to the necessity of becoming. They think that evil and suffering are but deplorable steps toward becoming, steps that are inherent to its fulfillment. Thus according to Hegel, those who are aware of what time demands, the great men, are led to crush "many an innocent flower and destroy much that lies in the way."[6] But we do not have to blame them since the private individual and his suffering must pay their debt so that Essence can be fulfilled.

The ideal that is implied in this thought must be conceived on the model of being and its self-sufficiency. It is necessary to struggle "for a better being, for a harmony between ourselves and the world or for the improvement of our own being. Ontologism's ideal of peace and balance presupposes the sufficiency of being."[7]

This sufficiency is "only conceived in the image of *being*, such as it is offered to us by things. They *are*. . . . This reference to oneself is exactly what is said when one speaks of the identity of being."[8] Such is, according to Hegel, "the burning zeal" of essence that works for its own fulfillment. And on this view evil is only a limit in being.

Now this invincible persistence of essence, of this "strength that goes on," that goes past any gap of nothingness that might interrupt it, pleads for a being that no value can transcend and judge, and Levinas writes that we must find in this strength "the very virility of the universal and conquering logos." He writes:

> Grain and flax are taken from nature by the work of man. They testify to the break with spontaneous life, to the ending of instinctive life buried in the immediacy of nature, the given. They mark the beginning of what one can accurately call the life of the mind. Nevertheless, an insurmountable crudeness is left in the products of our conquering civilization. The world in which reason becomes more and more self-conscious is uninhabitable. It is hard and cold like those warehouses where the merchandise which cannot satisfy: while there it neither clothes those who are naked nor feeds those who are hungry; it is impersonal, like the factory hangars and industrial cities where the manufactured goods remain abstract—true with the truth of calculation and brought into the anonymous realm of the economy that proceeds according to knowledgeable plans which cannot prevent though they

can prepare disasters. There it is—spirit in its masculine essence. It *lives outside*, exposed to the fiery sun that blinds, to the winds of the open sea which beat it and blow it down—on an earth without inner recesses, removed from its homeland, solitary and wandering, and even as such alienated by the products that it has created which rise up untamed and hostile.[9]

The ontological function of the feminine

Let us continue our reading:

> Woman does not come to someone deprived of companionship simply to keep him company. She answers to a solitude interior to this privation and, which is stranger, to a solitude which subsists in spite of the presence of God— to a solitude in the universal, to the inhuman which wells up again and again when the human has mastered nature and has raised it to thought. So that the inevitable uprooting of thought, which dominates the world, be reconciled with peace and quiet by returning home, into the geometry of infinite and cold space must enter the strange failure of sweetness. Its name is woman. The return to oneself, this introversion, this appearance of *place* in space, does not result, as in Heidegger, from a builder's labour, from an architecture which shapes the countryside, but from the interiority of the Home—the reverse of which would be "any place," without the essential moderation of feminine existence living there, which is habitation itself. She makes the grain into bread, the flax into clothing. The wife, the betrothed, is not the coming together in a human being of all the perfections of tenderness and goodness which could have subsisted without her; everything indicates that woman is the original manifestation of these perfections, kindness itself, the origin of all kindness on earth.[10]

Thus to welcome someone in one's dwelling is a feminine characteristic even if there is in fact no human being of the feminine sex. Without this ontological characteristic of the feminine it would be impossible for the *conatus*, for its virile persistence in being, for its permanent self-satisfaction, for its self-conceit, and for its claims to be reasonable, to turn into this being for the Other where ethics begins. The feminine is thought of as what puts into question the easy conscience of this rationality of self-conceit. Let us see how.

Levinas describes the feminine as what is required in order to commune with oneself and to be capable of an ethical act. The feminine as the cardinal point of interiority, as the dwelling, as the silent language, aids the dissipation of the virile and helps find its way toward the unity of a silent interior life. The feminine compels the conquering and virile attitude to stop and to start thinking. It stops the project of being, a project that is deaf and blind to all that does not belong to the strength that persists. She who welcomes in her dwelling helps to find the way of interiority that stops this blind strength. "The woman is the condition for recollection, the interiority of the Home and habitation."[11] Levinas writes: "And the Other whose presence is discreetly an absence, with which is accomplished the primary hospitable welcome which describes the field of intimacy, is the Woman."[12]

SPECIAL
SAVINGS OFFER!

BUSINESS REPLY MAIL

FIRST-CLASS MAIL   PERMIT NO. 365   BOULDER, CO

POSTAGE WILL BE PAID BY ADDRESSEE

Details

PO BOX 50264
BOULDER CO 80323-0264

So the feminine—but here he writes "the woman"—is necessary for the intimacy of recollection. As if this "haven" was absolutely necessary in view of a greater attention to oneself that turns into a greater attention to the Other, in view of a conversion: from the hardness of the being which is for himself to the gentleness of the being which is for the Other; from ontology to ethics.

In its virile essence, spirit stands for an absolutely alienating category of being. It gives birth to a wandering which forbids the care of the Other. The masculine creates different kinds of works but it does not know how to defend them. Its works are mute and left to those who will take possession of them. A work that is produced by a masculine spirit can never succeed. Moreover, spirit, in its virile essence, is so much absorbed by its own work and so much dimmed by itself that it never has time to look after the Other.

The feminine has to help it go beyond this alienation. Since the feminine function is not to create, it cannot be wrapped into its works. It has to give birth to "a place" in space that will allow man to learn how to turn his natural way of living into ethics. Without this silent presence, this discreet and almost evanescent presence of the feminine, the world would be doomed to a rough and spontaneous life, the life of "the strength that persists." Without the feminine, wheat would not be ground, flax would not be woven, the world would be uninhabitable, and an ethical life would be impossible. Thus the silent voice of the one who welcomes, the dimension of interiority that begins with her intimate familiarity, are both an ontological category and an ethical paradigm. It saves the human being.

However, the feminine welcome is but a condition of ethics. Intimacy and gentleness do not comprehend *height* which is, according to Levinas, the only authentic ethical dimension. It means that the feminine (and he often says "the woman") would be excluded from the highest destiny of human being. This highest destiny would be reserved for the masculine once it has been converted to ethics thanks to the feminine.

THE FAILURE OF BEING OR THE OPENING TO THE OTHER

Responsibility

According to Levinas, the struggle to get "a place under the sun" does not constitute a right in itself. It does not give any meaning or justification to life; on the contrary, it gives birth to injustice and violence. The human being —if it wants to be really human—cannot be rooted to a place, even if this place is a dwelling, and he writes on its door: "do not disturb". In Genesis 7:16, after the description of Noah's ark, we can read: "and the Lord shut him in," which is very remarkable, according to Levinas, because it means that Noah could not shut the door himself, could not be happy to be safe while the world was being destroyed. And we know that it is still being destroyed.

Responsibility is not a choice but a calling. Contrary to a philosophical tradition, Levinas thinks that there is "an antecedence of responsibility to freedom" and he goes so far as to say that this antecedence "would signify the Goodness of the Good."[13] This kind of responsibility has nothing to do with the pride of the masculine that realizes its own responsibility, but it has much in common with humility. Responsibility is a calling. Man is responsible over and beyond his freedom. He has always been responsible and he cannot remember when this responsibility started, as it has always been there.

Moreover, Levinas does not say that man is responsible before the others for himself and his doings, he says that he has been responsible since time immemorial for the Other, for the neighbor. Man has to care for his neighbor and the universe before looking after himself, which is contrary to the virility of being. He is responsible for the neighbor's destiny, for the neighbor's suffering. He is so much responsible that, in front of the Other, he can in no way be innocent.

This responsibility, this promptness to say "Here I am" (as Abraham did in Genesis 22:1, 7, and 11) to the Other without taking time to inquire about his reasons, is the very humanity of being. "No one can save himself without the Others":[14] it is not possible since the flood threatens and since the neighbor is always suffering and always disturbs my quietness, and even my own grief. This responsibility is infinite. It is because it is not dependent on my freedom that it is infinite. "Man is stitched with responsibility":[15] he cannot rest and think only of himself.

Responsibility as a calling is a well-known idea of those who are familiar with the Bible and the Talmud. Thus we can read in the Talmud: "We are all responsible for each other" (*Sanhedrin* 27b). It is said in the Talmud that the one who does not oppose evil will have to answer for it: "Anyone who is able to take a stand against the faults of the people living with him and does not do it, is responsible in their place. It will also be the case if these people are his neighbours or even people who are living wherever on the earth: he will have to answer for them if he does not interfere when they are doing wrong. Rav Papa says that the Princes of exile are responsible for the faults of the whole world" (*Chabbat* 55a). And Levinas says that he understands "responsibility for what is not my deed, or what does not even matter to me." He adds that "the I always has one responsibility more than all the others."[16]

No one can take refuge in the privacy of his easy conscience when facing evil. No one can save himself who is a member of the alliance of responsibility (*brit achariout*), who is linked to this alliance from an anarchic past and a "pre-originary susceptiveness."[17] This assignation does not give any rights; on the contrary, it gives an excess of duties, and this excess of duties enables one to know one's uniqueness: "The uniqueness of the responsible ego is possible only in being obsessed by another."[18] Such is the end of the virile ego who was so proud of himself and thus begins humanity in the service of the Other. It means that each has to tear himself apart from his interest in his own being in order to serve the Other. But this service is the true homeland of human being, a homeland that has nothing to do with becoming rooted or with being the first owner. It has to do with this "move towards the Other" which, according to Levinas, is of "Jewish essence."[19]

Substitution

Substitution fulfills responsibility. Levinas describes its structure as "a passivity inconvertible into an act," which means "to bear the wretchedness and bankruptcy of the Other, and even the responsibility that the Other can have for me," and above all to bear them without any free choice, to be bound to bear them. He writes that it is a "'religiosity of the self' which is beyond egoism and altruism."[20]

Substitution means that a human being encounters the meaning of *kenosis*: "The feat, for the being, of de-taching itself, of emptying itself of its being, of placing itself 'back to front,' and, if it can be put thus, the feat of 'otherwise than being.'"[21] That is to say, the exact contrary of the natural perseverance in one's being, the exact opposite of the *conatus*. Substitution means to support the weight of the world, the weight of the non-ego, to be bound to bear this weight without free choice. It has nothing to do with altruism, since it does not refer to freedom. This generosity is the very structure of the self, a structure which is a preoriginary susceptiveness, without any free commitment. Goodness of substitution is not the contrary of evil but the fact of the "otherwise than being" which describes the straightforwardness of the ethical finality of a subject.

This condition of being "a hostage" that does not rest on any free commitment goes so far as to command me "to give to the Other by taking the bread out of my own mouth, and making a gift of my own skin." It means "a denuding, an exposure to being affected, a pure susceptiveness."[22] Thus we have to understand the meaning of a self that is "for the Other."

In his more recent works Levinas proposes a new way of approaching this question when he speaks of the preeminence of the question of the right to be, a question that is much more basic than the ontological one. Substitution is linked to "the fear of all the violence and death that my being, in spite of its guiltless and conscious purpose, can bring about."[23] This fear strikes the self facing the Other. It does not mean that this self is any way "neurotic," it is the very straightforwardness of signification. This fear means that the self is aware of his election: no one can be substituted for the one that has to substitute for others—at least it is his vocation—"as if the whole weight of the creation rested on my shoulders."[24] That is the very meaning of the word election.

Levinas quotes Isaiah 53:4: "Surely he hath borne our griefs, and carried our sorrows: yet we did esteem him stricken, smitten of God, and afflicted." This "he" is a messianic figure. We know that in Judaism Menahem (the comforter) is one of the names of the Messiah. But Levinas adds that everyone has to behave as if he was the Messiah: "Messianism does not mean, to be sure, that someone will come who will put a stop to history. It is my power to support the suffering of the others. It is the moment when I recognise this power and my universal responsibility."[25]

Thus we can understand the link between the biblical ideas of Messianism and the strict concept of substitution. It is not a description of a mere fact but it is "the condition of all solidarity."[26] Without the condition of being hostage there can be no pity, no compassion, and no pardon. Moreover, it is the occurrence of a truly good act springing from this incomprehensible disinterestedness that can restore hope and support the whole world even during the darkest time. We can understand this idea when reading Etty Hillesum, a young Jewish woman living in Amsterdam during the *Shoah* and who was to die in Auschwitz: "Our teachers are in prison, a friend of Jan had just died under the blows, there were so many reasons for grief, but we were saying: it is too easy, this desire for revenge. This is the gleam of hope on this day." "Now there is nothing else to do but to give the Other all the goodness that is in ourselves." "It is a hard day, a very hard day. We have to learn how to support the weight of the 'fate of a multitude' with the others and we have to eliminate all the private trifles. Each one endeavours to save himself but he knows very well that, if he escapes, someone else will have to fill his place." "One would like to be balm shed on so many wounds."[27]

Maternity as the very pattern of substitution

We have just seen that subjectivity is not conscious of itself, but is "the reverting of the ego into a self, the de-posing or de-situating of the ego" which is "the very modality of disinterestedness."[28] Now the maternal body as "integral for the Other," with its anxiety for the one it protects, gives us the full meaning of subjectivity.

Levinas describes the maternal body as "a pre-original not resting on oneself,"[29] as a body of goodness that is devoted to the Other before being devoted to itself. In this unselfish and maternal body, subjectivity loses all the substantiality and identity that would already be acquired. As a subjectivity without substitute, the maternal body has to answer for the Other and is irreplaceable in this task. The maternal body suffers for the Other, it is "the body as passivity and renunciation, a pure undergoing."[30] It is the very contrary of the *conatus*. It is "signification for the Other and not for itself."[31] In spite of me, for the other.

As the maternal body answers for the Other and makes room for him or her inside itself, it is evicted from its harbor and disturbed so far as to be out of breath, and this is precisely the signification of subjectivity. It is the ethical signification of the maternal saying. The "pre-original not resting on oneself" of the maternal body entails anxiety and listening but it lacks free choice. It is the time of an inalienable mercy for the Other, an infinite patience when facing an election that gives birth to the self in the very moment that it interrupts its essence.

The maternal body is ruled by the Good beyond being; it has not chosen the Good but the Good has elected it. It is a passive body, a body that is a hostage since it is evicted from its own being. "Is not the restlessness of someone persecuted but a modification of maternity, the groaning of the wounded entrails by those it will bear or has borne?"[32]

Thus it seems that maternity is the ultimate meaning of the feminine, the very metaphor of subjectivity and, of course, not only a metaphor. We have to encounter this failure in the virility of being in order to understand the meaning of Other. The maternal body knows in its flesh and blood what subjectivity means. But we have to take note of the fact that, according to Levinas, ethics in its feminine achievement means to be a mother and nothing else. Can we agree?

THE FEMININE AND THE DISRUPTION OF BEING BY GOODNESS

A biblical figure of the feminine: Rebecca (Genesis 24)

Eliezer, Abraham's servant, has to find a young woman that will please Isaac and he chooses the *mitsva* (duty) of hospitality as a criterion by which to recognize her. The young woman will have to say "Let down thy pitcher, I pray thee." And she will say, "Drink, and I will give thy camels drink also" (Gen. 24:14). This criterion means that Eliezer cares less about the class of the young woman than about her feeling for the Other, her ability to perceive the Other's demand as a demand that is meant for her. Such is the ethical service in which one learns that the Other has a primacy over one so that natural egoism turns into the "Here I am" which is eponymous of concern to stay inside the covenant.

Rebecca is chosen because of her responsibility for this stranger, for this thirsty man who was begging her to give him water, and above all because of her responsibility for the thirsty animals that could not even ask for water. It is as if the highest expression of devotion was to feed the neighbor and to give water to him. Rebecca's election is that of a young Aramean lady who is not yet aware of the One God, an election that is founded upon her ability to give, on her feeling of duty toward the neighbor. To be able to greet and to give, to find love beyond profit, without caring how it will turn out, is what is most important according to Eliezer. The one who acts in this way will be able to be in the covenant.

She gives proof of her responsibility for the Other who, in spite of all his wealth, is but a stranger. "My position as *I* consists in being able to respond to the essential destitution of the Other, finding resources for myself. The Other who dominates me in his transendence is thus the stranger, the widow and the orphan to whom I am obligated."[33]

Rebecca is aware of the helplessness of the face of the Other in spite of all the gifts he brings. She is aware that she is the one that can help him even if it is at the cost of her own freedom and spontaneity. Such is the excellence of ethics, of the "for the Other" which characterizes the covenant.

She leaves her family, she does not want to linger a few more days, nor does she want to ask to be granted leave, according to Rachi. One does not have to be granted leave when one has to go toward the one that is waiting. And no one can replace her. She does not hesitate to go and meet the one who will free her from the weight of an identity that was but a heritage and who will show her the way to a new identity: the identity of utopia, the identity for the Other. But an identity without security and without guarantee. Such is the feminine as the disruption of being by goodness beyond maternity.

Conclusion

If there is a universal mission to interrupt the self-satisfaction of those beings who think that they are self-sufficient and reasonable, and who think that they do not have to wonder about their right to be; if there is a universal mission to put an end to this everlasting oversight of the Other, in his or her suffering and death, an oversight that helps one go on unconcerned and serene; if we have to shake the easy conscience of the beings who persevere in their being, in order to see peace occur, a peace that will be a life for the others, a peace that will be as concernful as love; then we have to understand the meaning of this disruption of being by goodness. Is this not the meaning of the feminine in the human being?[34]

Notes

1. Emmanuel Levinas, NP 104.
2. Emmanuel Levinas, DL 53; trans. E. Wyschogrod, "Judaism and the Feminine Element," *Judaism*, 18, no. 1, 1969: 33.
3. Emmanuel Levinas, AE 233; OB 185.
4. Vasily Grossman, *Life and Fate*, trans. Robert Chandler, London, Fontana, 1986, 407.
5. AE 222; OB 176.
6. G. W. F. Hegel, *Vorlesungen über die Philosophie der Weltgeschichte, vol. 1, Die Vernunft in der Geschichte*, ed. J. Hoffmeister, Hamburg, Felix Meiner, 1955, 105; trans. H. Nisbett, *Lectures on the Philosophy of World History*, Cambridge, Cambridge University Press, 1975, 89.
7. Emmanuel Levinas, *De l'évasion*, Montpellier, Fata Morgana, 1982, 69.
8. Ibid., 68–69.
9. DL 53; trans. "Judaism and the Feminine Element," 33.
10. DL 54; trans. "Judaism and the Feminine Element," 33.
11. Emmanuel Levinas, TeI 128; TI 155.
12. Ibid.
13. AE 157; OB 122.
14. Emmanuel Levinas, HH 97; CP 149.
15. HH 98; CP 149.
16. Emmanuel Levinas, EeI 101–2, 105; EI 95, 99.
17. AE 157; OB 122.
18. AE 158; OB 123.

19. NP 64.

20. AE 150; OB 117.

21. AE 149; OB 117.

22. AE 176; OB 138.

23. Emmanuel Levinas, DVI 262.

24. HH 50; CP 97.

25. DL 120.

26. AE 150; OB 117.

27. Etty Hillesum, *Une vie bouleversée*, Journal 1941–1943, Paris, Seuil, 1985, 103, 150, 159, and 229.

28. AE 65; OB 50.

29. AE 95; OB 75.

30. AE 100; OB 79.

31. AE 100; OB 80.

32. AE 95; OB 75.

33. TeI 190; TI 215.

34. I would like to thank Mrs. Josiane Sourlas for her generous help in reviewing my translation.

CHAPTER

8

ANTIGONE'S DILEMMA
Tina Chanter

I begin this article by introducing the question of woman in Derrida's work, and then move on to Levinas's treatment of femininity. A third area of discussion focuses upon Sophocles's *Antigone*, which I use to introduce some of the issues in current feminist thought, to which the final pages are devoted. By bringing to bear some of the considerations raised by the work of Derrida and Levinas, I hope to counter the argument that any attempt to affirm feminine specificity implicates feminists in essentialism.

During a seminar held at the University of Warwick, in the presence of Julia Kristeva, in which her essay "Women's Time" was being discussed, the following question was posed: "Is Jacques Derrida a feminist?"[1] Even though Derrida has as good as given the answer, it is still a significant question.[2] In an interview, Derrida answers a question which refers to his book on Heidegger's reading of Nietzsche, *Spurs*.[3] The questioner, a woman, asks Derrida, "If the question of sexual difference is not a regional one (in the sense of subsidiary [to ontology and truth]), if indeed 'it may no longer even be a question' as you [Derrida] suggest, how would you describe 'woman's place'?" (C 66) Before Derrida answers, he allows himself to digress, making a detour which is not insignificant for the issue of Levinas's writing of woman. Derrida says "Perhaps woman does not have a history" (C 68). She does not have a history, he is suggesting, in the sense that she can step back from history, history understood as "continuous progress." Perhaps there is, says Derrida, "a completely other history: a history of paradoxical laws and non-dialectical discontinuities, a history of absolutely heterogeneous pockets, irreducible particularities, of unheard of and incalculable sexual differences." The history Derrida invokes is not unlike that rhythmic cyclical time that Kristeva has described as women's time, the Nietzschean monumental time which subverts the idea of linear progressive history.[4] This discontinuous time also has affinities with the rupture of totality that Levinas's infinite effects.

But to come to Derrida's answer to the question about woman's place, which he reformulates as "Why must there be a place for woman? And why only one, a single essential place?" Derrida goes on: "This is a question that you could translate ironically by saying that in my view *there is no one place for woman* . . . it is without a doubt risky to say that there is no place for woman, but this idea is not anti-feminist, far from it; true, it is not feminist either" (C 68).

So, at least according to Derrida, his question is not a feminist one. I said that even though we know the answer, the question "Is Jacques Derrida a feminist?" is still significant. It is significant because the answer "No" is given within a discourse which does not confine itself to continuous history, is not contained within the time of the line, but moves between that linear history, and into an affirmation that there is another time, women's time.

The significance of the question "Is Jacques Derrida a feminist?" lies not so much in whether his own answer to the question is yes or no, but in the fact that it was a man who posed this question, and that the question is a different one, depending upon who asks the question and who hears it. Depending not only on whether the questioner is a man or whether the respondent is a woman, but also whether, if the questioner is a man, he asks the question as a man, and if the respondent is a woman, she answers as a woman. That is, whether the man asks the question from his own time, the time of history as progress, and whether the woman answers from her own time, a time which cuts across that history.

On this particular occasion of which I am speaking, the man who asked the question "Is Jacques Derrida a feminist?" like Derrida's interviewer, had been reading *Spurs*, and a discussion took place as to what it means for a man to want to write like a woman.[5] Whatever it means for a man to want to write like a woman differs significantly from what it means for a woman to want to write as a woman. I would want to insist on this. One might say that the question of woman, the woman-question, is one which would have to be addressed before one could begin to answer the question about what it means for a woman to want to write as a woman. But if, as Derrida has written, "there is no such thing" as "an essence of *the* woman or the sexual difference" in the same way that "there is also no such thing as an essence of the *es gibt* in the *es gibt Sein*, that is, of Being's giving and gift" (S 120/ 121) is it impossible to raise the question of woman? If there is no history of woman, in the sense of history as continuous progress, perhaps, after all, the writing of woman would have to be questioned before woman can be questioned. Perhaps this writing would provide a way of raising an impossible question. If there is no woman as such (S 100,101) perhaps the writing of woman is precisely the place to look for her, precisely where the question of woman raises itself, because, as Derrida has written in *Spurs*, "It is impossible to dissociate the questions of art, style and truth from the question of the woman" (S 70,71). The question would raise itself in different ways depending on whether it is a man's text or a woman's text.

Derrida begins his essay "En ce moment même dans cet ouvrage me voici" with the words "He will have obligated."[6] It becomes more or less clear, as he writes, that these words refer to Emmanuel Levinas. But on the last page of his essay Derrida asks the question: "If feminine difference presealed, perhaps and nearly illegibly, his work, if she became, in the depths of the same, the other of his other, will I then have deformed his name, to him, in writing, at this moment, in this work, here indeed, 'she will have obligated'?" (EM 59; AM). Within what movement does this shift from "he" to "she" take place? How is woman written into Derrida's text on Levinas? Derrida quotes a sentence which Levinas "will have written" as Derrida says "twice, in appearance literally identical." The sentence is this: "Work thought to the end requires a radical generosity of movement in which the Same goes toward the Other. Consequently, it requires an *ingratitude* from the other" (EM 24; AM). Must women, one might ask, be ungrateful for being written into Derrida's text? A few pages later Derrida announces:

> It is by starting from the Other that writing thus gives a place and forms an event, for example, this one: *Il aura obligé*. It is that response, the responsibility of that response, that I would like to interrogate in its turn. Interrogate, to be sure, is not the word, and I don't yet know how to qualify what is happening here between him, you and me, that doesn't belong to the order of questions and responses. It would rather be his responsibility—and what he says of responsibility—that interrogates us beyond all coded discourses on the subject.
>   Hence: what is he doing, how does he work (*oeuvre*) when, under the false appearance of a present, in a more-than-present (*plus-que-parfait*), he will have written this for example, which I slowly read to you, at this very moment, listen. (EM 28; AM)

What follows is a long passage which includes a reference, acknowledged by Levinas in a footnote, to a phrase in The Song of Songs, the phrase "I am sick with love."[7] Derrida comments that not only is this phrase, "translated and quoted (in a footnote, so as to open up and deport the principal text)" but that "it is torn from the mouth of a woman, so as to be given to the other" (EM 30; AM). "Why," asks Derrida, "doesn't he [Levinas] clarify that in this work?" The answer Derrida gives to his own question will be taken up later in the same text and, despite the strength of his conviction at the moment he says it, it will be put into question. The reason Levinas does not make clear that the phrase is torn from the mouth of a woman is, says Derrida, at this moment in his text "doubtless because that remains in this context, and with regard to his most urgent purpose, secondary." We are forewarned that Derrida might have to take back his words when he adds, on a cautionary note, "Here, at least, he doesn't seem to answer that question." The question has been raised—woman's place from this point on in the essay remains questionable. Is the feminine secondary for Levinas, or is it absolutely other, and as such primary? Eliding several questions into one we could rush ahead and ask is the feminine relation one of absolute transcendence or does it ultimately involve a return to the self?

Although Levinas insists on the secondariness of the feminine, Derrida also finds the opposite affirmation in Levinas's text. In Derrida's words, "The feminine is also described [in his text] as a figure of the wholly other." And with this, continues Derrida, "we have recognized that this work is one of the first and rare ones, in the history of philosophy to which it does not simply belong, not to feign effacing the sexual mark of his signature: hence, he would be the last one surprised by the fact that the other (of the whole system of his saying of the other) happens to be a woman, commands him from that place" (EM 56).

The question of priority between the feminine and the Other in Levinas's work is indeed a difficult one, as is the question of the priority between the I and the Other in the face-to-face relation. Which comes first, the ethical relation or the feminine relation? The I of elemental enjoyment who is welcomed, or the other who welcomes? The I who, from his position, in the stance of an instant, is commanded, or the Other whose eyes forbid his murder? Which relation, if one can put it thus, is more transcendent, the feminine or the Other? The question is not simple, not least because of the multiple accounts of the feminine in Levinas's work. Levinas draws upon the feminine as *eros*, as fecundity, as voluptuosity, in the dwelling, as maternal. How are these separate accounts to be understood, and how do they relate to the ethical relation of the face-to-face? Is my ethical relation to the other preceded by femininity as the erotic relation, as the way of the tender?

One might want to explain Levinas's differing accounts of the feminine by showing how a preoccupation with the erotic relation in his early work gradually gives way to a concern with the ethical. Certainly this explanation would gather support from the fact that *eros* and the feminine are predominant in 1947 (in *Le temps et l'autre* and *Existence and Existents*), whereas *Totality and Infinity* (1961) seems to privilege the ethical relation.[8] One could even argue that the disappearance of the feminine, which is coupled in *Otherwise than Being* with an increasing interest in maternity, is symptomatic of this shift away from the erotic toward the ethical. But an examination of a fairly recent text by Levinas disrupts this hypothesis.

A new preface to the second edition of Levinas's *Le temps et l'autre* was written in 1977 (but not published until 1979), thirty years after Levinas first published the lectures delivered under that title. The preface postdates the publication of *Totality and Infinity* by sixteen years and *Otherwise than Being* by three years. Levinas tells us he has not amended the text of *Time and the Other*, despite reservations about what he claims to be its "abrupt and maladroit" style—or "non-style." He did not revise it because he still holds to the principal project of which it is "the birth and first formulation" (TA 7–8; TO 29–30). In his new preface Levinas chooses to highlight two fundamental points from his 1947 text. Both concern "the way in which the phenomenology of alterity and its transcendence" was attempted in 1947 (TA 14; TO 35). There is the transcendence of alterity which is sought first of all "starting with femininity," and there is the "structure of transcendence" which was glimpsed in *Time and the Other* "starting with paternity." The first way of transcendence, femininity, Levinas says "appeared to me as a difference" which cuts across all other differences, "not merely as a quality different from all others, but as the very quality of difference." Paternity, on the other hand, is the relation between father and son, a nonindifference, "a possibility that another assumes: through the son there occurs a possibility beyond the possible" (TA 14–15; TO 35–37).

The fact that Levinas sees the project he outlines in *Time and the Other* as consonant with his later work indicates that we can expect to find the analyses of the feminine and paternity presented in *Time and the Other* confirmed in *Totality and Infinity* and *Otherwise than Being*. But contradictions emerge between the earlier and later texts. Not only between earlier and later texts but even within the same texts, Levinas at times appears to affirm the priority of the ethical, and at other times the priority of the feminine. While in *Time and the Other* the transcendent, which, one assumes, includes the ethical, is seen as a mode of the feminine (TA 15; TO 36), and in *Existence and Existents* the feminine is said to be the other par excellence (DE 145; EE 85), the status of the erotic relation becomes ambiguous in *Totality and Infinity*. Levinas says there, "In love transcendence goes both further and less far than language" (TeI 232; TI 254). That is, it is both more and less transcendent than the face in the ethical relation. The ambiguity is compounded when, having read in the section "The Dwelling" that Martin Buber's I–Thou relation is a relation with feminine alterity (TeI 129; TI 155), one then reads in the section called "Phenomenology of Eros" that the movement of love does not share the structure of the I–Thou relation (TeI 238; TI 261 and TeI 242; TI 264).

Despite his claim that women do not have to be empirically present to ensure the presence of the feminine dimension (TeI 131; TI 158), it could be shown in a number of ways that Levinas's use of terms such as "femininity" and "maternity" is sexually specific. For example, he criticizes the Platonic conception of *eros*, which he says "completely fails to recognize the role of the feminine" (DE 145; EE 85). By singling out the feminine Levinas makes clear that he is concerned to wrest it from the oblivion to which it has been subjected, and to invest it with a positive significance. Levinas no more uses terms such as "paternity," "filiality," "fraternity," "virility," in a neutral way than he does the term "feminine." He consistently aligns virility with the language of mastery which dominates the other.

In *Le temps et l'autre*, Levinas specifies the meaning of passivity as the "end of virility," where "there is no longer hope" (TA 61; TO 73). Levinas is opposing the Heideggerian analysis of authentic Being-towards-death, which he calls "a supreme lucidity and hence a supreme virility." Death for Heidegger, Levinas stresses, is possibility par excellence. It "makes possible all other possibilities" and thus makes possible "the very feat of grasping a possibility" (TA 57; TO 70).

In contrast Levinas refers the passivity which is "more passive than any passivity," "the passivity of the for-the-other in vulnerability" to "maternity" (AE 89; OB 71). Suffering is the "passivity of patience" (AE 93; OB 73), as a past "prior to all memory and recall . . . an irrecuperable time" (AE 133; OB 104–5). In passivity, woman emerges in the guise of the mother. Levinas says

In maternity what signifies is a responsibility for others. . . . Maternity, which is a bearing par excellence, bears even responsibility for the persecuting by the persecutor.

Rather than a nature, earlier than nature, immediacy is this vulnerability, this maternity, this pre-birth or pre-nature in which sensibility belongs. This proximity is narrower, more constrictive, than contiguity, older than every past present. (AE 95; OB 75)

A passivity more passive than any passivity, the responsibility which is prior to any questioning of the I marks a third way between the distinction of activity and passivity. It is a way of admitting the excluded middle.[9] Another way is Levinas's recognition of the presence of woman as simultaneity of presence and absence, an alternation between meaning and meaninglessness, signification and nonsignification. Levinas associates *eros* with the innuendo of Shakespeare's witches, "an order where seriousness is totally lacking." Here, says Levinas, "the beloved is opposed to me not as a will struggling with my own or subject to my own, but on the contrary as an irresponsible animality which does not speak true words." But far from relegating the feminine to the realm of meaninglessness and insignificance, these descriptions already refer to the origin of meaning, already refer to the face. Already one step ahead of the straightforward expression of the face, the feminine dissimulates meaning. Levinas says, "Equivocation constitutes the epiphany of the feminine —at the same time interlocutor, collaborator and master superiorly intelligent, so often dominating men in the masculine civilization it has entered, and woman having to be treated as a woman, in accordance with rules imprescriptible by civil society" (TeI 241–42; TI 263–64).

Whether this last description is a reference to Antigone, or whether Levinas refers to the equivocal laughter of Shakespearean witches; whether he has in mind the "eternal irony of the community," or whether he has in mind Shakespearean tragedy, which latter he invokes more often to ridicule the order of kings—these questions suggest themselves but we do not find them resolved in Levinas's text. It is still less certain that the last portion of Derrida's essay, the part of the text set apart from the rest, capitalized and widely spaced, refers to *Antigone*.[10] But whether or not Antigone's presence can only be assured in *Glas*, Derrida's marginal text on Hegel, or whether it can be read into his essay on Levinas too, despite the absence of her name, she haunts those pages.[11] Antigone makes her mark as having been deprived of the experience of motherhood, an experience which serves to bring these considerations into the arena of current feminist debate.

Sophocles's *Antigone* has largely been interpreted as a play demonstrating the irresolvable and therefore tragic conflict between two domains, the divine law and the human law. In his discussion of *Antigone* Hegel says that *Sittlichkeit*, the ethical order, "splits itself up into distinct ethical substances, into a human and divine law."[12] It is often assumed that Hegel sees the divine law as embodied in the individual action of Antigone, and the human law as represented in the person of Creon, King of Thebes. Critics, including Castoriadis and Steiner, have pointed out, however, that Hegel does not simply identify the divine law with Antigone's action and the human law with Creon.[13] It is true that Antigone represents the divine law, which finds its concrete manifestation in the family, and that Creon represents the human law, that of the community, which, says Hegel "has its real vitality in the government" (PG 323; PS 272). But it is equally true that each law contains the other, in a negative way. Consciousness has reached the stage of Spirit, and, unlike Reason, it is "conscious of itself as its own world, and of the world as itself" (PG 313; PS 263). That is, "both laws have within them the moment of consciousness." Each law must encounter its opposite in the other law; each is negated by the other. We find that there is "connection and transition into one another" (PG 323; PS 272). In other words, in the ethical world consciousness knows itself, it is self-conscious, but since it also contains its own negation, Hegel says it "is on the one hand ignorant of what it does, and on the other knows what it does." Like all the stages on the way to Absolute Knowledge, "as a knowing" ethical consciousness is "a deceptive knowledge." "It learns through its own act the contradiction of those powers into which the substance divided itself and their mutual downfall, as well as the contradiction between *its* knowledge of the ethical character of its action, and what is in its own proper nature ethical, and thus finds its own downfall" (PG 317–18; PS 266). Both Antigone and Creon are destroyed by their steadfast duty to their own actions, and neither are in a position to understand fully their own ethical stance.

Just as the here and now of sense-certainty gives way to an object such as a grain of salt which combines the several qualities—being cubical, white, tart, and so on—Hegel says that "for ethical perception a given action is an actual situation with many ethical connections" (PG 318; PS 267). The individual act of Antigone is not only based upon the divine, it also reflects a political meaning in the sphere of human law. Similarly, while Creon's decree may be based on the political authority of the state, it is not divorced from the divine law. Let us look first at the way Antigone's act embodies the dual character of ethical life.

In his account of Antigone's burial of her brother, Hegel refers to the "community" as the negative aspect of her act. In paragraph 451, he is concerned with the status of the family as not merely "natural" but also "spiritual."[14] In the previous paragraph, after reiterating that the human reflects the divine law, and vice versa—"each of the opposites in which the ethical substance exists contains the entire substance, and all the moments of its contents"— Hegel points out the difference between the immediate existence of the family (its "unconscious existence") and its actual existence (its "self-conscious existence"). He goes on to say that it is not the *natural* existence of the family that confers upon it an ethical character. The ethical character which is peculiar to the family goes beyond its natural existence. Hegel expresses the point specifically in terms of the brother-sister relationship. He says that when the "brother leaves the family" and "the sister becomes or the wife remains the head of the household and the guardian of divine law" then "the two sexes overcome their (merely) natural being and appear in their ethical significance" (PG 327; PS 275). Although the natural relationship between brother and sister is overcome, the identity of the sexes remains fundamentally determined by nature. Hegel says, "Nature, not the accident of circumstances or choice, assigns one sex to one law, the other to the other law" (PG 332; PS 280). Hegel goes on to show that those activities which take place in the sphere of the family are also rooted outside of the immediate private home. The point of the family is to provide a supportive background from which (male) individuals can launch themselves into the public domain of the polis. Hegel says,

> The acquisition and maintenance of power and wealth is in part concerned only with needs and belongs to the sphere of appetite; in part, they become in their higher determination something that is only mediated. This determination does not fall within the Family itself, but bears on what is truly universal, the community; it has, rather, a negative relation to the Family, and consists in expelling the individual from the Family, subduing the natural aspect and separateness of his existence, and training him to be virtuous, to a life in and for the universal. The *positive* End peculiar to the Family is the individual as such. (PG 320; PS 269)

The true significance of the family, then, is its expulsion of the individual into the polis. The brother-sister relationship is at "the limit at which the self-contained life of the Family breaks up and goes beyond itself" (PG 327; PS 275).[15] The culmination of the life of virtue is the end of that life. Hegel tells us that the object of familial relations is lived beyond that natural, blood relationship.

> The deed . . . which embraces the entire existence of the blood-relation . . . has as its object and content this particular individual who belongs to the Family, but is taken as a *universal* being freed from the sensuous, i.e., individual reality. The deed no longer concerns the living but the dead, the individual who, after a long succession of separate disconnected experiences, concentrates himself into a single completed shape, and has raised himself out of the unrest of the accidents of life into the calm of simple universality. But because it is only as a citizen that he is actual and substantial, the individual, so far as he is not a citizen but belongs to the Family, is only an unreal impotent shadow. (PG 321; PS 270)

Just as death is pivotal to Antigone's enactment of the divine Law, so death is the power on which Creon, as principal of the governing order, depends in order to maintain his position as head of state. In Antigone's deed of burying her brother we find the "perfect" accomplishment of divine law, a perfection which nevertheless has recourse to its opposite, i.e., the law of the community. As we have just seen, by taking upon herself her brother's death, "The Family" —in the shape of Antigone—"thereby makes him a member of the community," says Hegel. If the law of the community intervenes in the divine law exemplified in Antigone's act, it is the divine law that cements Creon's control of the state. Hegel explains that Government allows the family to flourish, giving each member "an enduring being-for-self of its own." "But" he goes on, "Spirit is at the same time the power of the whole, which brings these parts together again into a negative unity, giving them the feeling of their lack of independence, and keeping them aware that they have their life only in the whole." The state thus tolerates "special and independent associations" within its governance, but it achieves ultimate recognition of its own power by confronting its citizens with their need for the protection of the state. This is effected through the fear of death. Hegel says, "Government has from time to time to shake them to their core by war." Thus, through war, those who have become isolated from the state and caught up in pursuing their own private ends "are made to feel in the task laid on them their lord and master, death" (PG 324; PS 272–73).

The reason I have spent some time rehearsing the account Hegel provides of the divine and human law is because their interdependence, which is commonly overlooked, has crucial significance for Hegel's reflections on the role of Antigone. It is easy to conclude that Hegel elevates Creon over Antigone. If one takes as the key Hegel's assertion in paragraph 470, this conclusion seems unavoidable. There Hegel says, "The ethical consciousness is more complete, its guilt more inexcusable, if it knows *beforehand* the law and the power which it opposes, if it takes them to be violence and wrong, to be ethical merely by accident, and, like Antigone, knowingly commits the crime" (PG 336; PS 284). But this interprets Antigone's action merely as the result of "a sentiment or disposition," merely at the level of "pathos" (PG 337; PS 284), whereas a few paragraphs later, Hegel will point out that Antigone's action must be reassessed. Understood "as a moment of the visible community its activity is not confined merely to the underworld, or to its outer existence, but it has an equally visible existence and movement in the actual nation." He goes on to say that "what was represented as a simple movement of the individualized 'pathos' acquires a different look, and the crime and consequent destruction of the community acquire the proper and characteristic form of their existence" (PG 340; PG 287). Hegel continues, apparently confirming the priority of male (human) law over feminine (divine) law, but then going on to overturn this priority: "Human law in its universal existence . . . is the manhood of the community" which "maintains itself by consuming" the family. One reads on, with Irigaray in her essay "The Eternal Irony of the Community," to find that there is a sense in which Antigone has the last word after all. Hegel says,

> Since the community only gets an existence through its interference with the happiness of the Family, and by dissolving (individual) self-consciousness into the universal, it creates for itself in what it suppresses and what is at the same time essential to it an internal enemy—womankind in general. Womankind—the everlasting irony (in the life) of the community—changes by intrigue the universal end of the government into a private end, transforms its universal property of the state into a possession and ornament for the Fam-

ily. Woman in this way turns to ridicule the earnest wisdom of mature age which, indifferent to purely private pleasures and enjoyments, as well as to playing an active part, only thinks of and cares for the universal. (PG 340; PS 288)

However much woman ridicules the "earnest widsom" of her community at the expense of the government, it is not on her own account. For woman, Hegel says, "it is the power of youth that really counts." Woman might have the last laugh, but she still depends on the superiority of her male counterpart. It is the bravery and "physical strength" of youth that appeals to woman (PG 341; PS 288–89). It is still a male power in which woman invests her interest, albeit a rebellious male power.

However, while Antigone is conforming to one aspect of her traditional female role of subservience, in so doing she is denying herself another. Steiner acknowledges that the resurgence of interest in the figure of Antigone during the nineteenth century may have been related, among other factors, to the fact that the status of the rights of woman became an issue during the French Revolution. He concedes however that any improvement in the condition of women took place within a more general program of reform, and the limited effect this had leads one to think that any symbolic influence Antigone might have exercised only served as "a surrogate for reality."[16] The point I want to emphasize stems from precisely the inadequacy of focusing upon the issue of women in terms of rights. It is just because Antigone's plight is construed according to rights and duties that the tragedy of Sophocles's play obscures this plight.

In burying her brother Polynices, Antigone remains faithful to the law of the family in the private sphere of the home, and thereby finds herself posed against the public sphere of the political. This much is clear. What has received less attention is the fact that by executing her familial duty, she is, at the same time, forced to renounce her own capacity for motherhood. Although she declares herself prepared to go to her death from the first, for death is the punishment she knows she will incur if she disobeys Creon's orders in burying Polynices, still she rails against the curse by which she is doomed to her death.

There has been considerable discussion as to why Antigone says she would not have defied the civil edict of the king in order to bury a husband or a son. Antigone will suffer death only for her brother. She says:

> Father and mother lost, where would I get
> Another brother? For thus preferring you,
> My brother, Creon condemns me and hales me away,
> Never a bride, never a mother, unfriended,
> Condemned alive to solitary death.[17]

Hegel's elevation of sorority over all other familial relations can be seen as a response to Antigone's words. The priority of the sister-brother relationship over the wife-husband and mother-son relationships is discussed, for example, by Kojève in his interpretation of Hegel.[18] He points out that unlike the relationship between husband and wife, that between brother and sister is not based on sexual attraction; and although it is a blood relation, and in this respect it is akin to the mother-son relation, it is a purely disinterested relationship. It is based neither upon desire, nor upon the wish to reproduce. The value of the brother is invested entirely in his being or existence—that is, it is on the ontological plane that Antigone recognizes her duty to her brother. Neither a husband nor a son would have been related to her in such a pure way.[19]

Twice before, Antigone has mentioned the fact that Creon's punishment denies her the possibility of marriage (*Antigone*, 148, 149) but here, for the first time, when she specifies that she would not have given up her life for husband and son, but only for her brother, she adds that her capacity for motherhood is being denied her at the same time. Why must she bury her brother? In doing so and thus condemning herself to death, she is precisely renouncing the possibility of giving her life for a son or a husband, for she will have neither. Antigone, acting according to the directive of her familial duty, knowingly flouts the authority of the state. In burying her brother she elevates the rights of the family above the rights of the state. Hegel points out that she thereby embodies a principle of particularity, a feminine principle. But in *taking on* her brother's death, in performing the burial rights denied him by the polis, Antigone is precisely taking on a male role. In so far as she puts his honor before her fulfillment as a woman, she is not acting as a woman, but, in the courage that it takes to defy the king's command, she acts as if she were a man.[20] She may be remaining true to her feminine role as guardian of the family, but at the same time she is subverting the relationship between family and polis. Antigone takes on the public role to which, as guardian of the private familial sphere, she is usually subservient. For the law of the family, the private law, only makes sense insofar as it facilitates the functioning of the public realm of the polis. It is inconceivable, given this context, that Antigone should consider her own life apart from her role as a sister. Female rights only figure in relation to male rights. Although she laments her lost chance of motherhood, she never questions that she must bury her brother. For Antigone, there is precisely no dilemma. From the opening lines of the play she is set firmly on her course, never deviating from the line of duty, never wavering in her decision. And in adhering to her duty as a sister, she crosses the boundary between private and public. She elevates her duty to her brother above the political significance of his public action, and thereby transforms her familial duty into an act of political defiance. She refuses to subordinate her duty to her brother to the question of her brother's political honor. In other words she refuses to accept that her individual attachment to her brother ceases to be significant if her brother is not seen to fulfill his universal role in the political sphere.

Ironically, in adopting her course of action, in burying her brother and then committing suicide, Antigone simultaneously undermines the polis in yet another way. We have seen, and Steiner, among others, has pointed out, the ambiguous place of the family, standing between the individual and the state.[21] The state would wish to usurp the ties which bind together the family, in order to augment its own power. But at the same time it depends upon the procreative function of the family and therefore paradoxically it also needs the family to retain its independence from the state, in order to provide it with the military and political resources necessary for its maintenance. By killing herself, Antigone has renounced her procreative function before Creon can deprive her of it.

It emerges then, that far from being purely a matter of rights and duties, the tragedy of Antigone is that in giving up her life, she gives up motherhood. It might be argued that while she will not give birth to a child, she has, in a sense, conferred life upon her brother. By honoring his life, giving him the burial that Creon denies him, Antigone gives her brother's life meaning. She expresses her commitment to Polynices by restoring honor to his life through performing burial rites at his death. But in order to do so she gives up her betrothal, and her hope to be a mother. She acts unselfishly, one could say. But, one could also say, that insofar as she does not question her obligation to Polynices, neither does she question the superiority of the state. The fact that she expresses her love for Polynices by honoring him in death reveals the efficacy not only of the divine law, but also of the human or political law.

I have pointed out that to impose a simple dichotomy between divine and human law on Sophocles's play fails to recognize that the burial of the dead is dictated not only by divine law but also by human law. That Antigone chooses to honor her brother and to give up her chance of motherhood demonstrates not only her devotion to divine law and familial ties, but also that she attaches no importance to her own individual wishes. Her compassion for her brother is inextricably linked with his political honor, and the fact that his public, universal, male honor takes precedence over her own private, individual, female destiny remains unquestioned by Antigone.

How does this stand with feminism? One of the arguments which has been developed in support of the case for equal rights for women is based on a distinction between nature and social conditioning. In the case of motherhood, feminists have differentiated the natural capacity of women to bear children, and the social expectation that women will become mothers. Perhaps the most famous formulation of the view that women are not defined biologically but have learned to conform to social norms is contained in Simone de Beauvoir's claim that one is not born woman, one becomes woman.[22] To concede that women are socialized into adopting so-called feminine values, opens up the possibility of changing the destiny of women. The separation of sex and gender is called for in order to liberate women from the social demand that their lives follow a traditional pattern. If femininity is socially constructed, and not biologically determined, then social change can bring about women's liberation. The ramifications of such a change affect the lives of men just as much as women, although in different ways. But precisely because the balance of power would be upset, as Toril Moi has argued, it is in the interests of patriarchy to equate gender with sex, thereby confusing role expectation, which is

socially constructed, with anatomical characteristics, which are biologically determined.[23] The implication is that the reverse is in the interests of feminism,
that feminists should strive to maintain the distinction between sex and gender,
so that biological make-up cannot be seen as determinative of women's roles.[24]

Understood primarily as a struggle for equal rights for men and women,
feminism tends to minimize rather than emphasize the differences between
the sexes. It is, for example, the lack of political rights, rather than biological
differences, that sets women apart as a group in what Kristeva has identified
as the first wave of feminism.[25]

Implicit in the rejection of their traditional roles is a devaluation of, for
example, motherhood. Child rearing is construed as a restriction of freedom.
Women are even made to feel guilty for apparently conforming to what has
traditionally been expected of them, for wanting to be mothers. The issue
is seen in terms of the dilemma of whether to conform, or to be liberated
—a dilemma not realized by Antigone.

It is against this climate that, in a second wave of feminism, feminine qualities are being reevaluated.[26] Traditionally feminine roles are reevaluated as
positive attributes to be affirmed, not eradicated. Instead of attempting to
diminish the differences between men and women, feminism would celebrate
these differences and embrace the values developed through traditional female
tasks such as mothering, nurturing, caring. But the legacy of feminist thinking,
whereby differences between the sexes are played down and similarities are
emphasized, has set up the feminist problematic in terms which see sex as
necessarily opposed to gender. From this perspective, any attempt to endorse
an identity specific to women risks defining women with reference to biologically determined characteristics. The insistence that women are not only different, but should strive to retain and develop their differences is therefore
viewed with considerable suspicion. The affirmation that women are irreducibly different from men is taken as a dangerous prescription for women's roles
to be dictated by their biological make-up. The argument amounts to a charge
of essentialism.

But why whould the feminism that celebrates the distinctive qualities of
women, rather than focusing upon the issue of sexual equality, entail biological
determinism? Isn't the suspicion based upon a conception of history which
is still dominated by the line of time as a unidirectional infinite series of nows,
still dictated by the linear concept of progress?[27] If women were to step outside
of history as progress into the place to which they have in fact been consistently
relegated, their vision would no longer be restricted by the view that success
comes through separating sex from gender, relieving women of the natural
burden of motherhood. It would not have to be a choice between femininity
and feminism.

In the chapter on Irigaray in her book *Sexual/Textual Politics*, Toril Moi
declares that "Irigaray falls into the very essentialist trap of defining woman
that she set out to avoid" (STP 142). A few pages later Moi concludes: "If,
as I have previously argued, all efforts towards a definition of 'woman' are

destined to be essentialist, it looks as if feminist theory might thrive better if it abandoned the minefield of femininity and femaleness for a while and approached the questions of oppression and emancipation from a different direction" (STP 148). That all attempts to define woman are inevitably essentialist seems rather a sweeping assertion.

Although the problem of defining woman raises issues of crucial importance, the definition of woman is not problematic for the reason Moi thinks. Her argument appeals to the importance of differentiating between the female sex as naturally determined and feminine identity as culturally determined.

But Moi formulates the same criticism in a more interesting way. Just as Derrida's deconstruction is, according to Moi, "self-confessedly parasitic upon the metaphysical discourses it is out to subvert," so Irigaray is hoist by her own petard. "Having shown that so far femininity has been produced exclusively in relation to the logic of the Same," Moi says of Irigaray, she "falls for the temptation to produce her own positive theory of femininity. But, as we have seen, to define 'woman' is necessarily to essentialize her" (STP 139).

Just as it is unfair to criticize Derrida for failing to go elsewhere than metaphysics, as if there ever could be some pure, anti-metaphysical realm, an outside which was not already governed by the rule of opposition which relates to the inside, as if he were naïve enough to think one could ever escape the inside/outside opposition, as if one could step outside of metaphysical language and leave history behind, as if a new language could be found which were not analogous to the old, so it is unfair to criticize Irigaray for essentializing woman in attempting to define her. Far from being unaware of the differences between defining women in respect of their biological sex and their socially learned roles, Irigaray is thinking through the problem of sexual difference on a different level. It is a level which takes account of—indeed almost takes for granted, and therein lies much of the confusion of Anglo-American responses to her work—the fundamental fact that our bodies are never simply biological facts.

In focusing upon multiplicity and otherness, embracing contradictions, women's difference, not only from men, but also from one another, and even within themselves, can be affirmed in a time of discontinuity. Consequently even the phenomenological language of experience is rendered inadequate to describe the complexity of feminine otherness. To put it negatively, it is the exclusion of women from linear history which gives women their specificity.

We have seen that Derrida asks whether Levinas, precisely in making sexual difference secondary, has not affirmed as neutral what is in fact masculine, has not mastered femininity by mastering its origin, sexual difference. Perhaps the impossibility of pinning down Levinas's account of the feminine is no accident, but rather an acknowledgment of the impossibility of raising the question "what is woman?" without already having decided her essence.

This does not mean that the question should not be raised. Only that it is a difficult question to ask, and that its formulation calls for careful thought. Whether or not to define woman is necessarily to essentialize women depends upon how one understands definition. If a definition is understood as stipulating the unchanging essence of women, then one would be on dangerous ground indeed. But the meaning of essence is one which must be brought under scrutiny, if Heidegger's questioning of Being is to be taken seriously. And not only Levinas and Derrida, but also Irigaray and Kristeva, take Heidegger's question seriously. The question of woman is indeed a risky question, but perhaps the risk involved is one which must be taken. The economy of such a question is not one in which returns are guaranteed, but how could such an economy produce anything other than another definition of woman's place? To fix that place would be to impose an alternative designation upon women, but one which would still be played out according to the same rules, one which would still be governed by its opposition to men.

Notes

1. Julia Kristeva gave a seminar in the department of philosophy at the University of Warwick in May 1986.
2. Christie V. McDonald, "Choreographies," Interview with Derrida, *Diacritics* 12, Summer 1982: 66–76. Hereafter referred to in the text with the letter C, followed by page numbers.
3. Jacques Derrida, *Eperons: Les styles de Nietzsche: Spurs: Nietzsche's Styles*, bilingual edition, London and Chicago, University of Chicago Press, 1979.
4. Julia Kristeva, "Women's Time," in *The Kristeva Reader*, ed. Toril Moi, Oxford, Basil Blackwell, 1986, 189. See Nietzsche's essay "Vom Nutzen und Nachtheil der Historie für das Leben," *Unzeitgemässe Betrachtungen II, Nietzsche Sämtliche Werke*, vol. 1, Nördlingen, Deutscher Taschenbuch, 1980, 258–65; "On the Uses and Disadvantages of History for Life," *Untimely Meditations*, trans. H. J. Hollingdale, Cambridge, Cambridge University Press, 1983, 67–72. I have developed the theme of feminist time in my paper "Female Temporality and the Futures of Feminism," in *Abjection, Melancholia and Love*, ed. J. Fletcher and A. Benjamin, Warwick Studies in Philosophy and Literature, London, Routledge and Kegan Paul, 1990, 63–79.
5. See *Spurs*, 127. Hereafter referred to by the letter S in the text.
6. Jacques Derrida, EM 21–60; AM. Hereafter referred to parenthetically in the text.
7. Levinas acknowledges the Song of Songs as his source in note 5 to chapter 5, AE 181; OB 198.
8. Emmanuel Levinas, TA; TO. Levinas, DE; EE. Hereafter referred to parenthetically in the text.
9. See John Llewelyn's discussion of the "middle voice" in his *Derrida on the Threshold of Sense*, London, Macmillan, 1986, 90–94.
10. At the conference "Re-Reading Levinas," in May 1987 at the University of Essex, Derrida said that the voices evoked at the end of his text "En ce moment" are neither male or female.
11. Derrida, *Glas*, Paris, Editions Galilée, 1974; *Glas*, trans. J. P. Leavey, Jr. and R. Rand, Lincoln and London, University of Nebraska Press, 1986.
12. G. W. F. Hegel, *Phänomenologie des Geistes*, Hamburg, Felix Meiner, 1952, 317; *Phenomenology of Spirit*, trans. A. V. Miller, Oxford, Clarendon Press, 1979, 266. Hereafter referred to with the letters PG and PS in the text.
13. Cornelius Castoriadis, "The Greek Polis and the Creation of Democracy," *The*

Graduate Faculty Journal 9, no. 2, 1983: 108. George Steiner, *Antigones*, Oxford, Clarendon Press, 1986, 34.

14. Hegel says, "Although the Family is *immediately* determined as an ethical being, it is within itself an *ethical* entity only so far as it is not the *natural* relationship of its members, or so far as their connection is an *immediate* connection of separate, actual individuals; for the ethical principle is intrinsically universal, and this natural relationship is just as much a spiritual one, and it is only as a spiritual entity that it is ethical." Neither can the ethical bond within the family take the form of love, since for Hegel "the ethical principle is intrinsically universal." The ethical principle, Hegel concludes, must consist in the relation between the individual and the family as the sole end of individual action. Hegel says "The ethical principle must be placed in the relation of the *individual* member of the Family to the *whole* Family as the Substance, so that the End and content of what he does and actually is, is solely the Family. But the conscious End motivating the action of this whole, so far as it is directed towards that whole, is itself the individual" (PG 320; PS 268–69).

15. See Derrida's *Glas*: "The brother/sister relation is a limit. There the family as family finds its own proper limit (*Grenze*), circumscribes itself in it. Without it, the family would not determine itself, would not be what it is. Or with it either. The limit being what it is—in Hegel—it is not what it is, gets clear of itself as soon as it attains itself. With the brother/sister relation the family is exceeded by itself. It 'dissolves itself and goes out of itself.' The family resolves itself in this limit, the very instant what enters into it goes out of itself, at once sensibly and insensibly, like a point in a null and infinite time, interminable" (187–88, 166).

16. Steiner, *Antigones*, 10.

17. *Antigone*, in *The Theban Plays*, Harmondsworth, Middlesex, Penguin, 1986, 150.

18. Alexandre Kojève in his discussion of Hegel's interpretation of Antigone, *Introduction à la lecture de Hegel*, Paris, Editions Gallimard, 1947, 100–101.

19. Derrida takes up only two themes in his discussion of Hegel's Antigone—the burial place, and "the liaison between brother and sister" (*Glas*, 161, 142). See also Luce Irigaray's observations about the brother-sister relation: "They are the same blood, but in them blood is at rest and in balance. Thus they do not desire each other, they have neither given nor received this Being-for-the-self from each other, they are free individualities vis-à-vis each other. What is it, then, that impels them to unite so that finally one passes into the other? What meaning does each have for the other that draws them thus into this exchange? Is it recognition of *blood*? Of their common allegiance to the power of the *same blood*? Could it be that a matriarchal type of lineage ensures in its purest and most universal being? In this sense the family of Oedipus would be quite exemplary because the mother of the husband is also his wife, thus re-marking the blood tie between the children of that union—including Polyneces and Antigone" (*Speculum de l'autre femme*, Paris, Les Editions de Minuit, 1974, 268–69; *Speculum of the Other Woman*, trans. G. C. Gill, Ithaca, New York, Cornell University Press, 1985, 216).

20. See Irigaray, who says, "If Antigone gives proof of a bravery, a tenderness, and an anger that free her energies and motivate her to resist that *outside* which the city represents for her, this is certainly because she had digested the masculine. At least partially, at least for a moment. But perhaps this will have been possible only at the time when she is mourning for her brother, just long enough to give him back the manhood he had lost in death and to feed his soul therewith. And to die in the act. . . . And her work in the service of another, of the male Other, ensures the ineffectiveness of any desire that is specifically hers" (*Speculum*, 274, 279; 220, 225). After reading this paper at the "Re-Reading Levinas" conference, a useful discussion of Hegel's Antigone in Patricia Jagentowicz Mills's book, *Woman, Nature and Psyche* (London, Yale University Press, 1987), came to my notice. She also makes the point that even though Antigone embodies a feminine principle in burying her brother and thus

remains loyal to familial ties, her act becomes a political one. She says, "Antigone must enter the political realm, the realm of second nature, in order to defy it on behalf of the family, the realm of first nature" (27). Mills attempts to show that Hegel, in comparison to Sophocles himself, has oversimplified the role that Antigone plays. It has not been my concern to make any claims about the inadequacy—or otherwise —of Hegel's reading of *Antigone* as compared to Sophocles's intentions. Neither have I attempted to give a full account either of Sophocles's play, or of Hegel's discussion of it. Those already mentioned go some way toward this. Irigaray, Derrida, and Steiner provide very different commentaries, all valuable each in its own different ways. See also Raymond Pietercil's article "Antigone and Hegel," *International Philosophical Quarterly* 18, 1978: 289–310.

21. Kojève says, "The family is the internal foe of the antique state; the family which this state destroys and the private person which it does not recognize; but it cannot do without them" (105, *Introduction*). I owe this reference to Steiner, who makes a similar point about Hegel's treatment of Aeschylus's *Eumenides*, in which he thinks Hegel is implicitly referring to Sophocles's *Antigone*. Steiner says, "Inevitably, the state will seek to absorb this familial sphere into its own governance and order of values. Yet if it did so completely, it would destroy not only the individual but the procreative units from which it draws its military-political resources" (26, *Antigones*).

22. Simone de Beauvoir, *The Second Sex*, trans. H. M. Harshley, New York, Vintage Books, 1974, 301.

23. Toril Moi, *Sexual/Textual Politics*, London and New York, Methuen, 1985 (hereafter references are to STP in the text).

24. Hester Eisenstein, *Contemporary Feminist Thought*, London and Sydney, Unwin Paperbacks, 1984, xiv.

25. Kristeva, *Kristeva Reader*, 193.

26. Kristeva, *Kristeva Reader*, 194.

27. Female temporality transgresses linear time according to Kristeva. Although Heidegger has shown that the linear model of time in fact assumes a non-linear conception, Kristeva is interested in "temporal modalities" which are "anterior" to any formal representation of time (*Kristeva Reader*, 192).

PART FOUR

Levinas's Readers: Derrida and Blanchot

CHAPTER
9

SKEPTICISM IN THE FACE OF PHILOSOPHY
Robert Bernasconi

Believe me, the skeptic finds contradiction and
imperfection in all that is thought, because he
knows the harmony of perfect beauty, which
is never thought. The dry bread that human
reason well-meaningly offers him, he disdains
only because he is secretly feasting at the
table of the gods.[1]

Arguments are not always as conclusive in philosophy as their proponents expect them to be, even when they are valid. It is said that the extreme forms
of skepticism have been refuted, but they continue to recur. In *Otherwise
than Being or Beyond Essence*, Levinas refers to this as "the alternating fate
of skepticism in philosophical thought" (AE 24; OB 19–20). He evokes it, both
in that book and elsewhere, in the context of two closely related questions.
The first is that of the conditions under which philosophy signifies truth. A
major part of Levinas's interest in skepticism derives from the fact that it contests the possibility of truth (AE 214; OB 168). For himself Levinas suggests
that neither philosophy nor truth find their ultimate justification within themselves. The order of the said (*le Dit*), to which they belong, must be referred
to what Levinas calls saying (*le Dire*), which takes place as the exposure of
oneself to the Other. This establishes a link with the second reason for Levinas's
interest in skepticism. One of the major objections against Levinas's thinking
is that in the course of articulating his claim that ethics is beyond being and
so unthematizable, he makes a theme of the unthematizable. Is there not a
fundamental betrayal of the *otherwise than being*, whenever it is cast in the
language of being? Is it not contradictory to affirm the independence of ethical
intelligibility from theoretical thought within a theoretical discourse?[2] Levinas
sees a parallel between this objection and the philosophical refutation of skepticism. The fact that the refutation of skepticism has failed to prevent skepticism's
return suggests to Levinas that this objection to his thought will prove similarly
ineffective. It is at this point that the second context in which Levinas refers
to skepticism combines with the first. For he again looks to the difference

between the saying and the said in order to elucidate the ineffectiveness of philosophical argument both against skepticism and, as he would like to think, against his own articulation of the good beyond being.

It is important to recognize that Levinas is giving skepticism and its refutation the status of a metaphor or "model" (DVI 268).[3] He is not himself adopting a skeptical position. He gives no indication of having made a detailed study of the history of skepticism. Nor does he attempt to situate historically the argument about skepticism to which he refers, except to locate it at the dawn of philosophy (AE 8; OB 7). Reliable historical evidence about early skepticism is in short supply. The first skeptics seem to have written nothing and said little. To take an example which is already relatively late, Clitomachus said, according to Cicero, that he had never been able to find out what Carneades thought. A curious state of affairs when one recalls that Clitomachus was not only one of Carneades's students but his successor as head of the Academy.[4] But it is in part explained by the fact that at this time skepticism, if one can legitimately use the word at all with reference to the dawn of philosophy, was as much a way of life as a philosophical position. Many of the difficulties philosophers have had comprehending skepticism arise because they overlooked this aspect of it.[5] Even when it is recognized, it is rarely shared. Metaphysical thought is understood by Levinas to be "attention to speech or welcome of the face, hospitality and not thematization" (TeI 276; TI 299). "Our relation with the Metaphysical is an ethical behaviour and not a theology, not a thematization" (TeI 50; TI 78).[6]

Levinas seems to uphold the view of skepticism as self-defeating as soon as its own argument is turned against it. He refers to that moment when skepticism does not hesitate to affirm "the impossibility of statement while venturing to *realize* this impossibility by the very statement of this impossibility" (AE 9; OB 7). Metrodorus of Chios, a disciple of Democritus, exemplifies what Levinas has in mind. He allegedly said that "None of us knows anything, not even this, whether we know or do not know."[7] Levinas is impressed by the fact that in spite of losing the argument skepticism returns unabashed. What, if I may put it this way, renders this impossibility possible? Levinas claims that this alternation points to a "secret diachrony" by which skepticism somehow escapes the synchrony of philosophy or—in a reference to the classical formulation of the principle of non-contradiction—escapes "the 'at the same time' of contradictories" (AE 9; OB 7). One recalls that the principle of noncontradiction in its classical formula states that "it is impossible that something should *at the same time* (*zugleich*) be and not be."[8] The diachrony of saying, whereby saying escapes presence, provides the basis for Levinas's attempt to explain how skepticism escapes the refutation which at another level it concedes. It also underlies his account of how the transcendent character of the face-to-face relation escapes every attempt to state it as a truth, but is nevertheless confirmed by saying it to the Other (TeI 196; TI 221). Nor does Levinas offer this account without recognizing that to do so is another betrayal of what is at issue. Diachrony is itself "a structure that no thematizing and interested movement of consciousness . . . can either resolve or recuperate in the simultaneities it constitutes."⁹ But the important point for Levinas is that skepticism provides a potent illustration of a signification which signifies beyond synchrony. The respectability of skepticism within philosophy provides a precedent for Levinas's own somewhat different attempt to thematize the unthematizable. It is perhaps for this reason that Levinas repeatedly calls skepticism the "legitimate child" of philosophy.¹⁰

As the "legitimate child" of philosophy, skepticism both is and is not philosophy. The question was already raised in *Totality and Infinity* where Levinas conceives of skepticism as a constant (albeit perhaps a somewhat clandestine) companion of truth. Skepticism's complicity in the question of truth separates it from "the ethical condition or essence of language" as it resides in the face of the Other.

> The presentation of the face is not true, for the true refers to the non-true, its eternal contemporary, and ineluctably meets with the smile and silence of the sceptic. The presentation of being in the face does not leave any logical place for its contradictory. Thus I cannot evade by silence the discourse which the epiphany that occurs as a face opens, as Thrasymachus, irritated, tries to do in the first book of the *Republic* (moreover without succeeding). (TeI 175; TI 201)

One should not be misled by the fact that in *Otherwise than Being* skepticism is introduced with reference to its contestation of truth (AE 214; OB 168). Skepticism, on Levinas's account, remains in love with truth.¹¹ Skepticism and the refutation of skepticism are a "couple." "Philosophy is not separable from skepticism" (AE 213; OB 167).

It should be clear that if the difference between the saying and the said relates to skepticism and its refutation, it is not in such a way that skepticism would be a saying, whereas its refutation would be a said. In *what* it says, in its said, skepticism cannot avoid being a philosophy. But by virtue of its refusal to abide by the refutation it has received, skepticism shows disdain for the *logos* which it itself employs. It shows that it is not prepared to abide by philosophy's rules, and yet its contestation of philosophy seems to be conducted on philosophy's own terms. How is this to be understood? Levinas in a formulation so careful that it is almost impenetrable writes, "It is as though skepticism were sensitive to the difference between my exposure without reserve to the other, which is saying, and the exposition or statement of the said in its equilibrium and justice" (AE 213; OB 168). Levinas does not claim to find a recognition of the difference between the saying and the said within skepticism. The claim that skepticism exhibits a sensitivity to their difference seems based on its inability to apply its denial of truth to its own claims. It is as if its saying did not occur "at the same time" as its said. Skepticism in this way shows itself to be divorced from the tendency of Western philosophy to regard saying as exhausted in the things said. It thus contests philosophy's supposition that the order of truth is the ultimate one (AE 214; OB 168). But just as skepticism ignores its refutation, philosophy for its part refuses to acknowledge that it has been interrupted by skepticism. Even though skepticism constantly returns, the *logos* must always have the last word. Philosophy carries on as if nothing had happened.

It is not only skepticism which is sensitive to the interval between the saying and said. When Levinas says that "language is already skepticism" (AE 216; OB 170), he means that all language resides in this difference between the saying and the said. And this has implications for the assessment of philosophy: "philosophical speaking . . . remains, as a saying, a proximity and a responsibility" (AE 214; OB 168). In other words, philosophy cannot simply be reduced to the order of the said, even if this is where it situates itself. This is important for two reasons. First, it withdraws philosophy from the oppositional schema into which Levinas sometimes forces it. Levinas is at his weakest when he sets himself up against individual philosophers or philosophy in general. He is at his most penetrating when he finds the otherwise than being within philosophy, as he already does in *Totality and Infinity* in the case of Plato and Descartes. In later works the examples multiply to include, among others, Aristotle, Kant, Hegel, Bergson, and Heidegger (DVI 185). Second, it follows that the evaluation of skepticism is not Levinas's primary concern. Levinas draws on the recurrence of (a certain form of) skepticism—in spite of the attempt of logic to exclude its return—in order to suggest that skepticism is witness to reasons that reason does not know. Levinas is not supporting skepticism as such. He accords no privilege to what is said in it (AE 218; OB 171). This marks a difference between skepticism and those other moments which Levinas has singled out from the history of philosophy. In the case of Plato's "good beyond being," Descartes's "infinite," or Kant's exaltation of practical reason over the theoretical, there was—even if it could not readily be thought within an intentional structure—a certain content by which the thought marked its interruption of ontology. That this is not the case with skepticism explains why Levinas is exercised by the question of its relation to philosophy. What draws Levinas to skepticism, to the point of proximity between his own thinking and skepticism, is its contestation of truth. In Levinas this takes place as the subordination of truth to ethics.[12] However, within its own limited sphere he seems to leave truth uncontested.

But these considerations which relate to *what* skepticism says, are in marked contrast to what is claimed for its saying. And yet does not that present a problem? How could any privilege be accorded to the saying of skepticism in particular—as opposed to other occurences of saying—once the said is disregarded? And is there not a privileging of skepticism not only in its use as a model, but also in the sentence "language is already skepticism"? What seems to intrigue Levinas about skepticism is reflected in the following sentence: "Skepticism, which traverses the rationality or logic of knowledge, is a refusal to synchronize the implicit affirmation contained in saying and the negation which this affirmation states in the said" (AE 213; OB 167). Skepticism is not just a denial or rejection of the possibility of knowledge. In its saying it is an affirmation which transcends the realm of the said at the same time as sustaining it. What Levinas says of all saying, that it is "both an affirmation and a retraction of the said," is thus preeminently true of the saying of skepticism (AE 56; OB 44). But what does skepticism affirm? How can it affirm *anything* when to do so would apparently amount to a return to the order of the said?[13] In fact, these considerations rehearse those which give skepticism its preeminence as a model. If the affirmation conflicts with what is said in skepticism, one might say that it is because this affirmation takes place on a different level from the said. Levinas does not take this route and instead looks to understand the affirmation as a saying where the Other is addressed. "The periodic rebirth of skepticism . . . does not permit us to confer any privilege on its said over against the implicit presuppositions of its saying" (AE 218; OB 171).

The difference—or rather nonsynchronicity—of skepticism's saying with its said opens the way to a reconsideration of skepticism's *self-refutation* as opposed to its refutation from outside. At the dawn of philosophy, the skeptics themselves were best versed in the refutation of skepticism. The formulation of Metrodorus of Chios quoted earlier that "none of us knows anything, not even this, whether we know or do not know" is an indication of how the early skeptics did not attempt to avoid paradox, as began to happen around the time of Sextus Empiricus.[14] Skepticism is saved not so much by formulating its statements with ever greater caution, but by differentiating levels. "The truth of skepticism is put on the same level as the truths whose interruption and failure its discourse states, as though the negation of the possibility of the true were ranked in the order restored by this negation, as though every difference were incontestably reabsorbed into the same order. But to contest the possibility of truth is precisely to contest this uniqueness of order and level" (AE 213–14; OB 168). However, these are not differentiations within the said, as would be the case if appeal to a metalanguage resolved the issue. Levinas insists on the diachronous difference of the saying and the said which, according to him, philosophy fails to mark explicitly.

I said earlier that Levinas introduced the discussion of skepticism and its refutation not only with reference to the contestation of truth, but also to address certain problems posed by his own exposition of the infinite. These problems were explored most thoroughly by Derrida in his 1964 essay "Violence and Metaphysics."[15] Derrida had insisted on the "unlimited power of envelopment" possessed by the Greek *logos* (ED 165; WD 112). He was provoked by some of Levinas's more dramatic formulations which claimed to have left the Western philosophical tradition behind. This is not the place to rehearse the argument as to whether "Violence and Metaphysics" is a critique of Levinas or already a double reading.[16] Whatever Derrida intended and however Levinas himself understood "Violence and Metaphysics," it was generally construed as a forceful critique and, as such, in need of some kind of answer. And yet Levinas nowhere responds explicitly to Derrida's "Violence and Metaphysics." It is not even mentioned when in *Otherwise than Being* Levinas attempts to reformulate the insights of *Totality and Infinity* without relying on the language of ontology or appealing to experience.[17] Nevertheless a case can be made on internal grounds that Derrida's essay played an important

part in leading to this reformulation. It is not simply that the questions of
thematization, of ontological language, and of experience were foremost among
Derrida's questions to Levinas. The very language in which Levinas addresses
these questions recalls Derrida unmistakably. So when Levinas in *Otherwise
than Being* allows that his language is a thematization, he is doing more than
repeating a point he had already conceded in *Totality and Infinity*. He is now
entering into a dialogue in which Derrida is his main interlocutor. The following quotation admits no more than had already been said in *Totality and
Infinity*: "The very discussion that we are at this moment elaborating about
signification, diachrony and the transcendence of the approach beyond being,
a discussion that means to be philosophy, is a thematizing, a synchronizing
of terms, a recourse to systematic language, a constant use of the verb *to
be*, a bringing back into the bosom of being all signification allegedly conceived
beyond being" (AE 198; OB 155). But when a couple of lines later he adds
the question, "Does not the discourse remain then coherent and philosophical?" the echo of Derrida is unmistakable.[18]

But if the considerations introduced by Derrida in "Violence and Metaphysics" are indeed under discussion in these pages of *Otherwise than Being*, two
striking anomalies arise. The first is the fact that in the very course of elaborating the considerations about the language he is employing, Levinas characterizes them as both "facile" and "familiar." That they are familiar follows from
the analogy he has drawn with the objections philosophy has always thrown
at skepticism. Not that Derrida's point is exactly the same as those used to
refute skepticism. Only that Levinas (according to Derrida) like the skeptics
(according to their opponents) cannot help but resort to the language he is
supposed to have renounced. "It is necessary to state infinity's *excess* over
totality in the language of totality; . . . it is necessary to state the other in
the language of the Same" (ED 165; WD 112). Levinas calls such objections
facile because they restrict the discussion to the ontological level and ignore
the means used to stand outside the coherence of philosophical discourse.
Levinas at this point cites the abuse of language and the ambiguity which
arises from the proximity of the neighbor (AE 198–99; OB 156). Insofar as
the diachrony of the saying and the said is indeed Levinas's response to the
problem of thematizing the unthematizable, it would certainly have been open
to him to respond to Derrida that it had already been given in *Totality and
Infinity* as part of the account of the "formal structure of language": "In discourse the divergence between the Other as my theme and the Other as my
interlocutor, emancipated from the theme that seemed a moment to hold him,
forthwith contests the meaning I ascribe to my interlocutor" (TeI 169; TI 195).
Nevertheless, had Levinas responded in this way it would have been open
to Derrida to reply in his own turn that he had not presented his questions
in the form of an external critique. He prefaced his questions by advising
that they were not so much objections as "rather the questions put to *us* by
Levinas" (ED 125; WD 84). And when he came to pose certain questions
of language in the third part of "Violence and Metaphysics," he repeated that

"all our questions belong to his own interior dialogue, are displaced into his discourse and only listen to it, from many vantage points and in many ways" (ED 161; WD 109). And yet if Derrida seems here to be disowning his questions and returning them to Levinas, a reading of "Violence and Metaphysics" would complicate, although perhaps not readily resolve, the question of ownership.

The second anomaly arises once it is recognized that Levinas's response to Derrida's "Violence and Metaphysics" can be found in the fifth chapter of *Otherwise than Being* where he treats the "birth of thematization, discourse and theory in ethical signification" (DVI 187n). That chapter will be the focus of the remainder of this essay, just as it was one of three or four texts scrutinized by Derrida in his second essay on Levinas, "At this very moment in this work here I am." The curiosity is that Derrida at no point seems to suspect that he is under discussion there.[19] Indeed, while Derrida focuses on Levinas's use of the phrases "at this very moment" and "in this work" which he then employs in the title of his essay, Derrida does not engage Levinas's discussion of skepticism which provides the context of those phrases. In order to understand how Derrida might have come to overlook this aspect of Levinas's discussion, it is necessary to recall some details of Derrida's essay.

"At this very moment in this work here I am" is Derrida's gift to Levinas, his contribution to a Festschrift published in 1980 under the title *Textes pour Emmanuel Levinas*.[20] Derrida specifically acknowledges the essay to be a gift, as a prelude to a consideration of the problems of giving something to Levinas. The problem arises in connection with the following passage quoted by Derrida from Levinas's essay, "*The Trace of the Other*": "Work conceived in its ultimate nature requires a radical generosity of the same who in the work goes unto the Other. It then requires an ingratitude of the Other."[21] Why? Because gratitude would return this movement toward the other back to the same and reduce the gift to a moment in an economy of exchange. If the only homage proper to Levinas would be one which conforms to what Levinas says of work in his work, then Derrida's essay must break the circle of the same. It must exceed the order of restitution. This is what Derrida is attempting to do by means of the transformation of the phrase "he will have obligated" through various stages until it becomes "she will have obligated." Derrida's essay seeks a way of reading Levinas which escapes paraphrase, imitation, and refutation. The essay is not a criticism of Levinas's perhaps unquestioned male perspective. It is rather an attempt to transform Levinas's text, so that it begins to appear differently. Derrida does not give to Levinas a commentary on his work which would retain Levinas's texts for himself. The texts are given to the Other. But this Other is not here Derrida's Other, who is Levinas, but Levinas's Other—woman. This leap to the Other's Other needs further examination beyond that which I can give it here.[22] One would need to consider this move in terms of Levinas's notion of illeity, "the third" who "looks at me in the eyes of the Other" (TeI 188; TI 213). What is important here is that Derrida's gratitude to Levinas is expressed as a gift which does not follow a path back to the origin, but is discreetly passed elsewhere to form a supplement to Levinas's discussion of woman.

This is the context in which Derrida returns to the issue of Levinas's writing. Derrida does not reiterate the questions he had raised in "Violence and Metaphysics." Rather, focusing on the section "Skepticism and Reason" from *Otherwise than Being* he examines the account Levinas gives there both of the way that saying interrupts philosophy and the way that philosophy succeeds in restoring continuity and suppressing the interruption. Philosophy's success is only limited, for the interruptions are conserved "like knots in a retied thread" (AE 216; OB 170). And yet, as I have suggested, Derrida seems to be wholly oblivious to the possibility that he is in these pages being brought face to face with Levinas's response to questions posed in "Violence and Metaphysics," questions whose source, as has already been noted, is uncertain. (Are they Derrida's questions? Or does Derrida only borrow them from Levinas himself?) In any event, far from defending the position he adopted in 1964, Derrida appears to reverse roles with Levinas without a moment's hesitation. No sooner has he posed the question of how Levinas inscribes the wholly other in the language of being—the question which dominates "Violence and Metaphysics" —than Derrida immediately withdraws it: "Shouldn't one reverse the question, in appearance at least, and ask oneself if that language is not *of itself unbound*, hence open to the wholly other, to its own beyond, and in such a way that it is less a matter of exceeding that language than of treating otherwise its own possibilities?" (EM 27; AM).

In this same vein, Derrida sketches a rich and sympathetic analysis of Levinas's title, *Otherwise than Being or Beyond Essence* (EM 29; AM). This is in marked contrast with the extreme caution with which Levinas himself introduces the phrase, a caution which again hints at a strange reversal of roles between them. Levinas expresses his own doubts about the efficacy of this "barbarous turn of phrase" (AE 224; OB 178) with considerations which recall the style of argument employed by Derrida in "Violence and Metaphysics." Does not Levinas sound more like Derrida of 1964 than Levinas of 1961 when he writes, "But one immediately wonders if in the formula 'otherwise than being' the adverb 'otherwise' does not inevitably refer to the verb to be, which simply has been avoided by an artificially elliptical turn of phrase" (AE 4; OB 4)?

One further example can be given of the way each has taken account of the other. In "At this very moment" Derrida observes how sensitive Levinas has become to the threat of contamination. He cites, for example, Levinas's remark in the preface to *Otherwise than Being* about the possibility of hearing a God uncontaminated by Being (EM 41; AM. Cf. AE x; OB xlii). Perhaps Levinas has become over-sensitive to this threat to the point where his concern about "contamination" begins to contaminate his discourse. What is peculiar about this is that one suspects that these worries are in some way a consequence of Levinas's reading of "Violence and Metaphysics" and that, to use another word from *Otherwise than Being*, they represent a "concession" to Derrida fully in conformity with the picture Levinas draws of Derrida at the start of "Wholly Otherwise": "Suspension of truths! Strange epoch! Perhaps in writing each of us feels this when we catch ourselves unawares using familiar notions with a surplus of precautions, while the new critique would challenge the sense of imprudence as the virtue of prudence. A new style of thinking is dawning on us in reading these exceptionally precise texts which are yet so strange" (NP 82; WO). Expression of the fear of contamination would then be an attempt on Levinas's part to engage with Derrida, one which Derrida himself seems to refuse by judging it misconceived: "Apparently he likes the tear but detests contamination. Yet what holds his writing in suspense is that one must welcome contamination, the *risk* of contamination, in enchaining the tears and regularly *resuming them* within the philosophical text or tissue of a *récit*" (EM 37; AM). But if Levinas's concerns about contamination arise from a reading of "Violence and Metaphysics," then do they not mark Derrida's own presence in Levinas's text? Not that they constitute what could be called with any precision a response to Derrida because along with the suppression of Derrida's name, the discussion in *Otherwise than Being*—as I shall try to show—does not reflect the proximity between Levinas and Derrida which emerges elsewhere.

It would appear therefore that Derrida makes occasional appearances in *Otherwise than Being*. They not only go unrecognized by Derrida in "At this moment in this work here I am," but Derrida even takes the reverse stance from the one Levinas might have anticipated from "Violence and Metaphysics," although a more careful reading might have prepared him for this insofar as it is dictated by the exigencies of double reading. The most sustained of the discussions of Derrida in *Otherwise than Being* occurs where Levinas entertains certain "familiar" and "facile" objections to his thematization and likens them to the objections philosophy has "thrown" at skepticism (AE 198; OB 155). Does this mean that the model of skepticism and its refutation has been taken a stage further, with Derrida now cast in a role parallel to that of philosophy's attempted—but never completely successful—refutation of skepticism? Such a picture might fit the image of Derrida that many readers take away from a reading of "Violence and Metaphysics" where Derrida appears to employ "the unforeseeable resource of the Greek logos" with its "unlimited power of envelopment" to hold Levinas in check (ED 165; WD 112). But a more complicated and much richer interpretation emerges from "Wholly Otherwise," a brief essay on Derrida by Levinas which is contemporaneous with *Otherwise than Being*. Levinas observes that Derrida has "in his polemic" not always disdained from following the path of the refutation of skepticism. Furthermore Levinas again recalls that "although at first crushed and trampled underfoot, skepticism got back up on its feet to come back as the legitimate child of philosophy" (NP 86; WO). It looks as if Levinas is preparing to say that his own thought can survive what he understands to be the "polemic" of "Violence and Metaphysics," just as skepticism returns following refutation. In other words, it looks as if he is about to bring to the surface a debate with Derrida which elsewhere remains only implicit. However, this argument is placed in a context different from that to be found in *Otherwise than Being* and one which transforms its meaning. In "Wholly Otherwise" Levinas also threatens Derrida with the same argument which "Violence and Metaphysics" employed against him. That is to say, Levinas entertains the idea of accusing Derrida, in his turn, of resorting to logocentric language. The passage reads:

> One might well be tempted to infer an argument from this use of logocentric language against that very language, in order to dispute the produced deconstruction; a path much followed by the refutation of skepticism, but where, although at first crushed and trampled underfoot, skepticism got back up on its feet to come back as the legitimate child of philosophy. A path, perhaps, that Derrida has not always disdained from following in his polemic. (NP 85; WO)

If Levinas refrains from using the argument, withdraws even as he rehearses it, it is not because its employment would be foreign to his style of thinking. Nor is it simply that he well knows that Derrida has always acknowledged the vulnerability of his thinking to his own strategies, so long as those strategies are not recognized as strategies. More important here is the fact that the susceptibility of deconstruction to its own arguments suggests that in terms of the model of skepticism and its refutation, deconstruction should be cast in the role of skepticism, rather than that of the philosophy which strives to refute skepticism. Levinas does not anticipate those, mainly in literary theoretical circles, who today would construe deconstruction as a form of skepticism. Rather he thinks of Derrida as occupying a place *like* that held by skepticism insofar as both are vulnerable to their own arguments. Of course, Derrida has always known of this vulnerability which governs many of his strategies. The so-called double reading associated with Derrida would not be the same as a Levinasian reading in terms of "the non-simultaneity of the Said and the Saying," but it is *as if* Derrida were in some way *sensitive* to the difference between saying and the said. A reading of the section "Skepticism and Reason" which saw in it only attempts to answer Derrida's objections would, therefore, be severely one-sided. Most importantly, it would neglect the extent to which Levinas could be said to recognize in Derrida's way of reading philosophical texts a sensitivity to diachrony which parallels that found in skepticism. Deconstruction was as good a model for explaining how his thinking is sustained as skepticism was. And from this perspective there is nothing familiar or facile about a thinking which marks a stage in the "growing awareness of the difficulty of thinking" (NP 81; WO), a thinking it would be ridiculous to want to improve (NP 89; WO).

What then lies behind Derrida's inability to recognize the impact of his thinking on Levinas as the cause of the latter's fear of contamination? And why is Derrida blind to the way that "Skepticism and Reason" addresses "Violence and Metaphysics"? Does some necessity underlie his silence on the question of skepticism in spite of his detailed commentary on pages devoted to this theme? It is hard to believe that Derrida could have taken up the discussion of skepticism without recognizing that he himself was meant. Had he done so he would have found himself within Levinas's text and this would have reversed the whole movement of the essay which is, as I have said, directed neither toward himself nor Levinas, but toward Levinas's Other—woman. In other words, had Derrida succumbed either to mere commentary or to refutation he would have reduced the face-to-face encounter with Levinas to some kind of tête-à-tête and he would have had to have recognized himself as an author of Levinas's discourse. Derrida would thus have been obliged to acknowledge his gift of "Violence and Metaphysics" as one which Levinas had already accepted and returned to him in *Otherwise than Being*, so reducing this thought to the order of the same.

Or to put it another way, Derrida would have been obliged to write of chapter 5, section 5 of *Otherwise than Being*: At this very moment in this work here I am— *At this very moment* of this reading *in this*, Levinas's, *work here I*, Jacques Derrida, *am.* So Levinas's refusal to name Derrida in *Otherwise than Being*, with the exception of a single footnote reference to *Speech and Phenomena* (AE 46 n. 23; OB 189 n. 23), his non-acknowledgment of the gift of "Violence and Metaphysics," his absolute ingratitude (if that is what it was), maintained the gift. And brought forth another.

Early in "At this very moment" Derrida writes that he does not know how to qualify what happens between Levinas, the feminine partner in the exchange, and himself (EM 28; AM). At the end the unidentified writer says to the feminine partner: "I don't know whether you are saying what his work says. Perhaps that amounts to the same. I don't know any more whether you are saying the contrary, or if you've already written something entirely other. I can't hear your voice any more, I can hardly distinguish it from mine, from any other, your fault suddenly becomes illegible to me. Interrupt me" (EM 59; AM). The discussion between Levinas and Derrida which is so often assimilated to the standard models of argument—refutation and response—and thereby enclosed within philosophy, bears the marks of another kind of encounter, one not governed by the model of knowledge or even of truth. Levinas writes in *Otherwise than Being* that "to require that a communication be sure of being heard is to confuse communication and knowledge" (AE 212; OB 167). The messages passed between Levinas and Derrida are not always sure of arriving; Derrida does not acknowledge Levinas's discussion of him in "Skepticism and Reason" in spite of his detailed commentary on its final pages and Levinas has, so far as I am aware, nowhere taken up or even referred to "At this very moment in this work here I am." And yet at one point Derrida— or at least one of the voices of "At this very moment"—announces, apparently without knowing that it is at the very limits of knowing as much as it can know without knowing what it cannot know: "I am still ignorant of what happens here between him [Levinas], you [the woman] and me. It is not of the order of questions and responses" (EM 28; AM).[23]

Notes

1. Friedrich Hölderlin, *Sämtliche Werke*, ed. F. Beissner, Stuttgarter Ausgabe vol. 3, Stuttgart, Kohlhammer, 1957, 81; trans. W. R. Task, *Hyperion or the Hermit in Greece*, New York, Ungar, 1965, 93.

2. "Façon de parler," DV 266.

3. Notice that Levinas also offers another model for the refutation, that of Plato's *Parmenides* (DVI 266–67).

4. Cicero, *Academics*, Book 2, 139, trans. H. Rackham, Loeb Classical Library, London, Heinemann, 1979, 649. See also Gisela Striker, "Sceptical Strategies," in *Doubt and Dogmatism*, ed. M. Schofield, M. Burnyeat, and J. Barnes, Oxford, Oxford University Press, 1980, 55.

5. On skepticism see especially Michael Williams, "Scepticism without Theory," *Review of Metaphysics* 41, 1988: 547–88. Also *The Skeptical Tradition*, ed. Myles Burnyeat, Berkeley, University of California Press, 1983; *The Modes of Scepticism*, ed. Julia Annas and Jonathan Barnes, Cambridge, Cambridge University Press, 1985; and *Doubt and Dogmatism*.

6. See R. Bernasconi, "Levinas: Philosophy and Beyond," in *Philosophy and Non-Philosophy since Merleau-Ponty*, ed. H. J. Silverman, New York, Routledge, 1988, 236–37.

7. Fragment 1, *Die Fragmente der Vorsokratiker*, ed. Hermann Diels, vol. 2, Zurich, Weidmann, 1985, 233–34.

8. Immanuel Kant, *Kritik der reinen Vernunft*, B 191. See also Aristotle, *Metaphysics*, 1005a 19.

9. "L'Ancien et le nouveau," *L'Ancien et le nouveau*, ed. Joseph Doré, Paris, Cerf. 1982, 37; TO 137.

10. One might imagine that the return of skepticism is illegitimate because of the weight of the arguments against it. Indeed this impression is so striking that on the three occasions in *Otherwise than Being* when skepticism is referred to as philosophy's legitimate child, the English translator renders it as "illegitimate" (AE 9; OB 7) or as "bastard" (AE 108 n. 18; OB 192 and AE 231; OB 183). But skepticism is the *legitimate* child of philosophy insofar as the question of skepticism is still construed as a question about truth. Levinas attaches some importance to the dignity accorded to skepticism by philosophy in spite of its refutation (DVI 267), presumably because it shows philosophy abiding by rules other than those it declares.

11. "Tout Autrement," NP 84; WO.

12. In *Totality and Infinity* Levinas says that "truth presupposes justice" (TeI 62; TI 90). However, this refers to the subordination of truth to ethics and not to justice in the technical sense that it later develops.

13. It might seem that skepticism, by seeking to minimize its own content, has even managed to attain a level of purity which Levinas's own exposition has renounced. Skepticism's alleged purity is, however, a neutrality, the denial of that "fine risk" which sets metaphysics (in the sense Levinas gives it in *Totality and Infinity*) apart from skepticism (cf. AE 213; OB 167). The purity of skepticism might in this way be likened to that of the beautiful soul which, as Hegel already demonstrated in the *Phenomenology of Spirit*, is ridiculous because its purity is sustained only on condition that it continues to deprive itself of the means to act (cf. AE 61; OB 47).

14. On skepticism's self-refutation see Williams, "Scepticism without Theory"; David Sedley, "The Motivation of Greek Scepticism," in *The Skeptical Tradition*; Myles Burnyeat, "Protagoras and Self-Refutation in Later Greek Philosophy," *Philosophical Review* 85, 1976: 46–69; and Mark McPherran, "Skeptical Homeopathy and Self-Refutation," *Phronesis* 32, 1987: 290–328.

15. In ED 165; WD 112.

16. See the Editors' Introduction above.

17. "Signature," in DL 379; trans. Mary Ellen Petrisko, "Signature," ed. Adriaan Peperzak, *Research in Phenomenology* 7, 1978: 189.

18. Later in this essay I shall indicate other points in *Otherwise than Being* where "Violence and Metaphysics" has left its mark. Further examples could be cited, but I shall limit myself to one more which is relevant to the issues I shall be discussing later. When Levinas suggests that signification signifies beyond synchrony, this is his way of providing an answer, or at least the beginnings of an answer, to the objection that "the philosopher finds language again in the abuses of language of the history of philosophy, in which the unsayable and what is beyond being are conveyed before us" (AE 10; OB 9). That Levinas is recalling certain arguments put by Derrida is perhaps confirmed when Levinas concedes soon after that "negativity, still correlative with being, will not be enough to signify the *other than being.*" That seems to suggest that he has in mind Derrida's insistence that "the positive plenitude of classical infinity is translated into language only by betraying itself in a negative word (in-finite)" (ED 168; WD 114). For some indication of how complex the discussion of the notion of the infinite is, see Robert Bernasconi, "The Silent Anarchic World of the Evil Genius," in *The Collegium Phaenomenologicum*, ed. J. Sallis, G. Moneta, and J. Taminiaux, Dordrecht, Kluwer, 1988, 257–72.

19. That the section "Skepticism and Reason" answers objections formulated by Derrida has already been proposed by Jan de Greef in "Scepticisme et raison," *Revue philosophique de Louvain* 82, 1984: 365; trans. Dick White, "Skepticism and Reason," in *Face to Face with Levinas*, ed. Richard Cohen, Albany, State University of New York Press, 1986, 159. My presentation differs from de Greef's on a number of points. I shall briefly mention four issues of interpretation. First, I have focused not simply on skepticism's refutation, but on its self-refutation as the key to Levinas's discussion. Second, Levinas does not seek to privilege skepticism in the way de Greef claims. Third, de Greef neglects Levinas's claim that "language is already skepticism." This leads de Greef to attempt to solve the problem posed by skepticism, "to find another outcome than that proposed by Levinas." Levinas insists that "the return of skepticism . . . would be pure nonsense . . . if the truth about the diachrony could be collected in a theme without thereby refuting itself" (AE 217–18; OB 171). By contrast, de Greef wants to save Levinas from refutation by reason and to do so he feels obliged to deny that skepticism is ever refuted. Although de Greef appeals to Levinas's phrase the "enigma of philosophy," it is evident that he means something very different by it —almost anodyne in comparison—from the fact that he is so insistent on avoiding paradox.

20. EM; AM.

21. "La trace de l'autre," in EDE 191; TTO 349.

22. For a more detailed consideration of Derrida's essay see Simon Critchley's "'Bois' —Derrida's Final Word on Levinas," chap. 10 below.

23. An earlier version of this paper was delivered at De Paul University, Chicago, on 25 March 1986.

CHAPTER

10

"BOIS"—DERRIDA'S FINAL WORD ON LEVINAS

Simon Critchley

10. And the servant took ten camels of his master, and departed; for all the goods of his master *were* in his hand: and he rose and went to Mesopotamia, unto the city of Nahor.

11. And he made his camels to kneel down without the city by a well of water at the time of evening, *even* the time that women go out and draw *water*.

12. And he said O LORD God of my master Abraham, I pray thee, send me good speed this day, and shew kindness unto my master Abraham.

13. Behold, I stand *here* by the well of water; and the daughters of the men of the city come out and draw water:

14. And let it come to pass, that the damsel to whom I shall say let down thy pitcher, I pray thee, that I may drink; and she shall say, Drink, and I will give thy camels drink also: *let the same be* she *that* thou hast appointed for thy servant Isaac: and thereby shall I know that thou hast shewed kindness unto my master.

15. And it came to pass, before he had done speaking that, behold Rebekah came out, who was born to Bethuel, son of Milcah, the wife of Nahor, Abraham's brother, with her pitcher upon her shoulder.

16. And the damsel *was* very fair to look upon, a virgin, neither had any man known her: and she went down to the well, and filled her pitcher, and came up.

17. And the servant ran to meet her and said, let me, I pray thee, drink a little water of thy pitcher.

18. And she said, Drink, my lord: and she hasted, and let down her pitcher upon her hand, and gave him drink.

19. And when she had done giving him drink,

she said, I will draw *water* for thy camels also,
until they have done drinking.
20. And she hasted, and emptied her pitcher
into the trough, and ran again unto the well
to draw *water*, and draw for all his camels.

Genesis 24[1]

1.

"Bois"—this is Derrida's final word on Levinas. The final word of his text *for* Emmanuel Levinas (EM 60; AM).

"Bois"—"drink," understood verbally, Derrida's final word articulates an imperative, it places us under obligation. It is an imperative written without a point of exclamation in the intimacy of the second person singular. "Bois" is not directed from a position of height to an anonymous multitude, it is not the impersonal "Buvons!" or "Buvez!" which, in a spirit of exclamation and camaraderie, commands the others to join in a toast or partake in a symposium. The imperative "bois" does not call us to take on board nourishment, an operation that Levinas has already described (TeI 100–103; TI 127–30) and which always remains within the circuit of the separated ego and its *jouissance*. To utter the imperative "bois" is to give to the other, to let down one's pitcher and offer drink to the other; it does not mean "eat, drink, and be merry." Such a giving is inadequately described through the image of friends nourishing themselves and their individuation in a spirit of collectivity and bonhomie. To utter the final word—"bois"—is to nourish the hunger of the other and is akin to the tearing of bread from my own mouth. I interrupt my ego through fasting and breaking the other's fast (cf. AE 72; OB 56).

"Bois"—"drink," what is being given here? What is being offered to drink? Derrida's final words on Levinas are the following, "I WEAVE MY VOICE SO AS TO BE EFFACED THIS TAKE IT HERE I AM EAT—APPROACH —IN ORDER TO GIVE HIM/HER (*LUI*)—DRINK (*BOIS*)." The textual voice here speaks of weaving itself in order to be effaced. As such, the textual voice is not in the process of disappearing, rather it effaces itself before an other; the voice is addressed to an interlocutor. In the act of effacement, where the self is possessed by the other, the voice persists and says "HERE I AM . . . EAT . . . DRINK." The voice offers something to the other, its arms outstretched and its hands full, asking the other to approach. Upon the other's approach, the voice holds out its gift and says "bois"—"drink." The gift of drink is being offered here. Derrida's final word on Levinas offers the gift of drink to the other, a giving which, as I shall show, describes the generous movement of the ethical work. Derrida's final word on Levinas describes that ethical work, where Derrida's text is given to Levinas.

"Bois"—"drink," the ethical work must be given in radical generosity. The work must be sent out from the same to the other without ever returning to the same. Levinas writes in "The Trace of the Other," "*The Work (L'Œuvre)* thought radically is indeed a movement from the Same towards the other which never returns to the Same. To the myth of Ulysses returning to Ithaca, we would like to oppose the story of Abraham leaving his homeland forever for a still unknown land and even forbidding his son to be brought back to its point of departure" (EDE 191; TTO 348). Levinas thus opposes the nomadic wanderings of Abraham to the well-rounded narrative of the *Odyssey*.[2] The ethical work must possess a movement which exceeds the circle of the self and goes unto the other without ever turning back. Consequently, the work of the word "bois," the final word in Derrida's work *for* Levinas, describes the generous giving of the work to the other, letting down one's pitcher in order to let the other drink. The woman that shall marry Abraham's son Isaac, must fulfill the duty (*mitsva*; cf. ND 156)[3] of hospitality. Abraham's servant recognizes the woman when she lets down her pitcher and offers drink to him and his camels; her name is Rebecca. Thus it is in her responsibility to the stranger, by offering drink, that Rebecca fulfills the duty of hospitality and performs the ethical work. "Bois" is the very event of the ethical work, giving to the stranger without hope of return or remuneration. Derrida's final word on Levinas is the first word of responsibility, the establishment of the ethical relation.

However, this ethical and textual structure must begin to be complicated in order to describe adequately what is at work in "At this very moment." I rejoin the quotation from "The Trace of the Other": "The Work (*L'Œuvre*), thought as far as possible, demands a radical generosity of the Same who, in the Work, goes towards the other. In consequence the Work demands an *ingratitude* of the other. Gratitude would be precisely the return of the movement to its origin." In order to stop the ethical work returning to the Same, the Other must receive the work *ungratefully*, because the movement of gratitude returns to the Same, as is the case in philanthropy. Therefore, one should not be grateful for ethical works, Eliezer should be ungrateful to Rebecca, and the addressee of Derrida's final word should show ingratitude. Should one then be grateful to Emmanuel Levinas?

To approach this question let us briefly consider the status and function of "At this very moment." The essay originally appeared in *Textes pour Emmanuel Levinas*, a collection of essays, where each text is, in a very obvious sense, *for* Emmanuel Levinas, is destined *for* him, to pay him homage, and forms part of a Festschrift, a commemorative work where friends praise the author like guests seated at a symposium. Derrida's text forms part of an act of commemoration, where the author's life and work are collectively recalled. Thus, "At this very moment" is a text that is addressed to an interlocutor or other who is known, addressed, and recalled in the work. Such is the conventional structure of homage.

The situation becomes more complex when one begins to consider the ethics of this textual structure. What ties the authors of *Textes pour Emmanuel Levinas* together in this act of commemoration is the fact that they can all recall Levinas's work; Levinas has worked for them and they would like to pay him homage. But what work does Levinas's work perform? How does his work *work*? As was shown above, Levinas opposes Abraham to Ulysses, claiming that the ethical structure of the work is one which goes generously from the Same to the Other without ever returning to the Same. Thus (and one must note from the outset the continual slippage that occurs in "At this very moment" between the notion of the work that Levinas discusses in "The Trace of the Other"—the good work—and a textual work written and signed by Emmanuel Levinas), on Derrida's reading, Levinas's work *works* by going out generously from the proper name and signature of Emmanuel Levinas toward the other. Levinas's work is not circumscribed by the proper name of Emmanuel Levinas, it is a work that continually exceeds itself and opens itself to that which comes before and after nominalization. To employ a word favored by Derrida, Levinas's work is possessed of a *dehiscence* (EM 43; AM) where the work bursts open and goes unto the other without return, allowing it to perform the ethical.[4]

Levinas's work has worked for Derrida and the other authors in *Textes pour Emmanuel Levinas* precisely to the extent that it has let the work go unto the other, allowing the other to drink without the self quenching his or her thirst in the Other's grateful eyes. The logical and ethical necessity that haunts Derrida's essay is that by writing a text *for* Emmanuel Levinas, by paying homage to his work and recalling how his work works, one would return the work to its author, thereby betraying the ethical structure that Levinas's work tries to set to work. How, then, does one write a text for Emmanuel Levinas? "Suppose that in giving to you—it little matters what—I wanted to give to him, him Emmanuel Levinas. Not render him anything, a homage for example, not even render myself to him, but to give him something which escapes from the circle of restitution or of the 'rendez-vous'" (EM 24; AM).

Derrida cannot pay homage to Levinas by giving his own text back to him, he must be cautious to avoid rendering to Levinas what is Levinas's, for in so doing, he would make the ethical relation correspond to the time of the "rendez-vous" ("'that common time of clocks,'" ibid.), where the Other would render itself up and return to the Same. "I would like to do it faultlessly (*sans faute*), with a 'fault-lessness' (*sans-faute*) that no longer belongs to the time or logic of the rendez-vous. Beyond any possible restitution, there would be need for my gesture to operate without debt, in absolute ingratitude." Returning to the theme of the quotation from "The Trace of the Other" and the question of ingratitude, Derrida would like to sew a seamless and flawless work and then give it to Levinas with a flawlessness that would escape the temporality and speculative logic of the rendez-vous. However, the only way in which a text *for* Emmanuel Levinas can be written which would return Levinas's act of radical generosity is by being *ungrateful* and by writing a *faulty* text. Ingratitude is the only mode in which one can write a text *for* Levinas, if that text is going to maintain the ethical structure that Levinas's work sets to work.

> If I must conform my gesture to what makes the Work (*L'OEuvre*) in his Work, which is older than his work, and whose Saying according to his own

terms is not reducible to the Said, there we are, engaged before all engagement, in an incredible logic, formal and non formal. If I restitute, if I restitute
without fault, I am at fault. And if I do not restitute, by *giving* beyond acknowl-
edgement, I risk the fault. (EM 24; AM)

This is indeed an incredible logic, a faulty logic or logic of the fault. Yet
it is a logic whose "necessity" or "fatality" (EM 56, 58; AM) is irreducibly
ethical. In order to write a text for Emmanuel Levinas, I must not give it
to him; I must make the text faulty in such a way that it does not return
to the Same but goes unto the Other.

"Bois"—"drink," I let down my pitcher and the other drinks from out of
my own thirst. Levinas's work *works* insofar as it is given to someone other
than Emmanuel Levinas. To write a text for Emmanuel Levinas, to create
a work that maintains the Other in its otherness, entails, therefore, that the
text or the work must not be given back to Levinas's name. To write a text
for Emmanuel Levinas is to write a text that is not *for* him but for the Other.
Consequently, it is ethically necessary for "At this very moment" to be ungrateful, faulty, and, to recall a word from Derrida's first essay on Levinas, *violent*
(EM 56; AM).

Yet, it is important to point out that ingratitude, faultiness, and violence
are not directed *against* Levinas; they are not moments of an external critique
which would naïvely oppose itself to the supposed generosity, flawlessness,
and peace of Levinasian ethics. Ingratitude, faultiness, and violence are the
necessary conditions of a fidelity to Levinas's work, a work which works precisely to the extent that it cannot be returned to the proper name of Emmanuel
Levinas. To schematize this, one might say that it is only in ingratitude, faultiness, and violence that the ethical Saying is maintained. To write a text *for*
Emmanuel Levinas is to create a work that is neither *for* him nor *against*
him, but where the modalities of for and against become inseparable yet
inassemblable conditions for the possibility of ethical Saying.

"Bois"—"drink," an imperative directed at a singular second person, the
singular Other who is my interlocutor. But who is the Other? If Derrida does
not let his pitcher down so that Levinas may drink, but in order for the Other
to quench his or her thirst, then who is this Other? If Levinas remains thirsty,
then is "bois" Derrida's final word on *Levinas*? Indeed, is "bois" *Derrida's*
final word? Is the textual voice in "En ce moment même" that of Derrida
or that of an other? Can one still speak of proper names here?

I here approach a major theme of "At this very moment": the question of
the name. And if I am obliged to continue to employ the *proper* names of
"Derrida" and "Levinas," for clarity's sake but also because of the grammar
of propriety embedded in language, then it is with a provisionality that will
become increasingly apparent. The pattern of reading in "At this very moment"
can be said to articulate itself around the difference between the *Pro-nom*
(Pro-noun or Fore-name) and the *nom propre* (the proper name). Recall, that
Derrida's *first* word on Levinas in "At this very moment" is the pronoun "Il,"
which is the subject of the phrase "Il aura obligé." A phrase which resounds

throughout the early pages of "At this very moment" and which, to the knowledge of the textual voice (EM 23; AM), and my own, has never appeared in Levinas's work. Who is "He"? A clue can be found in the final paragraph of *Otherwise than Being*, a passage itself cited in "At this very moment" (EM 44; AM):

> In this work which does not seek to restore any ruined concept, the destitution and de-situation of the subject are not without signification: after the death of a certain god, dwelling in the hinter-worlds (*les arrières-mondes*), the substitution of the hostage discovers the trace—unpronounceable writing—of that which, always already past—always "he" (*"il"*)—does not enter into any present and to whom neither the names designating beings nor the verbs where their *essence* resounds are suitable—but who, Pro-name (*Pro-nom*), marks with his seal everything that can bear a name. (AE 233; OB 185)

In this work, which attempts to describe the ethical work, the self is understood as being taken hostage by the Other (AE 142; OB 112). In its relation to the Other, the self discovers the trace of that which does not enter into any present and which is designated with the pronoun "he." Thus, the "he" is the "Pro-nom," the Fore-name of that which comes before all named beings but which marks each being with its seal. The trace is that which escapes from the order of presence and the proper name. The Levinasian claim is that a trace is found in the face of the Other which is that of the *il*, the *Pro-nom* (EDE 214; CP 71). In "Enigma and Phenomenon" (EDE 207–9; CP 64–66), Levinas opposes an order of presence and phenomenality (from the Greek, *phaino*, to bring to light), where entities are cleared in their Being, to an order of the enigma (from *ainigma*, a dark saying or riddle), which attempts to set forth the otherwise than Being. For Levinas, the enigma of the beyond Being is expressed by the (masculine) pronoun of the third person singular (EDE 199; TTO 356), an enigma he seeks to describe with the term *Illeity*: "This way of leaving the alternatives of Being—we understand it with the personal pronoun of the third person, with the word *He*. The enigma comes to us from Illeity" (EDE 214; CP 71).

Thus the signifyingness (*signifiance*) of the otherwise than Being in a work entitled *Otherwise than Being* is ultimately borne by the "Il" of Illeity. Levinas's work *works* by giving the work to the "Il." Recalling the schema that was sketched above, the work of Emmanuel Levinas is possessed of a certain dehiscence to the extent that it is a work that goes unto the Other without returning to the Same. One can now see that the Other to whom the work is ultimately addressed is "Il," the trace of Illeity, who does not sign Levinas's work but who marks it with his seal. For Levinas, it is the trace of Illeity signaled in the "Il" that constitutes the first act of obligation, the foundation of the ethical relation. When I am faced with the other person, I enter into relation with the enigma of the trace of Illeity, and, in that "intrigue" which binds me to the "Il" from across the "toi" (EDE 215–16; CP 72–73), I am bound in an ethical obligation.

It is now possible to understand the first of the "one, two, three words

. . ." which form the leitmotif of "At this very moment": "Il aura obligé." The "Il" is the "Pro-nom" of the trace of Illeity. From the first word of Derrida's essay, "Il," the textual voice alludes to the way in which Levinas's work *works* insofar as it is addressed to the trace of the otherwise than Being. Derrida's first word on Levinas, like his final word, is a performance of the ethical objectives of the latter's work.

Before pursuing the question of the name, what can one make of the second and third words of the phrase, "il aura obligé"? The first thing one notices is that the tense or temporality of these words is the future anterior (or future perfect) which habitually describes an action that will have been performed by a certain time and which is formed in French (and in English) by compounding the future tense of one of the two auxiliaries *avoir* (to have) and *être* (to be) with the past participle of the main verb. The temporality of the future anterior is something that Derrida has exploited throughout his work and its logic pervades "At this very moment"; for example, "there is the future anterior, which I *shall have* frequently *used* nonetheless, having no other possible recourse. For example in the little phrase: 'He will have 'obliged'" (EM 48; AM, my italics; and cf. EM 38, 39; AM). The importance of the future anterior is that it is a tense that escapes the time of the present; it simultaneously points toward a future—*aura*—and a past—*obligé*—but never toward the present. Consequently, the subject of the phrase—*Il*—cannot be said to be a present subject, rather He/It is a subject that will have obliged in a time that is irreducible to the present.

At several points in "At this very moment," Derrida refers to "the dominant interpretation of language" employed by "philosophical intelligence" and which would seek to display all entities in the light of the determination of Being as presence. The significance of the future anterior is that it is a temporality irreducible to what Derrida would call "the metaphysics of presence," or what Levinas would call "ontology," and which envisages a language that would escape (or perhaps remain beneath) the dominant interpretation. The future anterior is the temporality of the trace of Illeity; it is the time of ethics.

One begins to see how much is already presupposed in the first words of Derrida's essay: "Il aura obligé." The subject of the phrase is the *Pro-nom* or trace of Illeity which provides the condition of possibility of all ethical obligation and which takes place in a temporality that escapes the metaphysics of presence or ontology. Derrida's first and final words on Levinas, "il aura obligé" and "bois," are ethical *performatives*.[5]

It has perhaps become clear by now that it would be misleading to interpret the Pro-nominal "Il" as a pronoun that could be substituted for the proper name of Emmanuel Levinas. "He" is not Levinas; "What I thus call—this work—is not, especially not, dominated by the name of Emmanuel Levinas" (EM 23; AM). Levinas's work *works* insofar as it resonates with the (masculine) third person singular pronoun that provides the condition of possibility of ethical obligation. Thus, Levinas's work should not be dominated by his proper name and he should not exercise authorial or signatorial (EM 47; AM) control over his work. Rather, Levinas's work sets the "Il" to work, "He" who will have obliged.

However, and here we return to the theme of the play between the pronoun and the proper name and to the question of ethical violence, it would also be a mistake to distinguish radically Levinas's proper name and the Pronominal "Il." A few lines below the last quotation one reads, "the subject of the phrase 'he will have obliged' might be (*soit*) Emmanuel Levinas." Thus although the "Il" is not dominated by the name of Emmanuel Levinas, the latter might be the subject designated by the pronoun. Continuing this thought in a slightly different formulation, the textual voice writes that it must renounce the supposed neutrality or anonymity of a discourse that employs the impersonal third-person pronoun. While the name of Emmanuel Levinas is rarely employed in "At this very moment," the textual voice makes it clear that the essay is not addressed to an anonymous addressee: "I will not pronounce your name nor inscribe it, but you are not anonymous at the moment when here am I telling you this."

Surprisingly, perhaps, what is at stake here is nothing less than the success or failure of Levinasian ethics. As has already been pointed out, for Levinas's work to work it must be directed toward the wholly other, the trace of Illeity that is signaled in the phrase "Il aura obligé" and which must not be allowed to return to the Same. To return to the Same is to return to the name, the proper name of Emmanuel Levinas. Conversely, if Levinas's work *does not* work, then it will return to or at least be indistinguishable from the name of Levinas. Derrida's strategy here is complex and is governed by a certain necessity which needs to be schematized: If Derrida simply showed how Levinas's work works by going unto the "Il," then he would merely be repeating Levinas's generous ethical gesture and thereby returning Levinas's work to its author. As has already been established, the necessary response to Levinas's work is one of radical ingratitude; thus, to reciprocate the generosity of the ethical gesture is to return the Other to the Same and consequently to deny ethics. Therefore, in order to maintain the ethical moment, Derrida must commit an ungrateful violence against Levinas's work: he must show how the work *does not work*.

One way of showing how Levinas's work does not work would be to argue that it ultimately returns to his proper name and to the logic of the Same. Yet this begs the question: does not the necessary violence of ingratitude which was intended to preserve the ethical, precisely deny the latter by returning the Pro-nominal "Il" to the proper name of Levinas? In order to circumvent this objection, the structure of Derrida's reading must be deepened once again. Let us ask: to whom should Levinas's work be returned in order to maintain ethical alterity? Might not the answer be *Elle* and not *E.L.*, the theme of the feminine that is developed in the final pages of "At this very moment"? Is "She" the Other to the wholly other, to whom the text is ultimately given?

"Bois"—"drink," the order of the Genesis narrative needs to be inverted and the roles reversed; Eliezer must let down his pitcher for her, Rebecca.

The shift from Levinas's name to the theme of the feminine is, once again, articulated around the difference between the proper name and the pronoun. Throughout "At this very moment," the textual voice replaces Emmanuel Levinas's proper name with the initials *E.L.* (see EM 24; AM for the first occurrence of this). At certain strategic points in the essay, *E.L.* is substituted for *Il* and the leitmotif of the essay reads: "E.L. aura obligé" (EM 45, 46; AM). Now, if one elides the pronounciation of the two letters "E" and "L" in order to produce one phoneme, two things occur: firstly, the word "El" is formed which, as Levinas points out in "Le nom de Dieu d'après quelques textes Talmudiques" (ND 158, a text which is referred to extensively in "At this very moment"—cf. EM 34–35, 38, 41, 56–58; AM), is one of the proper names of God in the Talmudic tradition. Secondly, one produces a homonym for the feminine third-person singular pronoun—"Elle." It is the second of these transmutations which opens up the ultimate horizon of "At this very moment." On the penultimate page of the essay the pronoun "Il" is replaced by "Elle" and the leitmotif of the essay is transformed into: "Elle aura obligé," "She will have obliged."

The structure of "At this very moment" can be said to move between three formulations of an ethical imperative or performative: "Il aura obligé," "E.L. aura obligé," and "Elle aura obligé." The transfer between the pronouns "Il" and "Elle" is mediated through the initialed proper name of "E.L." On three occasions in "At this very moment," Derrida employs the neologism "entr(el)-acement" (EM 49, 50, 51; AM), where the parenthetical "(el)"—the name of God, the name of Levinas—stands between the "inter" and "lacing," it stands on the threshold between the interlacing of two opposed terms, in this case the pronouns "Il" and "Elle." The deconstructive or, what I have called elsewhere, *clôtural*[6] fabric of Derrida's reading of Levinas is stretched across these two pronouns, where the threshold that divides both the masculine "Pro-nom" from the feminine "Pro-nom" and the pronominal from the proper, is continually transgressed.

There are two moments of reading at work in "At this very moment": first, Derrida tries to find out how Levinas's work *works*, and second, "he" tries to show how Levinas's work *does not work*. The first moment of reading shows how Levinas's text resists the economy of the Same or logocentrism and goes generously unto the Other: "Il aura obligé." Conversely, the second moment of reading is the necessary ingratitude and violence that are required in order to maintain the alterity of the first moment. The second moment is performed by showing how Levinas subordinates sexual difference to ethical difference and thereby encloses both the "Il" and the feminine with the economy of the Same. The work is not returned to "E.L." but to the other of the wholly other: "Elle aura obligé."

"Bois"—"drink"; is this how Derrida's work works? Is this the final word on Derrida's reading of Levinas? It has been shown above that Levinas's work must be possessed of a dehiscence which maintains the Saying of the pronominal *Il* or trace of Illeity. Levinas's work works insofar as it is interrupted by an alterity which refuses to return the Saying of the work to the proper name of Emmanuel Levinas. The claim of my commentary upon "At this very moment" is that Derrida's work is governed by a similar necessity: the work of Derrida's work is one that must not be returned to and circumscribed by Derrida's proper name. "At this very moment" is possessed of a dehiscence that allows it to resonate with an alterity which must not be reduced to the logic of the proper. Derrida's work works insofar as it returns the text to *Elle* and lets the voice of feminine alterity interrupt Levinas's work. To reduce the textuality of "At this very moment" to the proper name of Jacques Derrida (by saying, for example: "in this essay, Derrida says . . . ," "Derrida's final word is . . . ," etc.), as I will have often been obliged to do, is to foreclose the opening announced by ethical alterity and to cover over the ethical interruption that the text seeks to maintain.

This point can be reinforced by an examination of the narrative structure of "At this very moment." The text is not a monologue spoken by the signatory, Jacques Derrida; it is at the least a dialogue for two voices, and one might even call it a "polylogue" (cf. FC 8). The horizontal dash (—) that precedes the first word of the essay indicates that somebody is speaking in the text; the quotation marks denote a voice that is not necessarily that of the text's signatory. Turning the pages of the essay, one finds nine more of these dashes, each denoting a change in the textual voice. Furthermore, "At this very moment" is spoken or written by a number of voices that are sexually differentiated into masculine, neutral (*sic*), or feminine. Now, the interruption of Levinas's work occurs when the textual voice becomes that of a woman. This interruption can first be seen where the textual voice that begins the essay ("— il aura obligé") calls across to an other, "Where should you and I, we, let it be?" and is interrupted by a new voice, that of the feminine other, "— No, not let it be. Soon, we shall have to give it to him to eat and drink and you will listen to me" (EM 26–27; AM). The voice of the Other responds to its interlocutor (one might call the latter the voice of the Same) and promises that it will soon speak. This pattern of interruption is repeated on two further occasions: first during a discussion of the sexuality of the textual voice in the Song of Songs ("— He or she, if the interruption of the discourse is required?" EM 29; AM), and second during a discussion of the work of *Il* and its relation to the proper name of Emmanuel Levinas ("— Will it be said of 'this work' (*ouvrage*) that it makes a work?" EM 44; AM). As I show below, the most lengthy interruption (beginning, "— I knew" EM 51; AM), which constitutes the second moment of reading, is the response of feminine alterity, the interruption of the woman reader in Levinas's work.

"At this very moment" is not a monological text with one textual voice and one possible reading; rather there are at least two voices and two readings at work in the essay. As such, the text is structured as a double or *clôtural* reading. The first moment of reading, performed by the voice of the Same (a masculine reader), engages in a repetition of the Levinasian text, where the reader produces a commentary which says the same as Levinas and shows how his work works. The second moment of reading, performed by the voice of the Other (a woman reader), of the Levinasian text, interrupts the intentions and shows how his work does not work. The deconstructive pattern of "En ce moment même" is divided between the two moments of a double reading —repetition and interruption, Sameness and Otherness—which are performed by two sexually differentiated readers. As such, these two readings and readers do not constitute an opposition or antinomy, rather they maintain a relation of what was called above "entr(el)acement," that is, an ethical relation that would be respectful of the irreducibility of sexual difference.

"Bois"—"drink"; this is not *Derrida's* final word on Levinas, it is not governed by *him* and his proper name. The final word of ethical obligation is always uttered by the Other, in this instance "She" who interrupts Levinasian ethics and sets Derrida's work to work. Any consideration of the ethics of deconstructive reading must begin from this datum. But how should *I* read the work of Derrida's work in order to maintain the interruption? Does not the repetition implicit in *my* commentary foreclose any opening onto an ethics of sexual difference? How should I show gratitude to Derrida? Commentary is never neutral, and my-commentary-upon-Derrida's-commentary-upon-Levinas undoubtedly conceals the opening that is so carefully prepared by a double or *clôtural* reading. However, and precisely through the double passivity of a commentary upon a commentary, such a reading, no doubt only in its interstices and hiatuses, might reflect some of the oblique rays of the deconstructive opening where the injunction is announced and the interruption is maintained.

2.

I shall continue, then, in the manner of a commentary, by repeating the repetition of the first moment of reading. I begin with an illuminating misquotation. While endeavoring to understand and explain the workings of Levinas's text, the textual voice stumbles across one of Derrida's early texts.

> His [i.e., Levinas's] "text" (and I would even say *the* text, without wishing to efface an irreplaceable idiom) is always that heterogeneous tissue that interlaces both texture and atexture without uniting them. And whoever (as was written elsewhere of an other, very close and very distant) "ventures to plot the absolute tear, absolutely tears his own tissue, once again become solid and servile in once more giving itself to be read." (EM 38; AM)[7]

Two points need to be emphasized in relation to this passage. First, Levinas's text is a heterogeneous tissue,[8] that is, a substance composed of differing parts which are maintained in a relation of alterity. Levinasian textuality is composed of a certain texture and atexture, and it allows these opposing composite elements to maintain both their absolute alterity, while also interlacing them and bringing them into relation. Returning to the first parenthetical remark in the above quotation, one notices that the word "text" is given an italicized definite article ("*le* texte"). Although the textual voice is clearly hesitant here, as the use of the conditional tense would suggest, I believe that one would not be mistaken in inferring that when the textual voice speaks about Levinas's text, he is referring to *the* text. The structure of Levinasian textuality is a heterogeneous tissue similar to that which constitutes the structure of *the* text, of general textuality. Second, and this will confirm the first point, the textual voice proceeds to cite, strangely, and as if from memory, one of Derrida's early texts while giving no indication, however, of where the citation might come from. In fact, the quotation is drawn from the final three lines of Derrida's 1967 essay on Bataille and Hegel, "From Restricted to General Economy: A Hegelianism without Reserve" (cf. ED 407; WD 277). In the final pages of the latter, Derrida discusses Bataille's account of the Hegelian/Kojèvian text and concludes that it is one that can be read from the left or from the right, as a revolution or as a reaction. The text itself contains and maintains both these heterogeneous possibilities; it is a text whose tissue can be absolutely rended through an act of Bataillesque *souveraineté* only to solidify once more into what, for Bataille, is the servility and laboriousness of Hegelian/Kojèvian discourse.[9] This play of rending and mending, where differing elements enter into a relation where they remain absolute in that relation, here defines the heterogeneous structure of textuality. As I shall show, the structure of Levinasian textuality serves as an *exemplum* for general textuality, and a reading of the former gives one some insight into the latter.

How, then, does Levinas produce this heterogeneous textuality? How does his work work? How does Levinas's work (*ouvrage*) allow the Work (*Œuvre*) to be produced? What sort of writing does this require? The Work (*Œuvre*) that Levinas's work (*ouvrage*) performs is the setting forth of the *Il*, the wholly other. Thus the question becomes, "How does he manage to inscribe or let the wholly other be inscribed within the language of Being, of the present, of essence, of the same, of economy, etc.[?]" (EM 27; AM). If the linguistic resources of logocentrism or ontology are the only ones that are available to us, and if the trace of Illeity is wholly other to the language of Being, what was called above the "dominant interpretation of language," then how does that which is entirely foreign to logocentric or ontological discourse enter into it? In order to explain this enigma (which is the enigmatic possibility of ethics), shouldn't one *reverse* the question and ask oneself, "if that language is not *of itself unbound (d'elle-même déliée)* and hence open to the wholly other, to its own beyond, in such a way that it is less a matter of exceeding that language than of treating it otherwise with its own possibilities."

Although the dominant interpretation would claim that language is exclusively bound to Being and the Same, *perhaps* (and the modality of the *peut-être* in Levinas is something that intrigues the textual voice in "At this very moment" [cf. EM 34–35; AM]) language is from the start *unbound* and therefore capable of being bound to the otherwise than Being, the wholly other. It is not a question of replacing the present language of ontology with a language of ethics, but rather that of treating language in a manner that is otherwise than Being and presence. As is made clear later on in "At this very moment," for Levinas it is not a question of simply overcoming language in the name

of some irreducibly ontic "beyond." Language (*langue*) is as indispensable to
ethics as the tongue (*langue*) in the mouth of the one who tears off bread
in order to give it to the other (EM 31; AM). For Levinas, an ethics of silence
would be irreducibly violent.

In the first moment of reading, and in order to provide an insight into how
Levinas's work works, the textual voice seeks out those places where
unboundness or dehiscence are at work in Levinas's work. The textual voice
selects three examples of unboundness which, taken together, form the "cryptic" (EM 23; AM) title to the essay; they are the phrases: "En ce moment
même," "dans cet ouvrage," and "me voici." These phrases are quotations from
Levinas and occur in his work precisely at those moments when he is considering how his work works. In the following pages, I shall pass over the examples
of *ouvrage* and *Œuvre*, which have already been discussed, and elide the
me voici (cf. EM 28–29; AM). The privileged example, which will permit the
ultimate structure of Levinasian textuality to be discerned, will be the phrase
en ce moment même.

In order to elucidate the theme of unboundness, the textual voice quotes
extensive passages from *Otherwise than Being*, where Levinas employs the
phrase *en ce moment même* at the very moment when he is explaining how
his work works. I shall begin by citing the two passages as they appear in
Derrida's essay.

> Every contesting and interruption of this power of discourse is at once related
> by discourse. It therefore recommences as soon as one interrupts it. This
> discourse will affirm itself as coherent and one. In relating the interruption
> of discourse or my being ravished by it, I retie the thread and are we not,
> *at this very moment* [my italics, J.D.] in the process of barring up the exit
> which our whole essay is attempting, and encircling our position from all sides?
> (EM 32; AM, AE 215; OB 169)

And secondly,

> The discourse which suppresses the interruptions of discourse in relating them
> together, does it not maintain the discontinuity behind the knots where the
> thread is retied?
> The interruptions of discourse, recovered and related within the immanence
> of the said, are conserved as the knots in a retied thread.
> But the ultimate discourse, where all the discourses are uttered, I still inter-
> rupt it in telling it to the one who listens and is situated outside the Said
> that discourse says, outside all that it embraces. Which is true of the discourse
> that I am in the process of holding *at this very moment* [my italics, J.D.].
> (EM 33; AM, AE 216–17; OB 170)

One should firstly note and underline the repetition of the same phrase,
"*en ce moment même*," in these quotations. For it is a repetition which involves
a dislocation or displacement, where the same phrase, when repeated in two
different but related contexts, interrupts itself and says something wholly other.
In the first passage, Levinas raises the theme of interruption which occurs

in *Otherwise than Being* (AE 24, 214–15, 216; OB 20, 169, 170, and cf. EM 38; AM). For Levinas, the interruption of essence or Being occurs in the reduction of the ontological Said to the ethical Saying (AE 56; OB 44). Such an interruption of the Saying within the Said denies the closure (*"fermeture,"* AE 24; OB 20) of the Said and, for Levinas, represents the only end (*"fin,"* ibid.) that can be envisaged for philosophical discourse. There is no simple and radical overcoming of ontological or logocentric language through the ethical Saying of the otherwise than Being, rather the ethical is the momentary interruption of the *logos*. As such, any attempt to thematize ethical interruption will always retie the thread of philosophical discourse. Thus, Levinas asks himself whether, in thematizing the ethical Saying within the ontological Said of a book, he is, *at this very moment*, denying the ethical breakthrough that *Otherwise than Being* attempts.

However, another picture of interruption emerges from the second quotation. Levinas appears to be saying, first, that although the ethical interruptions of essence are retied in the thread of the ontological Said, they are preserved as knots in such a thread. And second, that the ultimate or final discourse, where all discourse is uttered, is still interrupted by a Saying that is addressed to the one who listens, the other or interlocutor who is situated outside of the Said. Levinas's claim is that this ultimate interruption occurs in the discourse that he is holding *at this very moment*.

Thus, in the interval that separates the repetition of the *en ce moment même*, a certain dislocation has occurred. The repetition of the same phrase has wholly other consequences.[10] In the first instance, at this very moment, I enclose the ethical interruption of essence within the ontological Said; while in the second instance, at this very moment, I ultimately interrupt the Said. At the very moment when Levinas is explaining how his work works, one is confronted by an absolute heterogeneity, where Levinas, through a repetition of the Same, says something wholly other. Indeed, one might say that it is precisely through such a heterogeneity that Levinas's work works.

But how are these two instances of the *en ce moment même* related? To approach this question it is necessary to examine the metaphor of the retied thread (*le fil renoué*) that is employed in both these passages and which so intrigues the textual voice. In the first passage, the interruption of discourse is akin to the breaking of a thread which is itself retied in the ontological thematization of the Saying in the Said. In the second passage, the interruptions of discourse, although retied into the thread, are preserved as knots in the thread and, indeed, at this very moment, in addressing myself to the one who listens, I break the thread. Thus the two heterogeneous instances of the *en ce moment même*, linked together through a dislocating act of repetition, are related and tied together through the metaphor of the retied thread. The picture that is beginning to form is that of a single thread with a series of knots running its length. These knots would represent the moments of the ethical interruption of essence, each of which could be interrupted, at this very moment, by addressing myself to an interlocutor.

Recalling the metaphor of the tissue or fabric that occurred in the passage from the essay on Bataille, one might say that Levinasian textuality is a fabric that is continually rended and mended and where the rending that takes place in ethical interruption is retied back into the body of the text as a fault or a flaw. As I shall show, the fabric of textuality is explained and deepened in "At this very moment" through the image of a *series (série)* of rends and mends, an unbound seriality of discourse.

But is the seriality which binds together these two instances of the *en ce moment même* one of reciprocity and strict equality? Does the play of rending and mending take place without priority? To address these questions it is necessary to turn to a second example of the *en ce moment même* from "Le nom de Dieu" that is also cited at length by the textual voice,

> Responsibility which, before the discourse bearing on the *said*, is probably the essence of language.
> It will of course be objected that if any other relation than thematization may exist between the Soul and the Absolute, then wouldn't the act of talking and thinking about it *at this very moment* [my italics, J.D.], the fact of enveloping it in our dialectic, mean that language and dialectic are superior with respect to that relation?
> But the language of thematization, which we are using *at this moment* [my italics, J.D.], has perhaps only been made possible by means of that Relation and is only ancillary to it. (EM 34–35; AM, ND 167)

One immediately notices the same unboundness that was in evidence in the previous examples. After tentatively establishing that responsibility—*for* one's fellow humans *before* the self-effacement of the transcendent God (ND 164) —is the essence of language, Levinas raises the objection as to whether this essence is enveloped within the thematizing language that is being employed *at this very moment*. But he immediately goes on to claim that the language of thematization that is being used *at this very moment* is only made possible by the essence of language revealed in the relation to the other. One thus rediscovers the same heterogeneous fabric that was discussed above, with the subtle but important difference that one instance of the "en ce moment même" is given priority over the other. In the passages cited, the second instance takes precedence over the first: although the language that is being used *at this very moment* is that of thematization (where the ethical rending of the fabric is continually mended by the hand of Being), this language is, *at this very moment*, only made possible by the ethical relation which constitutes the essence of language (where the fabric is torn from the hands of Being).

In the repetition of the *en ce moment même*, a subtle, almost inapparent, yet crucial dimension of alterity opens up, unbinding the language of the tradition. The heterogeneous structure of textuality gives an absolute priority to alterity, to the otherness in which the conditions for the possibility of ontology and logocentrism are located. With specific reference to the two instances of *en ce moment même* from "Le nom de Dieu," the textual voice writes. "The second 'moment' will have forced the first toward its own condition of possibility, toward its 'essence' beyond the Said and the Theme. It will have, in advance—but after the fact in the serial rhetoric—torn the envelope" (EM 37; AM).

The ethical interruption of essence which must, of necessity, envelop itself in the language of thematization, will always, of necessity, tear that envelope. The double necessity that is at work here obliges one to employ the language of the tradition, but, at the very same moment, one *will have been* obliged to interrupt this language and bear it toward its own condition of possibility. The fabric of discourse is not simply the play of rending and mending that was discussed above, because Levinas finds a way of retying the knot which does not mend the thread and which produces an irreducible *supplement* to ontology. The structure of textuality becomes yet more complex, "But there is in his text, perhaps, a supplementary nodal complication, another way of retying without retying. How is this supplement of the knot to be figured?" (EM 40; AM).

How indeed? As is remarked upon a few pages further on, the singularity of the Levinasian text is due to the way in which it binds itself together at the very moment when its discursive structure is unbound. The fabric of the text is both bound and unbound. The bound language of thematization, which is employed in order to thematize the nonthematizable, must not be allowed to envelop the nonthematizable "essence" of language. An irreducible nonthematizability *must* (and one must, as always, be continually vigilant as to the ethical modality of the *must—il faut*) stand apart from the thread of the ontological Said where the moments of ethical interruption are preserved as knots. There must be an "interruption between interruptions" (EM 40; AM), a threadless supplement to the knot which cannot be retied back into the ontological thread of the Said. The picture that now emerges is one where, within the knot of each ethical interruption that has been tied back into the ontological thread, there persists an irreducible supplement to the knot which is the very interruption of interruption.

The fabric of the text, a texture of threads and knots, contains what the textual voice calls a "hiatus" within each knot, which constitutes what I called above *atexture*, a threadless moment in the fabric. This moment of *atexture*, whether it be called "the hiatus," "the interruption of interruption," or "the supplement of the knot," is the point of ethical priority within the text, the Saying that is the condition for the possibility of the Said. As the textual voice points out, this supplement to the knot is not unique, "a sole interruption does not suffice"; there must be a multiplicity or plurality of knots, what is called a *"series"* ("I have chosen to name this structure by the word *series*"). One imagines a series of knots, connected by a continuous thread, and upon or within each of these knots would be a nodal point of supplementarity. Indeed, this image of the text as a play of binding and unbinding, where the mended interruption of essence is itself interrupted by a moment of irreducible ethical priority, is the way in which Levinas's work works. The textual voice introduces the neologism *sériature* in order to explain the complex textual structure of obligation, "An interrupted series, a *series* of interlaced interruptions, a series of *hiatuses* that I shall henceforth call, in order to formalize in economical fashion and so as not to dissociate what is no longer dissociable within this fabric, *sériature*" (EM 48; AM). With the word *sériature*, defined as the movement of binding and unbinding, the play of texture and atexture, a formal designation of the workings of Levinas's work has been attained. Formally and thematically, Levinas's work works as an interrupted series or a series of interrupted interruptions, where the continuity and repetition of the series is continually placed under erasure (*série + rature = sériature*) by the energy of an ethical interruption.

The concept of *sériature* describes the relations between binding and unbinding, between being bound to ontological or logocentric language while at the same moment being unbound to that language. The fabric of Levinasian textuality is a *sériature* insofar as it maintains a tension between the thread (the ontological Said), the knot (the ethical Saying or interruption), and the hiatus (the interruption of interruption); where what is unbound, nonthematizable and wholly other to ontology and logocentrism can only be articulated through a certain repetition of ontological or logocentric language, a repetition that interrupts that language. Levinasian textuality (and perhaps textuality in general, *the* text) obeys a *sériatural* rhythm of binding and unbinding which preserves the absolute priority of ethical obligation.

3.

The first moment of reading has shown how Levinas's work works, and, as such, does not leave the order of commentary, where the internal exigencies of the text are repeated and left intact. Commentary always belongs to the text that is being commented upon and derives from a choice which has decided not to disturb or dislocate the order of the text (a principle which extends, of course, to the commentary-upon-a-commentary that I am writing at this very moment—"Bois"). To repeat or comment upon a text is ultimately to return that text to its author. Now, for reasons discussed above, to return Levinasian textuality to the proper name of Emmanuel Levinas is to deny the structure of ethical obligation and reduce the Saying to the Said. It is therefore ethically and, I would claim, deconstructively necessary for the repetition and commentary of the first moment of reading to be violated and transgressed in the second moment, a reading that leaves the order of commentary.[11]

The form of this violation and transgression is the ungrateful response which maintains the responsibility of ethical interruption by returning the text to "Elle" and not to "E.L." The transition from the first to the second moment of reading is marked by a shift in the grammatical gender of the textual voice. It is the woman reader who leaves the order of commentary and makes "At this very moment" a double reading.[12] The textual voice concludes its commentary by writing that it is "impossible to approach his work without first of all passing, already, by the re-treat of its inside, namely, the remarkable saying of the work" (EM 51; AM). The voice of commentary faithfully traces the inside of Levinas's work and detects its ethical Saying. Yet, at the very moment when the ultimate sense of ethical Saying becomes manifest, when we finally understand how Levinas's work works, the voice of commentary addresses itself to an other and asks for a response, "you (come), obligated woman reader (*lectrice obligée*). You can still refuse to grant him that sense." The textual voice calls to the feminine Other, the woman reader, asking her to come (*viens*),[13] to approach and refuse the sense of the ethical Saying.

"Bois"—"drink"; from across the wide line space that divides two paragraphs and two voices, the feminine Other responds in responsibility: "I knew. In listening I was nonetheless wondering whether I was comprehended (*comprise*), myself, and how to stop that word: comprehended (*comprise*)" (EM 51; AM). In virtue of the gendered status of French grammar, the additional "*e*" on the neutral (i.e., masculine) past participle "*compris*" indicates that the gender of the textual voice is female. One finds further confirmations of the femininity of the textual voice in the subsequent pages of the essay, where the textual voice repeatedly refers to herself as a woman: "Why should the son be more or better than the daughter, than *me*," "The other as feminine (*me*)," "their common link to *me*, to the other as woman," "I speak from *my* place as a woman" (EM 52, 54, 56; AM; my italics).

If the transition from the first to the second moment of reading is effected by the shift from a neutral (masculine) reader, a *lecteur*, to a woman reader, a *lectrice*, then how does the woman read in order to return the work of Levinas's work to "Elle"? She begins with an apparently innocent example of Levinas's *sériature*, an example of the work: "I shall give or take an example of it. More or perhaps another thing than an example, that of the 'son' in *Totality and Infinity*, of the 'unique' son or sons: 'The son is not my work (*oeuvre*), like a poem or an object'" (EM 51; AM and TeI 254; TI 277).

The example of *sériature* is the son, "he" who is my "work." Of course, such an example is not at all innocent, because by choosing the question of the son, the woman reader opens up the problem of the relation between sexual difference and ethical difference in Levinas. It is precisely this theme that will be the subject of the second moment of reading.

After giving the page reference to the above quotation from *Totality and Infinity*, the woman reader casually throws in the following aside, "I assume that the context is re-read." But what is the context of this context? There are two contexts to which I shall briefly return before continuing with the commentary: first, *Totality and Infinity*, and second, "Violence and Metaphysics." In the fourth and final section of *Totality and Infinity*, entitled "Beyond the Face," Levinas, as he does elsewhere in his work (TA 85–89; TO 91–94 and DE 157–65; EE 92–96), posits fecundity as the access to a domain of existence that breaks with the Parmenidean unity of Being. In fecundity, I both am my son and I am not my son; he is both the fruit of my loins and a being with a separate and independent existence. There is a *sériatural* logic at work in fecundity, where I am both bound to my son and unbound to him. Although the personage of the son should not be immediately conflated with the "He" of the trace of Illeity, one can see why the woman reader chooses fecundity as an example of Levinasian *sériature*. In fecundity my being is interrupted and doubled and I enter a *pluralistic* domain that cannot be reduced to Eleatic monism. Thus, Levinasian ethics works insofar as it sets the son to work.[14] It is through fecundity that the "dream of a happy eternity" (TeI 261; TI 284) or a "victory over death" (TA 85; TO 90–91) cannot simply be discarded as aberrations.

The second context is "Violence and Metaphysics," where a strange point of continuity relates that text to "At this very moment." As her reading gets underway, the woman reader parenthetically quotes Derrida's final words on Levinas in "Violence and Metaphysics," from the final footnote of the latter work.

> To himself, his text marks its signature by a masculine "I-he," a rare thing, as was elsewhere noted "in passing" a long time ago, by an other ("Let us note in passing on this subject that *Totality and Infinity* pushes the respect for dissymetry up to the point where it seems to us impossible, essentially impossible, that it could have been written by a woman. The philosophical subject of it is man (*vir*)"). (EM 52; AM and ED 220; WD 320–21)

The woman reader notes "in passing" that which Derrida footnoted "in passing" some sixteen years earlier: namely, the masculine determination of ethical difference in Levinas's work. One might therefore read the second moment of reading in "At this very moment" as a continuation of this final footnote, as "A Note to a Note in 'Violence and Metaphysics.'" The woman reader takes up a position of alterity ("by an other") *not only* with respect to Levinas's work, but also with respect to "Violence and Metaphysics." In addition to the necessary ingratitude shown toward Levinas's work, might one not consider the second moment of "At this very moment" as a double reading of "Violence and Metaphysics," as a re-reading of Derrida's early work in terms of the ethics of sexual difference?

Provisionally and schematically, in order to approach the second moment of "At this very moment" as a double reading of "Violence and Metaphysics," it would be necessary to show how the latter text is inhabited and dislocated by the former. To take an "innocent" example of this, consider that after the opening two expository sections of "Violence and Metaphysics"—"The Violence of Light" and "Phenomenology, Ontology, Metaphysics"—the textual voice closes its commentary with the following footnote:

> We will not go beyond this schema. It would be useless to attempt, here, to enter into the descriptions devoted to interiority, economy, enjoyment, habitation, femininity, Eros, to everything suggested under the title *Beyond the Face* and which the situation would doubtless merit many questions. These analyses are not only an indefatiguable and interminable destruction of "formal logic," they are so acute and so free as concerns traditional conceptuality, that a commentary running several pages would betray them immeasurably. (ED 161; WD 315)

Although "Violence and Metaphysics" mentions some of the above themes, for example those of pluralism (ED 132; WD 89) and fecundity (ED 127; WD 86) discussed in "Beyond the Face" and the question of the feminine raised above, one might say that the text *forecloses* a detailed discussion of them and erects a frontier or limit to its conceptual schema, a frontier that is crossed by the phenomenological descriptions of the later sections of *Totality and Infinity*. I suggest that the reason why they have to be excluded is not just because "a commentary running several pages would betray them immeasurably"— a statement which, for the reasons discussed above, has more truth than might at first be imagined—but also because they would betray the conceptual schema of "Violence and Metaphysics." Now, if the governing intention of Levinas's work, that of the break with Parmenides, is achieved in those descriptions of *eros*, fecundity, and pluralism ("Existing itself becomes double. The Eleatic notion of Being is overcome" [TA 88; TO 92]), the very descriptions which the commentary of "Violence and Metaphysics" cannot but betray— and which would betray the order of its commentary and of commentary itself —then does not their omission mark a serious flaw in the fabric of "Violence and Metaphysics"? And is this a flaw which only the woman reader, both the betrayed and the betrayer, could discern? I suggest that it is plausible to read the second moment of "At this very moment" as a supplement to "Violence and Metaphysics," whose supplementary logic would be to inhabit and dislocate the latter text, betraying its conceptuality through a double reading and opening the text to an economy whose necessity would be ethical.

Returning to the context of the second moment of reading in "At this very moment," the woman reader is seeking to interrogate the link, in Levinas's work, between sexual difference—the other as another sex—and ethical difference—the other as "He," the wholly other (EM 52; AM). It is important to stress from the outset that the woman reader will not simply claim that Levinas's work is antifeminist, patriarchal, or sexist, but rather that by subordinating sexual difference to ethical difference and by trying to maintain the latter in a sexual *indifference* or *neutrality*, Levinas gives a privilege to the masculine. How does this come about?

On the same page of *Totality and Infinity* where Levinas speaks of the son as the work which attains a plurality within Being, he proceeds to substitute the word "child" (*enfant*) for "son" (*fils*): "I do not have my child, I am my child" (TeI 254; TI 277). Of this silent act of substitution, the woman reader asks, "Is it that 'son' is another word for 'child,' a child who could be of one or the other sex?" (EM 52; AM). If this were the case, if the work of the child is sexually indifferent, then "why couldn't the daughter play an analogous role?" If the neutral work can be as well described by the word "child," then why should the word "son" (*fils*) mark this indifference or neutrality more ably than the word "daughter" (*fille*)? The work of the son in *Totality and Infinity* establishes an absolute ethical difference which is sexually indifferent. The *sexual* difference that is so evocatively described in "Phenomenology of Eros" is ultimately *aufgehoben* by the fecundity which establishes a meta-Parmenidean *ethical* difference.

The question now becomes: if ethical difference is sexually indifferent, then "how can one mark as masculine the very thing that is said to be anterior or still foreign to sexual difference?" (EM 52; AM). It has already been established that if Levinas's work works, then it is precisely to the extent that it allows the trace of Illeity, the "Il" of the wholly other, to glimmer in the face of the Other (*autrui*). Now, if this "Il" is sexually neutral, how can it be marked with a masculine pronoun? The silent slippage that occurs between "child" and "son" reveals that the supposed neutrality of ethical difference is marked, in Levinas's work, by a certain priority of the masculine. The sexual indifference of ethical difference treats masculinity and neutrality as synonyms. However, this is not the only pair of synonyms at work here, because by making sexual difference secondary to ethical difference and by marking the latter with a masculine pronoun, the secondary status of sexual difference becomes synonymous with the secondary status of the feminine. The problematic that ultimately guides the second moment of reading is given in the form of a question. She writes,

> I come then to my question. Since the work is under-signed by the Pro-noun He (before he/she certainly, but He is not She), could it be that in making sexual alterity secondary, it becomes, far from letting itself be approached from the Work, his or the one that says itself there, the mastery, mastery of sexual difference, posed as origin of femininity? Hence mastery of femininity? (EM 54–55; AM)

Does not the sexual neutrality of ethical difference lead ineluctably to a mastery of sexual difference and, synonymously, to a mastery of the masculine over the feminine? If this is the case, then how can Levinasian ethics be considered ethical?

These questions take us right to the heart of the second moment of reading. The claim is that Levinas makes sexual difference secondary with respect to the sexually neutral wholly other. To mark the neutrality of the wholly other with a masculine pronoun is to make sexual difference secondary as femininity. Yet this state of affairs is about to undergo a reversal and be exposed to the supplementary logic of the double reading: "The secondary status of sexual, and therefore, says He, of feminine difference, does it not thus come to stand for the wholly-other of this Saying of the wholly other, within its *sériature* here determined and within the idiom of this negotiation?" By making sexual difference secondary to ethical difference and by equating sexuality with the feminine, does not the feminine, then, become wholly-other to the Saying of the wholly other? If "She" is the other to "He," and if "He" is the wholly other, then "She" is the other to the wholly other. The question then becomes: as the other to the wholly other, as a being that possesses greater alterity than the wholly other, does "She" not demand greater ethical respect and priority than "He"? "The other as feminine (me), far from being derived or secondary, would become the other of the Saying of the wholly-other."

The reversal that the woman reader is attempting here is one where priority is given to that which was secondary. If "He," the wholly other, "will have obliged" us to an absolute obligation, then may not "She," the other to the wholly other, have put us under an even greater, more primordial obligation? For the woman reader, the theme of the feminine constitutes "a surfeit of un-said alterity" (*un surcroît d'altérité non-dite*) within the *sériature* of Levinas's work. One might say that sexual difference is Levinas's "blind spot." But what economy governs this blind spot? How does Levinas remain blind to sexual difference? Two *enclosures* can be detected in Levinas's work: (1) By making sexual difference secondary and by seeking to master the un-said alterity of the feminine, the "Il" of the wholly other would risk *enclosing* itself within the economy of the same. (2) By seeking to enclose sexual difference within ethical difference, the feminine is *enclosed* within the economy of the Same. She writes, "Included within the same, it is by the same stroke excluded: enclosed within, foreclosed within the immanence of a crypt, incorporated in the Saying which says itself to the wholly other." Feminine alterity becomes enclosed within the Saying which says itself to the wholly other; the feminine is foreclosed within the immanence of a *crypt*.[15]

The economy of the blind spot is governed by these two enclosures, where Levinas's work encloses the trace of Illeity within the economy of the same and encloses the feminine within a crypt. Levinas remains blind to the priority of feminine alterity by circumscribing her within the economy of the ethical and by inhuming her within the crypt of the same. For the woman reader, the desexualization of the wholly other is a way of making the feminine secondary and, hence, of failing to recognize "Her" as the other to the wholly other. To recognize the absolute alterity of the feminine is to realize that "She" replaces "He" as the "Pro-nom" of Levinas's work: *"Elle aura obligé"*: "Then the Work apparently signed by the Pro-noun He would be dictated, inspired, and aspired by the desire to make She secondary, therefore *by* She."

The conclusion to the second moment of reading is that feminine alterity, as the other to the wholly other, "pre-seals" (EM 59; AM) Levinas's work in such a way that it *does not* work for "Him." Levinas's work can only go unto the wholly other on the condition that feminine alterity is circumscribed and inhumed. The strange consequence of the latter is that Levinas's work is itself engaged in a denial of (feminine) alterity and thus remains enclosed within the economy of the same which it has continually striven to exceed.

If, during the first moment of reading, it was discovered that the way in which Levinas's work worked was best described in terms of *sériature*, then the second moment has discovered a second *sériature* which shows how Levinas's work does not work for *Il* but for *Elle*. At the very moment when, with one hand, I weave the delicate fabric of the ethical text, another hand, a woman's hand, undoes my work. The question now becomes: how exactly does the repetition and commentary of the first moment of reading combine with the violence and interruption of the second moment in a text *for* Emmanuel Levinas? How do these two moments preserve the gift of the ethical? "Bois"?

4.

The woman reader freely admits the violence of her reading, "What I suggest here is not without violence" (EM 56; AM). It is a faulty violence, which leaves a flaw in *his* name and *his* work, "Violence faulty in regard to his name, his work." Yet who is "he" in this context? Against whom is the violence committed? Is it against "him," Emmanuel Levinas, or is it against "Him," the wholly other?

As I noted above, the logic of the fault, of violence and ingratitude, is not accidental but essential to the ethical event of the text: "bois." Ingratitude does not arise like an accidental evil, it is a necessity or fatality within ethical Saying. The necessity of Levinas's work is that its *work*, the "Il," must be ungratefully received in order to maintain ethical alterity. In the second moment of reading, this alterity is maintained by returning the work to "Elle" and not to "E.L." Consequently, the violence that the woman reader commits is directed against "Him," Levinas's work, and not against "him," Emmanuel Levinas. Ingratitude and violence are committed against the body of the wholly other and not against Levinas: "It isn't him, but Him, that my fault comes to wound in his body."

"Bois"—"drink"; the fault has been committed, the violence has been done, the body of the "Il" has been wounded, the text for Emmanuel Levinas has been written, and ethical alterity has been maintained. Yet how can this violent, wounding text be given to Emmanuel Levinas? What will become of this faulty text? "If I wanted to destroy or annul my fault, I should have to know what becomes of the text that is writing itself at this very moment, where it can take place and what can remain of its remains." *If* (and the hypothetical character of this conjunction must be noted) the woman reader wanted to annul her fault and give her text to Levinas in a way that would still maintain the ethical, then what will she have been obliged to do? At this point, the text takes a further and final detour into "Le nom de Dieu." Levinas remarks that in the Talmudic tradition it is expressly forbidden to efface any of the names of God. If one does, by some fault, efface one of His names, if one's hand slips on a page of the manuscript bearing His name, then, "the entire page upon which the error that motivates the erasure or effacement of the Name figures, must be placed in the earth like a dead body" (ND 157).[16] The Torah is a body of writings which are given as much respect as the living body of a human being, and when that textual body is violated or fatally flawed it must be buried in accordance with the same ceremonies that accompany human burial. The woman reader is intrigued here by the analogy between textuality, embodiment, and the act of burial. The body of the faulty text is not censorially burnt and reduced to a pile of ashes, rather it is inhumed like a corpse where it is allowed slowly to decompose. The fault within the text slowly disappears as the text decomposes.

The woman reader finds a correspondence between this Talmudic anecdote and the status of her own text. To wound or violate the trace of Illeity by replacing the pronoun "Il" with "Elle" constitutes an act of effacement or erasure. The woman reader effaces the Pro-noun or Fore-name of God and replaces it with "Elle." Now, in order to annul or destroy this fault, this text *for* Emmanuel Levinas must be placed in the earth and allowed to decompose. Thus, the faulty text is given to Levinas by burying it in the earth, where it is preserved in a process of slow decomposition. However, the burial of the text does not render it faultless and thereby deny ethical alterity by returning the text to its author. On the contrary, the fault is not erased, it is preserved in the process of decomposition. Ethical alterity is maintained because the fault, although inhumed, is still preserved and therefore the text is returned to "*Elle*" and not to "E.L." It is "She," the feminine body, the body of feminine alterity, who is buried. It is she, the woman reader, who gives the dead body of the feminine to Levinas. "His" work has been violated and given back to Him in the buried form of the feminine body because this is the only way in which the ethical work can be maintained. After the burial, the text *for* Levinas becomes an absent work, what is called "a work of mourning" ("*un travail de deuil*, EM 57; AM).[17] Consequently, the ethical work is a funereal work of mourning over the dead body of the feminine. The final scene of "At this very moment" takes place at a funeral.

The woman reader brings her reading to a close with the words "*elle aura obligé.*" However, the text does not end there, for another voice comes to interrupt the text: "— I no longer know if you are saying what his work says. Perhaps that comes back to the same. I no longer know if you are saying the contrary, or if you have already written something wholly other. I no longer hear your voice, I have difficulty distinguishing it from my own, from any other, your fault suddenly becomes illegible to me. Interrupt me" (EM 59; AM).

Whose is the voice that interrupts and says "I" here? It is clearly not that of the woman reader, for it is she who is interrupted. Returning to the hypothesis of the double reading that has been argued for in this essay, I would claim that it is most plausible that the "I" denotes the return of the masculine voice of the Same, the voice of commentary that showed how Levinas's work worked. On this reading, the second person singular pronoun "you" would refer to the woman reader, and the possessive pronoun "his" would refer to Levinas's work. Thus, the masculine textual voice no longer knows if the woman reader is saying what Levinas's work says. To say the same would doubtless return that work within the economy of the Same ("Perhaps that comes back to the same"). On the other hand, the textual voice also adds that it no longer knows if the woman reader is saying the contrary to Levinas's work, or whether she has written something wholly other. The masculine voice no longer knows if she is saying the same or something other to Levinas's work, the voice no longer knows how to read the reading. Unreadable and unknowable, he no longer hears the woman's voice and it becomes difficult to distinguish it from his own or from that of any other. It is at this point that the textual voice engages with plurality, the male voice becomes indistinguishable from that of the woman, the two moments of reading become intr(el)aced and, at that very moment, the fault within the woman's reading becomes unreadable. The textual voice is unable to read Levinas's work in terms of one moment or the other. The two moments or lines of the double reading suddenly cross and form the figure of a chiasmus. It is from within this unknowing, unreadable, undecidable position that the voice demands of the Other, "Interrupt me."

The response to this final call for interruption leads into the last scene of "At this very moment," the strange final paragraph of the essay. How is one to comment upon it? In fact, despite its obscurity, the final paragraph resonates with many of the themes that have already been discussed. It can be approached as a liturgy ("THE THING OF THIS LITURGY . . . "), in the Levinasian sense, that is, as a *leitourgia*, the Greek term which describes the movement of the work (*ergon*) from the Same to the Other (EDE 192; TTO 350). It is a liturgy spoken at a funeral, the funeral of the feminine Other: "HERE AT THIS VERY MOMENT I ROLL UP THE BODY OF OUR IN-TERLACED VOICES CONSONANTS VOWELS ACCENTS FAULTY IN THIS MANUSCRIPT." The "I" that speaks here is the woman reader. It is she who rolls together the interlaced voices and moments of reading into the body of the text. It is she who gives the text to Levinas by burying it in the earth: "I MUST PLACE IT IN THE EARTH FOR YOU—COME LEAN DOWN." It is she who calls ("COME") to the Other to lean down over the place where the gift is buried. One imagines a man and a woman leaning over a grave at a funeral and looking down at the earth. The woman speaks, "IT'S OUR MUTE INFANT A DAUGHTER PERHAPS OF AN INCEST STILLBORN."

The faulty text that wounds the jealous body of the *Il* is *Elle*, the stillborn daughter whose fatally flawed body is buried and allowed slowly to decompose, rendering the fault illegible. "She" is the faulty body, the inhumed stillborn daughter. "IN THE BOTTOMLESS CRYPT THE INDECIPHERABLE STILL GIVES ITSELF TO BE READ." The only way in which the daughter can be contained within ethical difference is by enclosing her within the bottomless crypt of the Same, within an economy that makes sexual difference secondary. The voice of feminine alterity speaks out from the closure of this crypt, the woman reader pleads, "WE MUST HAVE A NEW BODY AN-OTHER WITHOUT ANY MORE JEALOUSY THE MOST ANCIENT STILL TO COME."

The faulty text has been buried, the stillborn daughter decomposes within the crypt. Above, a woman's voice weaves ("*TISSE*") and effaces itself ("*M'Y EFFACER*"). The gift has been given, the text for E.L. has been returned to "Elle" and buried, ethical alterity has been maintained. The woman's voice calls to the Other, "TAKE IT . . . APPROACH"; she beckons to the Other to come closer and receive the gift. Again, one imagines a woman and a man leaning over a grave, the man, the elder of the two, plunges his hands into the earth and takes his stillborn daughter into his arms: "BOIS."

21. And the man wondering at her held his peace, to wit whether the Lord had made his journey prosperous or not.

22. And it came to pass, as the camels had done drinking, that the man took a golden earring of half a shekel weight and two bracelets for hands of ten *shekels* weight of gold;

23. And said, whose daughter *art* thou? tell me, I pray thee: is there room *in* thy father's house for us to lodge in?

Notes

1. This passage from Genesis (King James translation) is discussed in Catherine Chalier's essay in this volume, "Ethics and the Feminine."

2. On the theme of the *"cercle ulysséen"* of philosophy, see Derrida's "Ulysse Gramphone: l'oui-dire de Joyce," in *Genèse de Babel*, Etudes présentés par Claude Jacquet, Paris, C.N.R.S., 1985, 227–64. Reprinted in *Ulysse Gramophone*, Paris, Editions Galilée, 1987, 57–143. Page references to the original text. In this essay, through a reading of Joyce's *Ulysses*, Derrida tries to show that there is a preoriginal *"oui"* or *"yes"* which breaches the circular movement of the Odyssey, the en*cyclo*paedic dialectic of philosophical appropriation. For Derrida, this prelogocentric, preontological opening of the *"oui"* is the *responsibility* which all discourse presupposes, "The autoposition in the *yes* . . . is pre-ontological, if ontology says what-is or the Being of what-is. Discourse on Being presupposes the responsibility of the *yes*" (257).

3. Cf. Chalier, "Ethics and the Feminine."

4. For occurrences of this word in relation to Heidegger, see *Eperons: Les styles de Nietzsche*, Paris, Flammarion, 1978, 95.

5. On the question of the performative, see EM 46–47; AM and the reference to speech act theory, EM 33–34; AM. The relation of Levinasian ethics to speech act theory is discussed by Jan De Greef in "Skepticism and Reason," trans. Dick White, in *Face to Face with Levinas*, ed. Richard Cohen, Albany State University of New York Press, 1986, 181–202.

6. I have attempted to elucidate Derrida's practice of reading through an account of the concept of closure (*clôture*) in his work and have advanced the notion of *clôtural* reading. See "The Problem of Closure" in "The Chiasmus: Levinas, Derrida and the Ethics of Deconstructive Reading," Ph.D. diss. University of Essex, 1988, 72–142.

7. Strangely, when the textual voice copies the phrase from the Bataille essay into "At this very moment," it is misquoted. The quotation marks that surround the words "absolute tear" and "solid" suddenly rise like the curtain in a theater, as Derrida is wont to say (*De l'esprit*, Paris, Editions Galilée, 1987, 53–54; trans. Geoffrey Bennington and Rachel Bowlby, *Of Spirit*, Chicago, University of Chicago Press, 1989, 31), a fact made all the more ironical because Derrida makes so much of Heidegger's misquotation of quotation marks when the latter cites his 1933 Rectoral Address in his 1935 *Introduction to Metaphysics* (*De l'esprit*, 57; *Of Spirit*, 34).

8. On the notion of the text as a tissue (*textus, texere, textile*), see the unoccasioned paragraph that is appended to the bibliography of *L'écriture et la différence* ("*texte veut dire tissu*" ED 437). This note is discussed at length by Alan Bass in the translator's introduction to *Writing and Difference* (WD ix–xx).

9. For Bataille's reading of Hegel, see the few fascinating pages devoted to the subject in *L'expérience intérieure*, Paris, Gallimard, 1943, 127–30.

10. Is it through the act of repetition that one gains access to the wholly other? I would like to let this question suspend itself over the entirety of the present essay. What interests Derrida in Levinas's use of language is precisely this repetition ("The possibility of this repetition is the very thing that interests me" (EM 23; AM). In the

repetition of phrases like *en ce moment même*, and also in the repetition that takes place within a Levinasian phrase like "a passivity more passive than all passivity" (EM 47; AM), a certain dimension of alterity opens up, where traditional terms like passivity begin to say something otherwise than their traditional signification. The repetition of traditional language prepares the saying of something wholly other to the tradition. In following the path of the repetition of the tradition one eventually crosses the path of something wholly other to it (*De l'esprit*, 184; *Of Spirit*, 113). On repetition in Derrida, see John Llewelyn's recent essay "The Origin and End of Philosophy," in *Philosophy and Non-Philosophy Since Merleau-Ponty*, ed. Hugh J. Silverman, New York, Routledge, 1988, 209). See also Blanchot's remarks on repetition in *L'écriture du désastre*, Paris, Gallimard, 1980, 14–15, 20, 72.

11. I have argued elsewhere that Derridian deconstructive reading is characterized by its traversal of the space between commentary and interpretation. See "The Chiasmus: Levinas, Derrida and the Ethical Demand for Deconstruction," *Textual Practice* 3, no. 1, April 1989: 91–106.

12. One might and perhaps *should* read the second moment of "At this very moment" in conjunction with Irigaray's essays on Levinas; both the subtle and evocative reading of "Phenomenology of Eros" (TeI 233–44; TI 256–66) undertaken in "The Fecundity of the Caress" (in *Ethique de la différence sexuelle*, Paris, Editions de Minuit, 1984, 173–99; trans. Carolyn Burke in *Face to Face with Levinas*, 231–56), and the more directly critical reading contained in this volume in "Questions to Emmanuel Levinas: On the Divinity of Love" (above, chap. 6). In the latter text, Irigaray articulates many of the themes raised in the second moment of reading: the function of the son (*fils*) in the relation of sexual pleasure (*volupté*) and the notion of the son as a work (*oeuvre*); the subordination of the feminine to the *telos* of paternity; the question of the fault (*faute*) and the faultiness of (male) ethics; the subordination of sexual difference and carnal love within monotheism, particularly Judaism.

The difference between Irigaray (at least in her second essay) and Derrida is that she does not attempt to *read* Levinas, rather she engages in a powerful, necessary, and compelling feminist *critique of* Levinas which speaks with a woman's voice. Derrida is a man, and, furthermore, in the second moment of reading, a man speaking with the voice of a woman. But is such a *mimesis* of the feminine by the masculine really plausible? Is it politically dangerous? Should it too become the subject of feminist critique?

On the question of whether a man can and should speak with the voice of a woman, see Kelly Oliver's "Nietzsche's Woman," *Radical Philosophy* 48, Spring 1988. For a more subtle and stratified discussion of the question of the feminine in Levinas, with reference to wider feminist issues, see Tina Chanter's "Antigone's Dilemma" (above, chap. 8) and "Feminism and the Other," in *The Provocation of Levinas*, ed. Robert Bernasconi and David Wood, London, Routledge, 1988, 32–56. For a helpful discussion of Irigaray, see Margaret Whitford's "Luce Irigaray's Critique of Rationality," in *Feminist Perspectives in Philosophy*, ed. Morwenna Griffiths and Margaret Whitford, London, Macmillan, 1988, 109–30.

13. On the important theme of *viens* as the name for that which cannot be contained within philosophy, metaphysics, or discourse upon Being and which calls beyond Being and from the Other, see *Of an Apocalyptic Tone Recently Adopted in Philosophy*, Paris, Editions Galilée, 1983; trans. John P. Leavey in *Oxford Literary Review* 6, no. 2, 1984: 3–37. For example, Derrida writes, "For want of time, I shall limit myself to the word, if it is a word, and the motif "Come" ("*Viens*") that occupies other texts written in the meantime, in particular 'Pas', 'Living On' and 'At this very moment in this work here I am', three texts dedicated, one could say, to Blanchot and to Levinas" (87; 31).

14. Although this is doubtless true of the works up to and including *Totality and*

Infinity, one wonders whether its conclusions extend to *Otherwise than Being*, and in particular to what Levinas says of *maternity* as a metaphor for the ethical in that work (AE 130–39; OB 102–9). A careful and sensitive approach to these issues has been broached by Catherine Chalier in *Figures du féminin*, Paris, La nuit surveillée, 1982; see especially 126–33 and 139–49.

15. On the theme of the crypt in Derrida's work, see: "Fors: Les mots anglés de Nicolas Abraham et Maria Torok" in *Cryptonymie: Le verbier de l'homme aux loups*, Paris, Aubier-Flammarion, 1976; trans. Barbara Johnson, *The Georgia Review* 31, 1977: 64–116. See also the discussion of Hegel's interpretation of Antigone in *Glas* (Paris, Denoël Gonthier, 1981 [1974], vol. 2, 198–263; trans. John P. Leavey, Jr. and Richard Rand, Lincoln and London, Nebraska University Press, 1986, 142–88), where Derrida focuses specifically on the theme of the crypt or sepulcher.

16. In the transcription of this sentence that appears in "At this very moment," the textual voice mistakenly substitutes "manuscript" (*manuscrit*) for "page" (*feuillet*), and writes, "The whole manuscript then has to be buried" (EM 57). Levinas writes that only the page that contains the fault must be buried.

17. This reading should be closely shadowed by Derrida's *Mémoires for Paul de Man* (Paris, Editions Galilée, 1986. Trans. Lindsay, Culler, and Cadava, New York, Columbia University Press, 1988), and in particular the first lecture, "Mnemosyne," which deals with the theme of an impossible mourning. "Or is it that of the *impossible mourning (deuil impossible)*, which, leaving the other his alterity, in respecting the other's infinite remove, refuses or finds itself incapable of taking the other within oneself, as in the tomb (*tombe*) or the vault (*caveau*) of some narcissism?" (27; 6)

CHAPTER
11

3 2 1 CONTACT
Textuality, the Other, Death
Ruben Berezdivin

Consequent zu sein ist die größte Obliegenheit eines Philosophen . . . (To be consequential is what is most incumbent upon a philosopher . . .)
Kant, *Critique of Practical Reason*

The enigmatic title that has imposed itself upon me should perhaps first be clarified, so that the reader may—follow along. (To *follow along*, the logic of sequences, consequence, will be at issue here, will be part of the stakes of this paper.)

The title, then.

(1) 3 2 1 . . . [0], a diachronic countdown signifying the setting off, the triggering away, explosive happening, of an "event"—this event, replacing, substituting for the missing (and Arabic, Semitic) "0," may well be called, following Levinas, "contact," since that event, if it happens, and entailing with it the issue of where and how it could have happened, will have established a contact among us of responsibility and substitution for the Other, here, exemplarily, with Levinas and his "thought"; followed by a synchronic structure which the contact, it will be argued, entails, namely the inscription of *guilt* (but it is the German *Schuld* which attracts that English word and sets it in motion) as indebtedness, debt, demanding infinite reparation, the "consequences" of which remain to be taken into account in what follows.

(2) This chain, or sequence of natural numbers, 3 2 1 itself, can be separately interpreted as phases or moments, *tokens* of the count-down.

3 will have multiple meanings, to be sure, but first and foremost, and by now not surprisingly, it will mean, or bring to presence, represent, the philosophy of a certain questioning Heidegger, during the period or phase of *Sein und Zeit*, and here standing for the exemplary philosopher.

3 also means, "derivatively," philosophy itself as that which is required along with, and as consequence of, the entry of the third party or person, witness and judge, philosophy as justice and justification, provoked by the demands and cries for justice to make an appearance on the stage.

Finally, 3 means mediation, or better, conjoining Hegel and Freud, trans-ference. Heidegger would be the instance of transference for the text we are to read.

For it is a single text, which however inextricably links 2 texts, that we are attending to or talking about, to wit, Derrida's "At this very moment in this work here I am," Derrida's self-presentation before Levinas in the form of the issue of the gift of the other, the other gift and the other's gift which we would say is *engaged* with Levinas's *Otherwise than Being* in a way that is "wholly otherwise."

2 would then be Derrida and Levinas in their respective texts, but also the face-to-face dual relationship *before*, uncontaminated by, the coming along and the consequences drawn from the coming along of the 3rd, and it also means, if you will, the dual mimetic relation of antagonism or violence as its alternative but inevitable other side (I refer here to Girard and Lacoue-Labarthe on mimesis and violence).

To double business bound; or better, to "triple" business. 2 may also (and inevitably must) mean Heidegger and Levinas, especially in their encounter, at the time when *Being and Time* became inscribed within the polemical expo-sition of *Time and the Other* in 1947. For I will briefly try to indicate how these two texts can generate a structure inscribed in the other text, inscribed in that other dual relationship.

Finally, and perhaps less persuasively, the 1: take your pick, and bearing in mind the group's insistent desire, perhaps even demand, for a "negative" rapprochement with some sort of Plotinian philosophy, it could mean the Plotinian or the Platonic 1, or, let us say, to draw things along more quickly, the *proper name* of God: the unique and only 1 ("Shema Israel Adonai Elohenu Adonai Echad" as the Jewish prayer has it).

I would then signify what excludes being numbered. As we all know, for the Greeks, the founders of philosophy, counting began with 2, hence 1 is what escapes comparison, synchrony, gathering together, in its uniqueness and total otherness, ab-soluteness. Such that it cannot be counted, it must be by-*passed*, leading the sequence along to that contact it precedes and inscribes or entraces, disappearing in its arrival like illeity.

Contact, the "key" word of the title, would name the event which this con-ference, this coming together in the name of Levinas to think his otherness, would achieve. What happens when Derrida and Levinas are, albeit textually?

This event is eerie, and its passage, if it happens, is traumatic and instantane-ously anterior, eerie, and, as if we had been visited by the ghost of an other, strange, uncanny—*Unheimlich.*

Hence: 3 2 1 CONTACT.

3.

Does not the most affirmative fidelity . . . involve us with an absolute past . . . : the dead-being who will never itself return. . . . The self has that relation to itself only *through* the other, through the promise (for the future, as trace of the future) made to the other as an absolute past, and this *through* this absolute past, thanks to the other whose sur-vival, i.e., mortality, always exceeded the "we" of a common present? . . . Memory stays with traces . . . of a past that has never been present . . . and which always remains . . . to come—come from the future, from the *a-venir*, the to-come. Resurrection, which is always the formal element of "truth," a recurrent difference between a present and its presence . . . *engages the future.*[1]

Il aura fait loi, he will have set forth an example: an example, here, that obligates us to think, write, live, otherwise, differently, engaged otherwise with difference. Engaged being a figure for an alliance or bind with the future and its promise, its promissory, resurrective, reiterative, prodigious capacity.

The law being, operative as obligation, will have been the issue of this text, and its mode of operation our primary concern, one that is both properly philosophical and in excess of its formal and material bounds.

For Derrida's text, "At this very moment," concerns the performance of a certain inscription of a contact with Levinas's obligatory text, with the question—without-question—of the contact between 2 texts, here (exemplarily, perhaps) those of Derrida and Levinas.

2 texts, Derrida's and Levinas's, come, have come into contact, the one inscribed as a trace of otherness within the other. This contact which occurs without a phenomenological present, this exemplary confrontation, implies and invites a philosophically disturbing event, namely the *Auseinandersetzung*, the setting apart, between ethics, in Levinas's nonontological sense, and textuality, in Derrida's grammatological sense.

Derrida's "he" in "At this very moment"—for the text is a fictional dialogue between a grammatically male and female persona—already stresses the *issue* of the text, which will also be its destination or emission, at the beginning of this context-less *assertion*: "If you hear me, you are already sensible to this strange event," namely, that in a past without present capable of having been experienced and hence epistemologically *assumed*, something has taken place, the Other has already effracted, already broached his passing by the present conversation of the fictionally set interlocutors.[2]

This "passing by," this leaving of the trace of a passing by the Other, will have already constituted, before the conversation even gets started, an obligatory event, "strange" (an adjective repeated during the conversation) because of its anteriority to any presence or present discourse that would wish to absorb its para-doxicality, but strange also because alien, because it is an event in which the Other makes his presence and absence felt from "beyond" the context.

Yet it is not the strange "logic" of that absolutely prior alienating event that is to be thematized in the fictional dialogue of Derrida's essay; rather, following the awareness of that absolute passing which *has already obligated*, the text will be the attempt to bind itself to the obligation and to return it, but not within the circulation exchange of a debt—an obligation incurs a debt as well

—but a return that would be a gift responding to the gift of the obligatory passing of the Other, one could say the attempt to *give* thanks for the gift that has already, strangely, obligated.

That return of the gift or gift of the return that re-turns the logic of returns in returning to the Other to give him a sort of thanks, that return will take on a form conforming to the attempt to give a return gift that doesn't simply return to the *same* other who gave the gift but rather to another other—and it will be one of the claims of the text, of its consequences, that the others are multiple and multiply diverse, not unique —to another other with whom the "he" must make communicational contact in the text itself, within its very fictional web: "At the moment when here I am telling you this, sending it to you like a letter, giving it to you to hear or to read, *giving* it to you mattering to me infinitely more than what it might transmit."

What "he" is trying to give "her" seems to be the obligatory phrase or text itself, inscribed like a foreign or alien body, always in quotation marks, *"Il aura obligé,"* he will have obligated, but the giving or gift is only accomplished if he touches her with this obligatory phrase coming from another *Il*, thus obligating her, though perhaps otherwise, in turn, an event that can only happen if she is herself open to that phrase, able to receive its obligatory passion and import within her body and herself, in order, then, and con-sequentially, to return it in turn by offering a gift of obligation of her own, another gift.

This is not an analysis of that text, "At this very moment," I am simply sketching in some traits belonging to its structure. In that text, which is a *mélange-à-trois*, the "he" who receives the obligatory phrase from the other, from Levinas's work, and beyond it, is already himself drawn by a bind, bound to an obligation as the text commences. He will proceed to explicate the con-sequences of that a priori obligation, but the explication is itself offered to another, "she," and offered not in order to explain the phrase but to *bind* her to it, to give her that obligation as a gift from the other by means of which he may establish contact with her and the obligation at one and the same, anterior, time.

(Before I regress further, I want to say that the fictional structure of Derrida's essay is *mimetic* insofar as it stages the telegraphic or postal contact which obligates the "he" to the "she" and both through the prior event, the "strange" event, signified and opened forth by the inscribed [context-less] phrase, coming from another outside this text; whence the *mimesis*, since the contact between he and she in the fictional text mirrors the contact between self and other in the face-to-face as recounted in Levinas's text, and also mirrors the face-to-face between Levinas's and Derrida's texts by enacting such a contact within the fiction of a dialogue at the same time entracing Levinas's text into the text by means of the insertion of the phrase and its obligatory instance as alien, within and yet without his own text.)

The issue that we must bear today, that must today bear issue, is that of a textual contact, the "face-to-face" between two *corpora* or two bodies inscribed and as it were dead, as to how such contact takes place, if it does, and what that contact would signify, ethically assymetrical contact, caressing each other, between 2 texts, such as Levinas's and Derrida's.

Derrida's text, then, already stages a sort of confrontation with Levinas's by trying to let itself be affected by the obligatory event, by tracing out how the event might happen, and by in turn setting to work, elaborating, the trace of obligation of and for the other within his text. Thus there are at least 3 and not 2 persons in "At this very moment," Levinas, "he," and "she," and the face-to-face of responsibility for and to the Other becomes inscribed in the text-to-text as responsibility for the signed and signing *seriasure* that allows a text to inscribe the trace of otherness—as obligatory, ethical instance—within the fabric of what would otherwise be an ontological *récit* of an event, the making and constitution of a book.

Which leads me, finally, and conclusively, to my 3, the number three and its settling of accounts, its justification, and the text or instance of the 3rd, the witness and judge.

3 in 3 2 1 Contact is the start of a sequential count-down terminating in the strange event whose issue we've been recounting. But it signifies as well the impossibility of being with 2, with the Dual, upon which it will inscribe or stamp a necessarily con-sequential third text which stands in a relation I am calling transferential in regard to the other two (this will remain only a sketch, of course).

That 3rd text or text of the third is here Heidegger's, taken as it informs the issues at work in both Levinas and Derrida, who here have stood for the 2 in the title (the 1 would then refer, nonnumerically, to the referential dimension of discourse, confronting ethics and textuality, and *hence* to the Other and death and to the death of the Other. That 1 must indeed disappear, must be by-passed, so that contact may take place according to it and through it. 1 is the issue, the event-condition—the good, god, being, *Ereignis*, the other, death, the text—and what in the count-down leads to the moment or instant before contact, which transfers the 2 into contact, par-achieves it, thus both achieving and destroying contact. That would then be linked, sequentially, to the impossibility of singularity, of uniqueness, of death, except by means of some other factor which in accusing and evoking it must ipso facto disappear leaving an absolutely past trace of itself behind, death-as-such for instance, thus becoming the death of the other standing as the obligatory law behind the contact with the strange, accounting for the necessary *deflection* which gently leans my regard to the other from the unrepresentable majesty of the 1 itself.)

2.

Turning toward the encounter between Heidegger and Levinas in 1947, let us try to graft *Being and Time* onto *Time and the Other* by first disengaging those traits that bear examination in the respective trajectories of those two texts.

(My "thesis," or *assertion*—tying and bringing into a chain—would then be: Only in projecting unto my death, death-bound, and being re-jected to "assume" [*Übernehmen*] my lack of ground in the consequentiality of a codestination with other *Daseins*, could I be opened up to the obligation of the Other *Dasein* facing me, and that, further, the other's obligation stems from his own place as mortal and bound to die, death-bound.)

The following traits may be disengaged from Heidegger's *Being and Time* with due caution in order to set them moving into Levinas:

(1) *Geworfenheit*, as the absolute anteriority of my insertion into being before any possible resumption of it in the reiteration (*Wiederholung*) of my past in "resolution" (*Entschlossenheit*). Hence: the inscription of the absolute past within and before thinking.

(2) *Schuld*, guilt/debt: The elucidation of the necessity of "assuming" guilt by reinsertion into the absolute anteriority without the possibility of mastering it.

(3) Death: The necessity of projecting toward my "utmost" possibility in order, in my re-jection from it, to encounter fully and without subterfuge my *Geworfenheit* and reiterate it by directing it to those missed but inscribed possibilities within the con-sequence of my "generation," as a *Geschick* drawing together, each in their death-boundedness, mortality, the various *Schicksale* of the *Daseins*. Bound to die hence bound, obligated, ethically commanded by and to "death" and hence re-bound to the past, bound to rebound upon and to the past and make it binding, engaging myself within the consequential chain.

(4) *Temporality*: The future controls the process of temporalization, by open-ing me up to my absolute impossibility which throws me back to resume my indebtedness to others as my absolutely anterior past:

> Willing to have a conscience is rather the most original existentiell presupposi-tion for the possibility of a factical being-guilty. In understanding the call [of conscience], Dasein lets its ownmost self act in itself (*in sich handeln*) from out of the potentiality-for-Being which it has chosen. Factically, every action, however, is necessarily "conscienceless" . . . because it has already become guilty to others in being-with others on the null ground of its null project.[3]

The "null ground" refers to that prior pastness upon which *Dasein* is *geworfen* and which it must assume in order to be, while remaining unable to found it, whence a "null" or lacking ground, which one must *be* without attaining mastery of it.

In this re-jection to my *Geworfenheit* in the rebound from the crash against death, the "present" is *by-passed*, as we pass from what, in coming, ever futural but closing off further future, destroys my potency as being-able-to and leaves me in, shall we say, *dis-may*—the word signifying here both the lack of open-ness to my possibilities and the evanescence of the present subject precisely as subject to the anonymity of the lost everyday—rebounding to a past I must assume (*Übernehmen*) and resume as having-already-passed but *calling* for its reiteration, bound in that reiteration to what is inscribed in the past *as already futural and resurrective*, promising and compromising at once.

Thus: the by-passing of the present in the adjoinment or adjournment of death bound to death requires a con-sequential resolution in order to resume each possible instant of falling into the chain or sequence of my projected rejection, binding that present to the others and to my death.

This extension or stretching out of time is consequentially indebted and thus reinserted in its guilt by the *dismay* in which death binds our evanescent subjectivity and opens *Dasein* up to its past from which the casting forth of the future must thenceforth proceed.

(5) Hence the consequence of guilt is being bound to reiterate the absolutely anterior debt in projecting it within a sequence of nows resumed and bound together, *with* and *to* other *Daseins*, to a possibility ultimately bound to and by the dying of each *Dasein* bound to die and living upon that bind.

(6) The priority of futurity in *Being and Time* concerns the sense of guilt's consequentiality in resolution—ethics—in its bind to dying, obligated by death as my dying, my absolute catastrophe.

One could then say: my death-bind binds me and opens me up genuinely to the death-bind of the others. I suggest that it is at that spot that the instance of ethics affects the text *Being and Time*, albeit in an unorthodox manner. Death is obligatory and consequential, obligating to a sequence along with (*con*) others, and to a consequential drawing of the past in full awareness of its consequences: consequential ethics as temporally finite.

1.

This sketch should now be attached and grafted onto the conception of obligation that emerges from Levinas's text, *Time and the Other*, chosen because of the clarity of the logic of its argument (story).

Let us review that text from the point of view of how death functions in its relation to the other.

(1) The other as total alterity replaces death as what annihilates my mastery over possibilities, my initiative. But only insofar as the other replaces death as what is essentially futural and to come. Thus Levinas says, in passing from suffering to death:

> The principal trait of our relation with death, . . . that it makes impossible any assumption of possibility. It is why death is never a present. . . . it marks the end of virility . . . that turning around of the activity of a subject into passivity. . . . Death is thus never assumed; it comes. . . . What is important in death's approach is that at a certain moment we are no longer *able to be able*. It is precisely in that way that the subject loses its very mastery as a subject. . . . An event happens to us without our being able to have the least project. . . . Death is the impossibility of having a project . . . [it] indicates a relation to something absolutely other, something bearing

alterity. . . . Consequently, *only a being arrived at the crispation of its solitude through suffering and in relation to death is placed in a position where the relation with the other becomes possible* . . . the future is absolutely surprising . . . it is what cannot be grasped, what befalls us and takes us over. The Other is the future. The relation with the Other is the relation with the future.[4]

(2) Thus, since and because death shatters my *comprehension*, my grasp, my *Verstehen* as projecting possibilities, since it shatters my powers as possibilities of initiative—my virility—it makes room for the dimension of the other; it allows me access to the dimension of alterity; absolute alterity. The access to the wholly other, nonsynchronic with the same, requires the dissolution which death effects and the absolution of all power and emprise.

(3) The other as absolutely other obligates me only through the gap or interval left open by that catastrophe in which I experience the impossibility of *my* death. Contrary to Heidegger's thesis, it is precisely as "myself" that I cannot die, that I reach an impassivity vis-à-vis death. The impotence encountered in facing death surrenders my virile activism of comprehension and renders me passive and capable of hearing a wholly other voice, which obligates in enjoining me not to murder him or her.

(4) The future is the encounter with the other, the other is the openness to a wholly other instant or instance, and is encountered in the instantaneity of a nonpresent interval across the abyss of death, not my death, which I am incapable of assuming—but that of the other(s), whose death I can experience as the substitutes for the impossibility of my own death.

Insofar as the other is the future, the other delimits my dimension of being. Heidegger was wrong to believe that I cannot be substituted for another's dying since he thought that each I could die for itself; but if no one can die for himself, we can only die in lieu of each other, for each other as each other.

The substitution "even to the uncondition of hostage" which Levinas later elaborates means that I must be able in my absolute passivity and patience to experience death always as the other's death, in mourning the death of the other whose death allows me the "experience" of the absolutely alienating.

(5) Thus the other's face takes the place, in Levinas, of my death, as the shock of an obligatory future that is never present but rather bounces back to an absolute past in whose trace the passing of the other will have already obligated me to face him and care for him in absolute rectitude and to the point of tendering and assuaging his suffering and hunger, and keeping him company until he dies in my stead, in the steadiness of my mortal substitution of care.

To summarize: Obligation from the other and his phenomenal rupture with the temporality of my initiative, my projecting, can only take place because in trying to project my death I become impotent of possibilities and lose my virility, suffering (becoming open to) the destitution of the other, which is ultimate and absolute in his dying in my stead.

The obligation which the face-to-face incarnates, I before you where you claim priority over me in your mortal transcendence, comes from the place of death; it is only *as* dead and dying, already dead, that the destitution and suffering of the other obligates, the face-to-face as dual is a facing up to the image of the other's cadaver.

The destitution of the other obligates because it phenomenally, diachronically prefigures his being bound to die. The bind of the other's death binds me to the ethical call which accuses my irresponsibility and constrains me to obey his command: Do not murder me, or better: *Do not let me die, die for me*, an impossible double-bind (his death, my death) which leads inevitably to the infinitization of the obligatory command, erecting it as a law which categorically imposes its commands.

The command does not come from a prefigured beyond but from the abyss of his necessary but impossibly assumable death, to come, which I must assume from him; it comes from his bind to the coming of his death.

It could then be said that this is an a priori structure of mourning for the other that dictates the law from the place of the other's incomprehensible, forthcoming but already entraced in the abyss of a past, death, and thereby obligates me in its very incommensurability (sublimity). I must, in order for that to be possible, already be receptive, in absolute passivity, to the death germinating in the destitution, hunger and pain in the other, and must therefore always keep the image or phenomenality of the other distinguished from his cadaver-to-be, from his dead body. When his body incorporates death, then the image is redoubled with the body and the effects of uncanniness and ghosts arise, haunting the order of the imaginary, as Blanchot has shown in "The Two Versions of the Imaginary."[5]

This obligation stemming from the other's death—and the other is always a singular other whom I can meet singularly, something Heidegger's reference to other*s* effaces—binds me in the inseparable recognition of my death as substituted by his, whereby the consequence is my inevitable indebtedness, always already, to that other. For in order to be in contact, to receive the impress of the other, I must open myself up to his absolute passing away, a passing whose mark can only be remarked by means of a seriated inscription which is necessarily faulty, unorthodox, since the double bind to the other and to his death means that I must play my obligation within the law of the double bind, mourning his death in substitution, that I must obligate and link my impossible death before his cadaver, by the obsequies of a gift returned to the other in the face-to-face of a memorial (and a) friendship.

If the other's death is what obligates—my assertion in this paper—then the ultimate face-to-face *must* inscribe itself within textuality as *the living ethics of a dead other*, as the instance of the other in my corpus. Obligation cannot avoid justice, but justice and its thirds, transferentially, require inscription within a text that generalizes the obligation while leaving open the remarking of a consequential seriasure of traces and the singularization or signature of a text of obligation that obligates in *general* by means of a *singular* accusative.

Hence the need for the fault—guilt, indebtedness, but also false returns, false thanks—and its trace, for a fault that automatically contaminates the other's text—contact would be a priori contaminating, says Derrida with regard

to Levinas—in responding to it from the other shore. The fault would be consequential upon guilt before the other's death, binding the other to his law,
reinscribing his signature by accepting and reiterating his utter strangeness.

Only thus could a gift survive its inscription within the general textuality
of the same. The fault as guilt is thus a consequence of the necessity to follow
up contact with a response that confirms the other's obligation and counter-
signs it in whatever unique manner is consequential.

CONTACT

If then "At this very moment" is faulty, with respect to Levinas's corpus, it
is due to the necessity to respond to his obligatory gift by reinscribing the
gift so as both to save its survival chances and to disseminate it to multiple
aleatory deaths, texts, and obligations, without surrendering the accused singularity, a singularity whose faults must always remain unpredictable.

3 2 1: Levinas Derrida Heidegger: Contact: in the text we have before us,
a singularly intertextual debt or obligation is at work reinscribing guilt and
fault, as it must, *comme il faut*, in its consequential chain, letting yet another
third, "she," countersign the obligatory phrase which resumes the import of
Levinas's thinking as it inscribes itself in the text of the other.

In the trial or process, three texts, at least, have come into contact, and
the promise of their resurrection has been inscribed and disseminated.

The fiction of "At this very moment" leaves room in its haunted spaces for
thanking the other in the thinking that obligates us to understand obligation,
from out of the corpse of the other, as textual obligation inscribed within difference, which does not remove an iota from the essential *gravity* of living obligations, except to fully affirm our common, fraternal being as generally bound
to death, out of whose absolute passing away arises the engagement to the
future, still to come, always and again.

And thus with a gesture that I am not accustomed to make.

Thank you.[6]

Notes

1. Derrida, *Memoires: For Paul de Man*, New York, Columbia University, 1986,
66 and 58.

2. EM 21; AM.

3. *Sein und Zeit*, Tübingen, Niemeyer, 1949, 288; trans. J. Macquarrie and E.
Robinson, *Being and Time*, Oxford, Basil Blackwell, 1967, 334. Translation modified.

4. TA 58–64; TO 75–77. Levinas supplies an interesting retrospective introduction
to the work in which he does not disclaim it. In spite of changes in Levinas's thinking,
I think the core of what I extract from that work holds for later works, even if the
reference to death becomes more complicated in its conditioning the encounter with

the other. In *Totality and Infinity* the "dwelling" to some degree (along with its femininity) takes over the place of death, but that move was already inscribed in the program of *Time and the Other*, as its fourth chapter makes clear ("Alterity is accomplished in the feminine," TA 81; TO 88).

5. M. Blanchot, *L'espace littéraire*, Paris, Gallimard, 1955, 345–59; trans. A. Smock, *The Space of Literature*, Lincoln, University of Nebraska Press, 1982, 254–63.

6. One final remark: The title "3 2 1 CONTACT" is a sort of theft; it is the title of a television program in the United States which teaches "science" to "children." The word "Contact" occurs when the child is supposed to be contacted by the television transmission, at the moment when the program becomes alive for the child. It is thus communicating "knowledge" by means of a written, preinscribed program, which at the moment of contact cancels its distance and comes on "live." The count-down is presumed extrinsic to the effects of the contact and its programming; it is only preparative.

CHAPTER
12

A FINE RISK
Reading Blanchot Reading Levinas
Paul Davies

> Communication with the other (*Autrui*) can be
> transcendent [that is to say, for Levinas, can
> encounter the other *as* other in its "approach,"
> in "proximity"] . . . only as a fine risk to be
> run (*un beau risque à courir*).
>
> Levinas[1]

> Fragmentary writing (*l'écriture fragmentaire*)
> would be risk itself (*le risque même*). It does
> not reflect a theory, it does not give place to
> a practice that would be defined by or as
> *interruption*. Interrupted, it continues
> (*Interrompue, elle se poursuit*).
>
> Blanchot[2]

The concern in what follows is with some of the ways in which Maurice
Blanchot, in "Discours sur la patience" (1975),[3] *L'écriture du désastre* (1980),
and *Après coup* (1983), both reads or uses and cites or mentions Emmanuel
Levinas's *Otherwise than Being or Beyond Essence* (1974). The distinction intended here ("reading or using" over and against "citing or mentioning") is
purely heuristic. It is drawn between a *reading of* Levinas (that is, Blanchot
analyzing, commenting upon, and problematizing a whole series of terms introduced or developed in *Otherwise than Being*) and a *reading with* Levinas
(that is, Blanchot adopting some of those terms—along with others—and incorporating them, setting them to work in his own writing). This *reading with*
occurs, as we shall see, without Blanchot's necessarily notifying us of the fact.
I would suggest that some of the difficulties in understanding the presence
of Levinas in these texts (especially the *Discours* and *L'écriture du désastre*),
some of the difficulties, then, in reading them and in appreciating the importance of *Otherwise than Being* for Blanchot, are best met and dealt with by
attending to this double response: *reading of, reading with.*

These remarks might be said to address themselves to two groups. First,
those readers of Blanchot who remain puzzled by, and distrustful of, the alli-

ance with Levinas; those who feel that Levinas's name fits uneasily alongside Mallarmé's, say, or Kafka's, Hölderlin's, Nietzsche's, Char's, etc., the most important others *with* whom Blanchot reads and from whom he learns to read. But to concentrate only on the alliance—the shared and appropriated vocabulary, the references and exchanges—is to ignore the alterations Levinas's terms and concerns undergo when they are rewritten into Blanchot's text. It is to ignore, too, the specificity of the relation with Levinas; the way in which Levinas's is, for Blanchot, the unique proper name for a philosophical thought that *continues* where and when it would seem (and is) impossible to continue, a philosophical work characterized by a new and paradoxical *patience*.

Second, these remarks address those readers of Levinas who, initially accepting Blanchot as a fellow reader, are then confronted with what can only seem like a misreading. What is overlooked in this case is the influence Levinas has already had on the very inscribing of the space in which any reading (any reading of Levinas by Blanchot) is to take place.

In 1975, Maurice Blanchot published a text in *Le nouveau commerce* entitled "Discours sur la patience," subtitled, in parentheses, "en marge des livres d'Emmanuel Levinas." The text consists of forty-seven fragments. The longest, running for slightly over two pages, is a meditation on what is described as Levinas's "renewal" of the word "*responsibility*."[4] The shortest consists of just six words: "Le désastre prend soin de tout (*Le désastre* takes care of everything)."[5] Five years later, the forty-seven fragments reappear in *L'écriture du désastre*. Occasionally altered, added to, and rearranged, they are found, with just one exception, in the first quarter of the book. (The first words of the "Discours" are the first words of the book: "Le désastre ruine tout [*Le désastre* ruins everything].") The single exception is this one-line fragment from very close to the end of the "Discours": "Solitude qui rayonne, vide dans le ciel, mort differée: soleil."[6] We find it again, with two revisions, as the final line of *L'écriture du désastre*: "Solitude qui rayonne, vide du ciel, mort differée: désastre." A shining (radiating) solitude, the void in and/or of the sky, death deferred: sun and/or *désastre*. Thus fragments from the "Discours" both open and close the book. With this replacing of *soleil* by *désastre*, we are reminded of the thought, to which Blanchot introduced us a long time ago, of a catastrophic clarity, a clarity that both ruins and protects.[7] The last fragment of the "Discours" confirms the memory: "C'est le désastre obscur qui porte la lumière (It is the obscure *désastre* which carries [or sustains] the light)."[8]

We will need to say something about this "désastre," perhaps the most unusual and the most compacted of all the words with which Blanchot seeks to name the approach of what interrupts thinking (amongst which, of course, we must number "approach" and "interruption"). For it is not a word that thinking (philosophy) can recognize, rediscover, retrieve, or even learn to use. To identify one or more of its various sources (most notably, Mallarmé) is to beg the question.[9] What sort of reading (of Mallarmé, say) would ever lead to such a strange adoption, such a cryptic redeployment? Those texts of Blanchot's in which "désastre" is written must be read several times before its manoeuvres (or, better, its nonmanoeuvres, its *désoeuvrements*) begin to show themselves. But we will want to say something especially about its being written into the "margins" of Levinas's books, and about how we might begin to read it there.

Over and against this writing of "le désastre," over and against our preliminary remarking of the point of greatest difficulty in Blanchot's reading relation with Levinas, let us look at what would appear to be a far more straightforward gesture, a surprising appropriation of one of Levinas's most difficult words, "le Dire."

Three years after *L'écriture du désastre*, Blanchot writes an afterword to a new edition of *Le ressassement éternel*, itself a collection of two stories (*récits*) from the 1930s: "L'idylle" and "Le dernier mot." The title of the afterword becomes the title of the book, *Après coup*. On the face of it, the writing and discussion here are far more accessible, both in tone and content, than the fragments concerning "le désastre." Almost unusually accessible, the text seems marked with a confidence one would rarely, if at all, ascribe to Blanchot. With respect to "L'idylle," Blanchot notes (having already posed the problem of what it is for a writer to note anything, after the fact [*après coup*] about what he has written) how the questions and issues with which the story might be said to deal are contained in the story "only on condition that the story not be reduced through them to a content, to anything that can be expressed in any other way." We then read the following paragraph:

> ["L'idylle" is] a story in every respect unhappy. But, precisely, as a story which says all it has to say in enunciating itself (*qui dit en s'énonçant tout ce qu'il a à dire*), or, better, which announces itself as the preliminary clarity anterior to the serious or ambiguous meaning it also transcribes. . . . This would be the law of the story, its happiness and, because of it, its unhappiness, not because, as Valéry reproached Pascal, a beautiful form would necessarily destroy the horror of every tragic truth and make it bearable, even delicious (catharsis). But, because before all distinctions between form and content, between signifier and signified, even before the division between *énonciation* and *énoncé*, there is the unqualifiable *Dire*, the glory of a "narrative voice" which intimates clearly without ever being able to be obscured by the opacity or the terrible beauty of what it communicates.[10]

Much is familiar in this passage. The reference to Valéry's remark on Pascal returns us across forty years to the opening pages of *Faux pas* and to the notion of a writing that intensifies (essentializes) the very state it would seek to alleviate.[11] Such writing cannot simply be about that state. Blanchot's story can be read *as* such, that is *as* the story it is, if and only if we no longer think of reading as the taking on board of a message or content that we might subsequently communicate, differently and elsewhere, to others. Blanchot's story, this story "L'idylle," a story *about* a stranger and *about* the strange logic that obliges him to remain forever estranged, is itself a stranger to itself, subject to the same logic it would transcribe. The story does not circumscribe its content (and so is not, properly, *about* it), does not wrap it up for purchase, exchange, and consumption. Rather, the story draws me into the space in which it gives itself. It alters the space of communication understood as the space of exchange. The story is not a gift that can be easily received, if it can be said to be received at all, and what it is about cannot be thought apart from the manner in which it gives itself, incessantly and always.

Each of these themes or thoughts has been present, in one form or another, in Blanchot's work since the late 1940s. What is of particular interest, though, in the paragraph from *Après coup*, is that in refusing to characterize the story in terms of a certain formalization, in terms familiar to philosophy, terms that would organize it as the object of a particular type of experience (an aesthetic object and an aesthetic experience), Blanchot employs Levinas's term "le Dire," a term from a work of philosophy, as a synonym for his own "narrative voice." Not quite a synonym, however, for we should take seriously the fact that Blanchot's phrase is: first, preceded (qualified) by another Levinasian word, "la gloire" (glory);[12] second, and unusually for Blanchot, accompanied by the indefinite article; and third, and most importantly, quoted. In these respects, amongst others, this passage (at least the sentence beginning "But . . . before all distinctions between . . .," and perhaps the whole of the afterword) is unlike any of those in which the notion of the narrative voice is so carefully introduced, developed, and described. That notion is, from the first, caught up with the thought of an incessant giving, with the thought of a voice that continues to speak when no further speaking or (story)telling is possible. It is caught up, then, with the issues Blanchot is describing in the afterword. Yet, the phrase cannot be written directly, as though it had to keep its distance from this sort of presentation. It is interesting to see how Sarah Kofman, precisely in order to employ Blanchot's self-commentary, chooses to incorporate this passage in *Paroles suffoquées*. She holds the phrase "narrative voice" outside the quotation—*la "gloire" de la voix narrative*—so that its being quoted by Blanchot need not be quoted by her, and in the process returns it to the definite article. Meanwhile "le Dire," the unquoted, unacknowledged word of another in Blanchot's text, is written without Levinas's capitalization ("le dire inqualifiable") and so effectively dropped altogether.[13] Effectively dropped because, so written, the phrase does not surprise us. It does not sound so unlike Blanchot. Consider, for example, the final page of the essay "The Narrative Voice," where we read of the possibility of (a) "saying that would say without saying being and yet without denying it either (*de dire qui dirait sans dire l'être et sans non plus le dénier.*"[14] Elsewhere in "The Narrative Voice," when proposing that that voice "marks the intrusion of the other (*l'autre*)," Blanchot insists that this other (*l'autre*) not be "honored with a capital letter." To do so would be to "establish it in a majestic substantive, as though it had some substantial, even unique, presence."[15] It is inconceivable that "le Dire," any more than "l'Autre" or "l'Autrui," could ever be Blanchot's word.

We would have to say that, for Blanchot, "the narrative voice" and "le Dire" do not quite say the same. They are not quite the same way of saying *difference* or *irreducible alterity*. And yet Levinas's word clearly does allow Blanchot to say something, something other than or in addition to "the narrative voice." In our conclusion, we will need to ask what that something might be. Note, however, that "le Dire" has a twofold function here. On the one hand, it allows Blanchot to comment, in an unprecedented manner, on the re-reading and re-presenting of his own story ("L'idylle"). On the other hand, it also describes the way in which that story continues to signify, to intimate, to call for other readings, or at least an *other* reading. "Le Dire" thus says uniquely the unique saying of a particular type of "story." In this regard and to those familiar with *Otherwise than Being*, such a use must seem only to compound a misreading of Levinas.

With the aim of clarifying Blanchot's introduction of both the word "désastre" into a reading of Levinas and the word "dire" into an account and a presentation —a reading—of his own work, the paper now proceeds in two stages. (1) In the first, we continue to emphasize the exemplary role accorded Levinas's philosophy in the "Discours," *L'écriture du désastre*, and *Après coup*. But we do so only after an extended detour: A detour enabling us to consider that role in the context of Blanchot's references to other philosophers—most notably, *the* philosopher, Hegel—and to philosophy itself. At times, Levinas's name, and/or his vocabulary, seems to give rise to a type of formulation that the wider context (the way Blanchot has, from the first, read and alluded to "philosophy") would surely undermine. (2) In the second stage, we move to the reading of *Otherwise than Being* and attempt to follow the operations of what we have called the double response to Levinas. Our aim, here, will be to mark a curious circularity: Blanchot writing the word "désastre" into (the margins of) the *philosophical* text that best helps us to read the word, and, even more curiously, best helps Blanchot to write it.

1.

The question, then, concerns Blanchot and philosophy.

When Blanchot claims that a writer who writes "in ignorance of the philosophical horizon" necessarily writes with facile complacency, we might ask how a knowledge of that horizon is to manifest itself. What would count as such knowledge? What would be the criteria for determining the awareness or lack of awareness on the part of a work or writer? The most cursory reading of Blanchot makes it clear that it is not a matter of the work's dealing with "philosophical" issues or themes, or of the writer's being a "philosophical" poet, novelist, or whatever. Nor, a more careful reading would show, is it primarily a matter of the (literary) work's addressing, challenging, or even frustrating the traditional "philosophical" accounts of literature and literary activity. Blanchot's references to philosophy are never arbitrary. If his writing has always sought to hold itself at a *distance* from philosophy, it has never ceased to investigate that distance, inquiring into its effects both on and within philosophy. Indeed, it is not going too far to say that that distance *is* its effects on and within philosophy.

To write with an eye on the philosophical horizon. Blanchot makes his claim in the following lines. "To write in ignorance or rejection of the philosophical horizon—a horizon punctuated, held together, or dispersed by the words which delimit it—is necessarily to write with a complacent ease and fluency (the literature of elegance and good taste). Hölderlin, Mallarmé, many others, do not permit us this."[16] Here is no simple critical preference for one type of literature (the poetry of Hölderlin, Mallarmé, etc.) over another ("the literature of elegance"). Before considering this passage in the context of the fragment in which it appears, let us draw out the complexity belying the apparent accessibility of Blanchot's terms. We can discern, in that reference to the literature of good taste, an echo of an earlier remark about a self-serving and surface eloquence.

In *L'espace littéraire*, Blanchot speaks of that writing which concerns itself with the production of *les beaux morceaux* and *les belles phrases*, a writing which seems to conceal from itself the fact that it has been written, a writing about which we can only say that it is "readable."[17] Blanchot sees this production of fine phrases as one of the ways in which the writer seeks protection from an encounter with the specific and unsettling nature of *literary* production. In such instances, the writer writes as though he were the reader and so imagines that what the writer writes and what the reader reads are one and the same object, an object which circulates within an economy of exchange, a book, for example. However, to write is to produce something that only becomes the thing it is in the hands of another, an other of whom the writer is never the contemporary and over whom the writer has no authority. When Blanchot uses the notion of "the work" (*l'oeuvre*) to name the literary object, he insists that its only positive characteristic is its *approach*. We say the work as the approach of the work, as that which in approaching excludes or expels the writer. The work, as the approach of the work, is never yet the thing (the book) the writer sought to produce and so its production is never yet *real* production. The work is thus distinguished by an essential worklessness (*désoeuvrement*). What stands between the writer and reader is not an object that binds them together. A provider of neither symmetry nor commensurability, what stands between them is the refusal of any determinable relation. The special force Blanchot gives to the words "literature" and "writing"—the strategic privileging of these words—must always be understood in terms of this logic of the approach, in terms, then, of the perpetual alteration of communicational space.

L'espace littéraire follows and describes these operations and simulations —these simulated operations—with an extraordinary rigor and in extraordinary detail. But it does so not in order to serve a phenomenology of literary activity or to add to our understanding of what it is that writers and readers do. Blanchot attends to, and argues for the historical significance of, a moment in which writing discloses to itself the condition of writing. Writing or literature as a particular activity or undertaking—and so writing or literature as possibility—confronts within itself an essential impossibility. We might say that this activity realizes itself to be essentially not an activity. In this moment, a moment that yields the thought of the approach, writing is said to pose a question to itself, a question that also and crucially implicates philosophy. Literature, in Blanchot's strategic sense, begins when it becomes this question, and it obliges us to think together what cannot be thought together, a relation without relationality, a *rapport sans rapport*.

There would be several ways of formulating the question literature or writing embodies, the "gift" it brings to philosophy. In "Literature and the Right to Death," Blanchot speaks of it as the question literary language poses to language, the question literary activity poses to activity, where "language" and "activity" are heard as quintessentially philosophical terms. Blanchot lets these questions unfold in and from a reading of Hegel (a reading of the *Phenomenology*). Literature, at a certain moment in history, marks or experiences its distance from (the discourse of) history, from (the discourse of) real production and real activity.

L'espace littéraire continues to think this distance with respect to Hegel. It describes the worklessness that defines the literary thing in contradistinction to the labor of the negative in and as history. The major reference, however, is to the *Aesthetics* rather than the *Phenomenology*, and Blanchot considers Hegel's well-known statement that "art is for us a thing of the past."[18] What if the *end* of art were not a real end, or, rather, what if art continued despite its real end and, in this continuing, proved problematic for philosophy: problematic but unthematizable *as* a problem?

Hegel knew that works of art would continue to be produced, that people would continue to practice the arts, to exhibit and respond to them. But art had realized itself, had come into its truth and disclosed itself as art to history. The concept of art, from which everything that might continue within the various individual arts could be derived, takes its place in the *system*. Blanchot, however, hears in the continuing of art something which refuses the cloak of the universal concept. In this continuing, there is a stepping beyond the realization of truth. A step and a beyond that are no step and beyond at all since their domain can only be "outside" the truth. Hence the attempts, in such a time, to initiate a new search (*recherche*) for art. A quest which leads, for those who take the matter seriously, to an experience of what is called the "infinitely continuing outside."

This "outside" can be detected, or, better, is given to thought in very different ways, for example, in the work and the experience of Mallarmé (the infinite quest for *le livre*) and in the work and the experience of Kafka, whose parables, tales, and novels provide so many supreme instances of the space Blanchot is looking to define. In Kafka's "The Burrow,"[19] the construction of the perfect and the most intricate of dwellings leads by a slow and inexorable logic to the paradox in which its creator first moves from outside to inside and vice versa, and then comes to feel the presence of a wholly other nondialectical outside. In the first moment, the outside belongs to the burrow and stands in a relation to it. Having built it for security and having begun to live inside it, the builder desires to watch over the entrance to the burrow and so to ascertain whether the feeling of security he would have had were he inside is or would have been justified. In the second moment, toward the end of the tale, while lying in the "castle keep," the site of greatest security, whose pathways and exits are known only to its owner and inhabitant, the owner and inhabitant begins to hear a noise unlike any other. At various moments in the tale, the burrower has thought almost nostalgically of the days before the building of the burrow. Then, constantly terrified of being caught and eaten, his terror had an object and an origin. At the close of the tale, there is only the steady advance of a noise and a terror with neither object nor origin. The outside that is *its* region is not the outside onto which the burrow opens, and so not the outside into which the owner might step. And yet it is, nevertheless, the burrow's outside, and its advance is heard only by the one who builds, by the one who, in desiring the perfect and invincible domicile, has made a place where no one else can be. Would literature not stand to the (Hegelian) system, to the (philosophical) thought of totality, as this other and monstrous outside stands to the burrow? If so, we could only read and hear it from inside the system. And is that not what Blanchot, in "Literature and the Right to Death," attempts to do? It is not a matter, then, of opposing Hegel, the thinker of the system, to the writer, but of beginning to read Hegel as the writer. Recall, for example, the manner in which Blanchot reads Hegel's line concerning "the life that endures death and maintains itself within it."[20] It is now heard both as the final and most confident expression of philosophy's mastery, the very possibility of thought's thinking the totality, *and* as the approach that says the impossibility of dying, the impossibility of there being a proper end.[21] Putting it a little fancifully, it is as if one were to read Hegel's words as being also Kafka's words. Less fancifully, it is as if one were to hear Hegel's words as the index not only of history and of thought's capacity to know that history, but also of the non-event that befalls the burrow, of the slow advance of what removes from the burrower the promise of an end, any end at all, whether peaceful or violent. Hence, the final line of the tale and its capacity to disturb: "——But all remained unchanged.—— (——*Aber alles blieb unverändert.*——)."[22]

Now none of this is to be understood as a collapsing of philosophy into literature or as any sort of "blurring" of genre distinctions, a move that would simply turn the word "literature" back into the most familiar of designations. To begin to hear in the Hegelian text the approach of what continues outside the workings of the Hegelian dialectic (an approach which we say strategically as "literature's question"), to begin to read the Hegelian text as effected and altered by that outside, is for philosophy to encounter the possibility of reading otherwise. It is for philosophy to be altered, yes, insofar as this other reading is not one of the readings previously available to philosophy, and even now cannot become a "philosophical" reading. But, in being altered, philosophy does not become anything else. Altered, it continues.

We have cheated a little here, presenting Kafka's story in a way Blanchot would not quite allow. After all, if we could employ "The Burrow," say, as a means of exemplifying the condition of literature or writing, would we not simply be perpetuating philosophy's making of literature an endless source of examples for, and aids to, thinking? Nonetheless, our introduction of the story was slightly more complex than that, letting it not so much exemplify the condition of literature as *perform* the implicating (the altering) of philosophy by literature. This is what interests Blanchot, and this is what he tries to show in the accounts of the *recherches* and the "itineraries" of Kafka, Mallarmé, Hölderlin, and Rilke, that we find in *L'espace littéraire*.

Hölderlin, Mallarmé, and many others, amongst whom we can certainly name Kafka, do not permit us to write in ignorance or rejection of the philosophical horizon. Let us return to the fragment that prompted these reflections. (Our remarks here will necessarily be a little awkward and repetitive, circling the difficulty of presenting or of giving an account of Blanchot's relation to philosophy.) It is not that the writers Blanchot so admires possess, or that their work displays, a particular knowledge of interest to, or recognizable by, philosophy. In this sense, it is not, say, Kafka's relationship to philosophy that is at issue, but rather the relationship of those who would attempt to comment on what is given in Kafka's text ("What Kafka gives us—the gift we do not receive").[23] What is given is the thought of the approach, a thought that is not a thought or not primarily a thought, but rather the alteration of thought. There is a moment when writing, giving rise to the *thought* of the "outside," the "approach (of the work)," necessitates this alteration: a moment when, disclosing its essential difference from production, from action, and so from the essential as such, writing (literature) announces itself as exile and as perpetual openness to a future it can never announce.

To write with an eye on the philosophical horizon is to think what is given *as* literature's gift to philosophy, where philosophy must also name (although Blanchot would not encourage such a schematization) the discourse that has always saved literature from its self-discovery by variously: distinguishing and analyzing it solely in terms of its genres (poem, novel, epic, etc.), subordinating it to the higher term (art), and thereby assigning it a place, a law, a historical role, a function. It is a matter, *now* (i.e., after Kafka, Mallarmé, Hölderlin) of writing in such a way as to introduce (to insinuate) the *thought* of this outside and the *thought* of this other future into philosophy. To accompany philosophy, obliging it to acknowledge both this outside and its own inability to turn that outside into an object of knowledge. In other words, to write together what cannot be thought together. But who can genuinely be said to have written in such a way and to have attempted such a thing? Who has given his name to a writing that can be described, however clumsily, in such a fashion? Surely, and uniquely, it is Blanchot. This fragment, from *L'écriture du désastre*, whatever else it does, also describes the concerns of the fragments in that book. It gives a clue, albeit a fragmentary one, as to how to read them. Elsewhere, Blanchot has said that the gift the poet brings to thought is the *fragment*.[24] A gift that can only go on giving itself, it fragments any attempt to situate or read it. The fragment we are considering situates itself in relation to philosophy in order to say the impossibility of a fragment's being so situated. It thus grows opaque and withdraws from our reading—becomes unreadable—at the very instance of its helping us and of our beginning to read through and beyond it. We can never have done with it, and this is perhaps the point; to write alongside philosophy, insinuating and becoming the *thought* with which the philosopher (the philosophical reader) can never have done.

Blanchot writes (is not permitted not to write) with an eye on the philosophical horizon, and also, we are told, with an ear for the words that mark its limit, the words that "punctuate," "hold together," and "disperse" that horizon. What are these words? The fragment actually begins with a list of words and phrases that only later are shown to be the limit words in question: "last witness, end of history, epoch, turning, crisis,—or else, end of (metaphysical) philosophy."[25]

These words come to the fore when philosophy begins to detect the effects of the disclosure of the condition of writing. That is to say, writing implies these words. Writing, we might say, leads philosophy to compile a vocabulary with which to express or diagnose the disturbance that is its (writing's) coming to thought. In such a way, the words protect philosophy. But if writing implies them, it also revokes them, draws them out of work. The words that mark the limit of the philosophical horizon are ambiguous: on the one hand, they are names, philosophical names, asserting the possibility of philosophy's continuing to name whatever confronts it; and, on the other hand, they are responses, responses to what—*now*—ceaselessly calls philosophy into question. Blanchot expresses this ambiguity, in *L'entretien infini*, when he describes philosophy as "naming the possible and responding to the impossible."[26] His own writing, his own fragmentary writing, is caught up with this latter gesture, for it is a writing grown aware of itself as response. It asks what writing must become in and from that awareness, and its answer, as we have seen, has something to do with the writing of this response into the text of philosophy.

We must be careful here for it is a matter of discerning differences and degrees that Blanchot will never thematize as such. Note that a twofold difference would seem to have come into play. First, there is a difference between philosophy and writing (literature), and second, a difference within philosophy itself (the difference between naming and responding). An awareness of the former would seem to show itself in terms of a movement in the latter (from naming to responding, a drawing out of work). Blanchot allows, in the course of two essays on Nietzsche, that we can conceive of the former difference in terms of two languages, the language of philosophy (the language of the totality, *du tout*) and a "wholly other language" (the language of the "fragment").[27] If philosophy, if Hegel, can be read as both naming (mastering) and responding, Nietzsche's text is slightly different and so not quite, or not only, a philosophical text.[28] Nietzsche is the only philosopher Blanchot will also call a "writer." If he enables Blanchot to make the strategic distinction between two languages, and we must be careful not to abuse or overwork it, it is because, in his text, philosophy and this other language are held and given in an impossible coexistence. It is this coexistence, and so Nietzsche's text, that bequeaths to Blanchot the very notion of "fragmentary writing"; Nietzsche would seem to be paradigmatic for a writing that sought to "accompany philosophy," to attend to the giving of the gift that literature gives philosophy.[29]

The approach of the other language, the approach that *is* the other language, allows us to detect, in the names with which philosophy confronts and handles the possible, the "structure" of a response.

If Blanchot would perhaps claim that we sometimes touch a point where we cannot overlook this complex strangeness at the heart of literary communication—the strangeness that makes communication literary and the space of communication, literary space—he is always aware of the difficulty of thinking it. Such a thought, he will say, *interrupts* or *fragments* thought. No one is better than he at showing just how strange a word, a phrase, an incident, or a character in a poem, a tale, or a novel is. But that strangeness is never allowed to become a value or criterion by which a work or writer might be judged. The reading *encounter* with this strangeness, the *encounter* that alters reading (reading conceived of as either "active" or "passive"), is what Blanchot calls "the reading of passivity" or "passivity's reading."[30] Its *time* is the time in which I (the philosophical reader) respond to what resists reading, to what is unreadable, but to what signifies despite my inability to domesticate, appropriate, or translate it.

Blanchot's fragmentary writing, in particular the fragments of *L'écriture du désastre*, can be said to "operate" in a variety of ways. Tentatively, and for the sake of formulating our question, we might discern two such "operations" under the following headings. Many fragments, perhaps all, would fit under both. What we have in mind, though, is no more than a slight difference in tone or in *inclination*. (1) *Those fragments which signal ("faire signe") to the system (to philosophy)*: This signaling binds the fragment to an essential undecidability, a version of which we have already considered. The fragment signals to the system, the system fragments. What we read when we read the fragment can be seen as either the signaling fragment or the signaled—and so fragmented—system. (2) *Those fragments which speak of fragments as signaling to the system (to philosophy)*: A fragment can also serve as a meditation upon fragmentary writing, as an investigation into its effective undecidability. Such a fragment considers how a fragmentary writing signifies and how it might be read. When a fragment gives us that which we cannot simply receive, it displays the first *inclination*; when it considers this impossibility of receiving the gift (as in the formulating of the phrase "the reading of passivity"), it displays the second.

Blanchot's relation to philosophy would be examined by referring to the fragments under our first heading; those fragments which are philosophy's being accompanied by the other language. Here are the fragments into which Blanchot releases one of his special words, words to which he has given a special, strategic status, words for the most part with a long and complex history in his own texts. In *L'écriture du désastre*, he identifies four such words, calling them "the four winds of spirit's absence": "outside," "neutre,"[31] "désastre," "retour."[32] (It is interesting that only one of the four has been developed in a text other than Blanchot's and introduced as a result of that development: *retour*, from Nietzsche's impossible thought and heaviest burden, "the thought of eternal return"). These words, we are told, can form no system. They are "the names of thought when it lets itself come undone, by writing, and fragment." (Again, there is a sense of the undecidability characteristic of the fragmentary. These words belong to the other language but name thinking (philosophy) in its response to that language.) Blanchot's words interrupt any context into which they might be introduced. We should add that his fragments often address, and so fragment and interrupt, his own work ("Upon reading this sentence from years ago . . .");[33] in one instance, quoted as one of our epigraphs, displacing the very notions of "fragmentary writing" and "interruption" at the point where they would seem about to harden into a theory and a practice. The fragments under our first heading, insofar as they consist of the writing together of philosophy and the outside (to continue to use the word we have seen at "work," at work drawing out of work, in our discussion of Hegel and Kafka), should exhaust everything that could be said about Blanchot and philosophy, at least everything Blanchot would seem to want to say.

What interests us now, however, is the philosophical vocabulary that Blanchot knowingly employs (or employs while knowingly sharing it) in those fragments falling under our second heading; those, for example, which speak of the four words as special words, those which describe the reading (the reading of passivity) that is the reading of the fragmentary. Why, and how could Blanchot justify, the reference to a philosopher here, where it is a matter of remarking the scene of the most complex and unsettling encounter with philosophy, where it is a matter, precisely, of remarking the writing together of what cannot be thought together? These fragments are not to be envisaged as second order fragments, as a sort of meta-fragmentary writing. In attempting to gesture toward the "writing of the *outside*" or "the writing of *le désastre*," they draw that writing away from the contextualizing grasp of the philosophical reader. Insofar as they are successful, of course, they fall back under our first heading. This is where our distinction collapses. But it is a matter of using it simply to recognize the words that come into play when the fragmentary, the writing together, is itself the issue; in other words, when Blanchot's text considers the giving of its own gift and, accompanying that giving, frustrates any attempt to receive it.

The vocabulary employed in such instances is, it seems to us, either uniquely Levinas's or else, at least, uniquely shared with Levinas, and its major philosophical application and exposition is *Otherwise than Being*. It is, in part, a shared vocabulary ("response," "passivity," *the* words with which the other language, the language of the fragment, is described), and one developed over the course of fifteen or sixteen years, but also, and most importantly, it hinges on a word that, as we know, is never anything but Levinas's ("le Dire"). We would say, too, that despite the temptation, Levinas's exemplary presence cannot be likened to Nietzsche's because, more than any other work, it is *Otherwise than Being* that *L'écriture du désastre* (incorporating the "Discours") subjects to thorough and frequent fragmentation. With respect to the first *inclination*, then, Levinas's text—unlike Nietzsche's—is treated solely as a "philosophical" work. And yet, fragmented, *Otherwise than Being* nonetheless provides the word that best says fragmentary signification.

We believe that this extended detour was necessary to enable us to appreciate the singular nature of these references to Levinas. The aim now is to begin to read them.

2.

It is important, for Blanchot, that Levinas's work—even to the extent of seeming unfashionable, out of step with its time—remains and retains the name *philosophy*. It is important that it remains something to be approached, accompanied, and fragmented. And therein would seem to lie the problem.

Into the margins of Levinas's work, Blanchot writes, as we have seen, the following two lines: "*Le désastre* ruins everything," "*Le désastre* takes care of everything." The implicit violence of a more euphemistic "taking care of" in English perhaps suffices to suggest the ambiguity here: the sense of something both destructive and protective. On the basis of our preliminary account of fragmentary writing, we might propose an interpretation. *Le désastre* is and says the approach that ruins the totalizing discourse of philosophy. Yet it also attests to a certain transformation in and of that discourse. In being opened to what approaches, philosophy *responds* and comes to realize (although this realization registers as neither a moment of enlightenment nor a Hegelian step [*Aufhebung*]) that its language is not only a totalizing language. *Le désastre*, the writing of *le désastre*, in confronting philosophy with the approach of another future, a future philosophy can never master and a future that will thus never be philosophy's own, is protective of that future. "Writing" names the passivity that protects what cannot be thought and what, in approaching thought, remains always other. As we put it earlier, to write alongside philosophy or into the margins of a philosophical work would seem to mean the insinuating of a radical alterity, one to which that work can only respond. But what could such a move entail with respect to Levinas and to a work that already centers on and derives its inspiration—its reason—from just such an alterity? How do you approach a work that already attends to everything the approaching would wish to introduce?

But before concluding either that Levinas's "philosophy" is impossible (and so simply dismissing or "celebrating" it), or that Blanchot's "fragmentary writing together" is irrelevant, we should note that we have not really done justice to the ambiguity of the ruining, protecting *désastre*. In our reading, there was a change of object: the ruining of philosophical language, the protecting of the other future. What we should add or re-emphasize is that, in being ruined as a totalizing discourse, philosophy *continues* in and as a responding discourse. What is protected in the protecting of the other future is also philosophy in its *continuing as response*. It is this responsiveness—and the difficulty but necessity of philosophizing with and from it—that is Levinas's concern. What is vital here, and what Blanchot never ceases to applaud, is precisely Levinas's insistence on continuing to philosophize. Levinas's uniqueness, for Blanchot, seems to lie in his fidelity to the question of this originary response, or better, his fidelity to what that response does to, and means for, our questions and our questioning.

Earlier we noticed Blanchot's reluctance to capitalize the other (*l'autre*), his wariness about substantiating alterity. From the first, or perhaps at first, what most intrigues him is the alterity Levinas invokes under the heading of the *il y a*, a phrase that fluctuates bewilderingly between them. The *il y a*, a neutral, continuing existence without existents (and so never capitalized), might be fairly described for both as a drawing out of work, as the ruin of any ontology and any totalizing project. Levinas proposes the *il y a* as a synonym for Blanchot's *outside* and *neutre*, thereby seeming to provide us with a useful means of situating Blanchot's work within his own.[34] Elsewhere, we have examined the way in which Levinas would sometimes seem to subordinate the *il y a* to a certain linearity; thinking it between ontology and "ethics," the ruin of the former and so entrance to—or expression of the desire for —the latter.[35] Our aim in that paper was, in part, to question this subordination, not only in Blanchot's terms but also in Levinas's. For, in *Otherwise than Being*, Levinas comes to complicate any presentation of the move into "ethics," the retrieval of "ethics," as a linear narrative.

It is certainly not wrong to detect in Blanchot's readings of *Totality and Infinity* and *Otherwise than Being* perpetual reminders to Levinas of the repercussions for thought of the nonsubstantial alterity that is the *il y a*, its repercussions for any attempt to step beyond it. He does this again explicitly in the latter part of *L'écriture du désastre*. But these reminders do not exhaust those readings. Blanchot's aim is not simply to read the *il y a* against Levinas's other vocabulary (his vocabulary pertaining to *the* [capitalized] *Other*). His aim is not to argue that that vocabulary and the new thinking it would serve are impossible, where impossible would mean their being deemed philosophically worthless or no longer philosophical. It is rather to have us attend to the impossibility within them, the impossibility they protect and introduce (introduce philosophically) to philosophy. We will need to see what this means.[36]

Perhaps it will help if we envisage two commands as guiding and determining the course of Blanchot's readings of Levinas. First, do not read the step (*pas*) into "ethics," and Levinas's various retrievals, as part of a linear narrative. Read them, in other words, in terms of the logic of the *pas au-delà* (the logic of the *approach*). Second, do however read them! Do not imagine that that "logic" abolishes the "ethics" and its concomitant vocabulary. With reference to the first command, Blanchot will show just how strange, how "impossible," Levinas's words are. With reference to the second, he will show their necessity, the necessity they acquire in direct proportion to their "impossibility." Blanchot's readings do not impose these commands, but show how they are already implied by Levinas's texts and how—and herein lies its uniqueness —in *Otherwise than Being* they become explicit.

Let us follow Blanchot in his meditations upon Levinas's philosophical renewal of two words: patience and responsibility.

Patience: Toward the end of *Otherwise than Being*, Levinas, drawing on the semantic chain that so preoccupies Blanchot, suggests that we cease to think of *patience* as a straightforward postponing of action, as a way of handling or not handling finitude (our ontological condition), as *peace (paix)* defined solely in opposition to war. The obligation to be patient can only apply to me. In being patient, I cannot demand it of anyone else. Patience, the peace I wage for the other, is the absence of commensurability. Passivity necessitates asymmetry. Patience is thus not a more or less tragic encounter with my self, my finitude, or with what impends as my future. It is exposure to the Other.

Blanchot, taking up this thought, comments on the way in which such a patience can no longer simply be opposed to impatience. There are, he says, two types of patience, two ways of hearing the command to *be patient*. First, patience is called for in situations where and when it is possible, albeit frustrating or boring, to be patient. Such patience is an achievement brought about by our co-operating with time, a co-operation that bequeaths us all the time in the world. Here, we can say, letting be and waiting have results. They get us somewhere. But there is another patience and another command. One that finds me and claims me when I have no time or, rather, one that draws me "outside" a time I might, from a certain position and in the name of a certain power or mastery, call my own. At the heart of this patience is impatience, precisely the impossibility of being patient.

Responsibility: The relation of asymmetry in which I find myself always already opened to the Other is written, in *Otherwise than Being*, in such a way that it can never be undone or reappropriated by a higher or more fundamental intersubjectivity. I am ("I" is) not only one of the terms in the relation but the relation itself. The subject (subjectivity) is throughout the book written *as* the response to alterity; the response on the basis of which everything will be said. From the first, or prior to the first word, I am held in the accusative and written as *"me voici."* The "I" that establishes itself in language and the content of all it says is forever haunted by this preoriginal response. Language as communication, communication as reciprocal exchange, and "I" (the subject) as the guarantee of unification (of any unification at all) are *first* exposure to and solicitation of the Other. Just as philosophy, vulnerable to the same anarchism (the same primal scene?), is *first* "ethics."

Blanchot is much taken with the paradoxical singularity that characterizes the subject in response, the "me voici." If responsibility, like patience, means that I and only I can answer for the Other and if I, bound to the "me voici," am nothing but "for the Other" ("the one for the Other"), then I am both absolutely unique (the chosen *one*) and absolutely anonymous (for the Other). What I do *for the Other* must only be done by me but could be done by anyone. It is done by me as anyone, where this "anyone" is not the result of an abstraction from the thought of what I might do to a general or universalizable principle. This "anyone" is what, in Levinasian responsibility, I always already am. Here is how Blanchot writes it:

> Responsible: this word generally qualifies—in a prosaic, bourgeois manner —a mature, lucid, conscientious man, who acts with circumspection, who takes into account all elements of a given situation, calculates and decides;

the successful man of action. But now responsibility—responsibility for the other (*autrui*), for everyone, without reciprocity—is displaced. No longer does it belong to consciousness; it is not an activating thought process put into practice, nor is it even a duty that would impose itself from without and from within. *My* responsibility for the Other (*Autrui* [*Here, then, is the full Levinasian "renewal"* PD]) presupposes a change an overturning such that it can only be marked by a change in the status of "me," a change in time and perhaps in language. Responsibility, which withdraws me from my order (perhaps from all order [*de tout ordre*]), which separates me from myself . . . and discloses the other (*l'autre*) in my *place*, requires that I answer for absence, for passivity. It requires that I answer for *the impossibility of being responsible* (our emphasis), to which it has always already consigned me by both holding me accountable and discounting me altogether. And this paradox leaves nothing intact, not subjectivity any more than the subject, not the individual any more than the person.[37]

In these readings of "patience" and "responsibility," Levinas's text is fragmented. Let us say that there can be no question of its replying to Blanchot's interventions. Those interventions are not wrong and the paradox (the "impossibility") they affirm is in no way added to the text. It is already there at its center. Through the logic of the *approach*, the *pas au-delà* (through what we will call in a moment the "logic of *le désastre*"), Blanchot reads that which inside *Otherwise than Being* interrupts and fragments it. Here the reading, the fragmentation, might be thought as ruination. For some readers of Levinas (sometimes perhaps for Levinas himself) it will seem as though Blanchot has gone too far, has remained insensitive to the organization of *Otherwise than Being*, and has once again released the nonspecific neutral alterity of the *il y a* into each of Levinas's descriptions.

But Blanchot's readings are not objections to Levinas, nor are they simply affirmations. He is not suggesting that *Otherwise than Being* would have possessed a greater consistency or integrity had it been written as the "Discours" or as *L'écriture du désastre*. If Blanchot is especially drawn to those places in *Otherwise than Being* where the argument and exposition seem on the very edge of fragmentation, and if his reading in part performs that fragmentation and so confirms the text's precariousness, how does he address the fact that the text continues, that the argument and exposition survive?

Blanchot speaks of the *need* to understand the word "responsibility" as it has been "renewed" by Levinas. In this renewal "it has come to signify (beyond all meaning [*au-delà de tout sens*]) the responsibility of an other philosophy." What is this other philosophy? Blanchot insists that it remains "eternal philosophy." It is, then, we might say, the continuing of philosophy on the brink of fragmentation. These cryptic remarks in the "Discours" are accompanied by a footnote by the time they reappear in *L'écriture du désastre*. There we read that, in Levinas, we can find no break with Greek philosophy, with the language of the universal: "what is pronounced or rather announced (*ce qui s'énonce ou plutot s'annonce*) . . . is a surplus, a singularity which can be called Jewish and which *waits* to go on being thought (*qui attend d'être encore pensée*)."[38]

In his readings of *Totality and Infinity*, we occasionally get the feeling that Blanchot has to do far more work to draw out the strangeness of the project. He worries over some of Levinas's terms—including "ethics," "ethical," "face to face," "height"—because what is making them, or endeavoring to make them, ring so strangely is in danger of being submerged. In other words, and this will no doubt surprise many of its readers or would-be readers, *Totality and Infinity*, although it need not be, is perhaps too easily read. This, it seems, is not the case with *Otherwise than Being*. Although Blanchot has one or two reservations, something has clearly changed. What makes the difference seems to be the distinction between the saying (*le Dire*) and the said (*le Dit*); the saying as *responsible passivity*: "before anything is said and outside of being (*avant tout dit, et hors de l'être*) . . . the Saying (*le Dire*) gives and gives the response, responding to the impossible and for the impossible."[39]

Le Dire, the responsible passivity that turns philosophy (Greek philosophy) toward another future and makes it responsible for that future: In terms of the text of *Otherwise than Being*, in terms of *Otherwise than Being* as a book, *le Dire* is protective both of its continuing and of what would persist in threatening (fragmenting) it.

In *Totality and Infinity*, as much as *Otherwise than Being*, language is first solicitation. Language is itself the relation to infinity, the *rapport sans rapport*. In the preface to *Totality and Infinity*, Levinas comments on the link between this relation, between language as this relation, and the question of the book in which it would be introduced. The prefatory word which "seeks to break through the screen stretched between the author and the reader by the book itself . . . belongs to the very essence of language."[40] To read while remembering that word is to hear the continual undoing of the thematizations that necessarily follow it. The prefatory word unsays the said. This is a profound and difficult lesson, a warning that *Totality and Infinity* does not excuse itself from the obligations it detects in the relation to which language opens us, the relation which demands a change in our understanding of language.

In *Otherwise than Being*, this once only prefatory word is however explicitly recalled and reactivated at every stage of the argument and exposition. Although, as we shall see, there is a unique call-word, it is of another sort and, dare we say it, of another language. The subject in saying will be written differently with every twist and turn. Moreover, the distinction between the saying and the said, the account of the former's necessary betrayal in and by the latter, the attempt to "reduce" that betrayal as though to catch it in the act, as though to hear it happening, all of these hard-won distinctions and careful exercises will be shadowed by the specter of an "invincible skepticism." With time, one could follow the development. To begin with, the attempt to retrieve or to disengage the relation to the other from the totalizing language of philosophy (to disengage the subject in saying) is likened to the attempt to detect, within skepticism, that overriding movement when, although refuted, the skeptical utterance signifies and, in signifying, returns. But skepticism is not simply an aid to our understanding the main terms of Levinas's work. The "fine risk" that the skeptical *énoncé* and *le Dire* are said to run binds the former ever more closely to those terms. Toward the end of *Otherwise than Being*, we read that "Language is already scepticism,"[41] Blanchot uses this sentence on several occasions in *L'écriture du désastre*; not, however, in the "Discours." He will also write that "the invincible scepticism that Levinas admits shows that his own philosophy . . . affirms nothing that is not overseen by an indefatigable adversary, one to whom he does not concede but who obliges him to go further, not beyond reason . . . but towards another reason, towards the other as reason."[42]

What of "Après coup"? Here the work done by Levinas's words is of a slightly different order. But then "Après coup" itself is of a slightly different order. It is, as we have said, an unusual text for Blanchot, this "commentary" on two early stories, written on the occasion of their being reprinted. Let us try to clarify the nature of this "commentary." Again we propose a detour, but a much shorter one. It might help us draw out some of the more specific associations of "le désastre," and to begin to identify some of the senses of the "event" *after* which "Après coup" is written, if we pause to recall the complex presentation or autopresentation of *La folie du jour*.

The "récit" opens with an affirmation of sight. The one who sees (the one who tells the tale, the one whose voice—on first reading—convinces us that we are in fact reading an account of something) derives great happiness from that seeing: "I see the world—what extraordinary happiness! I see this day, and outside it there is nothing."[43] Yet this self-description is the introduction to an account of the "madness" or "frenzy" that befell both this day and this one who saw it, the one who continues to see it, a madness to which there were no (other) witnesses. The voice which tells this tale is thus the only one qualified to tell us of this event. This is the only voice we who were not there will ever hear. The event (the madness at the center of the tale) is described as a terrible attack on the teller's eyes. This moment of extreme violence, this attack on sight itself, breaks the bond that ties seeing to saying, the bond that enables us to think of saying as a metaphorical seeing and telling as a metaphorical showing. Elsewhere, Blanchot sometimes uses the following formulation: "to speak is not to see."[44] Hence the painful movement connecting the difficulty of speech with the bandage placed over the eyes after the incident. Hence, too, the animal cries, at the very instance of the attack, that are only afterwards thought to have been "mine." Now these things, we think as we read the story, are indeed terrible. But they are, at least (for how could it be otherwise?), events which either did or did not happen and which are now being recounted. Later the injunction on talking will be lifted and the *witness*, the "I," will be obliged to tell what happened, to describe the events themselves and *the* event itself. But that event has robbed events of their perviousness to being told, and everything "I" say (everything the one who says "I" says, everything the only witness says) will not be what the interrogators wish to hear. On the last page, we learn that the tale we are reading is the very tale proffered to the interrogators. Or rather, we learn that it is both that tale and something more. It is then, in part, the very tale they will not accept as *the* tale. The event, the catastrophe, seems to expand. For it is no longer an event itself (the attack on seeing that made saying painful) that disturbs in the tale, but the telling itself. In *this* tale, which can be neither told nor accepted, there is no distinguishing between the event and its telling. The event, we might say, is what is done to telling as a *result* (but this is too quick, too clumsy) of the coming to pass of what cannot be told. Blanchot's "tale" (and what have we added when we write the proper name? One of the first titles for this piece seems to have been "Un récit?")[45] thus tells of the violence of the command to tell: to tell what was seen. The difficulty the teller or would-be teller has here would be exacerbated by even the kindest of entreaties.

On a first reading, *La folie du jour* tells of the untellability of an event. To stop there, however, would be to align ourselves with the doctors, the organizers of the institutions. It would leave us with the sense of needing to find other means of encouraging the speaker to say what happened. It would leave us with the sense of an event (perhaps the most traumatic of events) about which the witness, the sufferer, the subject, is *as yet* unable to speak. But *La folie du jour* is not circular and, in addition to our realizing that what is being told is what the official listeners reject as a tale, we realize that that rejection cannot suffice to silence the telling. We are aware, too, that apart from this other and unacceptable telling, nothing (no thing, no event) will ever be told. On all the subsequent readings called for by these few pages, the event they might once (to another reader and in another time) have been about, becomes the telling of the untellable *as* untellable. An endless telling, attested to by the "final," and now famous, line: "Un récit? Non, pas de récit, plus jamais." The voice that keeps on coming, the voice that installs in Blanchot's *pas* and *plus jamais* the promise of a future without release and without catharsis (the *pas* of this *récit*, again and again), is what Blanchot calls "the narrative voice." He distinguishes it from "the narrating voice," the voice the doctors sought to hear and the voice we (always philosophical readers) thought we heard when we began to read *La folie du jour*.

The tale opens up a space in which the untellable remains untold. In this space (this "orphic space") the tale is already turning into its impossibility. Now, solely as a means of access, as a way of hearing the word, let us say that "désastre" names that which, in the tale, calls attention to the tale; that which effaces the division between the tale and its content (between the tale and what it tells); and that which is disastrous for the tale conceived of as a "bringing to the light of day." For it is precisely the "light of day" which this tale, turning into its impossibility, infuses with another light. Recall the catastrophic clarity referred to in our opening pages.

In our account of *La folie du jour*, we made use of the phrase "the narrative voice." We did so in a way consistent with Blanchot's introduction of it. But of course, Blanchot will never read *La folie du jour* for us, will never let the nonfictional works provide the theoretical vocabulary for explaining the practice of the fictional works. And how quickly each of these oppositions comes to seem untenable (theory/practice, nonfiction/fiction). His own discussion of "the narrative voice" will be marked by a complexity every bit as troubling as that found in *La folie du jour*, *L'ârret de mort*, "L'idylle," etc. In all of Blanchot's writings, we could detect the structure of an excessive giving: in the stories or non-stories, the fragments, the readings of others; in the invoking of philosophy, in the gesturing toward an other language.

What then of "Après coup"? It would seem to entail our moving from a discussion of the autopresentation of *La folie du jour* to one of the re-presentation (Blanchot's re-presentation) of "Le dernier mot" and "L'idylle." Do we not here catch a glimpse of what makes "Après coup" different; namely, Blanchot seeming to provide *a way of* reading, seeming to employ his own terms as theoretical terms? As delicate and as sensitive as her own reading of Blanchot always is, this is how Kofman would presumably have us interpret it. As we have seen, Blanchot does not quite use his own terms in this presentation of his work. Nonetheless, on first reading, perhaps also on second, it is hard to see why this text, this after word, is not going against the grain of Blanchot's writing. It is hard to see why it is not letting something be said that should not be said, something that would surely minimize or detract from the *risk* that is fragmentary writing. Does "Après coup," in its commentary, problematize itself? Is its giving in any way excessive? In closing, we will suggest (and what follows is no more than a suggestion) how the borrowing from *Otherwise than Being* allows Blanchot, in "Après coup," to undo—to fragment—a certain reception of "L'idylle."

We have avoided translating "le désastre," choosing instead to let it ring out as a word, so that the "writing of le désastre" means the writing of a word into the margins of philosophy and a particular philosophical text. But our reading of *La folie du jour* has shown us how *le désastre* is also something like an event: an event about which there is writing, and an event productive of a writing that is no longer *about* anything. The genitive in the writing *of* this event, *L'écriture du désastre*, is double and, in this doubling, the event is robbed of its event character. *Le désastre* is both what is written and what writes. It is thus more than a term in a relation, more than a possible term in a possible relation. It is the relating or the relation itself. It has a formal similarity, then, to the *Dire* in *Otherwise than Being*. *Le désastre* says something that philosophy cannot thematize or fix as an event. It names something philosophy cannot name; what, in having happened once, continues to happen and what, in continuing to happen, constantly affects the distance at which philosophy would hold itself. *Le désastre* is what lingers, what remains, but never as a determinable presence.

In *L'écriture du désastre*, we sometimes come across fragments that seem to be on the verge of telling a story: italicized fragments describing a scene, a "primal scene" ("Une scène primitive?":[46] This "title" is not italicized; note the question mark [*un récit?*]). They tell of a child who one day lifted up his head and saw the sky, the ordinary daytime sky, turned black; black without stars, a de-starred sky. An event, always past, that would perhaps rewrite the story of the gaze of wonder directed at the stars; the gaze that is said to inaugurate philosophy. Throughout *L'écriture du désastre*, the relation to the star connotes religious and nostalgic desire.[47] *Le désastre* effects a break with that relation, rendering relationality as such opaque. The gaze that *once* saw a starless sky ruined forever the thought of a beyond. To look beyond (*au-delà*) and see the absence of a beyond: here is Blanchot's *pas au delà*, and it is ruinous of any possible relation I or philosophy might have to the future. In *L'écriture du désastre*, we are occasionally on the verge of a story that would alter the story philosophy tells itself about its origins. The thought of philosophy's being called into question, the thought of its beginning and end, would here perhaps take on a different meaning. What calls philosophy into question—*both interrupting it and obliging it to continue*—is something like an event, from which philosophy cannot, any longer, keep its *own* distance.

In his essay on *La folie du jour*, in his reading of the institution in and from which the telling resounds (the place in which all telling is refused and from which there comes another, disastrous, telling), Levinas refers to or invokes (writes) the word "Auschwitz."[48] For Blanchot, too, *"le désastre"* is caught up with the question of writing and saying this terrible name. Auschwitz, the violence that befell the other (the Other) there, is an event from which philosophy will never be able to gain a distance, is thus something like an event. Its name, the most singular of names, also names the violence that continues; the violence against the other to which Auschwitz awakened philosophy and for which Auschwitz made philosophy responsible. So written (written through the logic of *le désastre*), "Auschwitz" makes philosophy aware of its (philosophy's) responsibility *there*, responsible both for that violence and for the future in which that violence and those suffering others are always to be remembered. Blanchot and Levinas would have everything in common here. To hear this name, not as the *once* that becomes a general term for all subsequent and similar atrocities, but as the *once* that alters the very way in which philosophy names events, is to hear it in terms of the logic (the writing) of *le désastre*.

In "Après coup," Blanchot begins by recalling the perilous between (from the "not yet" to the "no longer") that is "the path of what we call the writer," the between that serves to dismiss the writer from having any say in the work's reception and future.[49] He recalls it in order to show the full force of the embarrassment facing the writer who attempts either to look back or to look forward. But he recalls it, too, for the sake of another between. Between the writing of "L'idylle" and this reading of it, between a time when events could be recounted, could be told *about*, and today, falls Auschwitz.

The stories Blanchot re-reads in "Après coup" were written before Auschwitz, but then all stories from now on will be from such a time. There can be no stories *about* it. Hence, Levinas's reading of that non-story *La folie du jour*. In "Après coup" Blanchot looks back, noting the embarrassment of such a move, and sees between him and the elusive "L'idylle," Auschwitz, where this name names the relation that from now on binds us to all we would write, say, and think. In looking back at "L'idylle," Blanchot begins to hear another voice, one that rises from between himself and "L'idylle." The between *is* that voice. And yet, in an uncanny way, "L'idylle" seems to have allowed for such a voice. It gives rise to the thought of a telling that is no longer about something and so gives rise to the thought of an event (something like an event) that prompts such a telling. Is "L'idylle" evidence, then, of a future possibility? Does it speak to, or give a preliminary echo of, the violence that will make us yearn for just such a possibility? No, again not quite. In re-presenting "L'idylle," Blanchot goes to great lengths to deny us the opportunity of calling it "prophetic." He thereby denies to his work a future in which it might be regarded as holding a privileged standpoint or as speaking with an authoritative voice (as though his work might be the authority on the impossibility of authority, etc.). It seems to us that this denial is also a *fragmentation*.

In re-reading, re-presenting "L'idylle," Blanchot insists on the disastrous relation that binds the writer to what he writes. He insists, too, on the violence, the actual violence, against the other, that always stands in and as that relation. But if "L'idylle" (the work) must now always be heard as tied to that violence, it has no special critical, aesthetic, or moral status. We cannot speak for its being a more successful work than others. It and that violence—"L'idylle" and Auschwitz—are not to be thought together. They are to be written together, but once again written together *as* what cannot be thought together. In "Après coup," unlike La folie du jour and L'écriture du désastre respectively, it is neither "L'idylle," the tale itself, nor Blanchot's own most intricate vocabulary that does that writing. It is Levinas. "[B]efore all distinctions between form and content, between signifier and signified, even before the division between *énonciation* and *énoncé*, there is the unqualifiable *Dire*, the glory of a 'narrative voice.'"

In always lying on the hither side, however, a story can still open up a space in which "a voice comes from the other shore." This text, which more explicitly than any other raises the question of the relation of a story—of story-telling—to Auschwitz, only says the "possibility," only says the *rapport sans rapport*, in the words of another. It is not, then, strictly speaking, Blanchot's possibility. "A voice comes from the other shore": these words too are Levinas's. "Le Dire" says the opening of the space, the very way in which a story (turning into its impossibility) might signify otherwise. The last two words of "Après coup" are the name "Emmanuel Levinas." On the only occasion that Blanchot explicitly and apparently straightforwardly re-reads and re-presents an earlier tale, he effectively takes that tale out of work. He shows that the *désoeuvrement* at its center does not allow us to think it in relation to the "event" alongside of which it must now forever be read.

"Le Dire," Levinas's preoriginal saying and that which is "put forth in the foreword (*le propos de l'avant-propos*),"[50] would be a strange word to invoke *après coup*, in an afterword. But the issue of this anteriority and the part played by a foreword (a once only call-word) perhaps give us the clue as to why it is Levinas's word(s) to which Blanchot turns.

At the close of "Our Clandestine Companion," the piece Blanchot wrote for Levinas in 1980 (note that the clandestine companion might be heard as "philosophy"), we read:

> I would like to add an obsessional touch (*un rappel d'obsession*) . . . *Otherwise than Being* is a philosophical work. It would be difficult not to take it as such, since philosophy, even if it concerns discontinuity and rupture, nonetheless solicits us philosophically. This book begins with a dedication, however, that I here transcribe: *"To the memory of those who were closest among the six million assassinated by the National Socialists, and of the millions on millions of all confessions and all nations, victims of the same hatred of the other man, the same antisemitism."* How can one philosophize, how can one write within the memory of Auschwitz of those who have said, oftentimes in notes buried near the crematoria: know what has happened, don't forget, and at the same time, you won't be able to.
>
> It is this thought that traverses, that bears, the whole of Levinas's philosophy and that he proposes to us without saying it, beyond and before all obligation.[51]

"Obsession" is already one of the ways in which *Otherwise than Being* describes the relation with the other.[52] Obsession is "anarchical." If I say I am obsessed by the other, then it is not a matter of needing or being able to provide reasons. Obsession acknowledges an accusation without foundation. If I am obsessed by the other then I do not say "I" but "me voici." "An obsessive touch" thus situates what follows within a writing of or from the *rapport sans rapport*. Blanchot obsessively transcribes what is obsessively put forth in this foreword, in these few lines before the book starts. We have seen that *Otherwise than Being* is a book under a sort of threat. It is always about to be fragmented, always about to come undone. It handles that threat not simply by warding it off, but by continually transforming it into an obligation, the obligation to continue. And yet perhaps what "organizes" this book, what holds it together, *is* an obsessive touch. This dedication, in its specificity ("the memory of those who were closest"), is also to be read in terms of *le désastre*. We see that logic "at work" in the spreading of this most specific memory to all "the victims of the same hatred of the other man." This dedication obsessively sends *Otherwise than Being*, the book in its entirety, with its discussions, analyses, and endlessly incipient fragmentations, toward the only future philosophy can henceforth know: the future of the other. And it is surely with an eye on this dedication and this future, that Blanchot finds in *Otherwise than Being* the word that both says the fragmentary as such and, when written into the margins of his own work, witholds from that work any privileged (i.e., conceivable) relation to the "event"—*le désastre*—that *now* gives philosophy its future as response.

Notes

1. AE 154; OB 120.
2. *L'écriture du désastre*, Paris, Gallimard, 1980, 98. *The Writing of the Disaster*, trans. A. Smock, Lincoln, University of Nebraska Press, 1986, 59. Hereafter EDD and WOD.
3. *Le Nouveau commerce* no. 30–31, Spring 1975.
4. EDD 45ff. Unless otherwise stated, that is, unless the passage in question has been altered or relocated, all references to the "Discours" will give the page numbers of EDD and WOD.
5. EDD 10; WOD 3.
6. "Discours," 43.
7. So many references might be made here. For one of the earliest introductions of this thought and one that invokes two of its sources (perhaps the two major sources), cf. *Faux pas*, Paris, Gallimard, 1943, 47. The first discussion of Bataille, written in 1943, it opens with the figure of Nietzsche's "great noontide": "L'heure du Grand Midi est celle qui nous apporte la plus forte lumière; l'air entier est échauffé; le jour est devenu feu; pour l'homme avide de voir. . . ."
8. The last words of the "Discours"; EDD 17; WOD 7.
9. Appropriately enough, Blanchot's first essay on Kafka, "La lecture du Kafka," introduces us to this word. See *La part du feu*, Paris, Gallimard, 1949, 9. See, more importantly, the following sentence toward the end of that essay: "Les récits de Kafka sont, dans la littérature, parmi les plus noirs, les plus rivés à un désastre absolu," 18. Recall, in all that follows, that *L'écriture du désastre* would also say something about Kafka's work. For another earlier reference in Blanchot see *L'espace littéraire*, Paris, Gallimard, 1955, reprinted in Gallimard Collection Idées (page references are to the latter edition), 332. See also *The Space of Literature*, trans. Ann Smock, Lincoln, University of Nebraska Press, 1982, 332. For the more cryptic references to Mallarmé see "L'alphabet des astres" in "Quant au livre," Mallarmé, *Oeuvres complètes*, Paris, Gallimard, 1983, 370. And this line from the fifth section of *Igitur*: "sur les cendres des astres," *Oeuvres complètes*, 443.
10. *Après coup*, Paris, Editions de Minuit, 1983, 97–98; *Vicious Circles*, trans. Paul Auster, New York, Station Hill, 1985, 68.
11. *Faux pas*, 9.
12. Note that in "La puissance et la gloire" (1958), the essay which closes *Le livre à venir* (Paris, Gallimard, 1959), Blanchot, citing Rilke, offers a very different interpretation of the word: "Glory is the manifestation of being as it advances in its magnificence of being, liberated from all that conceals it, established in the truth of its unconcealed presence" (333). The essay (and the book) ends with the words "ni la puissance, ni la gloire" (340). Hints in *L'entretien infini* notwithstanding, "la gloire" reappears with its altered sense in *Après coup* surely on the basis of Levinas's use of it.
13. S. Kofman, *Paroles suffoquées*, Paris, Galilée, 1987, 23.
14. *L'entretien infini*, Paris, Gallimard, 1969, 567; "The Narrative Voice," in *The Gaze of Orpheus*, trans. Lydia Davis, New York, Station Hill, 1981, 143.
15. *L'entretien*, 567; *Gaze*, 143.
16. EDD 160; WOD 103.
17. *L'espace littéraire*, 268; *Space of Literature*, 200.
18. Ibid. 286; 214 and *Le livre à venir*, Paris, Gallimard, 1959; reprinted in Gallimard Collection Idées (references are to the latter edition), 265ff.
19. "Der Bau," in *Beschreibung eines Kampfes*, Frankfurt, Fischer, 1969; "The Burrow," trans. Willa and Edwin Muir, in *Description of a Struggle and The Great Wall of China*, London, Secker and Warburg, 1933.
20. *Le part du feu*, 331; *The Gaze of Orpheus*, 41.

21. It is difficult to read this notion of an existence continuing beyond a proper or determinable end without being reminded of Levinas's "il y a." I will return to this question later in the paper. For the moment, however, it is worth noting that Blanchot cites Levinas's *De l'existence à l'existant* toward the end of "Literature and the Right to Death," and that there are other, important, and mutual references. Yet, there is at least one crucial difference. For Levinas, the thought of this continuing existence produces a polemic against Heidegger, indeed signals the very ruin of the "fundamental ontology" of *Being and Time*. Levinas wants to say, too, that Blanchot's work, especially *L'espace littéraire*, shows that art (literature), opening thought to this neutral dissembling outside, is ruinous of any attempt on the part of philosophy (again, Heidegger) to conceive of, or hope for, a rapprochement between thought and poetry. (In this connection, see Paul Davies, "A Linear Narrative: Blanchot with Heidegger in the Work of Levinas," in *Philosophers' Poets*, ed. D. Wood, London, Routledge, forthcoming.) For Blanchot, however, there is no easy opposition to Heidegger, and if the primary reference is to Hegel it is only to suggest that the discourse of totality, at a certain moment (and the tension between Heidegger's and Blanchot's meditations perhaps lies in their respective interpretations of this "moment"), shows itself to be accompanied by its own uncanny echo.

22. "Der Bau," 165; "The Burrow", 220.

23. EDD 213; WOD 141.

24. "Parole de fragment" in *L'endurance de la pensée: Pour saluer Jean Beaufret*, Paris, Plon, 1968, 103.

25. EDD 158; WOD 101.

26. *L'entretien infini*, 68.

27. The two Nietzsche essays are "Passage de la ligne" and "Nietzsche et l'écriture fragmentaire." From the first, see the following: "Philosophy is shaken (*s'ébranle*) in Nietzsche. But is it because he would be the last of the philosophers? Or because (here there is someone) called by a wholly other language?" *L'entretien infini*, 226. From the second, see the reference to the "language *du tout*" and the "language of the fragment," 228. See also "Le 'discours philosophique,'" *L'Arc* no. 46, 1971.

28. Let us insist on the tentativeness of our formulation here. For perhaps the most explicit, and most condensed, statement on the difference between Nietzsche and Hegel see *Le pas au-delà*, 34–35.

29. Our aim here has been to draw attention to the slight nuances in the references to Hegel, Nietzsche, and eventually Levinas in Blanchot's writing. In doing so, we do not intend to rule out other nuances in Blanchot's approach to and conception of philosophy. For example, in the fragment we have been reading, Blanchot goes on to show how Heidegger's word *Ereignis* both implies (or at least allows) the thought of a certain representation of the history of Being, the history of the withdrawal of Being, so retaining a positive sense for the thought of the end of that history, and revokes it by demanding a more insistent and more obscure withdrawal. *Ereignis* both is and is not a limit word, both comforts and disrupts this limit vocabulary. If Blanchot argues for the preeminence of the latter, it is because, since 1947, what have most intrigued him in Heidegger's thought have been those moments when it has opened itself to another future, to the *outside*. Not *its* outside however, and here would be a difference between the references to Hegel and Heidegger. The outside in Blanchot's work discloses itself as a surplus to the system, and so to Hegel (the proper name for the system). We read the outside both inside and outside of the Hegelian text. Hegel occupies a unique position here. We cannot, accordingly, as Levinas might wish, speak of the "outside (of) the Heideggerian world" (cf. *Sur Maurice Blanchot*, 26). Blanchot's "outside" would accompany and undo Heidegger's texts differently because Heidegger would already be implicated in that outside, caught up in the question as to what to do now that this surplus to Hegel has come to thought. Blanchot is especially drawn, of course, to those moments when Heidegger has thought the need for, and the scene of, a new encounter with the poem, with the opaque word in the poem.

Nonetheless, there is a sense that, to put it crudely, something has to be done to Heidegger's text, just as it has to Hegel's, for these moments to be detected. Consider the ongoing meditation on Heidegger's "etymologies" in the latter half of *L'écriture du désastre*. Consider, also, the reference to Hegel in our fragment, and the identifying, in the Hegelian text, of a tension similar to that found in *Ereignis*.

30. EDD 158; WOD 101.

31. The *neutre* in its "relation" to the beginnings of philosophy is discussed in *Le pas au-delà*, 101–7. See also *L'entretien infini*, 119–31 and 441.

32. EDD 95; WOD 57.

33. EDD 97; WOD 59.

34. EeI 47–48; EI 49–50.

35. See "A Linear Narrative: Blanchot with Heidegger in the Work of Levinas."

36. In summary of the preceding two paragraphs, consider these two positions: (1) If Blanchot's *outside* and *neutre* are synonyms for the *il y a* and the *il y a* is subordinated to a linear development, then with respect to Levinas, Blanchot has his place and, again with respect to Levinas, need not trouble us. (2) If Blanchot's words are synonyms for the *il y a* and the *il y a* frustrates any subordination, then Levinas's texts are always vulnerable to Blanchot's readings. Now, if we are more sympathetic to (2), it is with one small but important disclaimer, one we derive from our earlier discussion. Blanchot's words (*outside, neutre*), to which we would now add *désastre*, also look to protect what is most extraordinary in Levinas's enterprise. In this sense, they are never quite the synonyms Levinas would suppose. And might not the wish to see them as such also be the wish to keep (1) open as a possible position? It is worth noting that the only occasion on which Levinas has cited or referred to a fragment from *L'écriture du désastre*, he has done so as an epigraph. The essay above which it stands seems at times to reimpose a linear relation, as though it were really being written on the other side of the fragment, providing a vantage point from which the fragment might be contextualized or read as a polemic. And given that the fragment in question continues the fragmentation (the fragmentary reading) of *Otherwise than Being* begun in the "Discours," it is as if in being returned to him in such a fashion, Levinas's words and thoughts have grown unrecognizable. Blanchot's *outside, neutre,* and *désastre* write or rewrite the *il y a* so as to insure the impossibility of its ever being subordinated.

37. EDD 45; WOD 25.

38. Ibid.

39. EDD 37; WOD 20.

40. TeI xviii; TI 30.

41. AE 216; OB 170.

42. "*Notre compagne clandestine*," in *Textes pour Emmanuel Levinas*, ed. F. Laruelle, Paris, Jean-Michel Place, 1980, 80; "Our Clandestine Companion," trans. D. Allison, in *Face to Face with Levinas*, 42.

43. *The Madness of the Day, La folie du jour*, trans. Lydia Davis, New York, Station Hill, 1981, 6/20.

44. See *L'entretien infini*, 35ff.

45. It was first published in 1949 in *Empédocle* no. 2. For a discussion of the question mark, see J. Derrida, *Parages*, Paris, Galilée, 1986, 130–35, 275.

46. EDD 117; WOD 72.

47. EDD 84–85; WOD 50.

48. *Sur Maurice Blanchot*, 60.

49. *Après coup*, 86; *Vicious Circles*, 60.

50. AE 6; OB 5.

51. "Notre compagne clandestine," 86–87; "Our clandestine companion," 50.

52. AE 140; OB 110.

PART FIVE

Levinas, Psychoanalysis, and Animality

CHAPTER
13

WHO SUFFERS?
Noreen O'Connor

Ethical philosophy, that which is concerned with responsibility, justice, vulnerability, puts the pathetic experience of mankind at the center of its reflection. This is a refusal to sublate love, hatred, hunger, desire, aggression, and sadness under categories of a will specifiable by reason. No longer do we imagine that we can intellectually grasp and fully possess the "meaning" of our death or the joy of our living. This is not to say that the end of philosophy as a rational enterprise releases us to a poetics of individual transcendence or transgression or to a psychology measuring our psyches. Poststructuralist philosophers have challenged the notion of the human construed as rational self-consciousness in favor of notions such as the subject of enunciation or the recurrent deconstruction of hierarchical dualisms.

Levinas and Freud both consider that the relationship between human beings is the most crucial issue to be elucidated in order to counter violence and heal suffering. Freud, despite the mechanistic and pseudoexplanatory character of his metapsychology, nevertheless shares with Levinas an emphasis on the primacy of the heterogeneity or asymmetry of human relationships. Freud privileges speaking and listening, the relationship of interlocutors which occurs outside of, yet challenges, the sedimentation of fixed "meanings" of sociopolitical classifications. One cannot become a psychotherapist only by reading texts or learning theories. Psychoanalysis highlights the fact that the time of each human being is not the time articulated by historiographers; rather, it is consistituted by the individual's relationships to other people. What is at issue is the difference yet relationship between people, separation and individuation.

Without elaborating a model of the genetic development of the psyche in terms of a drive economy, Levinas nevertheless also concentrates on the separation and yet the vulnerability of the "self": "The body is neither an obstacle opposed to the soul, nor the tomb which imprisons it, but that by which the self is susceptibility. The extreme passivity of 'incarnation'—being exposed to illness, suffering, to death is to be exposed to compassion."[1]

It is important to remember that Levinas is not engaged in a discussion of a relationship between the lived and the thematized. In stressing compassion, the susceptibility of the face-to-face, he is saying that in responding to the other whose face "speaks" to me and demands a personal response I am involved in a discourse which is an ethical act: "Moral consciousness is not an experience of values, but an access to exterior being—exterior being *par excellence* is the Other."[2]

If philosophy is ethical in Levinas's sense—concerned with suffering and substitution for the Other, then I believe that it is appropriate to examine the situation in which some people experience pain. In Bion's terms pain is the inability to suffer, that is, to be patient, where it is not a question of simply perceiving oneself locked within a self-preoccupation, a self-enclosed ego or state of narcissism.[3] Yet extreme pain results from the person being constituted as the image upon which an other projects his narcissism. François Roustang, a contemporary French psychoanalyst, presents such an account of pain in his paper "Towards a Theory of Psychosis."[4] He maintains that the psychotic has no relation with the other, yet is constituted by this relation. The psychotic only has thoughts implanted in him by the other; he is produced by thought. It isn't that he is repressing the other but rather that he has been expropriated. Roustang argues that the parent/parents themselves are without any relation to the other and make the child their project—he can think only what they invest in him. Roustang suggests that parents often use the child to settle a score with their parents by whom they have never felt loved. The child is put in the place of the unloving parents in order to replace a lack that was felt to be intolerable. Thus the child is placed in the past, in the passive. Roustang points out the paradoxical nature of psychosis, namely, that the psychotic does not know if he is other or himself; he is constituted by his parents/grandparents, yet his delirium cannot be connected with his generation—the other is both everything and nothing for him.[5] The psychotic does not speak in order to be understood, he cannot distinguish the statement from the enunciation. The enunciation is direct and does not express any desire. With the psychotic the analyst must listen to the cry of the "him" and not focus on his desire to be loved or understood. Roustang maintains:

> If there can be analysis of a psychotic, it is because the psychoanalyst knows that he himself is also a stranger and strange—two strangers meeting in a strange land. For the stranger who is the psychotic, the strange psychoanalyst becomes the possible, because he does not reject the other as a stranger and does not seek . . . to reintegrate him into the world of neurotic-normal beings.[6]

Is Roustang simply describing a pathological way of being-in-the-world which is properly confined to medical or scientific investigation? Or is it possible that by imagining that such pain is "safely" dealt with by experts who "know" the psyche and define rationality, we collude with and perpetuate the fragmentation of our psyches, our cultures? Do we have the patience to wait for the other whose "self" has been expropriated?

In *Totality and Infinity* Levinas argues that physical suffering is the situation where future evil becomes present at the limit of consciousness.[7] What he means here is that the acuity of suffering lies in the impossibility of escaping from it. Suffering realizes in the will the extreme proximity of the being menacing the will. At the core of Levinas's argument here is the point that just as there is ambiguity in the will, so also suffering is ambiguous. Suffering is the present of the pain acting on the for-itself of the will; but, as consciousness the pain is always yet to come. This is to say that the subject becomes a heroic will, because he can remain at a distance from the pain through consciousness. In such a situation consciousness is deprived of all freedom of movement and is at a minimal distance from the present.

For Levinas ultimate passivity is patience where the will is in subjection but still master. Thus, although the other being has power over me and does violence to me, he is still at a distance from me, and threatens from the future. In this extreme consciousness, the will reaches mastery in a new sense. In extreme passivity, death no longer touches me, so that the will becomes master. For Levinas, the supreme ordeal of freedom lies in suffering and not in death. He takes the phenomenon of hatred to illustrate this fact. In hatred, I desire the death of the other only in wanting to inflict death as a supreme suffering. While the aim of hatred is to reduce the other to the status of an object, yet he must recognize this reduction, which means that he must be a subject. Ultimately, hatred is absurd in that it is satisfied only when it is not satisfied, since the other satisfies it only by becoming an object. But he can never become object enough, since his witness is also demanded. On the other hand, in patience the will does not become absurd. Thus, while violence comes from the other as threat, yet it does not stop all discourse; it remains endurable in patience.

In *Autrement qu'être ou au-delà de l'essence*, Levinas elaborates the notion of suffering in the context of terms usually associated with pathology such as obsession, persecution, hostage: "Persecution is not added to the subjectivity of the subject and to his vulnerability; it is the very movement of recurrence. Subjectivity, *as other in the same*—as inspiration—is the putting into question of every . . . egoism arising in this recurrence."[8]

The other as the one who has meaning before one gives it to him is never reducible to my calculative schemes, yet I am obsessed with him. Obsession is neither a modification, nor a pathological exasperation of consciousness, but proximity. Although it is a refusal of both coincidence and mediation which synchronizes, nevertheless it is more determinate than relations ordered in a totality precisely because it is more immediate.[9]

The self and the other are outside of thematization, yet in the close presence of obsession. The other assigns me; obsession is a responsibility without choice, a communication without words or phrases.[10] Here a hermeneutical type of objection might be advanced to the effect that assignation must be simultaneously the experience, or consciousness of assignation. For Levinas, such an objection permits advertance to the anachronism in the representational model.

Here the question is how presence is presence to me; in other words, it is a question of the way in which presence is manifest and becomes representation. Further, it is to consign experience to the order of images and of knowledge. In representation, presence is already past. Levinas argues that assignation overturns the intentional realm. To be assigned by the other is to pursue that which is already present, to seek once more that which one has found. This is the displacement between presentation and presence, as is the tenderness of the caressed skin where passivity is absence.

The nonreciprocity of the face-to-face relationship is the uniqueness of the irreversible flow of time. This is the realm of obsession. Obsession is not in any sense a synchronic event, for it is concerned not with the self as specified within a conceptual landscape, but in its extracategorial ipseity. As obsessed I respond to the other's responsibility. Levinas argues that this notion of obsession breaks with the dialectical model of unity in difference. This is a rejection of the phenomenological notion of consciousness, which in Levinas's view substitutes the concept of the individual for the facticity of individuation and thereby loses singularity in a universal category.[11] As affected by the other, I cannot think that this affection should be reciprocal for I am simultaneously obsessed by the obsession I exercise on the one who obsesses.[12] Here there is a rupture of synchrony which is established by the difference of the same and the other in the nonindifference of the obsession exercised by the other on the same. This activity is outside of understanding but occurs as relationship of proximity. It is the singularity of the other that obsesses me. His singularity is his assignation—he assigns me before I designate him.

In "Useless Suffering," Levinas discusses suffering in terms of that which, although "given" in consciousness, nevertheless is, despite consciousness, unassumable: "As an 'experienced' content, the denial and refusal of meaning which is imposed as a sensible quality is the *way* in which the insupportable precisely is not support in a consciousness, the way of this non-supporting which, paradoxically, is itself a sensation or a given."[13] The passivity of submission in suffering is not the reverse of activity—it is more passive than experience, a pure undergoing. This is the challenge to pretensions of total meaningfulness. Suffering is absurd, for nothing. But

> the hurt of suffering—extreme passivity, impotence, abandonment and solitude—is it not also the unassumable and, thus, the possibility of a half opening . . . the possibility where a moan, a cry, a groan or a sigh, happen, there is the original call for aid . . . for the help of the other ego whose alterity, exteriority, promises Salvation?[14]

For Levinas, beyond suffering is not a self-conscious transcendence, not a rationalistic appropriation of my historicity with its hitherto hidden hurt but it is the inter-human. The ethical dimension of suffering is that of opening the difference between *suffering in the other*, where for me it is unpardonable and solicits me, and suffering in *me*, whose uselessness becomes meaningful as the suffering for the suffering of someone else.[15] This, I think, is why one can be a psychotherapist only through the interhuman emergence of one's own suffering.

The interhuman is made up of women and men—it is as sex-gendered human beings that we suffer. Psychoanalysis has emerged as privileged site for the investigation of sexual difference, but the problem is whether its development assumptions foreclose the alterity of adult desire. What has sexual difference got to do with suffering? I believe that there are two dimensions to suffering. First, the suffering due to narcissism—aggression, the totalizing pretensions of patriarchal power structures denying differences, this recurrently emerging as the glory of war—surely this is not a "useless suffering" with which we collude and inevitably endure? Second, I believe that Levinas's attention to the suffering of mortality—the otherness of aging—is very important and helps us to counter naïve teleological notions of arriving forever in a state of "psychic health" that would preclude all suffering—the dream of Western individualism.

Notes

1. E. Levinas, AE 139 n; OB 195 n. 12.
2. E. Levinas, *Difficile liberté: Essais sur le Judaisme*, Paris, Albin Michel, 1963, 326.
3. W. R. Bion, *Attention and Interpretation*, London, Maresfield Reprints, 1984, 19.
4. F. Roustang, *Dire Mastery*, trans. N. Lakacher, Baltimore, Johns Hopkins University Press, 132–56.
5. Ibid., 149.
6. Ibid.
7. E. Levinas, TeI 215; TI 238.
8. AE 141–42; OB 111.
9. AE 106; OB 84. E Levinas, EDE 229; CP 120.
10. EDE 229; CP 120.
11. AE 105; OB 83–84.
12. AE 106; OB 84.
13. E. Levinas, "La Souffrance Inutile," *Emmanuel Levinas: Les cahiers de La nuit surveillée*, ed. J. Rolland, Lagrasse, Editions Verdier, 1984, 329; trans. R. Cohen, "Useless Suffering," *The Provocation of Levinas*, ed. R. Bernasconi and D. Wood, London, Routledge and Kegan Paul, 1988, 156.
14. "La Souffrance Inutile," 331; trans. "Useless Suffering," 158.
15. "La Souffrance Inutile," 332; trans. "Useless Suffering," 159.

CHAPTER
14

AM I OBSESSED BY BOBBY?
(Humanism of the Other Animal)
John Llewelyn

Who is my neighbor? The discussion of this question throughout the ages has ranged from asking whether my neighbor is the Jew, through whether he is any and every other human being including my enemy, to whether he is God. It may enable us to clarify what Levinas's answer to this question would be if we ask not only whether his concept of the neighbor includes God, a question that, in the light of one interpretation of the belief in the death of God, might be deemed by some to be purely academic, but also whether Levinas's concept of the neighbor includes the nonhuman animal. This must be a live question for anyone who does not like the climate of utilitarianism and asks whether an alternative to it might be reached by taking the metaphysical ethics of Levinas as a guiding thread. For one of the attractions of utilitarianism is that it requires, in determining the morality of an action, rule, or institution, that consideration be given to the welfare of *any* sentient being. Among classical utilitarian statements on this matter, nothing is more eloquent than the words in which Bentham declares his hope that

the day *may* come when the rest of the animal creation may acquire those rights which never could have been withholden from them but by the hand of tyranny. The French have already discovered that the blackness of the skin is no reason why a human being should be abandoned without redress to the caprice of a tormentor. It may one day come to be recognized that the number of legs, the villosity of the skin, or the termination of the *os sacrum*, are reasons equally insufficient for abandoning a sensitive being to the same fate. What else is it that should trace the insuperable line? Is it the faculty of reason, or perhaps the faculty of discourse? But a full-grown horse or dog is beyond comparison a more rational, as well as a more conversable animal, than an infant of a day or a week, or even a month, old. But suppose they were otherwise, what would it avail? The question is not, Can they reason? nor Can they *talk*? but, *Can they suffer?*[1]

Is Levinas of the opinion that the question is, Can they talk? It is not easy to determine his opinion, because almost always when he touches upon the subject of animality he is thinking of the animality of man. There is, however, one place at least where he writes explicitly about a nonhuman animal. I am thinking of Bobby. Not Greyfriars Bobby of Edinburgh, the Franciscan Bobby, the terrier that mourned on his master's grave for fourteen years until he himself died, but the dog referred to in an essay entitled "Nom d'un chien ou droit naturel" published in 1975 in the collection *Celui qui ne peut se servir des mots* and reprinted in *Difficile Liberté*. No less eloquent than those words of Bentham's are those of the opening paragraph of this essay where Levinas mentions that according to Genesis Adam was a vegetarian and where he all but proposes an analogy between the unspeakable human Holocaust and the unspoken animal one. The reader of that paragraph may well feel his leather shoes beginning to pinch.[2]

I am thinking of Bobby in order to understand whom or what Levinas means by *Autrui*, the Other. Is *Autrui* a strictly personal pronoun? Can it stand for God? Can it stand for a dog? The question is not as rum as it may seem. Not as rum as the idea that occurred to George Borrow when, learning that the Romany word for God is *Duvel*, he mused in *Lavengro* "Would it not be a rum thing if divine and devilish were originally one and the same word?" We are not about to find Levinas arguing that the words "God" and "dog" have a common root. Although Bobby has his origins on the Egyptian side of the Red Sea, he is not a metaphorical Anubis. Throughout the entire essay about him Levinas tries to keep the metaphorical at bay, for the sake of the literal truth about the dog of the verse in Exodus 22 which his essay takes as its text: "neither shall ye eat any flesh that is torn of beasts in the field; ye shall cast it to the dogs." It is an uphill task, both for him and for the Talmudic interpreters of this text who explain what Levinas calls "the paradox" of a purely natural creature having a right, here the right of the dog to feed on this particular sort of meat, by referring to Exod. 11:7, which says that no dog shall move its tongue at the midnight when the first-born in the land of Egypt are threatened with slaughter and the Jews are about to be led into captivity. Threatened, be it noted, are the first-born not only of man, but of the chain of being "from the first-born of the Pharoah that sitteth upon his throne, even unto the first-born of the maidservant that is behind the mill; and all the first-born of beasts." But one of these beasts, the silent dog *sans* ethic and *sans logos*, by holding its tongue bears witness to the dignity of man. Man's best friend signifies a transcendence *in* its animality, "*dans* l'animal!" For which service he has the everlasting right mentioned in Exodus 22.

It makes a nice story, Levinas seems to say, but have not the Talmudic exegetes lapsed into merely rhetorical figures of speech? He decides that they have, no less than Aesop and La Fontaine, but he goes on to tell of another dog, the dog that strayed into the German camp for Jewish prisoners where Levinas himself and his companions had become accustomed to being treated as less than human, sometimes subjected to looks that were enough, as he chillingly expresses it, to strip them of their human skin. Yet Bobby, during the few weeks the guards allowed him to remain, was there every morning to welcome them with wagging tail as they lined up before leaving for work and, unconstrained by the prohibition placed upon his Egyptian ancestors, was there waiting when they returned at night to welcome them one and all with an excited bark. The last Kantian in Nazi Germany, Levinas comments, and one wonders if he intends us to take that comment as nothing more or less than the literal truth. How can we? How, any more than Aesop, La Fontaine, and the Talmudic exegetes, can Levinas be speaking otherwise than figuratively? For in the very same breath he adds that Bobby lacks the brains to universalize his maxim. He is too stupid, *trop bête*. Bobby is without *logos* and that is why he is without ethics. Therefore he is without Kantian ethics; and so he is without Levinasian ethics, since the ethics of Emmanuel Levinas is analogous to the ethics of Immanuel Kant in that each is an ethics with a God within the limits of reason alone, but without a dog or any other beast, except indirectly, if we are to judge by reason alone.

> To judge by reason alone, man has no duties except to men (himself or others), for his duty to any subject at all is the moral constraint by his will. Accordingly, a subject who constrains (obligates) must, first, be a person; and he must, secondly, be given as an object of experience, because he is to influence the purpose of a man's will; and such an influence can occur only in the relationship of two existing beings (for a mere creation of thought cannot become the cause of any purposive achievement). Since in all our experience we are acquainted with no being which might be capable of obligation (active or passive) except man, man therefore can have no duty to any being other than man. And if he supposes that he has such another duty, then this happens through an amphiboly of the concepts of reflection; and so his supposed duty to other beings is merely his duty to himself. He is led to this misunderstanding because he confuses his duty *regarding* other beings with a duty *toward* these beings.[3]

To judge by reason alone, Bobby cannot even say "Goodday," no matter how gaily he may wag his tail and how excitedly he may bark. If I think that I have duties to animals it is because I am failing to distinguish direct duties to or toward (*gegen*) from indirect duties regarding (*in Ansehung*). "Even gratitude for the long-performed service of an old horse or dog (just as if they were members of the household) belongs indirectly to man's duty, namely his duty *regarding* these animals; but directly considered, such a duty is always only his duty *to* himself."[4] If a man is not compassionate in his relations with animals he is likely to become insensitive in his relations with other human beings. According to Kant a man can have obligations only to a being that has obligations, which means, on his account of human experience, that human beings have obligations only to other human beings. The argument turns on the difference between doing something which falls under a single law and doing something which falls under two laws. The concept of obligation is that of something which falls under two laws, the law of human animality and the law of human rationality, and it is this duality that gives rise to the experience of constraint and tension which is implied in the notion of being bound. So a being which is a purely animal nature will have no sense of obligation, of oughtness. Nor will a being that is purely rational. Hence, Kant maintains, we can have no moral obligations to God. We have, according to Kant, duties of religion, that is to say, duties "of recognizing all duties as (*instar*) divine commands." The duty of religion, however, is correlated with an Idea of Reason that, from a theoretical point of view, helps us to make sense of the apparent purposefulness of nature; and, from a practical point of view, Kant holds, this Idea is of the greatest moral fecundity in availing an incentive to virtuous conduct. Thus what we take to be a duty to God is a duty to man himself, namely a duty each man has to himself, the duty to make himself virtuous.

Does Kant think that a man cannot have a duty to a being he does not know exists? He writes: "we do not . . . have before us (*vor uns*) a given being *to* whom we are obligated; for the actuality of such a being would first have to be made known by experience." He also writes, in the paragraph already cited, that we can have no duties except to human beings because "we are acquainted (*kennen wir*) with no being which might be capable of obligation (active or passive) except man." We can be under an obligation only to a being with whom we can be, as we say, face to face. In the very human world of Immanuel Kant, the other man is the only being with whom I come face to face. So too in the very human world of Emmanuel Levinas. The only face we behold is the human face and that is the only face to which we are beholden. Ethically, that is all that matters. In this, despite their fundamental disagreement over what it is for two human beings to be face to face, there is a considerable area of agreement between Levinas and Kant. Just as Kant maintains that I can have obligations only to a being that has, or (to cover the infantile and the senile) is of the kind that can have, obligations, so Levinas seems to imply that I can have responsibilities only toward beings capable of having responsibilities.

We have explained why Kant thinks that God can have no obligations. He thinks this because he thinks that the notion of obligation carries with it the notion of constraint, of a tie. So although we may coherently think of God acting according to the moral law, that law is descriptive, not prescriptive, of his action, and it is not a law for which He can feel respect or by which He can feel obliged. He can command but cannot be commanded. And this is what Levinas says, speaking of *Autrui*. I do not judge the Other. The Other judges me. I do not categorize him. He categorizes me. He picks me out, identifies and accuses me. I do not simply appear, but am summoned to appear before him (DVI 117). And in this court of appeal it is he who does the calling, calling me to testify: to testify to my responsibilities even for his responsibilities. So that where Kant allows that I have responsibilities to myself, namely to make myself virtuous, my responsibility toward myself according to Levinas is mediated by my responsibility for the Other's responsibility toward me. Further, in contrast to Kant's view that I have a duty to promote the happiness but not the virtue of others, Levinas holds that *I* go bail for the Other's obedience to the Law. "His business is my business" (ADV 106). But, Levinas goes on to ask, "Is not my business his? Is he not responsible for me? Can I therefore be responsible for his responsibility for me?" To this last question Levinas answers, Yes. For every responsibility that the Other has toward me and others I have a metaresponsibility. Somewhat like the little boy who, in order to be always one up on his playmate, declares "Whatever you say plus one," I have the last word even if I do not have the first, the dreadful glory of being chosen to be more responsible than anyone else. Only somewhat like the little boy, because I do not need to have a first preemptive word. It has already been dictated.

Starting from below, as it were, my responsibility toward the other man, an infinite progress is generated, an infinite that is not to be confused with the agent's infinite progress toward his moral perfection as postulated in the ethical theory of Kant, even though both Kant and Levinas call what gives direction to this progress an Ideal. In the Kantian Ideal happiness is commensurate with virtue. It is an Ideal toward which one strives by exerting a good will, and the realization of the Ideal would be a fulfillment. The Levinasian Ideal, as viewed from my subjectivity, recedes immeasurably further and further away the more I take up my responsibilities. The realization of it would be a derealization of my self, an emptying of myself, but a *kenosis* that could never be complete. And this taking up of my responsibilities is not an exercise of power, not even a power of the good will. It is a being taken up by the idea of Infinity and Goodness, the idea which is presupposed by the infinite progression-regression and which prevents it becoming the bad infinite that it would otherwise be. This explains the structure of Levinas's important essay "God and Philosophy." The first part of this starts from above with the idea of God, *En Sof*, the topic of Descartes's *Third Meditation*. Then, on pages 113–15 of *De Dieu qui vient à l'idée*, it starts again, this time from below, with the topic of the *First* and *Second Meditations*, subjectivity, and therefore in Levinas's text, since subjectivity is ethical subjection, with *Autrui*, the difficult pronoun that seems to do service for God in the meditations of Levinas rather as the name of God seems to do service for the scarcely mentioned "other minds" in the *Meditations* of Descartes.

Is God *Autrui*? Far from it, if by God we mean the God of positive or negative theology. The Other is not some Plotinian avatar of God. "The Other is not the incarnation of God, but precisely by his face, in which he is disincarnate, is the height in which he is revealed," revealed, that is to say, in discourse. "It is our relations with men . . . that give to theological concepts the sole signification of which they admit." "Everything that cannot be reduced to an interhuman relation represents not the superior form but the forever primitive form of religion" (TeI 51–52; TI 79). As indeed Hegel might have said, except that the infinity of the interhuman relation in his conception is an infinity that totalizes a symmetrical intersubjectivity. Hegel's God is beyond any gulf between subject and object, but it is, Levinas would contend, not beyond the participation of what according to Hegel too are primitive forms of religion, the mythological religions of faceless gods. The superior form of religion is one in which God is not numinous, and in which he is "in-himself," *kath auto*, only on the assumption of ontological atheism. Atheistic de-ontology, the atheism which results from the death of the pagan gods (TeI 115–16; TI 142) before which we are in danger of confusing God with the nocturnal stirring of the *il y a* (DVI 115). "The Other, in his signification prior to my initiative, resembles God" (TeI 269; TI 293). "The Other is the very locus of metaphysical truth, and is indispensable for my relation with God" (TeI 51; TI 78). But even when he is no longer conceived as the God of positive or negative theology, God is not the Other, *Autrui*. Far from it. He is closer to this farness. Not the impersonal *il* of the *il y a*, God is the third personal *Il* over and up there, *illic*, and, as Descartes says, echoing the *Symposium*, majestic, the eminence whose trace is inscribed in the face of the second person, the Thou or, more accurately and respectfully, the You, the Other, the idea of whom is the idea of Infinity thought by the first personal but never nominative me. The "in-" of this idea of infinity, Levinas comments, connotes both the being in me of the idea and the negation implied in the idea of my own finitude revealed to me a posteriori by my doubt and desire, and a priori by the immeasurable degree to which the "objective reality" of my idea of infinity falls short of the "formal reality" of its metaphysical and ethical origin. Infinity, the Desirable, God is the transcendence and holiness or distance that makes my nearness to my neighbor more than a relation of love, as for Kant, *mutatis mutandis*, love is that which unites while respect is that which sets a distance between us. "God is not simply 'the first other,' or 'the other par excellence' or 'the absolutely other,' but other than the other, otherwise other, other with an alterity prior to the alterity of the other" (DVI 113–15).

Concerning Levinas's phenomenological analysis of love, it must suffice to say here that it is a reflection on Plato's *Symposium* and Rosenzweig's *The Star of Redemption*.[5] Love is ambiguous. On the one hand it points to the exteriority of the beloved and to an exteriority beyond that exteriority, beyond the face. On the other hand it enjoys the interiority of sensation and return to oneself (TeI 244; TI 266), to the concupiscence that Pascal describes with the help of the proclamation of the first Epistle of Saint John 2:16: "Everything in the world is lust of the flesh, or concupiscense of the eyes, or vaingloriousness of life," *libido sentiendi, libido sciendi, libido dominandi*, the very same *cupere* that throws us back from the Cartesian idea of God to the *cogito* that would like to have everything under its command. There is a touch of the erotic in all love, says Levinas on one page. True, on the next occurs the phrase "Amour sans Eros." The pagan god is left behind as Levinas's thoughts turn from Plato to Rosenzweig. Rosenzweig writes of the love of a nonpagan God, God's love for man and man's love for God. In a footnote Levinas says that "Franz Rosenzweig interprets the *response* made by Man to the love with which God loves him, as the movement towards the neighbour." He probably has in mind the following sentences: "Since love cannot be commanded except by the lover himself, therefore the love for man, in being commanded by God, is directly derived from the love for God. The love for God is to express itself in love for one's neighbour. It is for this reason that love of neighbour can and must be commanded."[6] In the spirit of these sentences the love without *eros* to which Levinas once refers—and which Rosenzweig champions (on p. 163), though in treating of God's love for man—gets referred to henceforth as responsibility in order to mark its difference from ego-based desire and to mark that it is indeed a response.

But why must responsibility be limited to responding to a being that has the gift of speech? Why can we not allow an ethical responsibility to dumb animals? Responsibilities are responsibilities *toward*, at the very least, but among them not all are responsibilities *to* in the strict sense of answerability or response to a question or command. They may be responsibilities *for*, and it is of responsibilities *pour* or *de* that Levinas mostly writes, taking the trouble only twice, as far as I have noticed, to make the distinction between them and responsibilities *à*.[7] Of course, we could take up the question whether animals and, if so, which animals, can talk and whether they can talk to us. There is reason to believe that Levinas would consider it a crucial question whether Bobby merely barks or whether in so doing he can say "Bonjour." When asked about our responsibilities toward nonhuman sentient creatures, he is inclined to reply that our thinking about them may have to be only analogical or that the answer turns on whether in the eyes of the animal we can discern a recognition, however obscure, of his own mortality—on whether, in Levinas's sense of the word, the animal has a face. If this question is crucial, we may have to be satisfied with falling back on the need to appeal to spokesmen to speak on the animal's behalf, on analogy with what we do in the case of infants. However, the agent who speaks for the child says what he says on the child's behalf on the basis of something about which no one has any doubt: that the child does not enjoy being battered or starved. Is not the fact that this is also how it is with nonhuman animals enough to prove that I have responsibility for them? And that responsibility does not depend upon their having responsibilities, responsibilities, for example, to their offspring or to the humans they guard or guide. Let talk of their responsibilities be deemed anthropomorphism or rhetoric. As Bentham and other utilitarians say, the question is not, Can they reason? nor, Can they talk? but, Can they suffer?

We have seen that the first and perhaps second of these questions is all-important for Kant. However, the last is not for him morally irrelevant, as some of his readers infer. It is argued that Kant's concession that we have indirect duties to animals can be reduced to absurdity on the grounds that rationality is the only morally relevant characteristic that he can admit by which to distinguish animals from other nonhuman beings and that therefore, if we are to refrain from treating animals only as means because that is likely to lead us to treat fellow humans as means only, we should for the same reason refrain from treating only as means inanimate objects like hammers. This argument, I suspect, derives its plausibility from a failure to distinguish a necessary condition for moral agency, where the moral is opposed to the nonmoral, from a condition of the circumstances in which an action is performed that might determine whether the action is moral as opposed to immoral. The former condition is one that holds for any rational beings that may exist. The latter condition holds for the actions of those we know to exist, human beings. That Kant agrees that the animality of rational animals can be determinative of our duties toward them is implied by his claim that we have a direct duty to contribute to the well-being of other humans and to support them in distress, and an indirect duty to assure one's own happiness as far as one can consistently with one's other obligations.[8] The practical contradictoriness that makes some of my actions wrong depends on the fact that it is natural for men to seek their own happiness. The moral law is a test for practical, and that means teleological, consistency, and it applies to maxims prescriptive of how men can achieve that natural end. Since that natural end includes man's well-being as an animal, the maxim "Treat nonhuman animals as if they have no capacity for suffering" is not one that can be consistently conceived as a law of nature or willed to become one.[9] Such a conception is inconsistent with what one knows about animals from one's own experience of being one. This removes one obstacle preventing Kant from admitting that we have direct duties to brutes.

There remains the obstacle presented by Kant's doctrine that as far as we can tell on the basis of reason alone—by which I take Kant to mean that he is setting aside here matters based on feeling (other than the feeling of moral respect) and faith—man has no duties except to men because his duty to any subject is moral constraint by that subject's will. We should be well on the way to clearing Kant's path to admitting direct duties to animals if only this reference to the subject's will could be interpreted as what he wants or desires. If that were allowed, and if similar translations of the accommodating word *Wille* were permitted elsewhere in Kant's text, we should also be well on the way to converting Kant's theory of ethics into the tacit utilitarianism that Mill and others hold it to be. Kant himself is less accommodating than the word, taking pains to distinguish two of its primary senses. He remains adamant that we can have direct duties only to beings that have *Wille* understood as pure practical reason.

In the metaphysical ethics of Levinas I can have direct responsibilities only toward beings that can speak, and this means beings that have a rationality that is presupposed by the universalizing reason fundamental in the metaphysics of ethics of Kant. However, the protorationality of primary justice between two unequals anticipates the rationality of secondary justice among many, but without this entailing that I cease being more responsible than anyone else.

Both Kant and Levinas are so sensitive to the dangers of the *Schwärmerei* threatened by what Kant calls pathological love that they require an obligating being to be able to make a claim in so many words. No claim goes without saying, even if the saying is the silent saying of the discourse of the face— a silence not to be confused with the nocturnal silence in which the insomniac hears the menacing rustle of the anonymous *il y a* (TeI 236; TI 258–59). The Other only has to look at me. Indeed, what is expressed in his face may be expressed by his hand or the nape of his neck (TeI 240; TI 262). And for Kant at least the claim does not have to be a claim to a perfect right. I can have duties to others without any of those others having a right to require that

that duty be exercised toward him by me. Levinas, however, seems to be far more demanding. The very *droiture* of the face-to-face, its uprightness or rectitude, is the expression of the other's *droit* over me (TeI 10; TI 40). And in one place, at least, he says "I support the universe," "Je soutiens l'univers" (AE 152; OB 197). This might seem to augur well for Bobby. He is presumably part of the universe. So if supporting means being responsible for, I am responsible for, that is, obsessed by him. But Levinas distinguishes my support of the universe into two aspects. My support of the universe performs the role which Kant assigns to the transcendental unity of apperception, the role of giving the universe its unity. Prior to that transcendental unifying, Levinas says, is the unity of human society, the oneness of which is brought about by my responsibility. *Human* society. So there is no place for direct responsibility to Bobby here. What about the other aspect in which the unity of the universe is due to me? The other aspect of my unifying support is that which has to do with the unity of being. But this second aspect is derivative from the first and would therefore appear to be no more capable than it of accommodating responsibility for the nonhuman animal. The one space of the universe is the space of secondary justice, justice in the proximity of the third party. It is the ubiquity not of the geometrical space of the things at which I look, but of the pregeometrical space from which I am looked at by the face, the face which *me regarde* in both senses of the word, the face that looks at me and the face that concerns me; the face that *m'accuse* in both senses of that word: the face whose look picks out and accuses me (AE 147; OB 116). The face that calls me into question is not the face of the animal. It is thanks to human faces, Levinas writes, that "Being will have a meaning as a universe, and the unity of the universe will be in me as subject to being. That means that the space of the universe will manifest itself as the dwelling of the others." The door of that dwelling would seem to be slammed in Bobby's face, assuming that he has one.

This impression is confirmed by Levinas's endorsement of much of what he finds in Rabbi Haïm of Volozhin's *Nefesh Hahaïm* (The soul of life). In the doctrine expounded in this book Levinas recognizes a basis for his own teaching that man is responsible for the universe. The soul of the universe, according to Rabbi Haïm, is man and, significantly for our present question, man defined not Hellenistically as a rational animal, but man understood biblically as the being created in the image of God and, more precisely, Levinas hastens to add, of God as Elohim, God as the principle of justice, not God as principle of mercy indicated by the Tetragrammaton. Elohim is also the soul of the world. *Nefesh Hahaïm* describes a cosmology, cabbalistic and Hellenistic, in which is postulated a hierarchy of worlds with God at the top. But this cosmology has to be read ethically. The principle of justice at the head of this hierarchy of worlds is the source on which feeds the root of the soul of man. Thanks to this, man in turn nourishes the intermediate worlds. Man is dependent on Elohim, yet Elohim is at the same time dependent upon man as mediator (ADV 190). In Rabbi Haïm's ethical cosmology, man is *homo*

Israelis understood nonracially, and on the Israelite's obedience to the commands of the Torah depend the life and death of all the intermediate worlds, this "power" of life and death being man's responsibility or, as Levinas would say, his passivity more passive than the receptivity to which activity is traditionally opposed.

Does this responsibility include responsibility for the lower animal? The answer to this question would appear to be, Yes, if we are to go by the following statement cited by Levinas from *Nefesh Hahaïm*: "Just as the way in which the body moves depends on the soul that is interior to man, man in his entirety is the power and living soul of the innumerable worlds in his charge, above him and below" (ADV 194). And below. These two words get lost in Levinas's interpretation. On the very same page on which he cites them he writes: "It is at the lowest level (*au plus bas*), in man, that the entire fate of the universe is decided," and on the next page he cites from the Talmudic treatise *Aboth* "Know what confusion your action brings about in the worlds above you." That is to say: "It is not by substantiality—by an in-itself or for-itself—that man and his interiority are defined, but by the 'for-the-other': for what is above oneself, for the worlds—but also, interpreting "world" broadly, for collectivities, persons, spiritual structures. In spite of his creaturely humility, man is engaged in injuring them (or preserving them)." Is this broad definition of "world" not still too narrow to allow for responsibility to the lower animal? Where does he or she fit in? There is no sign that Levinas would place the lower animal "above oneself" among the collectivities, persons, and spiritual structures. It is as if the universe to which Levinas applies Rabbi Haïm's cosmology is the universe of discourse between the Creator and the human creature. The creatureliness of any creature more humble than man is a purely (or should we say "impurely"?) cosmological creatureliness, recalcitrant to production into ethics, whereas creation is the intake of ethical breath which Levinas calls *psychisme*: the reveille of the inner life by a *Wachet auf* that rouses it from the twilight of its dogmatic slumber, apparently re-creation but in fact older than cosmological creation as onto-logically understood—the very *pneuma* of the psyche.

In *Otherwise than Being or Beyond Essence* Levinas writes: "The soul is the other in me. The psyche (*psychisme*), the one-for-the-other, can be possession and psychosis; the soul is already the seed of folly" (AE 86; OB 191). Where the *conatus* of the synoptic ego is a desire to possess, ethical and metaphysical Desire is psychotic possession, possession not by being or language, but possession by God: sober (*dégrisé*) enthusiasm in which there is a response to the word of the Other. Levinas maintains that the first word addressed to me by the Other is "Thou shalt not murder/kill" where the oblique stroke signals the question, How are we to translate the Hebrew word *ratsah*? The answer to this question will have repercussions for the question whether I am obsessed by Bobby, whether I have responsibilities toward him. We have failed to discover any evidence that Levinas allows that Bobby and I can be face to face such that I could read in his own eyes "Thou shalt not kill." We must therefore retreat to the question whether in the face-to-face the other man addresses me not only on behalf of himself and other men, but also on behalf of the nonhuman animal; and to the question whether, if what the human face tells me is "Thou shalt not murder," the legal and quasi-legal connotations of the word "murder" prevent us saying that the commandment includes the nonhuman animal within its scope.

Commenting on Exod. 20:13, J. P. Hyatt states that *ratsah* refers to the murder of a personal enemy and that it is used much less frequently than two other words meaning to kill, *harag* and *hemît*. He adds: "It originally had nothing to do with capital punishment (administered by the avenger of blood or by the community), killing in war which was certainly sanctioned by the OT, or the killing of animals. Careful studies have shown that it is not confined, however, to intentional murder, but is occasionally used of unintentional homicide."[10] When we turn to Levinas's statements of the commandment we find that he sometimes formulates it as "Thou shalt not kill," but other times replaces *tuer* by *meurtrir* with no contextual indication that he would not be willing to use the latter in all his mentions of the commandment. This must not be taken to imply, of course, that he is not more aware than most of the strict injunctions of the Torah against causing animals unnecessary pain. He also knows very well that the later Priestly sections of Genesis that speak of man's dominion over animals have alongside them sections from the earlier Jahwist sections that speak of animals as man's companions and affirm that God's covenant is made between him and man and every living creature.[11] But what sort of relevance is to be ascribed to this sensitivity and knowledge on Levinas's part or indeed to any of the citations he makes in the course of his more philosophical writings of texts from the Jewish Bible or the Talmud? The face-to-face faces us with a dilemma. If the first word addressed to me derives its authority from, say, Sinai, does that not prevent Levinas making his claim that metaphysical ethics makes no appeal to the content of any positive religion? And if we allow such an appeal, what is to prevent one appealing to another positive religion? Even if Levinas's ethics cannot be an ethics of the other animal, even if Bobby cannot be my neighbor according to that ethics, we must take him seriously when he insists that the ethics of which he speaks is a humanism of the other man. This means that we must now ask how in the face-to-face the other man can say *anything at all* and how, without the constraints imposed by the importation of commandments from positive religions, he can be prevented from saying *anything whatsoever*.[12]

Notes

1. Jeremy Bentham, *An Introduction to the Principles of Morals and Legislation*, Oxford, Clarendon Press, 1907, 311.

2. See on the subject of shoes Emmanuel Levinas, *Du sacré au saint*, Paris, Editions de Minuit, 1977, 117– 18.

3. Immanuel Kant, *The Metaphysical Principles of Virtue* (part 2 of *The Metaphysics of Morals*), trans. James Ellington, New York, Bobbs-Merrill, 1964, 105.

4. Ibid., 106.

5. Franz Rosenzweig, *The Star of Redemption*, trans. William H. Hallo, New York, Holt, Rinehart and Winston, 1970.

6. Ibid., 214.

7. Emmanuel Levinas, NP 108; Emmanuel Levinas and Françoise Armengaud, "Entretien avec Emmanuel Levinas," *Revue de métaphysique et de morale* 90 (1985):302.

8. Immanuel Kant, *The Moral Law* (Kant's *Groundwork of the Metaphysic of Morals*), trans. H. J. Paton, London, Hutchinson, 1963, 67, 90–91.

9. Alexander Broadie and Elizabeth M. Pybus, "Kant's Treatment of Animals," *Philosophy* 49 (1974):376.

10. J. P. Hyatt, *Exodus* (New Century Bible), London, Oliphant, 1971, 214.

11. See Catherine Chalier, "Torah, cosmos et nature," *Les Nouveaux cahiers* 79 (Winter 1984–85):3–13.

12. Levinas's remarks about animals made in the interview included in Robert Bernasconi and David Wood (eds.), *The Provocation of Levinas: Rethinking the Other*, London and New York, Routledge, 1988, published since this essay was composed, are taken into account in chapter 3 of my forthcoming *The Middle Voice of Ecological Conscience: A Chiasmic Reading of Responsibility in the Neighbourhood of Levinas, Heidegger and Others.*

Contributors

Ruben Berezdivin obtained his Ph.D. in philosophy from Duquesne University under John Sallis. He also studied under Derrida at Yale. He taught at Sonoma State College and at Texas Technological University and has published articles on Heraclitus, Derrida, Heidegger, Nietzsche, and Levinas. He is writing two books, one on Heidegger's legacy, the other on Plato and fictionality and law. He currently works in Miami.

Robert Bernasconi is Moss Professor of Philosophy at Memphis State University. He is the author of *The Question of Language in Heidegger's History of Being* (1985) and is currently working on a book to be called *Between Levinas and Derrida*.

Catherine Chalier is professeur agrégé de philosophie in Paris. In addition to a number of articles, she has published five books: *Figures du feminin* (1982), *Judaisme et altérité* (1982), *Les matriarches* (1985), *La persévérance du mal* (1987), and *L'alliance avec la nature* (1989).

Tina Chanter is assistant professor of philosophy at Louisiana State University. She has published essays on Levinas, Derrida, and Heidegger and is currently writing a book entitled *Levinas and the Feminine* and researching a book on French Feminism and Simone De Beauvoir.

Fabio Ciaramelli studied for his Ph.D. with Jacques Taminiaux at Louvain-la-Neuve and is currently a research fellow at the University of Naples. He is the author of *Transcendance et éthique: Essai sur Levinas*, Brussels, Ousia, 1990. He has also published articles in Italian and in French on Levinas, Derrida, and Castoriadis. He is preparing an Italian translation of Castoriadis's *L'institution imaginaire de la société*.

Simon Critchley is lecturer in philosophy at Essex University. He studied philosophy at the Universities of Essex and Nice and wrote his Ph.D. dissertation on Levinas and Derrida. In 1988–89 he was university fellow at the University of Wales, College of Cardiff. He has published articles and translations in the area of Continental philosophy and is currently writing a book entitled *The Ethics of Deconstruction*.

Paul Davies is assistant professor of philosophy at Loyola University of Chicago. He has written essays on Blanchot, Levinas, and Heidegger.

Jean Greisch teaches philosophy at the Institut Catholique de Paris. He is a teaching researcher attached to the Centre National de Recherches Scientifiques in Paris. He is the author of *Herméneutique et grammatologie* (1977), *L'age herméneutique de la raison* (1981), and *La parole heureuse* (1987).

Luce Irigaray has a doctorate in philosophy and has worked for many years as a psychoanalyst. She also has a post at the Centre National de Recherches Scientifiques in Paris. Her first book, *Le langage des déments*, was published in 1973. She has published twelve books, of which three are available in English: *Speculum, This Sex Which Is Not One*, and "And the One Doesn't Stir without the Other" (in *Signs*, 1981). *Ethics of Sexual Difference* is forthcoming from Cornell University Press.

John Llewelyn was reader in philosophy at Edinburgh University until his recent retirement. His publications include *Beyond Metaphysics?* (1985) and *Derrida on the Threshold of Sense* (1986).

Noreen O'Connor teaches philosophy and is director of Friends World College European Centre. She practices analytical psychotherapy at the Philadelphia Association in London. She has published articles on contemporary European philosophy, feminism, and psychoanalysis.

Adriaan Peperzak studied philosophy in Louvain and Paris and has taught philosophy in the Netherlands, the United States, Italy, and Indonesia. His publications in English include *System and History in Philosophy* (1986) and *Philosophy and Politics* (1987).

Margaret Whitford is a lecturer in French at Queen Mary College, University of London. She is currently writing a book on Luce Irigaray. Her recent book, *Feminist Perspectives in Philosophy*, coedited with Morwenna Griffiths, is published by Indiana University Press.

Index

Abraham, 124, 127, 164
Aesop, 235, 236
Alterity, xi, xiv, 18, 31, 40, 42–43, 110, 133, 172, 196–97, 204, 213, 214
Anarchy, 80
Animals, xvii, 234–45 *passim*
Antigone, xvi, 130, 135–42, 145
Apel, Karl-Otto, 72
Aristotle, 80, 152
Art, end of, 207
Atheism, 239
Augustine, 53, 102
Auschwitz, 126, 221, 222, 223
Author, 15, 25, 36, 58–61

Bataille, Georges, 173, 176
Beauvoir, Simone de, 141
Being, xiii, xvi, 5, 6, 7, 30, 70, 77, 78, 87, 121, 225
Bentham, Jeremy, 234–35, 240
Berezdivin, Ruben, xvi
Bergson, Henri, 6, 152
Bernasconi, Robert, xiv, 90, 161
Bion, W. R., 230
Blanchot, Maurice, xvi, 6, 9, 98, 99, 105, 198, 201–26
Bonaventure, 53
Borrow, George, 235
Buber, Martin, 9, 139

Caress, 110, 113, 114, 116, 232
Carneades, 150
Castoriadis, Cornelius, 136
Chalier, Catherine, xv, 98
Chanter, Tina, xv, 188
Chiasmus, xiii, xiv, 6–8, 186
Ciaramelli, Fabio, xv
Cicero, 150
Clitomachus, 150
Cogito, 7, 20, 239
Compassion, xvii, 229–30
Conatus, 87, 88, 119, 122, 125, 126, 243
Consciousness, 62–63
Contamination, 26, 29–30, 31, 37–38, 44, 45, 46, 156–57, 158
Creon, 136–41 *passim*
Critchley, Simon, xiv, 161
Crypt, 43, 47, 183, 186, 189

Daughter, 39–40, 115–16, 181, 186
Davies, Paul, xvi
Death, xvi, 32, 134, 194–98, 231
De Beauvoir, Simone, 141
De Greef, Jan, 161
De Waelhens, Alphonse, 104

Deconstruction, xii-xiv, 4–7, 158
Dehiscence, 31, 165, 167, 170–71, 174
Democritus, 150
Derangement, 13, 18. *See also* Disturbance
Derrida, Jacques, 3–8, 90, 95, 97, 101, 130–33, 143, 144; *La Carte Postale*, 73; *Glas*, 135, 145; *Of Spirit*, 187, 188; *Spurs*, 130–31; "Violence and Metaphysics," xii-xiv, 82, 89, 149, 153–59, 180, 181; *Voice and Phenomenon*, 3, 4
—"At this very moment here I am": text of, 11–48; discussed, xiv, 67, 93, 135, 155–59, 163–86 *passim*, 191–94, 199
Désastre, 202, 213, 220, 223, 226
Descartes, René, 7, 71, 89, 152, 238, 239
Desire, 13, 15, 66
Diachrony, 7, 21, 27, 30, 60, 63, 64, 77, 93, 96, 150, 153, 154, 158, 190. *See also* Synchrony
Difference, xiv, 4, 5, 22, 24, 47, 133, 154; ethical, 170, 172, 179, 181, 182, 183, 186. *See also* Sexual difference
Disturbance, 24, 25. *See also* Derangement
Divinity, 6, 109–18 *passim*
Double reading, xii, xiv-xvi, 153, 157, 158, 171–72, 178, 180–81, 182, 186
Duty, 236

Election, 32, 42, 126, 127
Eliezer, 127, 169
Enjoyment. See *Jouissance*
Ereignis, 194, 225, 226
Eros, xv, 43, 133, 135, 239, 240; Platonic, 134
Eschatology, 37, 41, 53
Essentialism, xvi, 142, 143
Ethics, 23, 38, 62, 71–74, 85, 87, 89, 101, 123, 217. *See also* Difference, ethical
Ethos, 84, 89
Existence and Existents, 133

Face, xi, 45, 67, 68, 100, 114, 127, 135, 151, 238, 240, 241, 242
Face-to-face, xv, 133, 150, 193, 217, 232, 242, 244
Family, 128, 136–41
Fault, 12, 14–17, 30–33, 45–47, 112, 165, 166, 184, 186, 198, 199
Fecundity, xvi, 179, 180, 181, 237. *See also* Paternity
Feminine, xv-xvi, 40–44, 109–18 *passim*, 119, 122–23, 127–28, 132–35, 140–41, 169–71, 182–86. *See also* Sexual difference
Feminism, xvi, 130–31, 141–43
Feuerbach, Ludwig, 118
Fragmentation, 211, 212, 216